Subject of the Event

Subject of the Event

Reagency in the American Novel after 2000

Sebastian Huber

Bloomsbury Academic
An imprint of Bloomsbury Publishing Inc

BLOOMSBURY
NEW YORK · LONDON · OXFORD · NEW DELHI · SYDNEY

Bloomsbury Academic

An imprint of Bloomsbury Publishing Inc

1385 Broadway	50 Bedford Square
New York	London
NY 10018	WC1B 3DP
USA	UK

www.bloomsbury.com

BLOOMSBURY and the Diana logo are trademarks of Bloomsbury Publishing Plc

First published 2016

© Sebastian Huber, 2016

Library of Congress Cataloging-in-Publication Data
A catalog record for this book is available from the Library of Congress.

ISBN: HB: 978-1-5013-1712-5
ePDF: 978-1-5013-1710-1
ePub: 978-1-5013-1709-5

Typeset by Deanta Global Publishing Services, Chennai, India
Printed and bound in the United States of America

To Elias, who kept me going.

Contents

Acknowledgments

I thank Haaris Naqvi, Mary Al-Sayed, Grishma Fredric and everyone else involved at Bloomsbury for their help in putting this book into print

My thanks to the ProLit program in Munich for allowing me to start this book, as well as to the University of Alberta for granting me an ideal environment to finish it. Thanks to the Christie Travel Fund, I was able to present my findings on *The Road* at a conference in Langley, BC. I also thank the Munich's Graduate Center for funding the last months of my project. My special thanks go to my supervisors, particularly those who made it the hardest for me. Looking at the bright side, one could call them, with Malcolm Gladwell, a desirable difficulty.

Thanks to Jerry Varsava, the best support you can get.

Thanks to my friends and colleagues, particularly Sascha Pöhlmann, for always having an open ear and good advice.

Thanks to my ProLit fellow sufferers: Sebastian, Nadine, Sandra, Reinhard, with whom I had the pleasure to organize the conference "The Works. Of The Im/Possible" and have a lot of fun. The five of us indeed have taken up different fidelities toward our aesthetic-scientific-politic-amorous PhD event. No matter where we'll go from here, I just hope we keep faith in our friendship.

Cheers to Jan, who didn't understand why everybody was writing about "events."

Thanks to Mara for her reading of *The Time of Our Singing*, which helped me to clarify my thoughts on the novel in the conclusion.

Thanks to Russell and Leah for making me fall in love with the English language.

Thanks to my family.

Thanks to Amélie, a proper event, and our kids, true points.

List of Abbreviations

Alain Badiou
    Being and Event   *BE*
    Conditions   *C*
    Ethics   *E*
    In Praise of Love   *IPoL*
    Infinite Thought   *IT*
    Logics of Worlds   *LoW*
    The Rebirth of History   *TRoH*

Paul Beatty
    Slumberland   *SL*

Mark Z. Danielewski
    Only Revolutions   *S|H*

Cormac McCarthy
    The Road   *TR*

Thomas Pynchon
    Against the Day   *AtD*

Jess Walter
    The Zero   *TZ*

Introduction

America's Subjects of Events

What is going on?
Of what are we the half-fascinated, half-devastated witnesses?
The continuation, at all costs, of a weary world?
A salutary crisis of that world, racked by its victorious expansion?
The end of that world? The advent of a different world?
What is happening to us in the early years of the century
—something that would appear not to have any clear name in any accepted language?

Alain Badiou, *The Rebirth of History*.

Writing, as usual in the utmost provocative register, about the revolutionary events that have come to be known as the "Arab Spring," Alain Badiou addresses issues that are at the heart of this study and might be moved beyond the local dimension of a mere political diagnosis. Specifically, through Badiou's implementation of what Jacques Derrida has called in a different context an "apocalyptic tone,"[1] this epigraph very well might be transposed from its concrete geographical point of reference to the cultural milieu of the United States. The rhetoric of the "end of the world," of "crisis" but also the concomitant possibility of a "different," a new "world," is part and parcel of the American imagination from Christopher Columbus to Barack Obama. Hardly any other culture is so dependent on the perpetual oscillation between apocalypse and clean slates, which seemingly offers individuals liberation from various determinations.

The very concept of America, and particularly its literature, this study argues, is inexorably intertwined to the idea of emphatic events, be they conceived as "beginnings," "ends," or otherwise.[2] Given this predilection for events, I elucidate how the American novel after 2000 stands in this tradition, while offering a salient new conceptualization of events and subjects that arise out of such manifestations, I call with Badiou "subjects of the event." In inquiring into how Cormac McCarthy's *The Road* (2006), Jess Walter's *The Zero* (2006), Mark Z. Danielewski's *Only Revolutions* (2006), Paul Beatty's *Slumberland* (2008), and Thomas Pynchon's *Against the Day* (2006) craft a genuine conception of these terms, this book offers a critical exploration of how subjects are created in relating to the shattering experience of an event that endows them with reagency, a concrete form of subjective empowerment.

This line of argument obviously responds to a specific cultural domain in the United States. The relevance of investigating the status of events and subjects in America is thus specifically pressing when considering that American postmodernism, in particular, is haunted by the apocalyptic imagination of ends. Fredric Jameson begins his seminal *Postmodernism, or, the Cultural Logic of Late Capitalism*, published nine years before the second millennium came to a close—albeit already published as an essay five years before—with the observation: "The last few years have been marked by an inverted millenarianism in which premonitions of the future, catastrophic or redemptive, have been replaced by senses of the end of this or that (the end of ideology, art, or social class; the 'crisis' of Leninism, social democracy, or the welfare state, etc., etc.)" (1991: 1). However, while postmodernism for Jameson is thus the epitome of events in an eschatological sense on a level of *content*, the very *form* of this cultural period also hinges on the disposition of events. In ascribing to postmodernism itself the properties of a discontinuity with the modernist movement, Jameson opts for a literary historical approach that borrows the import of events as configurations that mark "some radical break or *coupure*" (ibid.: 1) with what has gone before, instead of addressing the various overlaps.[3]

If events assume a crucial place in the history of America and the discourse of postmodernism, this study accentuates one specific "end" that was proclaimed in this cultural era, but again, obviously harks back to a time before postmodernism.[4] What Jameson calls, among others, the "'death' of the subject" (ibid.: 15) and which implies the critique of the subject as a rational, self-same, *a priori* agent who is endowed with autonomy, freedom and agency, is indeed viewed by Jean-Luc Nancy as a profound event in the history of philosophy. In his introduction to the seminal essay collection *Who Comes After the Subject?* Nancy calls the deconstruction of the subject an "*event* that had indeed emerged from our history—hence the 'after'—and not as some capricious variation of fashionable thinking" (1991: 4, my emphasis). While emphasizing the break and relevance that this philosophical undertaking constitutes—it is not a mere variation but a proper disruption, an "emergence" if not an emergency—Nancy also calls upon various (French) philosophers to inquire into ways of how to think beyond this "wide spread discourse of recent date [that] proclaimed the subject's simple liquidation" (ibid.: 5).[5] Yet, although Nancy is eager to stress that "such a critique or deconstruction has not simply obliterated the object (as those who groan or applaud before a supposed 'liquidation' of the subject would like to believe)," (ibid.: 4) he only speaks of a philosophical/theoretical discourse.

Indeed, in Thomas Pynchon's *Gravity's Rainbow* (1973) that is often taken to be the apex of postmodernist literature, the protagonist Tyrone Slothrop is literally disappearing from the novel's diegetical world. First, he starts to "scatter" (Pynchon 2006: 517), then becomes "a cross himself, a crossroads, a living intersection" (ibid.: 637) until he finally disappears entirely.[6] However, the novel already calls into question the very concept of an autonomous subject and its disposition to act regardless of any corrupting restrictions when Slothrop is still "present." When still a child, Slothrop is conditioned by Pavlovian psychology to get erections before a stimulus is even perceivable; he continuously loses his identity and thus forgets his assigned missions by becoming more and more "variable" (ibid.: 517). All of this results, according to Timothy Melley's work, in "agency panic": "the crisis of apparently imperiled individual autonomy" (1994: 710).[7] If not eradicated *tout court*, a range of characters in such fiction find themselves stuck in a freeze-frame, "that last delta-t" (Pynchon 2006: 775) as in the case of Jacob Horner's "*cosmopsis*" (1988: 323) in John Barth's *The End of the Road* from 1958 or the pathological condition of "*Analysis-Paralysis*" (2006: 203) in David Foster Wallace's 1996 magnus opus *Infinite Jest*.

However, while the critique of the subject and its concomitant paralysis in such novels as *Gravity's Rainbow* is well established in the criticism, it is worth noting that Pynchon's novel also interlinks this subjective dissemination to its conception of events. In the context of this study, which is interested in a specific understanding of events and subjects that result out of such happenings, it is noteworthy that Slothrop's disappearance manifests itself at the very moment when he has reached the topological "order" of The Zone. The novel thereby not only comments on the conventional need for characters in narratives but also points to the insufficiencies of a narratological conception of events such as Jurij Lotman's influential definition in *The Structure of the Artistic Text*: "*an event in a text is the shifting of a persona across the borders of a semantic field*" (1977: 233). Ironically then, Slothrop disappears from the narrative when he has entered the heterotopic site of The Zone (which itself undermines the binary semantic fields of Lotman's account[8]). As soon as the "persona" has fulfilled its eventful transgression, *Gravity's Rainbow* lets it disappear.

If events are pertinent to American culture as such, narratology has stressed that they are even necessary for narratives in general. Particularly, narrative theory of the twentieth century has stressed the inevitability of events for stories: without events, that is, either extraordinary occurrences or an extraordinary manner of how to present occurrences, there remains nothing to be told.[9] Novels such as *Gravity's Rainbow* have, therefore, not only questioned the necessity for narratives to contain characters but also, on a more fundamental level, I would argue, undermined the need for narratives to mediate events at all and, rather, emphasized the dispositions of representation themselves. While this might seem counterintuitive, since the novel deals excessively with the most incisive "event" of the twentieth century, Pynchon intricately questions the stable identity of such happenings as the Second World War by integrating them in a larger scope of historical happenings where "*everything is connected*, everything in the Creation, a secondary illumination—not yet blindingly One, but at least connected" (2006: 717). This outlook of a constantly self-referring tapestry results in the loss of the emphatic character of events, since "events are all there in the same eternal moment" (ibid.: 637). Following from this, narratives no longer emphasize their mimetic commitment to communicate an extraordinary happening, or to extraordinarily communicate a happening—they make language itself the object of transgression, which has often led to the bemoaning of postmodernist uneventful metafictional reveries, as Tom Wolfe's or Jonathan Franzen's cultural pessimism has it.[10]

What is thus anathema for postmodernist literature is a coherent conception of the subject *as well as* an emphatic notion of the event. In fact, the starting point of my study insists that these concepts are inherently intertwined. That such novels undermine the ability of the subject to consciously and autonomously initiate a chain of events has to be viewed as related to the critique of theologocentric causations that reverberates in the traditional understanding of events. If Columbus's "discovery" of America is perceived to have opened up a new world, what are we to make of the fact that its "eventness" was used in order to legitimate the bloody history of America's "Manifest Destiny"? How does the possibility to escape the monarchical reign of Europe conflict with the oppression of the indigenous inhabitants of the American continent and the enslavement of Africans?

As fundamental the notion of events is for American culture, or maybe exactly because of this importance, postmodernism's reservations for this concept[11] because of its theological (Christian) and political (Imperialist) undercurrents are especially distinct in DeLillo's *White Noise* when the narrator-protagonist Jack Gladney converses with a "black man with . . . tracts" who tries to convert him:

> Is this the point of Armageddon? No ambiguity, no more doubt. He was ready to run into the next world. He was forcing the next world to seep into my consciousness, stupendous events that seemed matter-of-fact to him, self-evident, reasonable, imminent, true. I did not feel Armageddon in my bones but I worried about all those people who did, who were ready for it, wishing hard, making phone calls and bank withdrawals. If enough people want it to happen, will it happen? (1986: 137)

In commenting on America's desire for world-ending events that offer the uncertain but possible hope for redemption and clear identity patterns, "wicked" Preterite or "saved" Elect (ibid.: 136), *White Noise* points to the constructed nature of such events as part of America's *dispositifs* of control. The passage's emphasis on the ambivalence of such events that calls into question their singular, "stupendous" nature formulates a deep concern about a culture that clings to such mechanisms. As a consequence, literature particularly emphasized not only its own constructedness but especially pointed metafictionally to the discursive immersion of events and denied their pre-discursive reality. Slavoj Žižek gets to the heart of it when writing that this implies "the 'postmodernist' indefinite oscillation of 'how do we know this truly is the Event, not just another semblance of the Event?'" (1999: 159).

Decried as mere simulacra in such novels, there still seems to be an unabating pertinence of events that Gladney's cartoonish colleague Murray formulates in respect to the novel's media spectacle: "It's no wonder they call this thing the airborne toxic event. It's an event all right. It marks the end of uneventful things. This is just the beginning. Wait and see" (DeLillo 1986: 151). Tongue-in-cheek, Murray, the novel's representative of academic deconstruction, addresses a concern that my study investigates. Given postmodernism's crucial critique of both events and subjects, I argue that selected American novels after 2000 open up new ways of thinking about events and subjects that acquire reagency. With the awareness of the skepticism toward events and subjects, my study weighs in on this debate and argues that Cormac McCarthy's *The Road*, Jess Walter's *The Zero*, Mark Z. Danielewski's *Only Revolutions*, Paul Beatty's *Slumberland* and Thomas Pynchon's *Against the Day*, do not simply return to a nostalgic conception of a humanist subject and a theological event (in fact, they criticize such notions) but opt for different alternatives. Badiou's notions of events and subjects are helpful in this context, since they proffer a new conceptualization of these terms. Especially because of the ubiquity of the term "event" in everyday language, what is called for is a conceptual and theoretical delimitation that distances itself from the quotidian use of "events" that merely refer to everyday happenings. In contrast, for Badiou, events are fundamentally disruptive phenomena that are "excluded by all the regular laws of" (*E* 41) a situation and therefore not only absolutely contingent, since they "meant nothing according to the prevailing language and established knowledge of the situation" (*E* 43), but also crucially singular: events, unlike the apocalypse, for instance, undermine any logic of repetition.[12] As much as this notion of the event breaks with the tradition of that concept, so does Badiou's conception of the subject blaze a new trail. The subject, Badiou insists, is not an "abstract Subject" but only "*become*[s] a subject—or rather, . . . enter[s] into the composing of a subject" (*E* 40). Unlike a stable center for rational actions, Badiou suggests that a subject is rather a process that "compels us to decide a *new* way of being" (*E* 41): new precisely because it relates to the event, which casts forth a proposition that could not be discerned from the perspective prior to its pre-discursive eruption. Indeed, the major argument this study maintains, with Badiou, is that event and subject are inherently reciprocal phenomena. Only through the manifestation of a contingent, singular event that disrupts a particular situation can a subject be produced. But in order to be an event at all, there has to be a subjective process that affirmatively accepts the new imperatives that the event propels, which could not be discerned from the perspective prior to its manifestation and, indeed, call for an irrational wager of those who decide to act in fidelity to it. Instead of either yielding to the determining power of the event that subjects the subject *or* the autonomy of the subject that constructs an event, this theory implies a fundamental reciprocity that neither supposes the hierarchical dominance of one of these terms, nor lets them fuse in a dialectical *Aufhebung*. Both phenomena are dependent upon each other, without losing their constitutive importance.

In orienting myself along Badiou's thoughts in *Being and Event*, *Ethics*, and *Logics of Worlds* as well as his other writings about events as non-ontological, singular, and contingent ruptures that create various subjective procedures (reactive, obscure, and faithful), I argue that this philosophical undertaking offers a productive set of tools that helps us to read these five novels in their construction of events and subjects that relate to these singularities. However, while Badiou's theory presents a critical tool to read these novels in specific ways, these ways of reading do not simply adopt his insights as stereotypical "examples." In confronting Badiou's unique understanding of events and subjects with the cultural and literary traditions of the United States, this book shows how these novels help to negotiate this theoretical impetus, and thereby expands on Badiou's apparatus by offering new insights. By emphasizing the textual and literary qualities of these novels as works of fiction, I explore the scope of various subjects of events that are endowed with narrative, linguistic, political, or aesthetic reagency. While agency was a radically questioned capability in postmodernist literature and theory,[13] I argue that these novels do not *return* to a humanist notion of agency but stress the necessary *reciprocity* of event and subject, as well as the subject's *repetitive* "fidelity" to the propositions that an event evokes, which I term *reagency*.

Only by continuously reaffirming an event does a subject remain a subject and retain its reagency.

Badiou's introductory quote, therefore, also relates to a particular temporal setting in "the early years of the [twenty-first] century" that is marked by fundamental epistemological disorientation, especially, as this study exhibits, at the level of an individual and his or her experience of an event. Not only do Badiou's repetitive, paratactically aligned questions highlight a general form of uncertainty; they more emphatically articulate the crucial problems of how to face an event: What does a proper event ask us to do? Are we to conservatively uphold the "continuation, at all costs, of a weary world"? Are we to step up and engage in the new imperatives that such an event might bring forth? How can we even know if an event has happened, let alone what an event is? Do we have the language, "any clear name" to conceive of it at all? How can one not resort to paralysis confronted with such overwhelming stakes?

The epistemological crisis at the turn of the twenty-first century that Badiou addresses redirects a general dilemma to the concrete relation between subject and event, and, more importantly for this study, to the question of events and subjects in literature. In the wake of the "death of the subject" as a rational, *a priori*, stable agent within the various taproots of postmodernism, it becomes the question of how to formulate new trajectories that might offer a glimpse beyond this "discourse of the end" (*IT* 143) without obviously ascribing that different stance to a problematic notion of progress. However, the constellation of inquiring into the status of the subject in the literary field of the American novel after 2000 requires a concrete theoretical positioning, since this overlap has engendered a growing discourse that deals with this literary timeframe and conjoins it with the question of the subject. Emphatically, my project distances itself from the ubiquitous proclamations of "returns." I identify my project neither with a "return of the subject," nor with an "ethical turn."[14] Although my study is explicitly interested in "subjects" and "ethics," I reject a mere return of, and to, these concepts, which would imply that postmodernism was a road that should not have been taken and what is required now is a u-turn. This is amplified by Badiou's stance toward the "anti-humanism" of Foucault, Althusser, and Lacan. Instead of viewing these theoretical insights as unethical, or even unpolitical, Badiou maintains that "when those who uphold the contemporary ideology of 'ethics' tell us that the return to Man and his rights has delivered us from the 'fatal abstractions' inspired by 'the ideologies' of the past, they have some nerve" (*E* 7). Equally so, I would argue that when those who perceive the postmodernist novels of Pynchon, DeLillo, Kathy Acker, or Toni Morrison to be unethical, they have some nerve.

While there is a tendency of both postmodernist theory and literature to undermine notions of emphatic events and humanist subjects, my conception of the subject of the event and reagency do not explicitly involve a return to a seemingly edenic state *before* postmodernism. The subject of the event, rather, offers a new way of understanding the relation between a subject and an event by navigating the Scylla and Charbybdis of humanism and antihumanism. Becoming a subject of the event is not an *a priori* anthropological disposition but, rather, involves the contingent eruption of an event, which then initiates the possibility of this subject to be endowed with moments of empowerment beyond the determinism of poststructural theories.

Badiou's notion of an "ethics of truths" (*E* 40) also rejects the recent discourse of an "ethics of recognition."[15] What has become a prominent discourse in philosophy, sociology, and the humanities, and which, by and large, adopts the Levinasian idea of a respect of difference is in the context of this study too weak a basis for ethical analysis and praxis.[16] Instead of following the consensus forms of identity politics, my study affirms an ethics of truths as a situated form of ethical behavior that is sensitive to historical and cultural conditions, but is based on an event, and consequently eschews various identity groupings, since it is fundamentally "indifferent to differences" (*E* 27). Particularly, Beatty's *Slumberland* shows how identity politics may be surrogated by an evental politics that questions the multiculturalist or cosmopolitical dogma of respecting the Other. While an ethics of truth does not construct a timeless body of ethical rules that categorically helps the human to orient herself or himself in chaotic surroundings, it nevertheless offers a basis for ethical deduction, especially in matters of political responsibility.

Least of all do I subsume my analysis of five American novels that were published after 2000 in a grander gesture of literary periodization, which has often been labeled "post-postmodernism," or the like.[17] Grown out of the ennui with postmodernist literature and theory, a variety of critics have tried to blaze the trail of what is most often called post-postmodernism. Yet, such attempts that argue for an aesthetic and ethico-political detachment from postmodernism are often related to what Mary K. Holland aptly terms "an apparently growing appetite for forays into the similarly commitment-phobic debate about the end of postmodernism" (2013: 11–12). Although some critics, notably Holland but also Andrew Hoberek and Robert McLaughlin,[18] display a critical skepticism toward a wholehearted detachment from postmodernism, Stephen J. Burns observes that "for many critics the end of the century seemed to overlap with the end of postmodernism" (2008: 10). If there exists an inevitable arbitrariness in my study's delimiting starting point of "*after 2000*," this date seems appropriate for me since it addresses that "dreaded Y2K," as Pynchon's *Bleeding Edge* phrases it (2013: 302), that evokes the millennial relation between America and events. Besides the mere practical reasons for having a concrete temporal demarcation that is more precise than the ever-relative denominator of "contemporary," but also refuses to be as concrete in positing that September 11, 2001 serves as the historical point of inception for a shift,[19] I also choose the delimitation *after* 2000 as suggesting a new conceptualization of events that distances itself from its religious context in America.

The critical distance to arguments that call for a return of the subject; the political, the social, the ethical, the realistic, makes itself felt in this study, for one thing, in the choice of texts at hand. By explicitly interrogating household names of the American canon like Cormac McCarthy and Thomas Pynchon—the former seemingly at odds with postmodernism, as David Holloway, for instance, has argued (2002: 4), the latter apparently the synechdochal personification of this period[20]—my study rejects the turn toward such ostensibly "post-postmodernist" writers like David Foster Wallace, Dave Eggers, or Jonathan Franzen.[21] Indeed, the novels by Jess Walter,

Mark Z. Danielewski, and Paul Beatty could equally be termed postmodern because of their experimentation with form, play with irony, or reflection on history and its writing, for that matter. However, part of the argument of this study is that instead of mounting an approach of a return to the real,[22] it is explicitly the metafictional endeavor of these five novels that intricately engages in the reflection on events, as well as the production of subjects of events.[23] By emphasizing narrative, linguistic, formal, or diegetic breaks, these novels concentrate their energies on anti-mimetic forms of writing that are thereby particularly apt in negotiating the singular account of events and subjects and deny a naïve return of humanist narratives as well as a comprehensive determination of poststructuralist approaches. Instead of conceiving of ways of how "the subject [can] be put on its feet again" (Kurcharzewski et al. 2009: 2), I rather opt for a different conception of the subject as a subject of the event that points to the problems of "going back rather than going beyond" (Dunst 2009: 81) such theories.

Besides the fairly recent publication of these novels, I would insist that the scarce criticism that exists on these texts is partly due to what could broadly be called their metafictional tendencies, which renders them "merely" postmodernist texts and thus no longer worthy of consideration, or even to have anything to say about political matters. In tackling such a "serious" question as that of the subject, most studies take the more realistic novels of Eggers or Franzen as more apt to respond to such inquiries. However, it is my contention that the poetological reflections of such a novel as Jess Walter's *The Zero*, for instance, may point more intricately to questions of trauma and questions of representation, which it shows to be inherently connected to the ostensible event of "9/11" and its consequent biopolitical mechanisms, whereas Danielewski's *Only Revolutions* plays with form, but also criticizes a mere solipsistic form of subjectivity in the same breath.

While McCarthy's *The Road* has experienced by far the most elaborate account of tackling the question of the subject, most readings of the novel argue for a return to humanist ethics that the symbolic father and son constellation conveys. Exemplary for such a reading is Heather Duerre Humann's "Close(d) to God, Negotiating a Moral Terrain: Questions of Agency and Selfhood in *The Road* and *Sophie's Choice*." By adapting David Hume's notions of subjectivity and agency, Humann simply ignores postmodernist insights and lets the father act as an autonomous being.

Nicoline Timmer's *Do You Feel It Too? The Post-Postmodernist Syndrome in American Fiction at the Turn of the Millenium* is equally concerned with the question of the human. Although Timmer's text choice does not overlap with the novels in this study, her intention to interrogate a "new sense of self" (2010: 18) in contemporary American fiction addresses a similar question as this study. In following a recent turn to narrative psychological methodologies Timmer deals with the question of "what it means to be human" (ibid.: 13). By subscribing to Shlomith Rimmon-Kenan's call for a rehumanization of the subject in her *A Glance beyond Doubt*, Timmer similarly argues that subjects are endowed with "narrative agency" (ibid.: 41). Ultimately, her argument that humans have "the ability to navigate through different discursive communities and assemble their own story of the self" (ibid.: 41) by which they "regain 'control', the capacity to make sense of their experience of the world" (ibid.: 42) not only seems too fuzzy a definition of agency but also fails to adequately tackle the problem of discursive immanence. Positing that agency merely implies the infinitesimal relation to discursive regulations seems wanting and fails to circumnavigate determining structures beyond the ephemeral insistence on subversion. However, while Timmer acknowledges that her own undertaking "does not amount to a naïve return to the more traditional view of the self as centered and autonomous meaning-maker" (ibid.: 52), I would distance myself from such an interest in the "human" (13) by positing that my study is rather interested in the exceptional manifestation of a subject, which is an entirely different category.

Raoul Eshelman's *Performatism, or, The End of Postmodernism* is also a relevant study, since it addresses contemporary Anglophone art and argues that "we are now leaving the postmodern era with its essentially dualist notions of textuality, virtuality, belatedness, endless irony, and metaphysical skepticism and entering an era in which specifically monist virtues are again coming to the fore" (2004: xi). Such a monism could already be perceived, as I would argue, in such postmodernist novels as *Gravity's Rainbow*, but Badiou is also radically opposed to the belief in the One, as the very first meditation of *Being and Event* makes clear. While Eshelman also argues for a "new, positively conceived—but not unproblematic—type of subjectivity" that is a "reaction to the plight of the postmodern subject" and such subjects might incur the "enmity of its surroundings" (ibid.: 8), which is also the case for such subjects of events as in Pynchon's *Against the Day*, I maintain that only their fidelity to an event allows a form of "transcend[ing] a frame" (ibid.: 12) as Eshelman phrases it. Unlike the performatist subject that transcends a frame "by breaking through it at some point and/or reversing its basic parameters" (ibid.: 12), the subject of the event is not by itself able to enact such a " 'performance' " (ibid.: 12) but depends upon an event. Finally, although my study shares the emphasis on "transcending coercive frames rather than continually transgressing porous, constantly shifting boundaries" (as in the case of postmodernism), I explicitly distance this undertaking from a "distinctly *theist* cast" (ibid.: 13) and, rather, emphasize the atheist implications of a subject of the event.

Another text worth mentioning is Sascha Pöhlmann's introduction to the essay volume *Revolutionary Leaves: The Fiction of Mark Z. Danielewski*, since it insists on the political concerns of what is often merely denounced as experimental fiction, focusing on Danielewski's *Only Revolutions*. Pöhlmann reads the novel under the lens of Whitman's democratic poetics and politics, which informs my analysis of the novel's production of a subject of love that leaves behind the initial individual solipsism. Yet, while Pöhlmann sees the novel as "mov[ing] away from a notion of individualism that has rightly come under fire in the twentieth century, most notably in the discourse of poststructuralism and the 'death of the subject' which Foucault predicted in *The Order of Things*" (2012: 7), he argues that this critique of the subject results in a democratic outlook that is based on the Lévinasian relation to an Other. If for Pöhlmann the individual is always already in contact with an Other, I argue that the novel's event constitutes the crucial point where the two narrators' solipsisms are abandoned and the construction of an amorous subject is initiated in the first place.

That *Against the Day* marks a shift from Pynchon's other novels is fairly established in Pynchon criticism. Yet, the diagnosis that *Against the Day* is, in Heinz Ickstadt's words, "notably different from any of its predecessors" (2008: 218) has only tangentially been accredited to the status of events and subjects. What comes closest to my study's notion of subjects of events and reagency is Ali Chetwynd's talk on "Inherent Obligation: Ethical Relations and The Demands of Patronage in Recent Pynchon."[24] Chetwynd's reading of the novel distances itself from the critical commonplace about the critique of characters in Pynchon and argues that "crucial to the tone of Pynchon's work since *Mason & Dixon,* I argue, is the struggle of his characters to reconcile a sense of their own freedom from constraint with the inherent ethical obligations involved in fundamental relations like family, friendship and love" (2010: n.p.). Besides the fact that this question is not linked to the eruption of an event, I also insist that Badiou's notion of fidelity might be a more precise and productive concept that helps to understand how far Kit Traverse may transcend his obligations by becoming a subject of the event.

While I do insist that there are fundamental differences between such novels as *Gravity's Rainbow* and *Against the Day,* I refrain from seeing a movement toward a post-postmodernist aesthetics or politics. What this study is interested in is the positive analysis of how these novels conceptualize events and subjects instead of an *ex negativo* definition *against* postmodernism in a literary-historical framework. The mere fact that these novels, which certainly are not representative of "the American novel after 2000" as such, configure a different form of event and subject does not make me argue that this is an indicator for a wholesale departure from postmodernism in its many faces. To me, these novels continue the critique of the humanist subject, however, by offering a different alternative than mere paralysis or dissolution.

To this extent, whereas the novels under analysis could very well fit under the heterogeneous umbrella-term of postmodernism, the theoretical approach I pursue in this study is radically opposed to poststructural and postmodern theories at large. This question, of how to conceive of a concept of the subject without either fully determining it in the light of poststructuralist theories or relapsing to a naïve humanism is a salient methodological problem.[25] Particularly because postmodern literature and theory have comprehensively undermined the conventional notions of the subject and the event, I think it is necessary to acquire a different theoretical footing, which offers itself in Badiou's philosophy. To be sure, next to the fact that the humanities, and especially American Studies, have become skeptical of the continental import for its modes of analysis after the heyday of poststructuralism, a debate that was initiated by the so-called culture wars of the 1980s–1990s,[26] Badiou presents a special case in academia, to the extent that Jacques Rancière rightly calls him an "Unidentified Flying Object that has recently landed on our soil" (2004: 218). After a first vacuity in the critical response toward his thinking, which is repeatedly conceived as being radically opposed to postmodernism, or by himself declared to be "more-than-modern (given that the adjective 'postmodern' has been evacuated of all content)" (*TW* xvi),[27] and, as I argue, was and is still not accepted *because of* academia's theoretical inclination toward postmodern approaches (particularly deconstruction and constructivism in its various forms), Badiou's thinking has slowly but surely entered the awareness of scholarly research.[28] While Badiou's ontological approach that works with such conceptions as "truths," "fidelity," or non-ontological phenomena (events), is often all too quickly discarded as theological or idealist thinking,[29] and his mathematical approach seems suspicious from the other side of the Two Culture divide, his spectral place in twenty-first-century theory is also due to his political orientation.[30] Without being ignorant of the political undercurrents of Badiou's thinking, my study focuses more closely on his philosophical considerations and not his biographical past. While such a clear separation is arguably not always possible, my engagement with Badiou's analytical tools tries to construct a critical fidelity toward his concepts, which is particularly put to the test in the literary analyses. Since I refrain from simply applying Badiou's theoretical conceptions on the novels at hand, I show how the various novels also complicate his theory by extending its stimulus and creating a sensitivity to the American literary context that engages with the following methodological questions:[31] How can an abstract philosophico-mathematical conception of the event be made productive in a cultural context that is severely influenced by a religious undercurrent of such ideas? How can a collective notion of the subject be compatible with a strong individualistic notion of the subject as it is fostered in the United States? Equally so, one might ask how far Badiou, as another apparent installment of French intellectual "anti-Americanism" (*IT* 117), can be put into play with American literary and cultural concerns?[32] I argue that in bringing together Badiou's theory and the novels at hand, not only are the allegations against his theological, political, or abstract mathematical dispositions resolved but these concepts are also discussed by the five novels under investigation by foregrounding their literary quality, aesthetic disposition and, ultimately, political avail. By taking Badiou's theory as an event, if you will, these novels then become subjects of this event, which implies not a mere realization of his propositions. Instead, although they adhere to the general impetus of his theory to some extent, they critically engage in the literary adaptation of these terms that well go beyond the initial idea of this event.

While I generally conceive this study methodologically as a literary analysis that appropriates philosophical insights, interrogating various discourses on events that serve as points of contrast, I also suggest that close readings of the novels at hand are a specifically suited approach to analyze subjects of events, which thereby show that there are very close ties between this philosophical approach and the study of literature. Indeed, Mehdi Belhaj Kacem cuts right to the chase of the matter when he compares Badiou's methodological undertaking to that of a crime novel.[33] Instead of adapting Badiou's logical subtractions to the study of literary works of fiction, close readings manifest an important approach that investigates the ephemeral traces of events and attempts to "solve" the mysteries of these happenings. While there is obviously always room for interpretation in *how* I confront and read an event, this epistemological uncertainty is nevertheless already part of a hermeneutic act of detecting an event. There is no question of whether or not I relate to an event, since my ability to interpret it as such already implies that it is an event, as the next chapter will explain in more detail. A close analysis of the various situations that these novels conjure calls for the critical investigation of the novels' events, whose manifestation might sometimes be more apparent, sometimes less so. While *The Road* and *The Zero* mark their events in the very beginning of each novel and make the whole diegetic world dependent on these happenings, they nevertheless require a close analysis. In the case of the former, it is pertinent to grasp how the novel's event is distinct from religious or ecological notions of apocalypse; in the latter a close examination of the event is called for, since the novel unmasks the eventness of "9/11" as a simulacra. The events in *Only Revolutions*, *Slumberland*, and *Against the Day* are, in contrast, more inconspicuous. Detective work is required here in creating a distinction between the abundance of historical happenings that these novels depict and the authentic events that make possible the creation of subjects. Next to pointing to the parallels between Badiou's notion of events and subjects and American culture, my study also emphasizes the genuine realm of literature and how literary studies can inquire into a theory of the subject of the event with its tools of analysis.

Badiou's epigraph, which is first and foremost a diagnosis of current events, is therefore also adequate as a prelude and summary of this study, since it frames it in an explicitly political context. As a literary analysis, my study has certainly not the legitimate grounding of commenting on politics at large. Nevertheless, I insist that any discussion of subjects, events, and reagency cannot exclude the political in a time where democratic materialism, as Badiou phrases it, "only knows individuals and communities, that is to say passive bodies, but it knows no subject" (*LoW* 50). By undermining the clear separation that Badiou maintains between what he perceives to be the only possible realms of where a subject of the event may come to the fore (science, art, love, politics), my study's analysis of scientific, aesthetic, amorous, and political subjective processes not only always assumes a literary take on these concerns (thereby being scientific-aesthetic) but also inquires into the political undercurrents of such matters. In emphasizing the political implications of the novels under analysis, from ecological concerns, or issues of biopolitical control, to matters of racism and political persecution, each novel contributes to the literary discussion a concrete notion of politics. Instead of merely seeing politics as a form of revolutionary upheaval as in the case of the "Arab Spring," this study maintains that a novel's reflection on such debates also participates in a political praxis that implies the reader to a large extent. As a political literary analysis, my study therefore distances itself from the strict conception of politics as an emancipatory process that always implies societal revolution and locates this praxis in what Badiou would argue is the condition of art. Particularly through art's reflection on such issues as a formal revolution that is connected to political emancipation, the novel stands as a genuine discourse that engages in such an endeavor.

In this sense, I also emphasize the aspect of love, specifically as this condition is related to the aspect of fidelity.[34] By adapting the literary-theory of the subject of the event on a methodological level, what is required is a faithfulness to the text, paying attention to a narrative's structural, linguistic, and diegetical reflections on events that might often require the repetitive engagement of re-reading, as *Only Revolutions's* formal set-up emphasizes. This does not imply that there is only one reading of a text, which might suggest a uniform fidelity to it. On the one hand, fidelity always implies a dimension of irrationality, since the very act of deciding upon the existence of an event implies a fundamental "wager," "an unreasonable gamble or leap of faith" (Hallward 2003: 126). On the other hand, since there "are infinite nuances in the phenomenology of the procedure of fidelity" (*BE* 330), there can never be just one textual fidelity that dictates a categorical course of action (or interpretation). Nevertheless, the textual fidelity that this project assumes as its methodological approach is necessarily related to the reflection on events in these texts, since without such a manifestation, there could be no process of fidelity in the first place. As diverse as readings may be of these novels, they inexorably have to position themselves toward events. In a sense, the critic is, indeed, faithful to the text by falling in love with it, which might occasion moments of irrationality but is, indeed, part of a larger framework of a love of language: *philology* as such.

It is my contention that Badiou's notion of events, subjects, truths, fidelity, or points offers a rich and productive set of tools in the realm of philosophy as well as for the study of literature and American Studies in particular. As the first study that comprehensively engages with Badiou's concepts in the realm of a literary analysis, my book not only tries to introduce his ideas into a scholarly environment that is arguably still dominated by postmodernist theoretical and methodological approaches but also seeks to elucidate how it is particularly the novel that might adapt the somewhat abstract implications of Badiou's set theoretical approach that discusses ontological questions. Indeed, while Badiou himself focuses on all other artistic genres except for the novel,[35] I show that, specifically, the American novel contributes to this discussion, since subjects and events are an integral part of this tradition. In analyzing the American *novel* after 2000, I insist on its etymological origins: by evoking contingent, singular disruptive events, the novel, indeed, creates something *new*. If Johann Wolfgang von Goethe defined the novella as a "ereignete unerhöhrte Begebenheit" (1986: 203), this study opts for a more radical understanding of events that goes beyond a mere "unheard of," perfectly deducible "incident," and stresses that the novel here develops a theory of the subject of the event from within its literary scope and with the help of its textual, narrative, or fictional capabilities. While the books in this study do not radically innovate form, or entirely leave behind the traditions in what they write, they nevertheless poeticize the eruption of the new and thereby make possible the construction of various subjective procedures that are endowed with moments of empowerment, or reagency.

Besides the essential intellectual import that Badiou's philosophy offers for the study of the American novel in relation to its creation of events and subjects, I also suggest that the theory of the subject of the event can be related to existing research areas in American Studies. Far from simply following "the latest neo-Nietzschean mills flown from France" (2005: 19), as Green phrases it, I argue that Badiou, indeed, offers a genuine and enticing way of responding to existing problems of the research. To be sure, Badiou, who likes to see himself as the remedy for all of twentieth-century theory's aporias, does not produce a new grand narrative that subsumes all other discourses under its dominance. While also stressing various blind spots in his thinking, I nevertheless make the case that one can gain new insights in as diverse fields as ecocriticism, trauma studies, African American studies and identity politics, by bringing his philosophy into contact with these debates. His notion of the event critically engages with the powerful discourse of apocalypse in both its religious and ecocritical context. In adopting his ideas on ethics, one can arrive at productive insights in the political context of such incidents as the terrorist attack on September 11, 2001 that goes beyond the evocation of "trauma." By expounding a strong notion of collective subjectivity, the theory of the subject of the event also proves to engage in discussions of African American studies by raising issues of aesthetic and political empowerment.

In mirroring the conceptual duplicity of subject and event that are integral to this study, one might detect a similar division in the alignment of this book. As my title suggests, it is the compound between the subject *and* the event that guides not only the microscopic conceptual terminology of the literary analyses but also the structural architecture of this project. While the first chapter begins by obtaining a theoretical understanding that orients itself along Badiou's notion of events and the second chapter is dedicated to the literary investigation of various subjects, this is by no means a clear separation. Just as the event fundamentally depends on a subject that steps up to its propositions, so is the subject only produced through the manifestation of an event and may achieve reagency through the combination of these phenomena. This profound reciprocity, which Žižek fittingly calls a "circular relationship" (1999: 167), thus also makes itself felt in the alignment of this study. While I begin with a theoretical reflection on what constitutes an event, the question of the subject is always kept in mind. Equally so, whereas the "analytical" part of this project focuses on various subjects (reactive, obscure, and faithful ones), these chapters by necessity interrogate "theoretical" notions of events with a particular sensitivity to the American milieu of this concept. To this extent, I try to project the mutual dependence between subject and event onto the theory-analysis dichotomy of this book, for the "theory" part also involves "literary" examples—in a sense, already prefiguring the subjective constitutions—while the "analysis" chapters also do "theoretical" work: both engage in the theorization and negotiation of a subject of the event.

In establishing the theoretical instruments that are needed for the literary analysis of subjects of events, the first chapter examines Badiou's philosophy for its unique conceptualization of these terms. After defining events as non-ontological, contingent, and singular ruptures, I proceed to give an account of the notion of the subject that relates to this disruption and is faithful to it. After showing how this distances itself from both humanist and poststructuralist notions of the subject, I conclude the chapter by explicating my notion of reagency, a specific form of subjective empowerment that is, however, contingent upon the eruption of an event and the faithful incorporation of its propositions within the situation that strains to undermine its existence. By showing how this project transcends Badiou's rigid separation of the conditions of art, science, love, and politics, I establish an *ethics of reading* that specifically attunes to the novels to be investigated in the succeeding chapters. However, I want to stress that a neat distinction between a "theoretical" and a "literary" part is being avoided in this study. While Chapter 1 already considers literary cases, the following five chapters also do fundamental theoretical work. As novels, they are not only "examples" of Badiou's theory but they fundamentally adapt, extend, and even criticize what Badiou's philosophy has in mind.

Building upon these theoretical observations, Chapters 2 to 6 investigate the literary *refraction* of various subjects of events in five American novels of the twenty-first century. In this sense, the literary part of this book does not serve only as an illustrative mirroring of the blueprint that Badiou's theory offers. More emphatically, the novels under investigation refract Badiou's philosophical concepts to the extent that they add to his theoretization by deviating from his course, thereby breaking new ground.[36] Essentially, each chapter sheds light on the productivity of the theory of the subject of the event in responding to various discourses of American Studies and literary studies, and thereby not only contextualizes Badiou's theory in an American setting, but also shows how these contexts expand his thoughts (as in the case of the role of the event in American ecocriticism, for instance).

Moreover, each novel presents a different aspect of the theory of the subject of the event, without arriving at a clear and uniform picture. Yet, this is not only due to the literary works and their literary *work*, but also because Badiou's theory involves a variety of factors to successfully constitute a subject of the event that is endowed with reagency. The works under consideration exemplify how this theoretical concept is not an absolute paradigm that is readily applicable to every form of fiction published, which would result in a naïve "return of the subject." For if the subject of the event demarcated an unconditional disposition, this would imply that every fictional character in a novel after 2000 would become a subject. Indeed, my study is not interested in the question of "what it means to be human" (Timmer 2010: 13) but, rather, in the exceptional manifestations of subjects (of the event). Hence, rather than conceiving the subject of the event as a socio-historic approach to texts, irrespective of its aesthetic, political, or structural mechanisms, this study argues for its specificity as well as the particulate nature of its manifestation. While every narrative certainly contains happenings or characters, not every text contains an event, and thus not every text contains a subject; hardly any text contains a faithful subject of the event.

Badiou's types of reactive, obscure, and faithful subjects of events thus guide the analyses of Chapters 2, 3, 4, 5, and 6. Adapting more recent considerations of the various forms of subjects of the event that Badiou establishes in *Ethics* and *Logics of Worlds*, the constellation of these five chapters sheds light onto distinct ways of how a subject of the event might be created. On another level, these chapters are also aligned so as to explore the scope of the distinct spheres in which a subject of the event may be produced. Specifically, the faithful procedures in Danielewski's *Only Revolutions* (Chapter 4), Paul Beatty's *Slumberland* (Chapter 5), and Thomas Pynchon's *Against the Day* (Chapter 6) illuminate the four conditions of love, art, politics, and science. Yet, whereas *Only Revolutions* might be safely situated in the sphere of love, *Slumberland* and *Against the Day* fundamentally undermine the neat distinction between these rigid realms. Both *Slumberland* and *Against the Day* also attest that a subject of the event cannot always be contained in one hermetic "truth-condition." In the fictional negotiation of these concepts, the subjects in these novels transcend the rigidity of the four conditions and interrelate them without abandoning their fidelity. Badiou's penchant for logical purism, which is particularly evident in his separation of the four truth conditions is thus tellingly conveyed when he writes that "the crucible in which what will become a work of art and thought burns is brimful with nameless impurities; it comprises obsessions, beliefs, infantile puzzles, various perversions, undivulgeable memories, haphazard reading, and quite a few idiocies and chimeras. Analyzing this alchemy is of little use" (2003: 2). I think it is particularly the work of the literary critic to analyze these impurities and become an alchemist of sorts himself or herself. Only by traversing art or science into political domains do these fictions practice alchemy and conceptualize forms of reagency.

To this extent, the various subjects of events that I choose to analyze also exemplify "'untrue' subjects" (Toscano 2006: 16), where some constituent process that would create a faithful subject is amiss and which results in a literally corrupted, what Badiou provocatively calls "evil" (*E* 58ff.), subject of the event.[37] If the subject of the event is endowed with reagency, an emancipatory empowerment that only the manifestation of an event generates, these corrupted subjective forms attain their activity solely in negative terms, which makes me refrain from situating such moments of empowerment in the context of a reagency, a disposition that, rather, appertains to faithful subjective procedures. In contrast to Badiou's argument that the presence of a faithful subject is essential for the creation of reactive and obscure relations to this procedure, which he terms the primacy of the "Good" (*E* 60), I choose to imply the reverse structure, if only in order to go from the negative, corrupted, evil, to the positive, faithful, good.[38]

If Chapters 2 and 3 elucidate how the process of a subject being faithful to an event may be corrupted at the point of the subject's failed fidelity to an event (*The Road*) or the confusion of a mere happening with a genuine event (*The Zero*), there are also differences in the extent of an event. Whereas some events shatter the entire textual logic of a novel (*Only Revolutions*), they might also simply create a subject of the event as one of many narrative strands without affecting the entirety of a novel (*Against the Day*).

Chapter 2 thus inquires into a subject of the event that tries to conserve the world that existed prior to the eruption of an event, for which Cormac McCarthy's *The Road* is a paramount example. By trying to conserve the human order in spite of the radical imperatives of the cataclysmic event that the novel depicts, father and son become reactive subjects of the event that forfeit their claims to reagency. After establishing the extent to which the novel's event can be seen as an ecological event, which crucially distances itself from religious and ecological apocalypse as well as Badiou's scientific, aesthetic, political, and amorous conditions, I connect the father's perpetuation of human life, particularly through his clinging on to consumerism and the persistent trope of "carrying the fire," not to a return of humanist values but to the creation of a subject of the event that denies the truth of the novel's ecological event. The event is thus established as a crucial concept in ecocriticism that in the novel might, indeed, undermine the anthropological "question of the subject and its relation to the environment," which Timo Müller and Michael Sauter argue is "certainly one of ecocriticism's central questions" (2012: 8). Instead of adhering to the evental propositions, which call for the earthly abandonment of human life and life in general, father and son keep on clinging to the world before the event, which makes the father, in particular, an example of a reactive subject.

Another form of "'untrue' subjects" (Toscano 2006: 16) is interrogated in Chapter 3, which analyzes Jess Walter's *The Zero*. Dealing with notions of disruptive events in the American novel after 2000 means that one cannot circumnavigate the profound impact of the terrorist attacks of September 11, 2001. Yet, in undermining the discourse of trauma that has been circulating in the wake of the attack, the theory of the subject of the event shows how *The Zero* criticizes this discussion by unmasking "9/11" as a simulacra event. Despite the terrible implications of this happening, the novel undermines its status as an event and elucidates how an obscure subject of the event is produced, a subject that mistakes a mere happening for an event. As a consequence, the novel's narrative mechanisms, involving textual blanks that typographically comment on the discourse of trauma and suggest the instability of the protagonist's identity, are rechanneled as indicating a literary means to give expression to an "Evil" (*E* 8) form of the subject of the event. In denying the universal impetus of every event, this subject, rather, tries to exploit the happening for reclaiming biopolitical control in the United States.

After discussing these degenerate forms of subjective formation, I focus on three instances of faithful subjects of events who display their reagency in different fields and in different forms. Mark Z. Danielewski's typographically and conceptually virtuous *Only Revolutions* then marks the first case of a faithful subject of the event. In analyzing the novel's extreme play with form, this chapter's evocation of a subject of love lets the two solipsistic homodiegetic narrators move beyond the limited point of view of their individual worlds by adhering to their amorous encounter. It is specifically interesting here to see the interaction between the epistemologically and ontologically disruptive momentum of an event and the means by which a literary text may represent such a breakdown. Essentially, I argue that the novel gives the concept of reagency a particular formal expression by elucidating how Sam's and Hailey's fidelity to the event makes them perpetuate their story of love in a repetitive form that percolates into the realm of reception.

If *Only Revolutions*'s protagonists Sam and Hailey directly confront the event that shatters their egomaniac worlds, which makes them become a subject of love that consists of two individuals, Paul Beatty's *Slumberland* not only inquires into a larger outlook on the collective dimension of a subject of the event but also complicates the experience of events through its meditation on the resurrection of a bygone political event. The novel offers a literary exploration of a type of subject of events that Badiou introduces in *Logics of Worlds* and explicates only cursorily. While it already proves difficult to grasp how an individual comes into contact with an event that withdraws from the preeminent epistemological and ontological order, this subtype of fidelity even further problematizes this interaction by insisting that individuals might resurrect an event whose radiance has waned. Yet, *Slumberland* intricately engages in this problem by interconnecting this procedure with the persistent need for an emancipatory politics in the United States and its imperial outposts, in the novel's case, Germany around the fall of the Berlin Wall. In questioning the discourses of the end of history as well as the end of the Jim Crow era, the novel's reflection on the subject of the event creates a foundation for political and aesthetic reagency.

The sixth and last chapter deals with Thomas Pynchon's *Against the Day*. Whereas *Slumberland* also investigated the necessary interrelation between two apparently separate spheres (art and politics), *Against the Day* sheds light on the relation between science and politics. If all the other chapters focused on the construction of a single subject of the event, Pynchon's expansive scope in his sixth novel evokes two distinct scientific-political subjects of events. Thereby, the theory of the subject of the event is adapted to Pynchon's excessive novels of encyclopedic outlook by investigating the construction of two similar yet different instantiations of scientific subjects that are endowed with reagency through their fidelity to two scientific events. Against Badiou's claim that events and subjects are necessarily rare occasions, Pynchon juxtaposes a variety of such potential events and thereby mobilizes the poietical potential of literature to fictionalize as many events as possible, which could, indeed, be seen as a possible response to the very scarcity of "real-life" events. However, this plurality of events does not result in a similar conceptual dilution as in his former novels, where individuals remain paralyzed faced with the undecidability of how to recognize an event. Instead, Kit Traverse's fidelity to the Quaternionist event and Yashmeen Halfcourt's faithfulness to the Riemann event lets them leave behind specific determining forces and allows them to employ their reagency to undermine particular systems. Especially because these empowered subjects of events are faithful to scientific events, which clearly breaks with Slothrop's scientific incorporation in *Gravity's Rainbow*, indicates a shift in twenty-first-century literature's notion of subjects and events. By placing Pynchon at the end of this book, I want to suggest that while there is a notable shift in the conception of events, subjects, and reagency, this is not an absolute detachment from the US postmodernist novel.

In the conclusion, I take a glimpse at other American novels published after 2000. This final part intimates the fertility of the theory of the subject of the event beyond the five novels analyzed in detail in this study. Without suggesting that the discussion of subjects of events in a larger corpus makes it valid to argue for a literary historical or generic phenomenon, it is nevertheless worth noting that event, subject, and reagency are prominent concerns in American literature of the twenty-first century. If one wished to find answers to Badiou's questions—"What is going on? Of what are we the half-fascinated, half-devastated witnesses?" (*TRoH* 1)—this book shows that it is in the construction of various subjects of the events in the American novel of the new millennium.

1

The Question of the Event and the Question(s) of the Subject

Die Frage lautet: ob, wann und wie
wir Zugehörige des Seins (als Ereignis) sind.
(The question is: if, when and where
we are taking part in being [as event].) (My translation)

> Martin Heidegger, *Beiträge zur Philosophie (Vom Ereignis).*

The question of the event

While the term "event" abounds in contemporary, particularly Western, capitalist culture, and only has a fairly young history in the English language,[1] it is specifically the twentieth century that increasingly reflected on the concept, with philosophy and narratology standing out as the seminal discourses in the context of this study of literary texts.[2] What resulted from a multitude of philosophers, media theorists, sociologists, narratologists, and so on[3] trying to offer a concept of the event in order to make sense of particular cultural paradigms is an inflationary fuzziness: everybody intuitively seems to know what an event is, which attests to the concept's ubiquity and the resulting definitional vagueness. As a consequence, this chapter opts for an understanding of events that distances itself from these conventional conceptions by offering a variety of constructive insights that might be gained by a closer analysis of Alain Badiou's thoughts on events, insights that, as I argue, remain wanting in other conceptions of events. Conceiving them as non-ontological, contingent, and singular ruptures—which he defines in *Being and Event* in set theoretical terms as "ex = {x ∈ X, ex}" (179)—that open up the possibility of subjective constitutions and reagency, Badiou offers a unique concept of the event that not only breaks with a variety of other notion of events but also productively engages in the literary analysis of particular American novels after 2000.

Faced with the sheer abundance of concepts of events, emphasized by the apparent ubiquity and self-evidence of this term in ordinary language and theoretical discourses, this chapter does not offer an exhaustive overlook on the concept of the event. While one certainly would have to start and compare Badiou's notion of events to one of the most important thinkers of the event in the twentieth century, that is, Martin

Heidegger, I will leave this comparison to philosophical investigations.[4] Instead, I will immediately start with Badiou's notion of events and will cursorily point to how this conception differs from other definitions of events where necessary. As a literary study, this chapter is not trying to give a comprehensive account of the intellectual history of the event, which Marc Rölli claims is bound to fail in the first place.[5] While much has been said about the various parallels and differences between Heidegger's and Badiou's ontology, this part is deliberately entitled "the question of the event" and not "the question of being." Even though it is adamant to address, by detour and necessity, the foundational question of being at times, as a literary analysis, this chapter is rather interested in the ethics and aesthetics of subjects of events—the domain of the event and the subject, and not of being.[6]

Evental disruptions: Contingent, singular events of truths

Badiou is interested in how far a current situation may be affected by a fundamental rupture that essentially undermines the working premises of this order. In contrast to a creeping notion of constant becoming, which is a particularly important disposition in and of modernity, Badiou theorizes singular change.[7] By inquiring into the modalities of how change is possible, both theorize a concept of the event that is endowed with the potential to dismantle a particular order. While for Heidegger there is only a single event that takes place in the field of philosophy, Badiou suggests that there are multiple events that dismantle particular ontological orders (and not one single metaphysical system) in the extra-philosophical, what he calls the conditions or truth procedures of science, love, politics, and art. Unlike Heidegger, Badiou thus conceives of multiple events that, however, still retain their emphatic nature and thus distance themselves from the plethora of serial micro-events that Gilles Deleuze has in mind, for instance.[8]

Although Badiou places events in realms that are to him not philosophical, he is nevertheless very much concerned with the meta-philosophical concerns of ontology and critically distances himself from the epistemological orientation that has been ascribed to the various taproots of the linguistic turn.[9] In adhering to Heidegger's call for the primacy of ontology, Badiou, however, aspires to rethink the discipline not by trying to reinstitute a different beginning; his approach is, rather, one of subtraction that grasps the advances of Cantorian set theory (and the modulations of the Zermelo-Fraenkel system) and reveals them as already latent, though indiscernible, within what Heidegger would argue is mere metaphysical thinking, especially Plato.[10] Being crucially indebted to both analytical *and* continental philosophy, *Being and Event's* use of mathematics in order to give expression to beings as pure multiples still does not run in the same vein as the German-Austrian, or Anglo-Saxon tradition of cleaning language of its metaphysical baggage (which already becomes obvious by his ontological and not epistemological undertaking).[11] With the help of set theory, Badiou's most provocative claim that "ontology = mathematics" (*BE* 13) entails the thinking of being from a purely extensional, non-substantial, anti-theological, and immanent point of view, which helps to situate the event in intricate ways.[12]

By means of set theory ontology, he offers a stimulating approach, which makes it possible to move beyond a poststructuralist immanent sphere of constant self-reflexivity by charging the event with the potential of radical rupture, yet without relying on theologocentric causations. Badiou clarifies in *Theoretical Writings*:

> We must point out that in what concerns its material the event is not a miracle. What I mean is that what composes an event is always extracted from the situation, always related back to a singular multiplicity, to its state, to the language that is connected to it, etc. In fact, so as not to succumb to an obscurantist theory of creation *ex nihilo*, we must accept that an event is nothing but a part of a given situation, nothing but a *fragment of being*. (qtd. in Žižek 2006: 167)

Indeed, if one accepts the thesis that set theory as ontology fully accounts for the multiplicities of being without trying to unify them in a holistic structure, then the event is outside of this philosophical realm.

This is because, by definition, the event, as a multiple, counts itself as a multiple. As Badiou explains: "I term event of the site X a multiple such that it is composed of, on the one hand, elements of the site, and on the other, itself" (*BE* 179).

For now, it is enough to focus on the first characteristic of the event, that of its self-belonging, which guarantees the absolutely disruptive status of events by rendering them "external" (*BE* 184) to ontology. Badiou, therefore, conceives the revolutionary potential of events by designating them as non-ontological. Since the event counts itself as a multiple, it falls prey to Russell's Paradox (or as Badiou calls it in more advanced terminology: the axiom of foundation)[13] and is thus banned from ontology. As a set that contains itself, the event is illegal within ontology: "ontology declares that the event is not," since "there is no acceptable ontological matrix of the event." (*BE* 190). By means of the somewhat startling reconceptualization of ontology as mathematics, Badiou not only accomplishes a fundamental contradistinction between ontology and events but also implies a specific "negative" interrelation between the two. Events refrain from being integrated into ontology with ease and thereby incorporate a distinct momentum of rupture. While "ontology has nothing to say about the event" (*BE* 190), this does not simultaneously imply that one should apply Ockham's razor to the event: "It is not," as Hallward remarks, "that the event itself is nothing. It has the same (inconsistent) being-as-being as anything else. An event can be only a multiple, but it is one that counts as nothing in the situation in which it takes place" (2003: 115). As a consequence, these two realms do not suggest a materialist and idealist duality, which renders the latter an inexpressible transcendental domain, a line of critique that has often been launched against Badiou.[14] By expressing the event in the language of multiples, Badiou avoids the stipulation of a totally "Other" relationality, while still stressing the antithetical opposition between being and event. The friction that Badiou creates between an event and its potential to radically call into question, by its very definition, the entire situation of ontology, becomes the guiding impetus of how to think change. The event is, in Žižek's words, a "*skandalon*," a "chaotic intrusion that has no place in the State of the Situation" (1999: 159). Yet, the event not only has no place in the given ontological continuum but also emphatically disturbs the situation in which it manifests itself, "effectively undermining [its very] foundations" (Žižek 1999: 159).

However, an event is, for Badiou, not only defined by its non-ontological disposition, being excluded from the language of ontology. The second, crucial characteristic implies its formulation of an evental site.[15] While the first part of the definition "ex = {x ∈ X, ex}" (*BE* 179) has, for now, been covered (ex = {ex}), the matter of site-specificity is crucial for Badiou's historical understanding that establishes a variety of events, instead of a single one. In order to grasp the concept of the evental site, it is necessary to make a slight detour and explain the fundamental relation between belonging and inclusion that is the sole marker of relation within set theory.[16] Consisting merely of multiples, set theory can construct infinite multiples by relating them to each other through the simple and fundamental operation of belonging, which is written ∈. For example, a set "novel" could thus be said to contain other multiples, such as "words," "mountains," and "characters". The three multiples thus "belong" to the multiple "novel," which itself might belong to the multiple "art." Even though there may exist subgroupings between such multiples, the fundamental relation between these multiples is one of radical homogeneity, which secures the absolute equality between sets. For instead of conceiving relations between elements and parts, set theory rejects the hierarchical relationship that such an understanding would imply. This is underlined by the fact that each multiple might itself consist of multiples, and so on, which merely accounts for their extensional quantity rather than quality.[17]

Nevertheless, there exists a relationship between an initial set and its powerset that introduces a numerical form of domination, which is key to the understanding of the event. According to the axiom of the powerset, the multiple "novel," which, in this simple example, contains {words, mountains, characters} is made into a larger set that double-counts the various relations between these terms: {words, characters}, {mountain, characters}, {words, mountains}, but also {words}, {mountains}, and {characters} as well as the sum of these sets and the void set, since in set theory every multiple goes back to this initial multiple. The relation between an initial set and its powerset is thus, necessarily, one of quantitative domination, with the powerset always being bigger than the original set. While the first relation is thus termed "belonging," the second relation of "inclusion" relates to the subsets that can be constructed from an initial set. The abstract dimensions of this mathematical procedure become more tangible when considering a political example of such mechanisms. As Chapter 4 shows, the multiple "African Americans" has historically been seen as a "part" of American society, without implying a more fundamental notion of "belonging." If the American State—Badiou calls the set that double-counts the initial multiple "state of the situation," "representation," or "metastructure" (*BE* 93ff.), thereby clearly implying "a metaphorical affinity with politics" (*BE* 95)[18]—counted African Americans as part of its constituency, then it was only in order to express its power, "a clause of closure and security" (*BE* 98) over these multiples.[19] Through its "constitutive operations" of "*discerning*" and "*classifying*" (*BE* 328) such political minorities, the state expresses its literal power of representation. The relation between a specific situation and its metastructure is usually one that is marked by "excess" (*BE* 97) where the mere quantitative dominance of the latter secures its attempts by stabilizing such a situation.[20] In other words, the state of, to use another example, the mathematical situation around 1900 tried to construct a specific understanding of what counts as mathematics and what does not and thereby excluded particular discourses as outside of its legitimacy.

However, it is specifically the rare occurrence of "singular multiples" (*BE* 99) that is inherently connected to evental sites. A singular multiple is, for Badiou, a multiple "which is presented but not represented" (*BE* 99). In other words, while the usual double-count of the state integrates every sort of multiple in its metasituation, it cannot get a hold of this singular term. For "a singular term is definitely a one-multiple of the situation, but it is 'indecomposable' inasmuch as what it is composed of, or at least part of the latter, is not presented anywhere in the situation in a *separate manner*. . . . Although it belongs to it, this term cannot be included in the situation" (*BE* 99). It should be obvious to what extent this singular multiple relates to the event. By failing to be presented by the state of the situation, the event thus always has to contain such a "maximal singular" (Feltham 2008a: 96) evental site, which Badiou defines as such:

> I will term *evental site* an entirely abnormal multiple; that is, a multiple such that none of its elements are presented in the situation. The site, itself, is presented, but "beneath" it nothing from which it is composed is presented. As such, the site is not a part of the situation. I will also say of such a multiple that it is *on the edge of the void*, or *foundational*. (*BE* 175)

An evental site guarantees what can be termed the "new" that affects a particular situation. By pointing to the discrepancy of what the current metastructure accepts as terms of a native situation, such as a given scientific discourse, and what lies hidden within the situation without being recognized as a reality, such as imaginary numbers in the nineteenth century, for instance, events always imply a specific supplementary momentum. They strive to instill this multiple within the current situation that refuses to acknowledge that it lacks any representative claims over this multiple; they are, in Badiou's words, "the *inexistent* of the world" (*TRoH* 56). Thereby, events not only add a particular proposition to this situation but fundamentally restructure the current count of this order. As such, it is not only the non-ontological disposition of an event that creates the disruptive dynamic in relation to an ontological order; additionally, its capacity to point to a specific singular multiple that does not experience proper belonging also radically undermines the state's hegemony of counting each multiple. Again, thinking of a political example, where a government fails to acknowledge various minority groups such as African Americans, *sans-papiers*, and subalterns might facilitate the understanding of such abstract terms, which engage in constructing "existential injuries" (*TRoH* 68). Crucially, however, despite the "human" factor that an evental site composes in such instances, one cannot reduce a political minority as such to an event. Rather, the event carries with it the proposition that calls into question the process of representation (here also alluding to the mimetic crisis that such happenings unravel, which is analyzed more thoroughly in the following analyses) by highlighting the discrepancy between what belongs and what is merely included.

Especially because an event can only be discerned from the standpoint of a situation, the fact that it is simultaneously indiscernible from within the situation runs into some paradoxes and has to be examined in more detail; without getting ahead of ourselves, it is the crucial function of the subject to wager on this point of undecidability. Events, therefore, rely on the structural asymmetry between presentation and representation and thus hinge on "historical situations" (*BE* 173) that contain an evental site.[21] These evental sites, as Hallward observes, render a concept of history that is a purely structural "rather than an anthropological or a psychological" (2003: 120) one. Yet, this realist view of history neither parenthesizes the concept in favor of systemic inquiries (as structuralism had it), nor does it rely on a teleological driving force of History (as classical Marxism believed).[22] For Badiou, "there is no general history, only particular histories, or historical situations" (Feltham 2008a: 100).

Before elaborating on the aspect of radical contingency that undermines the Marxist linear movement to a classless *telos*, another important aspect that defines Badiou's events needs to be addressed more elaborately—their site-specificity. The evental site "localizes" an event within particular situations and achieves a concrete historicity. Badiou's evental site makes sure that events are necessarily tied to the circumstances in which they occur. Badiou thereby disperses the concept to account for a variety of other "singular multiples," effectively allowing the event to take place in other, specifically non-philosophical, contexts. Hence, Badiou stresses that an event is "local and does not take place across an entire situation, but occurs at a particular point in the situation" (Feltham 2008a: 100). This results, as I would argue, in a conception of events as more palpable, and individualized manifestations of change.[23]

The evental site, therefore, rejects the postulation of a meta-event that reigns across time and space by instilling evental manifestations with particular site-specificities. Be it the encounter of two lovers on the road in Danielewski's *Only Revolutions*, *Against the Day*'s state of science around the 1900s, or the political status of African Americans in Beatty's 1980s Germany, these novels always profess a sensitivity to the various structural givens of the world in which they manifest themselves. "A political event," Badiou observes with focus on his most outspoken condition, "occurring everywhere is something that does not exist" (*TRoH* 92). This means that what may be an event for some situation can be a mere trifle for others, as will become clear with the various juxtapositions of events with other happenings in the novels under investigation. *Only Revolutions*, for example, aligns its genuine amorous event with the presentation of such momentous historical (what Badiou might specify as "political") incidents as "The Abolition of Slavery," (S1) or "Kennedy's assassination" (H1). While this does not necessarily undermine the status of other happenings as potentially constituting events, particularly in their fictional modulation, as experienced from the situation that *Only Revolutions*' homodiegetic protagonists Sam and Hailey are parts of, such happenings do not qualify as events.

After having stated some examples of evental sites, particularly political struggles, or scientific developments, one might interject that such incidents are perfectly deducible from a larger perspective on the course of history. The French Revolution, one of Badiou's favorite examples of a political event, was thus already long in the making before the disruptive years around 1789–94. However, Badiou, in a similar vein as Michel Foucault, is not interested in a historical hermeneutics that tries to reconstitute a linear narrative of how specific changes are part of a larger continuum of becoming but, rather, is more interested in what Foucault, in reference to Gaston Bachelard termed "epistemological ruptures": such breaks "suspend the continuous accumulation of knowledge, interrupt its slow development, and force it to enter a new time, cut it off from its empirical origin and its original motivations, cleanse it of its imaginary complicities" (1972: 4).[24] This could be viewed in terms of the difference between historicism and historicity, as Žižek explains:

> Historicism refers to the set of—economic, political, cultural, and so on—circumstances whose complex interaction allows us to account for the Event to be explained, while historicity proper involves the specific temporality of the Event and its aftermath, the span between the Event and its final End. (1999: 153)

The historicity of events depends on their absolute contingent nature. For Badiou, the event is absolutely contingent. Symptomatically, he derives the logic of contingency in the eruption of an event from Stéphane Mallarmé's *A Cast of Dice* (1897).[25] By adopting, even *mimicking* as Mehdi Belhaj Kacem argues (2010: 29ff.), this trope of gambling, Badiou insinuates the absolutely contingent nature of an event:

> This gesture symbolizes the event in general: that is, that which is purely hazardous, and which cannot be inferred from the situation, yet which is nevertheless a fixed multiple, a number, that nothing can modify once it has laid out the sum . . . of visible faces. A cast of dice joins the emblem of chance to that of necessity, the erratic multiple of the event to the legible retroaction of the count. (*BE* 193)

Particularly the adjective "hazardous," which simultaneously implies the danger of an event because of its contra-ontological impetus, as well as the disposition of pure chance, is important here. While this metaphor of throwing a dice certainly offers some problems in respect of notions of probability and chance, Badiou tries to get across that events are, for one thing, modally not necessary, while they also simply cannot be anticipated. Feltham, indeed, points out that unlike chance, which can be "calculated and presented as belonging to the discursive situation of statistics" (2008a: 101), the event's contingency fundamentally exceeds such prognoses: it "is always an incalculable emergence, rather than a describable structure" (2005: 28) as Badiou notes in *Philosophy in the Present*. On the one hand, the sheer bandwidth of events denies any foreshadowing of their manifestation. By trying to work on a scientific problem, for instance, one might well be struck by the contingent encounter with a lover.

On the other, unlike such pseudo-events as "9/11," which have been pre-imagined in America's cultural unconscious, as Žižek argues (2002: 16), and which for Badiou were "perfectly intelligible (if not predictable)" (Norris 2009: 161), genuine events dodge not only the current modes of re-presentation. Indeed, particularly American culture, which is impregnated with the Puritan imagination of the absolute "event" of apocalypse, requires a crucial differentiation of the maximal contingency of the event, as the chapters on *The Road* and *The Zero* exemplify. This implies that the event surpasses the epistemological faculties of a specific situation and can therefore not even be imagined. While this is certainly true for fiction in general, to think the unthinkable is in the context of the event not a general poietic praxis but involves a fundamental moment of mimetic crisis, which has to be negotiated in literature's narrative, linguistic, and medial constraints. If events essentially strain the current epistemological foundations, since they "cannot be inferred from the situation," how does the novel interrogate and integrate such impasses through its typographic, narrative, linguistic, or ideological limitations? While this obviously breaks with more common notions of reality, particularly as conceived in constructivism, which posits that the entirety of reality is always relying on one or another kind of narrative/discourse and is thus always already mediated, events specifically engage in this realm beyond language and thereby surpass the linguistic givenness of a particular situation.[26] It is particularly the capacity of such works as Danielewski's highly self-aware novel, which negotiates representational impasses and modifies this mimetic *aporia* through specific typographic means, to inquire into the possibilities of how to represent something that refrains from being represented.

Given Badiou's postulation of maximal contingency, one might wonder about the appropriateness of his use of this gambling metaphor, for there are certainly other games of chance that would better account for the incalculable multiplicity of outcomes that remains unpredictable, such as the roulette. Yet, as Mallarmé's poem insists: "A throw of the dice will never abolish chance." The image of the hand throwing the dice thus emphasizes not the possibility of calculating the 1/6 probability of a particular number being thrown but focuses on the very act of throwing, from which point of view, there are specific results that are likely, yet one never knows the absolutely necessary outcome.[27] While Badiou therefore highlights, with Mallarmé, the contingency in the very act of throwing the dice, and not the calculation of its results, he also employs this metaphor for the reason that, even though "hazardous," the event is "nevertheless a fixed multiple, a number, that nothing can modify once it has laid out the sum . . . of visible faces" (*BE* 193). Although it is indiscernible from the point of the situation at the particular moment of its being thrown, the fixity of its result as just a number among others implies that the result that the event occasions is not a transcendental revelation. In fact, as *Only Revolutions* attests, the mere encounter between two lovers may amount to an event that initiates a fundamental ontological and epistemological breakdown. Despite the event's alterity, it can nevertheless be integrated within the situation and does not remain inherently other. The event is not, as Badiou insists, "barbarous, incomprehensible, or non-listed" (*BE* 329). "Although the being-multiple of the situation remains unaltered," Badiou observes in this respect, "the logic of its appearance . . . can undergo a profound transformation" (2009: 44). Accordingly, the event (and its site) only becomes a "fixed multiple," a term of this particular situation, by a specific action. Indeed, once it has been thrown, the dice installs a necessary incentive "that nothing can modify." In this respect, the event becomes an inevitable phenomenon that cannot be ignored by transforming a hitherto indiscernible proposition "visible."

This absolute moment of contingency thus undermines, on the one hand, a teleological conception that involves the prophetic anticipation of specific events, such as the apocalypse.[28] Equally so, it questions the constructivist notion of reality that does not allow the existence of such "meta-physical" concepts as Badiou's event, which takes its potential of inscribing something new into a situation by not being exactly inferable from the epistemological standpoint of a particular order. An event, therefore, distances itself from mere evolutionary change by raising obstacles to a specific situation's episteme. It "not only blocks knowledge," as Feltham remarks, "but also incites it to re-invent its categories" (2008a: 102). While the state of a situation often proves to readily absorb an event within its regime of representation, as *Slumberland* shows in the case of the end of Jim Crowe and the End of History narratives, an event's ontological alterity requires the fundamental reformulation of the very language that can account for such a multiple.

Lastly, by being totally unexpected, the event is also an unprecedented phenomenon, since if it had already happened before, it would lose its singular driving force. While a variety of the novels under investigation interrogate this disposition of contingency in their narrative presentation of the event, they also stress that, while events are singular, it is the practice of the subject that integrates a fundamental moment of repetition.

In this respect, Beatty's *Slumberland* renders an intricate negotiation of how a long bygone event may be resurrected after it has systematically been denounced by various discourses. If the event here does not return itself, since it is always singular, it is the resurrection of a subjective relation to this event, which, again, may produce a new event. Even though an event is pointed, a singular manifestation, the *truth* it evokes can be eternal. Badiou explains this property in *Logics of Worlds*, which again might seem stifling from the perspective of constructivism: not only does he add fuel to the fire by emphasizing the concept of "truths" (*LoW* 9), which he already stressed in *Being and Event*, but he also further specifies them as being "eternal" and "universal" (*LoW* 9–10), terms that are particularly contested within the theoretical milieu of postmodernism.[29] The matter of truth is thus one, among a multitude of aspects, where Badiou "is clearly and radically opposed to the postmodern anti-Platonic thrust whose basic dogma is that the era when it was still possible to base a political movement on a direct reference to some eternal metaphysical or transcendental truth is definitely over," (1999: 151) as Žižek observes.[30] Yet, instead of returning to an antiquated notion of truth as an objectively verifiable referent that transcends time and space, Badiou "adds a new definition of truth to philosophy's larder" (Feltham 2008a: 109). He is eager to extol the term for its distinction to the present state of knowledge that reigns within a situation, what he calls the "dialectic of knowledges and post-evental fidelity" (*BE* 331), that is, truth.[31]

While constructivist thought would vehemently disavow the existence of a realm beyond discursive knowledge, Badiou insists that truth is not an epistemological value, but an essential *praxis*: it is the "*process* of a truth" (*BE* 355, my emphasis) and not a static transcendental idealism, since truths "are not unifiable in a metaphysical system"

(2011: 1) as Quentin Meillasoux notes.[32] In contrast to the static state of the situation, truths are inherently dynamic and rely on an affirmative praxis. "Up to a point," Žižek remarks, "one can also say that Knowledge is constative, while Truth is performative" (1999: 157).

As a praxis this "truth-process" involves the positive discernment of all the multiples that are connected to an event within the situation it affects. It is a "gathering together" (*BE* 338) of all the propositions, which cannot be contained by the present state of knowledge. To this extent, a truth implies a negative demarcation of what is simply the old situation and what the event has added to its episteme, thereby fundamentally altering its perimeters and parameters.[33] It emphasizes the positivity of *"the terms of the situation which are positively connected to the event"* since "what is negatively connected does no more than repeat the pre-eventual situation" (*BE* 335). Whereas Yashmeen Halfcourt in *Against the Day* positively relates her reflections on geometry to the scientific event, the father in *The Road* merely and literally gathers together the signs of the situation before the cataclysmic event happened. In effect, this negative or positive relation to an eventual truth prescribes the various ways in which one may become a subject of the event, which is explained in more detail below.

Yet, this understanding of truth as a praxis of enquiring into the propositions of the event being "eternal" (*LoW* 66) or "infinite" (*BE* 333) might also be met with serious reservations, since it seems to reverberate with Platonist idealism or theology. In contrast to the often-launched allegations that Badiou is a Neo-Platonist,[34] his notion of truth breaks with Platonism, since unlike a transcendental realm of ideas, truths might be eternal, but this persistence crucially relies on the singular eruption of an event. Badiou observes that "a truth is not, but comes forth from the standpoint of an undecidable supplementation" (*BE* 355). Truths are only eternally true insofar as they rely on the contingent manifestation of an event that ushers them into the world: "All truth is post-eventual" (2011: 1) as Meillasoux notes. Like a line that might have a specific starting point but evolves into infinity, events could be seen as initiating such a trajectory that has a beginning but no end.

What is more, Badiou's notion of truth also distances itself from Platonist transcendentalism, since truths are fundamentally immanent. Badiou writes in *Ethics*:

> Essentially, a truth is the material course traced, within the situation, by the eventual supplementation. It is thus an *immanent break*. "Immanent" because a truth proceeds *in* the situation, and nowhere else—there is no heaven of truths. "Break" because what enables the truth-process—the event—meant nothing according to the prevailing language and established knowledge of the situation. (42–43)

While truths are fundamentally affecting a particular situation, they were present within this order, although this particular system did not have the "language" and "knowledge" to grasp its reality. As in the case of the Quaternions in *Against the Day*, which one day "descend, to take up their earthly residence among the thoughts of men" (561), so does an event manifest its ontological reality that lies beyond the given capabilities of thought.

The definition of truths as eternal stresses, moreover, the emphatic nature of events. Genuine events, for Badiou, elicit propositions that persist throughout time: "Of no truth can it be said, under the pretext that its historical world has disintegrated, that it is lost forever" (*LoW* 66). To avoid the event sinking into oblivion, Badiou therefore formulates an emphatic notion of events that may persevere throughout time. As Meillassoux remarks, Badiou here refuses "that there can be no eternal truth, all discursive statements being irremediably inscribed in a historico-cultural context that strictly delimits the scope of truth to the particular instance that it supports" (2011: 1). In *Slumberland*, for instance, the truth of human emancipation, which was inaugurated, according to Badiou, by the Spartacus slave revolt (*LoW* 65), is thus of pertinence even today as a fundamental political praxis. If the fact of universal human equality that this event elicits is still relevant, this does not mean that its propositions are simply transposed to, as in the case of the novel, the sociopolitical milieu of 1990s Germany.[35] As will become obvious in the case of *Slumberland*, this eternal appeal involves a very sensitive relation to the various situations in which it may be rediscovered as a truth. By the same token, a truth that an event brings into a world is infinite, which means that, since the event is itself an infinite multiple, there can be no end in discerning which multiples are positively connected to it. This has fundamental consequences for the status of the subject, which will be explained in more detail in the next part of this chapter.

Finally, it is worth noting that Badiou does not offer a naïve, collective account of truth when he further explains that, in respect of an amorous event, "love is thus a-truth (one-truth) of the situation" (*BE* 340). This "individual" (*BE* 340) capacity suggests that truths are not transcendent facts but relate to specific subjects in specific situations. Just as there is no meta-event, "there is no truth of truths" (12) as Badiou remarks in *Handbook of Inaesthetics*. In the case of love, "it *interests no-one* apart from the individuals in question" (*BE* 340) about what they take to be their event of love and the consequent truth it evokes. However, Badiou refrains from equating this to a merely phenomenological understanding of subjective truth. Even though truth is here decoupled from its meta-subjective position, it equally fails to be shrugged off as a mere flicker of an individual epistemology.

If it already proves difficult to accept that Badiou employs the term truth at all, it even more so invites criticism when he further argues that while there are individual truths, there also exist "mixed" and "collective" situations where truths appertain to a collective (*BE* 340). Universality hereby is again to be situated within the constraints of a particular situation. To repeat, there can be no universally acknowledgeable event *across* situations. Still, what is universal is the potential that the event harbors to be accepted by all those within this situation, irrespective of their class, race, gender, age, and, as the chapter on *The Road* will show, their being a human in the first place.

For now, the question of the event has been covered to some extent, having been defined as a non-ontological, disruptive singularity that is absolutely contingent. The next part of this chapter seeks to give a fuller outlook of the aspects that have already been touched upon briefly in the former but require further elaboration, most importantly that of the subject. Crucially, then, by establishing the question of the event as an active and affirmative praxis that is different from the philosophical question of being, this questioning, as the next part elucidates, is an inherently subjective endeavor.

Badiou's event implies a momentum of absolute systemic disruptions that become manifest in various situations (amorous, scientific, artistic, and political). In the following section, I want to focus more concretely on Badiou's notion of the subject, which is inherently tied to the event.

If one then accepts Badiou's notion of the event, there arises a variety of problems: What is the use of events if they are really non-ontological, excluded by definition from ontology, since it begs the question of how they manifest themselves? How does the stability of ontological situations change if these singularities cannot be deduced from the situations they affect? Are events thus more than mere Platonic ideas, cushioned in mathematical language, hovering in a transcendental sphere beyond epistemological access and, ultimately, ontological reality?

The question(s) of the subject

There is no super subject.

Alain Badiou, *Infinite Thought*

Indeed, the aporia of how to discern an event that is situated within a situation and simultaneously excluded from the representative scheme involves the fundamental participation of the subject. If the first part elucidated the ontological question of the event, the very crisis of knowledge that relates to the construction of a subject guides the second part. It is not only the question *of* the subject (What *is* a subject?) but also the act of questioning *by* the subject, as well as the *questionable* status of the subject upon which lies the focus of this part. Only through the seemingly paradoxical condition that an event is indiscernible from within the situation that it affects, the subject's questioning results in reagency and ethics. The *question*, it should become clear, is the prevalent motif in the sphere of the subject. Let me begin with examining the act of how the subject questions and raises the question *of* the event and its truth, which has already flashed up at some points. Then we may draw some general conclusions about what kind of subject Badiou has in mind, which offers, vehemently, not a naïve return to a humanist subject, while it concomitantly discards narratives of determination, disintegration, or deconstruction.

The question of the event, as has been elucidated in the previous part, is essentially an ontological one. Yet, how can an event be said to affect a situation if it remains clandestine from its perspective unless one wishes to invite theologocentric acts of a revelatory kind or a humanism that endows the human with the power to transcend these determinations? Emphatically, I would argue that the ontological question of the event becomes an epistemological *and* an ethical question of the subject. In fact, only by raising the question of the event, of how we are able to know it, a form of subjectivity is produced that ushers in the ethical. I start with the question of the subject in its epistemological respects before elucidating the ethical reverberations of this take on the subject.

The question of the question

The crucial paradox of the question of the event is thus the seemingly unbridgeable chasm between its manifestation and its discernment. By being "ultra-one" (*BE* 171), its exceedance of every count, that is, every access to it, seems to encumber its potential as a source of change within a world and its inhabitants. For, according to Badiou, an individual,

> being internal to the situation, can only know, or rather encounter, terms or multiples presented (counted as one) in that situation. Yet a truth is an un-presented part of the situation. Finally, the subject cannot *make a language* out of anything except combinations of the supernumerary name of the event and the language of the situation. It is in no way guaranteed that this language will suffice for the discernment of a truth, which, in any case, is indiscernible for the resources of the language of the situation alone. (*BE* 396)

In order to circumnavigate this conceptual deadlock, what is required to bridge the gap between the non-ontological status of an event and its appearance in a situation is an intervention. This crucial act of deciding whether an event has occurred or not can be seen as the first step of subjective constitutions. Yet, without going into the details of the mathematical background of this concept,[36] it suffices to understand that this procedure adopts the contingency that is latent in the eruption of an event and applies it on the process of its reception. Put differently, while the event cannot be foreseen, a process of intervention, which implies the recognition of a multiple as an evental multiple, is equally a gamble with chance. "Since it is of the very essence of the event to be a multiple whose belonging to the situation is undecidable," observes Badiou, "deciding that it belongs to the situation is a wager" (*BE* 201). The question of the event, which is ontologically and epistemologically uncertain, "invariably elusive" (*TRoH* 56), thus equally percolates in the questionable act of confirming it. Through the mere acceptance of a highly dubious wager, an individual makes a leap of faith in respect of an "*interpretative intervention*" (*BE* 181), which again reverberates with political undercurrents but more generally implies an act of decision. Besides the semantic connotation of literally inter-vening, a coming in-between, and thus distinguishing between a normal and exceptional state of affairs, the mere act of deciding that an event has happened concomitantly refrains from positing the mere affirmation of an extraordinary phenomenon. Again, since the event is, by definition, undecidable, an intervention is the very act of deciding upon this undecidability: "An intervention consists, it seems, in identifying that there has been some undecidability, and in deciding its belonging to the situation" (*BE* 202). In other words, what is being decided is, initially, not that the *event* belongs to the situation, but is the mere manifestation of an undecidable deadlock: "This event has taken place, it is something which I can neither evaluate, nor demonstrate, but to which I shall be faithful" (*IT* 47).[37] It should be clear to what extent this questionable act again fundamentally hinges on dispositions of chance, uncertainty, and faith. While this certainly echoes religious narratives of the epistemological uncertainty of both transcendental might, or transcending election, relying on a larger cause, Badiou critically distances himself from this notion.[38] He tries to construct a theory of the subject that does not endow it with heroic sovereignty but highlights its inevitably precarious status: "There is no hero of the event" (*BE* 207). Or, as Hallward summarizes it in apt words: "Badiou's subjects are always solitary, singular, always endangered" (2003: 124).[39]

It is worth noting that, while Badiou insists that the process of intervention is distinct from the subject and, rather, conceives it as a systemic operation within set theory,[40] I want to highlight the unmistakable anthropocentric semantics of this procedure. In the context of this study, it is specifically, but not exclusively, human characters that take a leap of faith and actively try to intervene by proclaiming the existence of an event. And it is their crucial "faith" in, for instance, an at-the-time highly dubious scientific field such as Quaternionism in the case of Pynchon's *Against the Day* that such characters are propelled into existentially precarious terrain. Since it will "always remain doubtful whether there has been an event or not, except to those who intervene, who decide its belonging to the situation" (*BE* 207), the fundamental uncertainty of such interventions particularly, but not exclusively, affects human beings.

The reason for seeing the intervention as connected to the subject is also because it implies a creative act of naming. "The initial operation of an intervention," writes Badiou, "is to *make a name out of an unpresented element of the site to qualify the event whose site is the site*" (*BE* 204). Given the fact that an event cannot be expressed within the terms of the particular situation it affects, giving it a name not merely "saves the event from oblivion by pinning a signifier on it" (Feltham 2008a: 103). "The intervention orientates the event towards the situation," as Feltham goes on to explain, "and by naming it draws it into linguistic circulation. In order to do so without reducing its eventhood, the name cannot be drawn from the multiples presented in the situation, but rather from unpresented multiples" (2008a: 103). To avoid naming the event with the present linguistic means, which would simply incorporate it within the present situation, it is thus required to draw its name from the evental site, since, as we have seen, those multiples are not represented in a given situation. Žižek notes:

> Badiou calls the language that endeavours to name the Truth-Event the "subject-language." This language is meaningless from the standpoint of Knowledge, which judges propositions with regard to their referent within the domain of positive being (or with regard to the proper functioning of speech within the established symbolic order): when the subject-language speaks of Christian redemption, revolutionary emancipation, love, and so on, Knowledge dismisses all this as empty phrases lacking any proper referent ("political-messianic jargon," "poetic hermeticism," etc.). (1999: 156)

This can be the mere first-person plural "We/Us" from the perspective of two lovers who, previous to their amorous event, could only think in terms of the first-person singular. Equally so, although one might certainly call two lovers a "couple," Badiou insists that this is trying to count this extraordinary happening from an outside perspective and does not employ terms that have been unrepresented from the point of view of the situation that has undergone a change.[41] The crucial extension of their subjective episteme gives a name to the event with a signifier that was unimaginable before their encounter, as Danielewski's *Only Revolutions* elucidates.

To be sure, there is no *right* name of an event, as a sort of ideal signifier-signified-referent relation; the name of the event explicitly lacks referential representation; it is a pure signifier. "The names 'Proletariat,' 'Christian,' and 'Revolutionary,'" as names of events, observes Hallward,

> are terms that incant their eventual [*sic*] referents, insofar as Proletariat is not the working class, Christian is not a particular kind of Jew or Roman, and revolutionary is not merely an advocate for the Third Estate. The same goes for individual proper names: as evental, the names Haydn, Schoenberg, Picasso, and Grothendieck refer to a process that, from the point of its presumed completion, converts an insignificant anonymity into the inspiration of a universal truth. (2003: 124)

The matter of naming the event is not seeking an essentialist term that creates a logocentric foundation but is more interested in the process of naming. While the name certainly cannot be entirely arbitrary, since it has to stem from the evental site, this aspect of the intervention focuses on the mere act of relating to the event, thereby already accepting its existence. The decision to endow this aberrant multiple, which is excluded from presentation, with a name, hence, refrains from entering the play of the signifier by highlighting the particularly non-referential disposition of the event and its name. That is, instead of viewing all signifiers as void, the name of the event constitutes a special signifier since it dodges all attempts of representation. "'The' term which serves as the name for the event, is," as Badiou insists, "anonymous. It has the nameless as its name" (*BE* 205). Against the poststructuralist argument that no signifier has any stable semantic correlative, which even undermines the very existence of a realm of signifieds at all, the empty name of the event, rather, relates to specific situations in terms of their unrepresented multiples. While the term "we" obviously exists in ordinary language, the event's specificity points to the lack of this term within a particular solipsistic situation and underlines the mere act of declaring the existence of an event as an initial wager.

In fact, the name and its naming are not merely indiscernible from the particular epistemological domain of a situation; they crucially undermine the present forms of representation. Like the event, which unshackles the ontological order of a world, so does its name, as an "illegal" (*BE* 205) action, "interrupt" and "endanger" the prevalent structure (*BE* 205–06). The mere act of naming the event, so to speak, involves a fundamental antagonistic potential.

This disruptive momentum latent in the act of naming the event, is, however, cushioned, once more, in a questionable framework. The only manner in which to express the name of the event, Badiou emphasizes, is the temporal mode of the *future anterior*, since it expresses the complex temporality in which a subject only retroactively "will have known" that an event has occurred. It is this intricate temporal mode, oscillating between future and past, between epistemological speculation and certainty, that becomes the conditional structure to bridge the two disparate realms of being and event and constitutes a subject. Norris notes in this respect that the subject's epistemological undecidability concerning the event hinges on the

> future-anterior tense and also . . . the conditional or subjunctive mode since it has to do with what cannot yet be formally proved or verified while none the less following by the strictest necessity from certain other propositions which, if true, will be recognized as lending decisive support to the given hypothesis or theorem. (2009: 232)

It should be obvious to what extent fiction generally engages in the production of such temporalities that makes it a fertile soil for such poietic processes, while this creative potential also endows literature with a crucial "realist" dimension. By assuming that narratives are especially invested in the linguistic and discursive interrogation of how to present a world that has experienced an event, this corrodes its mere position in a realm of subjunctives, of possible worlds. As I argue in respect of the novels under investigation in this study, literature here discards its reflection on just "possible worlds" by changing the focus on impossible worlds. Its as-if disposition is thus realigned not in a general poietic outlook of positing new worlds but in the construction of worlds that seem impossible, since they evoke an event.[42]

To return to the question of the subject: the ascription of existence of the event is necessarily an act of retroaction, which means that I can only *know* that an event has happened if I already know it attests to the crucial relation between subject and event. Since events, as mentioned earlier, are not Platonist ideas, they only *are* an event if a subject has discerned them to be so. Once more, one can detect in the epistemologically problematic mode of the "will have been" how the subject of the event enquires into forms of subjectivity that exceed traditional notions. Equally so, the act of naming an event is not a pure creative act of authorship, since the subject must inevitably resort to a specific pool that is connected to the evental site. Simultaneously, it requires the declarative intervention and acceptance of an event to become an ontological reality at all. This oscillation between realism and nominalism lets the pendulum swing between the notion that events exist beyond epistemological access to them, and the belief that grounds the very existence of events in a subjective perception of them. Yet, events are neither totally transcendent, nor absolutely dependent on a phenomenological awareness, but fundamentally dialectic without yielding to either the priority of one or the synthesis of each of these two poles.

What is more, this hysteron-proteron structure that wages on the existence of an event might seem to raise the chicken-and-egg problem, since it complicates the cause-effect trajectory of what came first, event or a subjective discernment of it. It is, however, precisely the rejection of this causality that the subject of the event tries to undo, since it founds the temporal simultaneity of these concepts. Once an event has occurred, a subject may be produced that discerns its existence; yet, for there to be an event at all, a subject must already have made the decision that something is an event. As the following chapters (particularly 2 and 3) show, this process is inexorable. *If* a proper event occurs, there is no denying it. For by denying it, one already has to have interrogated its eventness. In other words, once a genuine event has made itself felt, it is no longer a question of whether or not it is an event but simply one of deciding how to position oneself toward it. While there are infinite ways in how to relate to an event, the mere fact of its existence is inevitable.

The question of reagency

The last aspect that is part of the process of how a subject is constituted and sustains itself implies just these ways of how it expresses its "faith" to an event. After the initial process of an intervention, the mere wager on deciding upon the undecidable verdict if an event has occurred, which goes hand in hand with its naming, a third stage becomes manifest that assumes a crucial role in the upcoming analyses of literary subjects of events and pertinently relates to my notion of reagency.

What Badiou calls "fidelity" (*BE* 232) or being "faithful" (*E* 41) again addresses the disposition of uncertainty that runs throughout the various strata of the subject of the event. Just as the event's ontological status is dubious, and the process of naming it remains anything but secure, so is the very idea of how a subject may enact the propositions of an event within the situation it affects determined by uncertainty. Although this is expressed when Badiou argues that "to be faithful is to gather together and distinguish the becoming legal of a chance" (*BE* 232)—with an emphasis on chance and faith—he is eager to distinguish his concept from its religious context. Rather, he stresses that "the word 'fidelity' refers directly to the amorous relationship, but I would rather say that it is the amorous relationship which refers . . . to the dialectic of being and event, the dialectic whose temporal ordination is proposed by fidelity" (*BE* 232). Although this clarification, nevertheless, implies a certain degree of irrational devotion, fidelity crucially parenthesizes the dimension of uncertainty and intimates the wager of such a subjective process, as naïve as it might appear. By virtually leaving aside all doubts about the existence of an event, a subject risks "an unreasonable gamble or leap of faith" (Hallward 2003: 126). Fidelity or faithfulness to the event, as terms associated with myopic lovers or the religiously devout, thereby implies a particular aspect of irrationality, which clearly breaks with the rationalist strand of humanist subjectivity. For it would certainly be more circumspect, safer, to simply stick to "the ordinary run of affairs" (*BE* 233). But an event precisely calls this into question and calls upon those individuals who acknowledge its manifestation to enact its truth within the situation. To this extent, Badiou notes:

> A fidelity . . . is not a matter of knowledge. It is not the work of an expert: it is the work of a militant. "Militant" designates equally the feverish exploration of the effects of a new theorem, the cubist precipitation of the Braque-Picasso tandem (the effect of a retroactive intervention upon the Cézanne-event, the activity of Saint Paul, and that of the militants of an *Organisation Politique*. (*BE* 329)

Note how Badiou explicitly distinguishes the concept from scientific specialization, which would, on the one hand, require a specific environment that would deny the process of fidelity in its universal aspirations, while, on the other, it would also suggest the processual accumulation of knowledge. By employing this scientific metaphor, Badiou distances the notion of fidelity from the hermetic, rational setting of a laboratory and invokes an irrational, singularly contingent environment. Fidelity is thus not sustained by experts but by militants, yet another political term. What might appear as "feverish" madness in such individuals who explore an event and try to reformulate the situation according to its proposition, is, yet, as Badiou immediately clarifies, not solely a political praxis; it also generally involves the rigid "exploration" of new terrain. To this extent, this procedure rejects the postulation of "expert" capabilities, since it is absolutely democratic.[43] Instead of viewing fidelity as a particular ability of some elect group, it rather attunes to the event's universal impetus. As Žižek notes in his analysis of Badiou's *Saint Paul*:

> The interesting thing to note is how Badiou here turns around the standard opposition between Law as universal and Grace (or charisma) as particular, the idea that we are all subjected to the universal Divine Law, whereas only some of us are touched by Grace, and can thus be redeemed: in Badiou's reading of St Paul, on the contrary, it is Law itself which, "universal" as it may appear, is ultimately "particularist" (a legal order always imposes specific duties and rights on us, it is always defining a specific community at the expense of excluding the members of other ethnic, etc., communities), while Divine Grace is truly universal, that is, non-exclusive, addressing all humans independently of their race, sex, social status and so on. (1999: 170)

The truth that an event universally evokes is again, of course, not a general disposition but relies on the extraordinary eruption of a contingent event. From the standpoint of a situation that experiences the manifestation of an event, the truth that is constructed by a subjective fidelity does not discriminate between any qualitative dispositions. It is this particular universality that Badiou addresses when writing that

> a fidelity is always particular, insofar as it depends on an event. There is no general faithful disposition. Fidelity must not be understood in any way as a capacity, a

subjective quality, or a virtue. Fidelity is a situated operation which depends on the examination of situations. Fidelity is a functional relation to the event. (*BE* 233)

Depending on the eruption of an event, the process of fidelity is a particular process of such a situation. In undermining a generalizing account, Badiou stresses that there is no common quality of how a fidelity might be expressed. Nevertheless, what constitutes the common denominator of this process is that it positively affirms the truth that an event has elicited and tries to apply this within the situation it addresses. Since "a fidelity is conjointly defined by a *situation*" (*BE* 234), one can thus not posit a general mode of conduct, which renders the concept, just as the event, a local product of its concrete site-specific surroundings. In denying the possibility of a universal regulation of how to act when confronted with an event, Badiou's notion of fidelity (as well as the subject and the event) is inherently tied to his understanding of ethics, which will be discussed at the end of this part.

Albeit particular, there is virtually no end to the varieties of how to express one's fidelity. Since the only factor for a procedure to be counted as a fidelity is its "*thinking* (although all thought is a practice, a putting to the test) the situation 'according to' the event" (*E* 41), there opens up a myriad of different modes of action that may all relate to a single event. According to Badiou, there indeed "are infinite nuances in the phenomenology of the procedure of fidelity" (*BE* 330), where "in the same situation, and for the same event, different criteria can exist which define different fidelities" (*BE* 233). Truth be told, differing fidelities might even confront each other, as when "Stalinists and Troskyists both proclaimed their fidelity to the event of October 1917, but they massacred each other," or when "intuitionists and set theory axiomaticians both declared themselves faithful to the event-crisis of the logical paradoxes discovered at the beginning of the twentieth century, but the mathematics they developed were completely different" (*BE* 234). While Badiou does not ponder these counteracting trajectories at this point in *Being and Event*, both *Ethics* and *Logics of Worlds* offer a more refined and reflected spectrum of how an event may elicit positive and negative fidelities, which is discussed more elaborately in the chapters on *The Road* and *The Zero*.[44]

Additionally, there might not only be infinite ways of how to enact one's faithfulness to an event but the very process is also marked by infinity. Put differently, the processual dimension of a fidelity implies that it is an ongoing project with no end in sight. It requires absolute commitment to unravel the truth of an event, which, as has been noted, is infinite. "A truth alone is infinite," Badiou insists, "yet the subject is not coextensive with it. The truth of Christianity—or of contemporary music, or 'modern mathematics'—surpasses the finite support of those subjectivizations named Saint Paul, Schoenberg or Cantor" (*BE* 395). Thus, while it does not automatically imply that a subject who acts in fidelity toward an event is equally infinite, it simultaneously renders fidelity a praxis that is not done with once an event has been affirmed. Hallward gives expression to this when writing that a "truth is sparked by an event, but bursts into flame only through a literally endless subjective effort" (2003: 122). Despite the set theoretical implications of this argumentation, which involves the infinite amount of multiples in a situation and, consequently, the infinite acts of inspecting these multiples as being affected by the event, such a novel as Danielewski's *Only Revolutions* makes this more palpable when it shows that the fidelity of lovers toward each other might even surpass their respective deaths.

The endless act of being faithful to an event thereby denies the immediate and irrevocable constitution of a subject, once an event has occurred. To insist on the continuous reaffirmation of a singular event, then, addresses the necessary matter of repetition. For while an event only erupts once, the subjective fidelities to it are unmitigatedly iterative, which is expressed in the notion of "points."[45] For Badiou, "a point" is

> a particular moment around which an event establishes itself, where it must be re-played in some way, as if it were returning in a changed, displaced form, but one forcing you "to declare afresh." A point, in effect, comes when the consequences of a construction of truth . . . suddenly compels you to opt for a radical choice, as if you were back at the beginning, when you accepted and declared the event. (*IpoL* 50)

In order to maintain its fidelity to an event, a subject has to continually reaffirm the truth of the event. It amounts to a crucial reenactment that, however, not simply "replays" the event as a sort of simulacra of itself but attunes to the "changed, displaced" ecology in which its point is being affirmed. This amounts to "an attempt to preserve the characteristics of the event . . . when the event as such no longer possesses its initial potency" (*TRoH* 70). In fact, what could be perceived as a symbolic rite obviously has a dangerous past, particularly in the history of the American nation as a nation. How does one differentiate its desire for "new beginnings" that are likewise propagated in the perpetuation of such stories of origins of the "birth of the nation" and a reaffirmation of genuine events? Is there a difference between what in *Against the Day* manifests itself as the conflicting narratives of how to celebrate Independence Day, or doing "honor to the haymarket bomb, bless it, a turning point in American history" (*AtD* 115)? Faced with the conflicting narratives over historical legitimacy, it is a crucial undertaking to interrogate how the novels that are contemplated in this study offer critical reflections on what are unmasked in the case of Walter's *The Zero* as simulacra events, happenings that appear to be events for particular reasons, or how conflicting events and fidelities interact, as in Pynchon's *Against the Day*.[46] Crucially then, this study argues that these novels do not simply engage in a self-reflexive practice of writing alternating histories but come up with more cogent conceptualizations of genuine events and, necessarily, subjects of these events that acquire the abilities to move beyond the determining constrains of history.

What is at stake, then, is that in the notion of fidelity manifests a crucial act of empowerment, which I call, for the lack of a better term, reagency. By adding the prefix, I seek to crucially differentiate this form of subjective empowerment from the traditional notion of agency, even though there are obvious resonances, which is implied in their common stem. Equally so, this reflexive prefix does, crucially, not imply a *re*turn of agency but applies this to different ends. Unlike the humanist notion of agency, reagency is not an *a priori* "'property' of the subject—a sort of 'pure' autonomy and volition" (Melley 1992: 712), but rather an extraordinary operation that is essentially dependent on the eruption of an event (and a subject that declares its faithfulness). In fact, while fidelity to an event as reagency comes closer to the "older sense of the agent as 'middleman,' or 'factor'" (1992: 712) that Timothy Melley points out,[47] since a subject becomes a "middleman" between the truth of the event and its integration into a situation, the importance of the prefix details the necessary moment of re-action. In contrast to the idea of agency as the capability of a subject to initiate an event (or a chain of events) autonomously, reagency inverts this trajectory, for only through the eruption of an event does there open the possibility for a subject to profess its fidelity in the first place. However, to stress it once more, while the event constitutes a considerable factor in this process—a reagent if you will—it is more like a chemical reaction that requires the assemblage of two "substances" in order to effect the transformation of both constituents into a subject of the event. This metamorphosis is, however, not a mystical conversion: "An event is 'incalculable'," as Hallward notes, "but the truth it enables is not instantaneous or miraculous. Truth does not descend from on high, a ready-made revelation. If its occasion is indeed—for its subjects—experienced as a kind of grace, still 'only the work that declares it constitutes it' as truth" (2003: 122). Hallward here implies that although this form of empowerment may involve the transcendence of determining structures, it is, nevertheless, inexorably interconnected to the continuing adherence to an event's truth.

It follows that the notion of reagency also seems appropriate in relation to fidelity, since its prefix hints at the necessarily repetitive dimension of this process. Unlike agency, the faithfulness toward an event is not a general capability that may be applied to initiate various chains of actions; only through its repetitive activity is one's reagency and, thus, subjecthood sustained. In a sense, this subjective status is essentially performative: it does not ascribe an essentialist capability to specific agents but requires their active participation in the construction of a truth of the event; however, this is to be distinguished from postmodernist theories of performance, according to which one might simply choose one's identity within particular perimeters, since it specifically calls for the active affirmation of the truth of the event.[48] Only by working through the various points that integrate the event in the situation does a subject stay a subject.

While a subject is thus necessarily determined by an event, reagency still preserves the notion of empowerment latent in the concept of agency. Despite the questionable status of the event and the subject's enquiry of its truth, which may well propel subjects into precarious terrains, their fidelity always endows them with specific modes of emancipation. This is obviously not a wholesale transcendence of the structures that proved to determine such individuals through economic, racist, or ideological means, for instance. Nevertheless, the antagonistic potential that a process of fidelity offers entails various trajectories of resistance, which become more latent in the political contexts of Beatty and Pynchon. In exceeding the mere "subversive potential" of recent postmodern cultural theories, reagency empowers the subject in that it necessitates the active reconstruction of an alternative "counter-state: what it does is organize, *within* the situation, another legitimacy of inclusions. It builds, according to the infinite becoming of the finite and provisional results, a kind of *other* situation, obtained by the division in two of the primitive situation" (*BE* 238). The immanent appeal of such a different situation is, yet, not a utopic project but, as should have become clear with the revolutionary potential of any event, a critical reconceptualization of the entire situation according to the event. Reagency crucially raises the question of "how are we to be faithful to changing the world *within the world itself*?" (67) as Badiou writes in *The Rebirth of History*. It "compels us to decide a *new* way of being" (*E* 41). By abandoning the mere static and passive Spinozian "'perseverance in being' which is nothing other than the pursuit of interest, or the conversation of the self" (*E* 46), the active dimension of reagency implies, on the one hand, resisting the "worst kinds of inertia" that lure with the "permanent temptation of giving up, of returning to the mere belonging to the 'ordinary' situation, of erasing the effects of the not-known" (*E* 48). On the other, reagency also involves the strenuous work of not only transforming oneself according to the propositions of the event but also participating in the restructuration of the status quo that will not acknowledge any change. Therein lies the subjective component of reagency. A subject is certainly subjected *to* the event, but it is not a mere passive product of its incentive but obligates creative acts of participation.

After having elucidated to what extent the subject raises the question of the event and how far the processes of intervening, naming, and being faithful to the event are marked by profound uncertainties, yet construct a crucial form of empowerment, we are now in a position to draw some general conclusions about the question of the subject, and, in particular, what consequences these ruminations have for the status of the subject and, in conclusion, what kind of ethics this suggests.

The question of the Anti|Human

For Badiou, then, a subject is, as has repeatedly been intimated above, a *subject of the event*. As he puts it: "I term *subject* any local configuration of a generic procedure from which a truth is supported" (*BE* 391). In the following paragraphs, I elucidate how his subject as a processual enquiry into the truth that an event induces keeps both humanist and poststructuralist notions of subjectivity at bay, while offering a genuine account of how to enable it with the possibility of reagency. Besides summarizing the observations that have been made in respect of the subject's intervention, naming, and fidelity, I also make some additional qualifications that distinguish the subject of the event from its traditional conception.

First, it should have become obvious to what extent a subject, for Badiou, is an after-effect that crucially breaks with the humanist tradition that suggests that a human being is endowed with particular autonomous capabilities from the very start. As a subject *of* the event, Badiou's subject is only constituted through the eruption of an event: it is "convoked by certain circumstances to *become* a subject" (*E* 40). Against the humanist grounding of an *a priori* substantial entity (*BE* 391), Badiou therefore conceives the subject as an "exceptional" (Hallward 2003: 142) phenomenon that is inherently connected to the extraordinary status of an event. In reversing the modern conception of a subject that is equipped with the power to *cause* events, a subject of the event is, indeed, only *caused* by an event. The exceptional "rarity" (*BE* 392) of this process, which Žižek describes as "the local-contingent-fragile-passing emergence of subjectivity" (1999: 187), should, however, not be viewed as a form of Election, "a strange elitism, even more extreme than Nietzsche's" (Pluth 128), but it, rather, emphasizes the fact that there is a distinction between the mere being of an individual and the unique process of subjectivation. Hallward notes in this respect that

> what Badiou calls an ordinary "someone" (*quelqu'un*) is simply an indifferently infinite element already presented in a situation. By contrast, a subject in no way preexists the truth process that inspires him: subjectivation is the abrupt conversion of a someone. Although all someones *can* become subjects, Badiou offers no grounds for accepting the moralizing presumption that "every human animal is a subject." (2003: 142–43)[49]

While Badiou radically questions the humanist tradition of an *a priori*, self-same, autonomous subject, "a transcendental function" (*BE* 391) in the sense of Kant, a "psychological subject," or "the reflexive subject (in Descartes' sense)" (*E* 43), his conception equally rejects poststructuralist notions that undermine the subject as absolutely determined by discourse, desire, or capital. In fact, Badiou would see his undertaking in a lineage with "theoretical antihumanism" (*E* 5) elaborated by thinkers such as Louis Althusser, Jacques Lacan, and Michel Foucault.[50] Like the Foucauldian argument that the subject is always subjected and subjugated *to* power (1982: 781), Badiou positions the subject also to a specific point of reference, without, however, letting it be fully limited by such structures.[51] Even though a subject is thus the subject *of* an event, this relation allows it the potential of subjectivation in the first place. Rather than "subject to truth" (Hallward 2003) or "subject to the event" the expression "subject *of* the event" (*IT* 46, my emphasis) is more appropriate within the context of this study, since it articulates an affiliation that suggests the equal status of both concepts than the preposition *to*, which suggests the priority of the event and does not, as previously argued, account for the fundamental reciprocity between subject and event. Moreover, instead of emphasizing the notion of "truth" as Hallward does, this book is more interested in the concept of the event, even though the truth it evokes is inevitably linked to it.

Nevertheless, the subject is also not simply a "result—any more than it is an origin" (*BE* 392), which means that one should not take for granted the subject as an *a posteriori* but, consequently, stable effect of an event. The event does not evoke some kind of *rite de passage* that initiates an individual in the social order and endows it with subjecthood. As necessarily dependent on its fidelity to an event, it should rather be conceived as a process. Feltham also observes that Badiou's ontology has nothing to say about the *being* of a subject. What it can do, however, is to think the subject as an operation: "The subject is not so much an agent behind the work of change, but the work of change itself" (2008a: 112). On the one hand, Feltham here emphasizes the processual dimension of a subject, which has experienced a shift within Badiou's writing. While in *Being and Event*, he still "insist[s] that the subject is simply decided into existence, more or less instantaneously, he now [particularly in *Ethics* and *Logics of Worlds*] believes that the subject '*appears*' over time, over the course of a more articulated process" (Hallward 2003: 145).[52] It is particularly the infinite enquiry into the points of a situation that attests to a fidelity, and which has to be analyzed more elaborately in the following, that this processual dimension becomes more tangible.

On the other hand, Feltham's observation that a subject is not an "agent" but the "work of change itself" also implies that a subject may be constituted by more than a human being, or a textual character. While this study often reads characters as subjects of the event, it also enquires into a more complex interrogation of what Badiou calls in *Logics of Worlds* a "body" (35ff.). If Badiou explains his notion of a collective subjective body most of the time with political examples that are grounded in, yet crucially extend, Marxist notions of collectivity,[53] he also at times argues that an artistic body may, for instance, be constituted by a work of art itself: "The subject of an artistic process is not the artist (the 'genius', etc.). In fact, the subject-points of art are works of art" (*E* 44). Feltham sums this up:

> Those subjects that are posterior to the event are not heroic individuals, but enquiries and practices that take place *between and through individuals*—a political subject, Badiou says, is a meeting, a tract or a protest rally, not an individual, and an amorous subject is what happens in between two individuals, like moving in together, or surviving illness. (2008a: 106)

A subject usually exceeds the mere identification that one individual is one subject, where Badiou's Marxism makes itself felt but is also expanded. While each event thus has at least one subject of its truth, this denominator accounts for a variety of different enquiries that are simply subsumed under the greater and basic rubric of their fidelity or infidelity to the event. By the same token, besides Badiou's reconceptualization of the ordinary notion of an event, it here becomes clear how he equally strains the traditional identification of human and subject. Although he certainly has humans in mind when he speaks about the subject, he concomitantly refrains from a myopic anthropocentric perspective.[54] This complicated equivocation between subject and human is explicit in *Ethics*, when he writes:

> A "some-one" is an animal of the human species, this kind of particular multiple that established knowledges designate as belonging to the species. It is this body, and everything that it is capable of, which enters into the composition of a "point of truth"—always assuming that an event has occurred, along with an immanent break taking the sustained form of a faithful process. (44–45)

If his conceptualization of the human as an animal relates back to a specific philosophical tradition, which disavows the human a superior position, he, nevertheless, zeroes in on the human as a particular being endowed with the unique ability to enter into a truth procedure. While this is likewise confirmed when, in *Infinite Thought*, he insists that only "people are capable of truth" (53), the ambivalence between anthropocentric and anti-anthropocentric dispositions is deployed more thoroughly in this study's analysis of *The Road*, which focuses on an impetus that Badiou offers but never fully commits on, and thus considers a subject of the event that is not human *per se*.

Badiou's notion of the subject thus clearly breaks with both humanist and anti-humanist inclinations and extends the common understanding of subjects as individual human beings. By discarding the traditional notion of events and subjects, I conclude this chapter by examining the consequences for the status of ethics in Badiou's system, which makes Norris argue that Badiou is likewise " 'against ethics' in just about every currently accepted sense of the term" (Norris 2012: 40). Yet, ethics is not being discarded entirely. Like his unconventional conception of these previous terms, so does ethics prove to undergo a crucial reconfiguration that relates, as I have already intimated, to the evental constitution of a subject.

The question of ethics

For Badiou, "Ethics does not exist" (*E* 28). Despite the obvious controversial undercurrents of this claim, what Badiou implies by this radical rejection of one of the oldest discourses in philosophical thinking is, rather, to be viewed in the context of what he provocatively calls the " 'ethical' delirium" (*E* liii) of the present age.[55] What is perceived as one of his numerous polemical statements, which is condensed in his eponymous *Ethics*, however, tries to launch "a radical critique of 'ethical' ideology and its socialized variants: the doctrine of human rights, the victimary conception of Man, humanitarian interference, bio-ethics, shapeless 'democratism', the ethics of difference, cultural relativisim, moral exoticism, and so on" (*E* 90). He would thus not only subscribe to Jacques Rancière's critique of the supposed "ethical turn," in the latter's eponymous essay—what Badiou before Rancière already diagnosed as the "return to ethics" (*E* 2)—but also try to conceive of a reconceptualization of this discourse; in spite of these arguments, which also affect literary criticism,[56] Badiou seeks to give ethics a special place by undermining its etymological origination in "*ethos*." Against this understanding that, for Rancière, "signifies two things: both the dwelling and the way of being, or lifestyle, that corresponds to this dwelling" (2010: 184), Badiou intends to save ethics from its "fuzzy" (*E* 2), ubiquitous usage[57]—"no doubt a fashionable word," (2010: 184) as Rancière asserts—by making it a condition of exception. In order to criticize "today's socially inflated recourse to ethics" (*E* 2), Badiou, like in the case of the event and the subject, opts for a distinction between the ordinary "way of being," a mere passive dwelling, and ethics as a singular truth procedure that a subject engages in through his fidelity to an event. Thus, instead of implying the "search for a good 'way of being', for a wise course of action" (*E* 1), the ethical dimension of Badiou is transposed in his account not to the ordinary realm of being but to the exceptional process that an event inaugurates. Put differently, ethics is, for Badiou, the exception rather than the rule.

Badiou is thus "an anti-ethical thinker" (Norris 2012: 39) only so far. For he qualifies his denunciation of ethics as such: "There is no ethics in general. There are only—eventually—ethics of processes by which we treat the possibilities of a situation" (*E* 16). In tune with his conception of event and subject, Badiou attempts "to preserve this word *ethics*" (*E* 40) within the framework of his notion of singular truth processes. Ethics, for him, is the "ethics of truths" (*E* 40). As a consequence, ethics stops being a discourse of universal aspirations. By clearly rejecting Kant's categorical imperative, Badiou's notion of ethics relates, by means of his ontological exploration of events, always only to specific situations. Because of an event's site-specificity, ethics, as conceived as a process of fidelity, is equally inevitably local.

What is more, this ethical outlook also distances itself from Kant in terms of the status of the rational subject. "Above all," Norris notes in this respect,

> he [Badiuo] has resisted that Kantian conception according to which the imperatives of ethical (practical) reason are thought of as resulting from the moral agent's exercise of purely rational, autonomous, self-legislative will oblivious to the "pathological" promptings of appetitive desire or self-interest. (2012: 39)

Despite these obvious differences between Kant and Badiou on their ethical conceptions, I would argue that there is still a deontological aspiration that seems to run through both endeavors.[58] Although this dimension certainly differs from the universal and subjectively grounded maxims in Kant, the ethics of a fidelity toward an event could be said to equally raise the obligation to position oneself to it. Once an event has occurred, the utter necessity of an ethics becomes manifest. If one is part of the situation that the event perturbs, one has to take sides, "for or against the event" (Hallward 2003: 126). However, it is impossible to anticipate and prescribe just in what manner a subject proclaims its fidelity. While some subjects might affirm and integrate it into the situation in various ways, there may also unravel processes that corrupt it, as the following two chapters elucidate. The only ethical obligation one is responsible for is thus neither grounded in the self, a narcissistic reverie, nor in an other of political rationality, but only responsible to the event, which clearly runs against the grain of a variety of contemporary ethical philosophies, from Emmanuel Lévinas's respect for difference to Jürgen Habermas's communitarian discourse ethics.[59] The sole guiding principle that is thus articulated within Badiou's ethics of truths amounts to is simply the phrase: "Keep going!" (*E* 91). Since one cannot arrive at a universal rule of what deontological proscriptions a contingent event may invoke, all one can posit is to "do all that you can to persevere in that which exceeds your perseverance. Persevere in the interruption. Seize in your being that which has seized and broken you" (*E* 47). In other words, the ethics of truth that a subject of the event brings into being is the very transcendence of the ordinary *ethos*.

> Understood in terms of a philosophy of truth, "ethical" should simply describe what helps to preserve or en-*courage* a subjective fidelity as such. The ethical

prescription can be summarized by the single imperative: "Keep going! Or Continue!" For a truth is clearly difficult by definition. It implies an effectively *selfless* devotion to a cause. By going against the current, by going against the "natural" movement of time itself, it is vulnerable to various forms of erosion at every moment of its elaboration. (Hallward 2001: xi)

By the same token, ethics cannot formulate a general, normative guiding principle—or commit itself to more than the mere "Keep going!" (*E* 91)—since, next to being dependent on the contingent eruption of an event, the plurality of different truths that may be the basis for such enquiries also diverts to such an extent as to not allow any common denominator. "The only genuine ethics is of truth*s* in the plural," notes Badiou, "or, more precisely, the only ethics is of processes of truth, of the labour that brings *some* truths into the world" (*E* 28). By accounting for a plurality of evental truths, and by extension, of ethics, Badiou again simultaneously undermines the universalizing aspirations of a humanist kind, while also avoiding any indulgence in a relativist nihilism, which is particularly stressed through his evocation of "truths." Despite the context-specificity and plurality of truths, he nevertheless emphasizes their existence as processual acts of being faithful to events. Given the ultimate epistemological uncertainties of these processes, such an exceptional form of ethics certainly does not offer a cogent framework of how to live the good life but, nevertheless, gives this discourse an emphatic relevance, particularly because of its revolutionary appeal.

Thus, the general and single domain of "Ethics does not exist. There is only the *ethic-of* (of politics, of love, of science, of art)" (*E* 28). By ascribing ethics to the local procedures of politics, love, science, and art, Badiou therefore addresses what Rancière calls the "growing indistinction between fact and law" (2010: 185). These four spheres mark, for Badiou, the extraordinary practices of *subjective* (and not merely human) activity that enquire into that which is not fact and, as "generic conditions 'generate' propositions of the subject-language in which Truth resonates," as Žižek notes (1999: 166). In other words, it is only within these domains that eruptions of events are possible, since these practices probe, according to Badiou, into just these spheres of revolutionary change: "Every subject is artistic, scientific, political or loving . . . , for outside these registers, there is only existence, or individuality, but no subject" (1999: 91).[60] As Hallward further notes: "There can be no subject of athletics, of agriculture, of charity, of education" (2001: 182), since these modes of existence do not enquire into the genesis of events but merely sustain the ordinary ways of the world. Certainly, however, a farmer could pronounce his fidelity to a political event, or become a subject of love. According to Badiou, then, these four generic conditions "mark out the possible instances of the *subject* as variously individual or collective," as Hallward explains:

> Love, clearly, affects only the individuals concerned. Politics, by contrast, concerns only the collective dimension, the affirmation of an absolutely generic equality. And in "mixed situations"—situations with an individual "vehicle" but a collective import—art and science qualify as generic to the degree that they effect a pure invention or discovery beyond the mere transmission of recognized knowledges. (2001: xi)

It is certainly worth noting that Badiou extends ethics as a traditionally politico-philosophic discourse by enquiring into the ethical dispositions of other spheres of human activity.[61] That a political act can be ethical seems more commonsensical than scientific, artistic, or amorous enquiries into events, which for him, equally abound with such potential.

The question of conditions

I want to conclude this chapter by suggesting how the problem of conditions marks the main point of critique within the context of this study, specifically as attested by the literary works under investigation. This critique amounts to the problem of the distinctiveness of these conditions and their absoluteness, as well as the position of literary studies within these realms.[62]

While these fourfold conditions are certainly grounded in Badiou's penchant for structural clarity, to the extent that he often makes other subjective processes fit his static constellation in an uncannily simplifying manner (as when he considers Saint. Paul a "poet-thinker of the event" [2003: 2]),[63] the matter of the conditions assumes one of the most problematic postulations in the context of this study.[64] To be sure, taking art, science, politics, and love as the "four and only four fields of truth" (Hallward 2001: xi) where real change may happen certainly covers a great deal of human praxis (but again, only *human* praxis). And although the last three chapters that analyze faithful subjective procedures are to some extent following amorous, political, scientific, and artistic events, the very first analysis of the reactive subject in *The Road* elucidates a realm of evental manifestations in a context that seems as adamant in interrogating radical changes as the other spheres. In fact, within the diegetical world of the novel, an ecological event not only undermines the other conditions but also, at the same time, criticizes the anthropological orientation of these conditions. An ecological procedure thus supplements the strictly human conditions (although, as I mentioned before, its subjects may also be constituted by works of art or political tracts), and thereby fully extends the non-anthropological momentum that is latent in Badiou.[65]

What seems, moreover, wanting in this conception of four domains that make possible the construction of scientific, political, aesthetic, or amorous subjects of events is their mutually exclusive aspirations. As Badiou acknowledges himself in an interview, a crucial blind spot in his theory is the "problem of the connection between the different procedures" (*IT* 192).[66] While he at times seems to recognize the reciprocity of such a condition as politics and science,[67] or "love and art" (2009: 11), for instance, it, nevertheless, "seems absolutely crucial" for Badiou, as Clemens points out, "that love, mathematics, politics, they're absolutely separate, absolutely heterogeneous, they don't intermingle with each other in any way" (*IT* 191).[68] Although Badiou's argument that art creates its own truths that are "irreducible to other truths—be they scientific, political, or amorous" (2005: 9) disentangles art from its subordinated relationship to philosophy and opts for the singularity of art itself, it begs the question of whether art could not reflect upon these procedures as well.[69] Whereas this entire study is premised on the fact that the condition of art may negotiate ecological, amorous, political, scientific, and artistic subjects of events, the last two chapters of this book, in particular, show how the attempt at purifying these truth procedures runs into problems as expressed by Beatty's and Pynchon's novels. Only through the inter-generic fidelity toward an event, these novels suggest, can subjects of events "keep going" and apply the propositions to a situation that transcends the hermetic limitations of "artistic," "scientific," or "political" situations. The saliency of a scientific fidelity to an event may thus propel a political reaffirmation of an event's points. It is, as I would argue, particularly the hybrid capability of the novel to assimilate various (scientific, aesthetic, political, or amorous) discourses that makes it an especially profound and intricate domain for the inter-conditional implications of fidelities. The novel, as a crucial hybrid discourse, lacking any *"pertinent unity"* (2005: 10), shows how the logical purism latent in Badiou's theory might be negotiated, without forfeiting the potential to create subjects of events.

Even more so, while such works as *Slumberland* may incorporate political events in their diegesis, the very act of interpreting such literary works of art implies a specific orientation, an ethics of reading.[70] This last point of critique of Badiou's conditions projects itself on the entire question of this book as a literary study of subjects of events. Where is the place of literary analysis and critique within these procedures, if there is a place for them at all? Given Badiou's clear priority of the natural sciences in what he terms the scientific condition, and which exclusively are epitomized by examples such as Cantor, Einstein, or Gödel, while the condition of art only revolves around the aesthetic production of Schoenberg, Picasso, Mallarmé, or Beckett, the scientific *and* aesthetic (and one might well add *political*) implications of the study of literature should not be overlooked. As will be demonstrated within the particular readings of the novels that follow, the study of literature as a *science* that deals with the *aesthetic* and *political* implications of works of art combines the various specificities of these procedures and aspires to an ethical praxis. This is not to say that the study of literature, as such, assumes a sovereign position within these discourses, but its ability to combine the generic qualities of these fields makes it, nevertheless, an important site for ethical interpretation. Additionally, since ethics is the extraordinary coming into being of an event and subjects that are faithful to it, the study of literature is not a universal enquiry into the general laws of ethics and its negotiation in literature but becomes a specific, local analytics of the concrete textual worlds of a novel. This approach refrains from suggesting that the diegetical content of the American novel after 2000 crafts a specific ethical outlook in the sense of a possible-worlds game of make-belief that might serve as a foundation for a universal ethical imperative.[71] Since ethics and the imperatives that an event casts forth always only relate to the specific worlds in which the event occurs, one cannot simply deduce ways of action for the reader's lifeworld. Nevertheless, by delving into the specific textual situations that a novel conjures, the literary critic does become a part of that situation, tries to relate the eruption of an event, and analyzes the subjective constitutions that such an event may occasion. As should have become obvious within the course of this theoretical chapter, this is not a sovereign position, riding a high horse where one may haughtily look down from. By discerning the particular ethics-of-*The Road*, ethics-of-*The Zero*, ethics-of-*Only Revolutions*, ethics-of-*Slumberland*, and ethics-of-*Against the Day*, the literary scholar fundamentally raises the same (ethical) questions of the event and the subject and has to enter the uncertain waters of the subject of the event: an endeavor that is always contingent upon questions, and is itself, ultimately, questionable.

The concept of the subject of the event, as the theoretical part of this book has shown, implies the combination of two reciprocal phenomena: on the one hand, the contingent eruption of a singular, non-ontological event that crucially disturbs a particular situation; on the other, a some-one, who steps up to the radically changed environment that the event calls forth, giving this aberrant singularity a name and acting in fidelity to its propositions.[72] Only through the subject can there be said to be an event. Only through an event can there be said to be a subject. In what follows, I show how such subject-formations are negotiated in the American novel after 2000.

"You have to carry the fire"

The Reactive Subject in Cormac McCarthy's
The Road (2006)

You would like a hero of the road then?

Charlotte Brontë, *Jane Eyre.*

There is no hero of the event.

Alain Badiou, *Being and Event.*

There is no longer any world: no longer a mundus, a cosmos, a composed
and complete order (from) within which one might find a place,
a dwelling, and the elements of an orientation. Or, again, there is no longer the
"down here" of a world one could pass through toward a beyond
or outside of this world. There is no longer any Spirit of the world,
nor is there any history before whose tribunal one could stand.
In other words, there is no longer any sense of the world.

Jean-Luc Nancy, *The Sense of the World.*

To be sure, despite being a fundamental rupture, an *event* does not have to imply the emphatic dispositions that our ordinary use of the term at times seems to convey—as will become clear in the case of *Only Revolutions*, the mere encounter between two lovers may suffice for such a manifestation. Nevertheless, Cormac McCarthy's Pulitzer Prize–winning novel, *The Road* (2006), emblematizes the highest possible degree of an event's life-altering potential. In its imagination of a literally unimaginable world that is forsaken beyond recognition and its depiction of the ways in which humans relate to this happening, focusing in particular on the struggle for survival of an unnamed father and his son, the novel helps to grasp the rather abstract concept of a non-ontological singularity. At the same time, it shows that events do not simply amount to "positive" forms of emancipatory revelations for human beings, thereby illuminating an anti-anthropocentric dimension that addresses ecocritical concerns.[1] The novel's reflection on the devastating reverberations of an unexplained ecological event that has essentially transformed Planet Earth into a wasteland of bare life renders a "world" in which "there is," not only as Jean-Luc Nancy observes, "no longer any sense of the world" (1997: 4), but no world altogether. The event initiates the loss of the "world" as the era of human and biological beings; simultaneously, this chapter suggests that *The Road* shows how the event exiles the accompanying practices of "making sense" of this world.

As in the case of the other parts that follow, the methodological approach of this study follows the theoretical impetus of the subject of the event. Thus, this chapter begins with an inquiry into the nature of the event that *The Road* presents, testing its status as an event and trying to situate it within the four generic procedures that evoke a subjective process. Just as the subject has to wager on the existence of an event, so do my readings critically opt for the always uncertain and ephemeral interpretation of events. However, already the first novel under analysis extends Badiou's apparatus in that it gives narrative expression to an ecological event. The novel could therefore be seen as a historically sensitive contextualization of particular concerns that twenty-first century culture processes (but which have obviously been important before), addressing ecological issues that are absent from Badiou's account.[2]

After considering to what extent one may speak of an ecological event in *The Road*, how this type of event is to be situated within a larger discourse of an American apocalyptic tradition, and to what extent the novel's critique of this discourse is tied up with its reflection on the possibility of an ecological event, the second step consists in relating it to its subjective embodiments. In contrast to a variety of readings that celebrate the novel's persistence of life even in the face of "apocalypse," my reading suggests a more negative interpretation in relation to humankind. When positioned in the context of a theory of subjects of events, *The Road*'s two protagonists, the unnamed father and son, fail to live up to the propositions the event elicits. In tune with the radically thanatological ramifications that the ecological cataclysm evokes, Planet Earth exiles its human, and more generally, its animate beings.[3] *The Road* therefore imagines a diegetic world in which the "living" has been surpassed by an ontology of egalitarian dead objects, such as gray rivers, dams, corpses, and shopping carts. The novel's quite subversive vision could thus be seen as fictionalizing a radically anti-anthropocentric "world," an evental situation that exhibits the cognitive *aporia* of how to picture such a planet that resists any anthropocentrism and how an ethics of such a "world" could look like. By the same token, in reading *The Road* in line with McCarthy's whole oeuvre,[4] the novel perpetuates his generally bleak accounts of humans by depicting how a "subject" of the event does not necessarily have to rely on a human foundation. *The Road* shows that, given the absolutely universal and contingent impetus of events, even objects may become a subject of the event.

Yet, despite the unmistakable repercussions of the ecological singularity, the father nevertheless perpetuates his and his son's existence and instrumentalizes the faithful subject of the event, both his son's mother as well as the novel's inanimate beings. The father's clinging to the world before the event, as epitomized by his sacralization of consumerism and his repeated Promethean insistence to "carry the fire," as well as his perpetuation of narratives, render him, and by extension his son, reactive subjects. In spite of the radically changed environment, the father thus harks back to an essentially American ethos of relating to his surroundings in an exclusively anthropocentric manner, an exploitive praxis that here infringes upon the ecological event of the novel rather than a problematic notion of "nature." In contrast to the persistent argument that the *human* exploits *nature*, which constructs problematic conceptual binaries, I argue that the father is corrupted through his active rejection of the ecological propositions that the event elicits.

In Badiou's terminology, this then is an "evil" form of subjective procedure.[5] As he explains in *Ethics*, since to "fail to live up to a fidelity is Evil in the sense of betrayal, betrayal in oneself of the Immortal that you are" (71), the father's reactionary ethics has to be viewed critically within the context of the novel's event. As a reactive subject, father and son choose "a reasonable survival" that is "preferable to total failure and torment" (*LoW* 56), which would constitute a faithful subjective process. Instead of reading the novel as an allegory of human superiority, a quest narrative that leads them to a state of redemption, I seek to highlight their infidelity to the event, which undermines their self-professed goodness and renders them villains of the road.[6]

On a more abstract level, *The Road* sheds light on the concept of the subject of the event by showing that this subjective concept is not an *a priori* disposition but, rather, a radical submission to the event. However, this submission does not constitute a total passivity, which also manifests itself in the process of reception. The novel asks readers not only to interpret the propositions of the event and give it a name but also to be critical about the father's narrative manipulations. Whereas Jess Walter's *The Zero* shows to what extent a faithful subjective procedure may be corrupted in the realm of the event, urging us to inquire into the novel's happening and to demystify its alleged status as an event, McCarthy's novel elucidates a problematization within the context of the subject's relation to the event. In a sense, *The Road* also engages our hermeneutic fidelity to it, calling upon us to decode the event's manifestation, recognize its evental truth, and trace the subjective procedures such works engender.

The end of the world

The event in *The Road* emphatically initiates the end of the world. This is to be understood neither in a hyperbolic sense nor as a turn of phrase in which science fiction narratives, for instance, evoke post-apocalyptic settings only to show how humankind adapts to these radically different environments. Quite literally, the cataclysmic event of the novel ushers Planet Earth from its phase as a "world," derived from "wer-ald, 'the age of man'" (2010: 30), as Steven Connor observes, into an impossible world; in other words, the event's fundamental change of the earth's situation implies a crucial abandonment of anthropocentrism and biocentrism altogether, offering a "worldless world" (Carlson 2007: 58), or, as Randall S. Wilhelm puts it so neatly, a "new no country for old men, perhaps on its way to becoming no country for any men, women or children" (2008: 131). Depictions of the progressive death of all of the planet's life forms, the evacuation of its human and, even more generally, its animate content showcases that the event's non-ontological impulse has indeed radical ramifications for the world's being as well as for its beings. If events are to be conceived of as making the impossible possible, then *The Road*'s essentially ecocentric vision amounts to such a singularity in that the narrative "world" imagines a planet without human, animal, or botanical existences.[7] *The Road*, as will be argued in the following section, assumes characteristics of religious apocalypse but, crucially, extends these mechanisms in secularizing the concept and creating a planet that is essentially anti-anthropocentric and anti-biocentric. While the novel has been contextualized in the discourse of ecocriticism, I want to suggest that it critically reflects upon this discourse, positing not simply an ecological apocalypse but an ecological event. Before analyzing this ontology of objects, of detritus and waste—a "world as junk heap" (2013: 198), as Estes phrases it—it first needs to be settled as to what extent one can speak of an event, and an ecological event, in the novel at all. Both the religious inception of the concept of the apocalypse (with its traditional positive disposition of revealing and creating anew) and its modern transformation (with Puritan as well as ecological notions of destruction) prove helpful in sharpening the concept of the event that this study proposes and which *The Road* pursues.

Although *The Road* is remarkably silent about the inception of the catastrophe that has befallen Planet Earth, as has been noted frequently,[8] there are a variety of instances that serve as a hermeneutic grid from which one may grasp its status as an event. In fact *The Road*'s event meets the criteria of radically changing the situation it appertains to, since it is revealed without foreboding and ushers in a "world" that is based on essentially different grounds than the situation prior to its manifestation. While the novel unmistakably shatters the secure diegetic sphere of its represented world by reaching out into the cultural milieu of the reader's lifeworld for contrast and emphasis, the novel itself also describes this fundamentally altered world in its fictional realm.[9] In the novel's second sentence, the narrator not only describes the planes of destruction but also insinuates the manifestation of an event: "Nights dark beyond darkness and the days more gray each one than what had gone before. Like the onset of some cold glaucoma dimming away the world" (*TR* 1). By beginning the novel with a stark photologic juxtaposition that is structured as a movement from darkness to light, the novel instantaneously summons a religious context that is a particularly vibrant hypotext for the novel and very telling for its notion of events.[10] As in God's making of the world, the narrative poses the antecedence of darkness into which the "goodness" of light invades and thereby recalls one of the most influential founding "events" of Western metaphysics.[11] According to this rationale, the formless darkness, ("the earth was without form and void" [Gen. 1:2]) is negated by the incisive specificity ("each one") of quantifiable and numerable days; it manifests, in other words, the beginning of human time. This logocentric act of creation and separation performed by a transcendental being seems symptomatic for the novel's narrative situation, which will be discussed in more detail later in this chapter.[12]

While one could thus see parallels between a divinely incited event that serves as the beginning of the world as word and the act of narration that is authored by an ostensibly extradiegetic agency, the novel simultaneously undermines this logocentric undercurrent and, rather, conceives of an evental notion that denies the positioning of a transcendental origin. In acknowledging the anteriority of darkness before the metaphorical advent of day, the novel rejects the problematic acts of creation that guide Western metaphysics and that are also particularly fertile in an American context of positing clean slates and new beginnings. Instead, rather than supporting the binarism of day and light, a stone's throw from metonymical oppositions of "good" and "evil" that prove especially poignant for the novel's ethical semantics, *The Road* describes its event by integrating both dualities into a new situation. This is to say that *both* dispositions, the superlative darkness of nights *and* the monotony of gray daylight, constitute two sides of the same coin that mark the new situation after the event. Instead of positing a causality between darkness and then light, the novel's beginning describes the post-evental situation as a combination of both modalities. Yet, whereas there is a connection between both phases of the day that does not figure as a metaphor for a divine form of creation, the comparison ("more . . . than") that is drawn to "what had gone before" marks a difference that conveys the juxtaposition of the old and the new, post-evental setting. The new situation that is defined by a lack of lighting and, by extension, enlightenment, as well the oxymoronic colorless but punctuating particularity of gray days is contrasted with a state before the obscure event has taken place. Within just one sentence, the narrative thus conjures an ontological difference that serves to distinguish between these two situations.

Moreover, the event and its disruptive impact are also transported by the paratactical structure of the two phrases. This stylistic mode is equally used in the beginning of Genesis where it seems to function as a syntactical oscillation between the closed logic of each day's creation and the continuity between these acts that the conjunction "And" evokes. In other words, the paratactical structure of Genesis oscillates between the distinctive and independent quality of each day of creation that is then tied, through the use of anaphoric links, to a greater act of divine creation. In *The Road*, however, this syntactical logic supplements another sentence that insinuates the distinction between the days before and the days after the event for different reasons. By adding another comparison that is supposed to highlight the change that the event brought about, which is, however, marked by a syntactical ellipsis, the sentence intimates the disruptive force of the event on a linguistic level, symbolically interrupting the continuous flow of language.

Yet, while the ontological contradistinction that expresses the eruption of an event ushers in a process that "dims away the world," that is, the world as inhabited and perceived by human cognition, the event is not described as an ominous hellfire induced by religious or military catastrophe.[13] The simile that likens the event to a pathological condition that again undermines the divine movement from darkness to light intimates a reversed and slow but inevitable process of fundamental ramifications. By the same token, it is telling that this deteriorating process of eyesight relates to notions of lighting in its etymological conception also. Stemming from the Greek γλαυκός *glaukós*, meaning light, bright, this ocular disease once again suggests the eruption of a literally blinding event that fundamentally shatters any conception of the "I."[14] In fact, the likening to an ocular disorder not only generally embodies the structure of an event by stressing to what extent it crucially erupts and affects the "world," simultaneously disabling and enabling those affected by it; more specifically, one might also interpret this use of simile as symptomatic for the subjective process that the father engages in. While the event effaces the "world" and supplants it with a new situation, the father doubles this form of blinding in that he ignores its implications. He literally turns a blind eye/I to the event and chooses to reject its inexorability.

It is worth noting that the novel in its very beginning refers to an Old Testament context of events, but critically inverses a form of logocentric act of creation in framing its singularity as an act of destruction. While *The Road's* event thereby circumvents the problematic concept of original beginnings that Genesis sketches, it nevertheless interrelates to another form of event that assumes a decisive position within the biblical tradition and that, especially for American culture, finds its origins in the New Testament: apocalypse. Thereby, McCarthy's novel opens another discursive level in relation to its event that has crucially shaped American literature and essentially established its cultural imagination. Not as a counterpoint to the notion that America offered a new beginning but, rather, as part of the same structure,[15] this discourse of the "end of the world" thus serves not only as the cornerstone of a religious theme of an apocalyptic kind; particularly the twentieth century has appropriated this structural syntagma and filled it with different motives, most prominent among these being technological and environmental cataclysms, thereby also transforming the semantic connotations of the word.[16] While the basis for the eschatological considerations from Rachel Carson through Kurt Vonnegut, Phillip K. Dick and Kathy Acker to Don DeLillo hark back to a comprehensive imagination of the "end" in Puritanical writings, the historico-cultural context of the American Century undoubtedly played its part in rejuvenating this narrative, while also adapting its content to the environment of postmodernity.[17] However, despite the key role of narratives of apocalypse in American culture, the sub-genre of post-apocalyptic fiction assumes a special role in this imagination and *The Road* has to be viewed within the context of this discourse.[18] While the event in the novel recalls the notion of apocalypse in its religious understanding, it also implies characteristics that fundamentally differ from the biblical discourse. In fact, *The Road* proves to extend the religious concept by framing it in an ecological perspective, secularizing it in the vein of a post-apocalyptic imagination.

Indeed, both the etymological root of a "revelation" as well as the later semantic shift by which the ordinary usage of the term carries with it notions of grand-scale destruction are latent in *The Road's* event.[19] In the first sense, deriving from the "Greek *Apo-calyptein*, meaning 'to un-veil,'" (1996: 14) as Thompson observes, an event equally emphasizes a revelation of something that was nonexistent in the prior situation. The revelatory moment in the apocalypse thus engages with events on an epistemological and hermeneutic basis. Yet, while apocalypse as nestled in the typological Puritanical tradition is inherently connected to a "process of decoding scripture to unveil the date of the Second Coming" (ibid.: 3), the manifestation of the event can only function in hindsight. Although the religious hermeneutic that establishes the search for textual signs of orientation cannot avoid the fundamental component of contingency—the faithful never knowing for certain whether they would make it or not—the Puritanical desire for knowing and inquiring into the unknowable constitutes a remarkable cultural epistemology that is entirely excluded from the framework of events. Whereas New England Puritans such as Increase and Cotton Mather, Michael Wigglesworth, and Jonathan Edwards could invest efforts in trying "to find certain signs for the end of the world" (Elliott 2010: 24) and attempting to imagine what the apocalypse might look like,[20] as "The Day of Trouble is near" (1634), "The Day of the Doom" (1662) or "Notes on the Apocalypse" (1723) so vividly attest, the rationale of the event precludes any form of anticipation and, by extension, also undermines the overarching structure of predestination. If the apocalypse is imminent in the divine plan and "apocalypticism is inevitably bound up with imagination, because it has yet to come into being" (Garrard 2012: 94), events in general, as well as the one of McCarthy's novel, reject both transcendent determination and human prolepsis. In a sense, one could say that events and subjective relations to it, can always only be post-evental, that is, post-apocalyptic.[21]

The contingent nature of the novel's event is elucidated in one of the rare flashbacks that are focalized through the eyes of the father:

> The clocks stopped at 1:17. A long shear of light and then a series of low concussions. He got up and went to the window. What is it? she said. He didn't answer. He went into the bathroom and threw the lightswitch but the power was already gone. A dull rose glow in the windowglass. He dropped to one knee and raised the lever to stop the tub and then turned on both taps as far as they would go. She was standing in the doorway in her nightwear, clutching the jamb, cradling her belly in one hand. What is it? she said. What is happening? I don't know. (*TR* 54)

From the reactions of the father and his wife, one can tell to what extent they did not expect this to happen. Her persistent inquiry into the ontological dimensions of the event ("What *is* it?") and his inability to come up with rational answers are telling for both its disruptive singularity and the contingent nature of this eruption. This is also amplified by the man's failure to operate the technological appliances. The father, who is continuously characterized by a dexterous interaction with his environment (both "natural" and "technological"), here fails to operate the most basic equipment that supplies the most basic resources for living.

What is more, the eruption of the event is once more framed in an explicitly biblical setting. Not only does the separating motion of the "shearing light" again refer to God's initial schism but the stopping of clocks also indicates metaphorically the End of Time initiated by the apocalypse and thereby alludes to the New Testament. Paradoxically, if seen as a reference to Gen. 1:17—"And God set them in the firmament of the heaven to give light on the earth"— one gets another inversion of acts of creation and destruction.[22] For while the narrative content seems to refer to Genesis in its evocation of a lightning that crosses at some distance, the beneficial connotation of God's enlightenment is radically undermined in this passage. Here, light connotes not a positive symbol of human emancipation but, rather, its opposite.[23] As a harbinger of the coming destructions, the kinaesthetic traces of the event hint at the negative repercussions that it brings down on its animate inhabitants, again employing a term of medical discourse to transport the damaging effects upon substantial human organs.

In this sense, the passage also recalls another Old Testament scene that is also symptomatic for *The Road*'s event and its implications. The constellation of man and woman thus relates to the Edenic expulsion of Adam and Eve as told in Genesis 3 and suggests a similar topos in which the couple will have to evacuate the secure shelter they once inhabited. Contrary to the biblical narrative of the fall of man that is grounded in the transgression of divine law, however, the novel does not explicate any form of explicit hubris. Indeed, whereas the fall of man in Genesis causes their expulsion from paradise, in *The Road* it is the event that triggers their evacuation, thereby reversing the causal link between subject and event. The violation of God's imperative fashions an ethical framework in which the transcendental law provides a universal normative set of rules that has to be followed; in contrast, the ethical implications in the context of the subject of the event are always only event-specific. The transgressive actions of the father can only be assessed in their relation to the concrete propositions of the event.

While the discourse of biblical apocalypse is useful for elucidating and distinguishing the novel's event in respect to its radical change as well as the contingent manner of this eruption, ecocritical reflections on apocalypse prove an additional help in comprehending what "truth" this event brings forth and how it ushers in a "*new* way of being" (*E* 41). In order to grasp how the truth that this event evokes, a truth that insists on an abnormal multiple, which has been excluded from properly belonging to the particular world of the novel,[24] it is necessary to consider how the notion of apocalypse has been employed in a more recent discourse. By analyzing the close but problematic ties between apocalypse and ecological discourse,[25] one may better understand the radically new situation that *The Road*'s event evokes, which transcends a religious context. Still, rather than reading the singular happening of the novel as an ecoapocalypse, the following shows why it might be more appropriate to understand it as an ecological event. This, then, again harks back to the revelatory dimension of the novel's event. Not only is *The Road*'s ecological event differently structured in terms of its hermeneutic anticipation but the singular or abnormal multiple that the event brings to the fore as its site is intrinsically tied to a radical anti-anthropocentrism. What I would like to call an "inanimism" implies the exile of biological, animate organisms and thus offers a way of being that is itself an impossible thought for the discourse of ecocriticism.[26] By extension, the apocalyptic connotation of an unveiling also relates to the implicated subjective process that perpetuates the truth that is exposed by the event and maintained by subjects. It is only in the face of this encompassing truth and its grounding as a "new present" (*LoW* 51)[27] that the reactive status of the father may be discerned as a negative corruption of the faithful process that fosters this truth, since, as Badiou insists: "Without consideration of the Good, and thus of truths, there remains only the cruel innocence of life, which is beneath Good *and beneath Evil*" (*E* 60).[28]

Just as *The Road*'s event undermines its ready incorporation in a religious typology of apocalypse, so does it refrain from being a simple ecoapocalypse. I insist that the event in McCarthy's novel explicitly manifests not an ecological apocalypse but an ecological event. Certainly, one might see various intimations of the book's scenario as having experienced an ecological catastrophe, viewing "nature in terms of its capacity for being changed with amazing swiftness into its opposite through human agency" (Buell 1995: 307).[29] Although such an understanding of apocalypse crucially secularizes the religious inception by laying it into human hands, assuming the novel's singularity as an ecological event seems more appropriate and offers a variety of interesting observations. Because of the inevitable but highly problematic use of the apocalyptic trope and rhetoric for ecological discourse, the "single most powerful master metaphor that the environmental imagination has at its disposal" (1995: 285), as Buell phrases it, it appears more productive to conceive the novel's singularity in different terms.[30] In reading the novel's singularity as an ecological event, the novel's event not only rejects the circular structure of apocalypses that is latent in both religious and ecological instantiations, but this interpretation also refrains from the imminent aspect of nostalgia that most ecological apocalypses embody. In this sense, not only is the ecological event radically invested in the present, but its contingent eruption also disavows any form of pastoral ideology that, together with apocalypse, is the founding discursive paradigm of modern environmentalism.[31] On the contrary, the ecological event of *The Road* is a situation that neither allows romantic cravings for a lost Edenic past nor simplifies environmental change by myopically blaming the "human." As an ecological event, the novel's happening, rather, forces those affected by it to fully embrace its new propositions with utter vehemence, showing no interest in a genealogy of its inception.

Even though apocalypse seems to rely fundamentally on a teleological notion of time, apocalypticism as a cultural strategy functions in circular motions. While there is no question that Judeo-Christian temporality is different from circular philosophies in Asian and Hellenistic areas,[32] the actual mechanisms of apocalyptic discourses seem to rely on similar motions that are not exactly linear. As in Puritanical millennial jeremiads,[33] ecological apocalypse thus also positions an ultimate eschaton; however, this proleptic imagination (Garrard 2012: 86) only serves to effect change in the present. Garrard notes in this respect that "environmental apocalypticism, on this view, is not about anticipating the end of the world, but about attempting to avert it by persuasive means" (ibid.: 107–08). In very much the same sense as in utopian and dystopian novels, apocalypse thus functionalizes its prophetic imagination in order to exhort (ibid.: 108). Instead of a clear linear trajectory that is directed at a specific *telos*, the structure of apocalyptical rhetoric is therefore only interested in the future in order to reflect back onto the present, or as Cathy Gutierrez observes: "Like narrative, millennial systems use the promise of closure as the focusing lens of the present. Closure is anticipated as the end point that will retrospectively make sense of the past and present" (2005: 47).

This hysteron-proteron structure of ecological apocalypses (and also apocalypse in general) that Carson's Silent Spring established (Buell 1995: 285) simultaneously undermines temporal linearity by critically inflecting religious apocalypse in putting a positive accent on the time before the apocalypse has happened. If religious apocalypse cherishes the coming of the End Time for its promise of redemption, "less feared as an ultimate end than expected as a new beginning" (Freese 1997: 25), ecological apocalypse prioritizes the past in an often idealized manner—a "Nature" that needs protection if its Fall is to be averted. Ecoapocalypse thus not only projects a future in order to inspire changes in the present; it simultaneously uses a dystopian future in order to romanticize the past.

Although *The Road* certainly addresses ecological issues, I would argue that it does so on a subliminal level, since it does so without relapsing to a straightforward use of ecoapocalypse. Unlike many critics' opinion that "*The Road*, in the end, is a prophetic hieroglyphic of horror, an American jeremiad more terrifying than even the Puritan imagination could conjure" (2008: 60), as expressed by Edwards, I see the singular happening in the novel as addressing ecological matters in a more complex way than mere prophetic incitement of terror.[34] Its implication of an ecological event thus differs from ecoapocalypse in that it rejects any form of prolepsis, the event being fundamentally contingent, as already observed above.[35] Unlike "the apocalypse" that in Puritanical discourse "remained a welcome event" (Freese 1997: 25), or its negative projection in ecological discourse, where "the imagination is being used to anticipate and, if possible, forestall actual apocalypse" (Buell 1995: 285), there is just no room for anticipation in the case of events. They are essentially unrecognizable from the perspective of the situation that they affect.

The Road's event, however, avoids another problematic factor that is latent in the imagination of ecological catastrophe. As Garrard observes: "Apocalyptic rhetoric furthermore fosters a delusive search for culprits and causes that may be reductively conceived by conflating very varied environmental problems within the concept of a singular, imminent 'environmental crisis'" (2012: 115). As an ecological event, the novel assumes a mode of singularity without simplifying environmental processes into a singular happening. In fact, since hardly anything is actually said about the origins of the event, McCarthy stifles any attempts at pigeonholing the singularity into an environmentalist framework. Whereas the remarkable silence on the origins of the event relates intimately to the narrative situation and its relation to the father's status as a reactive subject, this avoidance of "culprits and causes" equally subscribes to seeing the happening as an event. Just as it is impossible to foresee the eruption of an event in the future, so is it beside the point of applying a historical hermeneutic to an event's manifestation in hindsight. Even though one might obviously speculate to what extent it was already perceptible and merely followed a deducible and inevitable path of causality, the logic of the event in *The Road* undermines this metaphysics of "simple becoming" in favor of "true change" (*LoW* 363).[36] Despite the fact that the novel plants various indices from which one may derive the actual quality of the event, it seems, indeed, to be part of the novel's endeavor to scatter traces of its causes without resolving to one definite explanation. By keeping quiet about the possible causation of the ecological wasteland, the novel thus not only enriches the process of reception; more crucially, this evasion equally subscribes to the singular and contingent eruption without the possibility of speculative anticipation. As an ecological event, in other words, the singularity cannot be reduced to a problematic reduction in which "humans" or "nature" caused it; the novel's event is not interested in possible origins, if there can be said to be any, but rather inquires into the post-evental effects of this eruption.[37] Understanding the novel's event as an ecological one, then, appertains to its ecological *implications*, instead of its clandestine sources.

This negative relation to the past is connected to a third reason why the novel narrativizes an ecological event rather than an apocalypse. The event, albeit dependent on the initial situation, nevertheless surpasses this stage and establishes a "new present" (*LoW* 51) without nostalgically looking back. Unlike the "pastoral ideology" that is latent in the master metaphor of apocalypticism and which "appeals to nostalgia, accomplishing their interventions by invocations of actual green worlds about to be lost" (Buell 1995: 301), the novel calls for an unmitigated embrace of the ecological event's new present. Indeed, in order to become a faithful subject, this process forces its subjective adherents to look ahead, simultaneously requiring them to bring this present into being. Before we are in a position to inquire into the faithful subjective procedures that *The Road* proposes and, more emphatically, analyze to what extent father and son deny this new present in favor of a pastoral past, it needs to be settled what kind of evental site this "world" evokes, whose acknowledgment produces a subject.

Events usher in new presents by supplementing the pre-evental situations with singular or abnormal multiples that these prior situations chose to ignore. If, for example, the event of African American emancipation introduced the multiple of the "oppressed slave" into the situation of the United States' political and cultural milieu, *The Road*'s abnormal multiple is to be situated within an ecological framework. By clearly referring to the negative repercussions of ecological pollution through such telling signifiers of capitalist culture as Coca Cola cans (*TR* 21) or empty gas stations (*TR* 5), the novel situates the narrative in an uncannily familiar environment of exploitation. Yet, if indeed the anthropocentric focus of the pre-evental world thus repressed and ignored a multiple, this is not simply a nostalgic form of "nature." In contrast to deep ecological and ecocentric approaches to an ecological practice that try to antagonize the blatant anthropocentrism of our world, the event does not opt for the common solution to current ecological problems in emphasizing the interconnectedness of the world's organisms, both human and non-human.[38] Unlike this other master metaphor of environmental discourse that uses a monistic understanding of an irredeemably encrusted "web," which "is central to the ethical force of the contemporary ecocentric critique of anthropocentrism" (Buell 1995: 282), the ecological paradigm that the novel's event evokes imagines a different form of being that radically rethinks the planet according to its suppressed singular set. Hence I suggest that the novel's event refashions the world as a situation previously dominated by human and generally organic beings in favor of its inanimate multiples—objects, waste, detritus, and also rocks, water, and dead bodies—thereby creating an egalitarian "inanimism." The novel's new ecology thus embraces a literal wasteland, actively exiling its animate inhabitants.

The radicality of this new situation not only attests to the inexorable and unmitigated repercussions that events may evoke; it also shows that events are not necessarily interested in the "human condition" as an indispensable carrier of its truth. By expanding Badiou's notion of an event in an ecological framework, *The Road* thereby also stretches the concept of the subject, reverting its strict anthropocentrism in favor of an "objective" subject.[39] In fashioning a situation that abandons anthropocentric perspectives and human beings altogether, the singular multiple of inanimate objects that was not "part of the situation" that might be called "world" (again indicating the etymological anthropocentrism of the word) is thus introduced into the situation, resulting in a fundamental change of its ontological prescriptions. Although such an imagination is certainly not beneficial for an environmental praxis, since as Garrard notes, "only if we imagine that the planet has a future, after all, are we likely to take responsibility for it" (2012: 105), *The Road*'s negative imagination is only negative in terms of its animate beings. Viewed from the perspective of a true egalitarian ontology that does not distinguish between subject-object and nature-culture binaries, McCarthy does not offer a simple narrative of ecological dystopia without hope.[40] Rather, the ecological complexity of the novel seems to foster a de-naturalization of our inexorably human world (and the biological world in general) by projecting and considering the possible consequences of a sphere beyond this paradigm.

A first indicator of *The Road*'s inanimism, its post-evental situation that perpetuates the existence/subjectification of inanimate beings, is addressed in the very beginning. Right after the novel has introduced the ecological event, the narrator goes on to explicate the man's dream from which he awakes in the very first line of the novel:

> In the dream from which he'd wakened he had wandered in a cave where the child led him by the hand. Their light playing over the wet flowstone walls. Like pilgrims in a fable swallowed up and lost among the inward parts of some granitic beast. Deep stone flues where the water dripped and sang. Tolling in the silence the minutes of the earth and the hours and the days of it and the years without cease. Until they stood in a great stone room where lay a black and white ancient lake. And on the far shore a creature that raised its dripping mouth from the rimstone pool and stared into the light with eyes dead white and sightless as the eggs of spiders. It swung its head low over the water as if to take the scent of what it could not see. Crouching there pale and naked and translucent, its alabaster bones cast up in shadow on the rocks behind it. Its bowels, its beating heart. The brain that pulsed in a dull glass bell. It swung its head from side to side and then gave out a low moan and turned and lurched away and loped soundlessly into the dark. (*TR* 1–2)

In line with the event's rejection of animate beings, this passage offers a first step in shifting the perspective from an anthropocentric point of view by creating an egalitarian ontology of human and non-human beings. Despite the notable human tint of the passage, with the platonic allusion to the cave and the anthropomorphic transformation of singing water framed in the prototypical genre of zoomorphical projection, one may also glimpse a shift of perspective concerning the priority of humans among these beings. The spatial dimensions that the passage conjures thus intimates the relative powerlessness of both father and son, "lost" in the intestines of a monstrous cavity. Moreover, this imminent terror that conveys their projected fear of the environment finds its apex in the horrific creature that is disturbed by man and boy. Interrupted in both habitus and habitat, it confronts the invading "pilgrims" with its symbolically "dead white and sightless" eyes, which suggests an animalistic transformation of a Tiresian figure that prophesies their imminent death. What is more, its status as an animate being is complicated by its description as being made up of granular mineral, while vital signs of organicism are contained in an inanimate "dull glass bell." This hybrid creature, however, does not simply undermine the distinctions between these two modalities. It, rather, incorporates an unconscious fear, being part of a dream, that embodies an ontology beyond pure organicism. The unconscious confrontation with a hybrid being thus attests the new present that steadily abandons "its bowels, its beating heart," slowly but inevitably, in a reluctant but conceding gesture, withdrawing "soundlessly into the dark." This creature, in other words, personifies an intermediate status in which pure organicism is being transformed according to its inanimistic evental site, a living *memento mori*.[41]

While such still living organisms are thus progressively exiled from the planet,[42] with birds perishing, trees falling, people dying, it is the perseverance of other beings that marks the continuation of the planet. Here, this persistence is represented in the element of water, which is depicted not only in its unabating endurance, having steadily carved deep flues into the cave, but also in an anthropomorphic celebrating mode. The acoustic rendering of the water, "singing," "tolling," gives expression to its reaction to the new present that finally acknowledges its being. Simultaneously, the water's tolling of the human clock also foreshadows the inevitable implications of this post-evental situation, with the sentence's structure paralleling the ongoing and penetrative progress of water, steadily slipping from one human unit of temporality to another. In this sense, the water embodies the new evental organization, literally adhering to the faithful subject's requirement to "'Keep going!' [Continuer!]" (*E* 52) that in this case wears the stone of anthropocentric time "without cease."

The persistence of the inanimate furthermore manifests itself in the novel's abundant depiction of "natural" materials, as well as in "cultural" waste and detritus, embodying a plane that according to Edwards "resists interpretation, for the landscape itself is largely mute, darkened, clouded, its color palette stripped of beauty and diversity and reduced to variations of gray" (*TR* 56).

Father and son attest this ongoing existence of the inanimate in two telling scenes. On their wanderings, they come across a dam. When the boy inquires into its function, the father replies:

> It made the lake. Before they built the dam that was just a river down there. The dam used the water that ran through it to turn big fans called turbines that would generate electricity.
> To make lights.
> Yes. To make lights.
> . . .
> Will it be here for a long time?
> I think so. It's made out of concrete. It will probably be there for hundreds of years. Thousands, even.
> Do you think there could be fish in the lake?
> No. There's nothing in the lake. (*TR* 19)

Unlike other anti-anthropocentric pastoral ideologies that insist on the perseverance of "nature," which guides a variety of deep ecological and ecocentric lines of argument, the novel here addresses the inevitable interconnection of nature and culture, what Donna Haraway calls "naturecultures" (qtd. in Garrard 2012: 17). Yet, it is not the mere deconstruction of this opposition that the father indicates by exhibiting the interconnection of these terms in the construction of a lake. The perseverance of the dam, being made to last another millennium and another possible chiastic event, more specifically indicates to what extent the post-evental situation does not discriminate between the persistence of natural or cultural artifacts. Both water and something that embodies the apex of human intervention in a "natural" environment as inanimate entities prevail within the framework of the ecological event. By defying an anthropocentic experience of time, the endurance of the dam marks its adaptation to the new situation, where its inanimate existence can no longer be measured in temporal units. Everything is being "consumed," as Carlson remarks, "by such a timeless time of 'ever,' the time of no time that we might believe operative not only in death 'itself' but indeed in the living death of a life without that shared openness of future and past" (2007: 58).

Instead of stressing the solely negative ecological repercussions of this construction—since the turbines produced clean energy—the post-evental situation of the novel is blind toward this distinction. It is, rather, the difference between living and inanimate beings that constitutes a new proposition that is addressed in the father's negative response to his son's question as to whether there are any living animals in the lake. Instead of a return to animistic "nature," the consequential ramifications of the novel guarantee the continuing existence of inanimate "naturecultures."

However, whereas this inanimate form of geo-graphy endures, the man's and the boy's inscriptions in the earth prove more ephemeral. Toward the end of the novel, father and son finally reach the coast, the goal of their wanderings. Sitting on the beach,

> the boy played in the sand. He had a spatula made from a flattened foodtin and with it he built a small village. He dredged a grid of streets. The man walked down and squatted and looked at it. The boy looked up.
>
> The ocean's going to get it, isn't it? he said.
>
> Yes.
>
> That's okay.
>
> Can you write the alphabet?
>
> I can write it.
>
> We dont work on your lessons any more.
>
> I know.
>
> Can you write something in the sand?
>
> Maybe we could write a letter to the good guys. So if they came along they'd know we were here. We could write it up there where it wouldnt get washed away.
>
> What if the bad guys saw it?
>
> Yeah. (*TR* 261–62)

Having been characterized as "pilgrims" (*TR* 1) before, the boy here subscribes to his status as a colonial vanguard, penetrating the land and transforming its savage chaos into an ordered and inhabitable place. Although simply a game of make-believe, the religious connotations of this act of creation suggest the boy's mimicking of a divine practice. In tune with the guiding ethical maxim that distinguishes between good and bad guys that requires further discussion, both father and son here recall the American context of the arrival of the founding fathers and the accompanying conquest of the continent. In contrast to this colonial project of settlement, however, father and son acknowledge the evanescence of their constructions in the face of the ocean, one of the new earth's inanimate subjects. It is tellingly no act of destruction that the water enacts on the items of the boy's small-scale imitation, which are equally part of this new order. The ocean merely "get[s] it" and thereby undermines the concrete place that the boy seeks to establish. The foodtin, another inanimate object of the post-evental world, floats in the sea without a clear destiny nor an anthropogenically fixed location.

Next to their architectural attempts to create order and uphold their human marks on the earth, they ponder a literally geographical practice that aims to ascertain their existence in the world. Yet, this act of inscription is equally denounced as futile, again unmasked in its impermanence that has to yield to the new paradigm that the ocean so comprehensively represents. Just as the sea will inevitably wash away the tin can, the stability of their alphabetical notes is never secure and ultimately, as a practice of human communication, excluded in this new present. While the father certainly enacts a form of logocentrism, not only asking the boy if he knew the "alphabet" but also being skeptical about the misapprehensions that might occur when the boy puts the "letter" into the sand, the novel is not merely opting for an alternative writing practice, a grammatology. Instead, *The Road* suggests that all forms of writing as acts of preservation, communication, mediation, or narration are necessarily anthropocentric and therefore have to be exiled according to the propositions of the ecological event.

Whereas the continuous trope of "carrying the fire" (*TR* 87) has to be viewed in this respect, yet with specific focus on their relation to the event and their consequent status as a reactive subject, the novel also addresses the superfluity of human cultural practices and particularly language as it becomes a redundant atavism:

> He [the father] tried to think of something to say but he could not. He'd had this feeling before, beyond the numbness and the dull despair. The world shrinking down about a raw core of parsible entities. The names of things slowly following those things into oblivion. Colors. The names of birds. Things to eat. Finally the names of things one believed to be true. More fragile than he would have thought. How much was done already? The sacred idiom shorn of its referents and so of its reality. Drawing down like something trying to preserve heat. In time to wink out forever. (*TR* 93)

Here the father is depicted as lacking not only the linguistic but also the cognitive means to communicate. Though epistemologically paralyzed for the briefest of moments, he glances at the event's imperative, the world as a man-made habitat transforming into a democracy of "parsible entities." Note, however, that he still assumes a constructivist stance toward reality by which the things disappear first and only then their signifiers.

Although this certainly highlights the father's anthropocentric perspective that cannot imagine a "world" without human mediation, the passage goes on to describe the constant process of inanimism by accounting for the qualitative or intensional reduction. It is simply colors, the names of birds, things to eat, all inherently human concepts that the event takes with it. While an anthropocentric perspective could not ascribe existence to the world without human perception of this world, the passage hints at an ontology of inanimate things beyond human access. By addressing a necessary aporia, *The Road* confronts us with a "world" without referents, simultaneously pointing to the impossibility of such an imaginative feat that the novel itself expresses: a "world," as Thomas A. Carlson notes in which "everything seems like a message or a means of exchange and connection now shorn of sender and purpose bereft of any recipient or destination" (2007: 57). It thereby again indicates the inexorably human notion of a referential reality where the event not only destroys the double-sided parts of a sign but also the third term that it ostensibly, extra-linguistically denotes. If the stability of both signifier and signified can by now no longer be taken for certain, the novel moves further and inquires into the ways in which we can envision a radically anti-anthropocentric "world," without even a notion of referents.

The necessary limitations of such an imagination are marked by the evocation of a religious context in which the "sacred idiom" once more intimates the presence of a divine act of destruction, in which God's word here teleologically ends the world in a reversed alternation of His Word in the beginning of Genesis. Although one might also interpret this in secular terms, denoting an alternative form of mediation in a world reigned by objects, it is still represented as a form of human mediation. Being not a coherent language, it is, nevertheless, an idiom that insinuates its reductive extensions but cannot avoid its anthropocentric stance. This is specifically important since this passage is focalized, if not narrated, by the father—a narratological interweaving that has to be analyzed in more detail in the next section. In one of the novel's repeated smooth transitions from external to internal focalization, the father's thoughts are not differentiated from the seemingly extradiegetic narrative voice. It is thus telling that while the father might anticipate an ontology without human access, he still can only approximate it and imagine it in terms of a linguistic model. From the necessarily human point of view of the father, it is thus impossible to grasp this ontology of objects. All he can do is acknowledge the perseverance of the inanimate "raw core" that antagonizes thermodynamic paralysis, preserving heat despite the wholesale abandonment of its human and animate constituents.

If the "sacred idiom" is still an anthropocentric attempt to conceive of the new situation, a final instance that represents this anti-anthropocentric order of inanmism situated at the very end of the book offers a cogent image for such an ontology. After the end of the novel's narrative action, we are presented with a seemingly random image, what Edwards appropriately terms a "pastoral coda" (2008: 55), whose narrative ontological status is anything but certain:

Once there were brook trout in the streams in the mountains. You could see them standing in the amber current where the white edges of their fins wimpled softly in the flow. They smelled of moss in your hand. Polished and muscular and torsional. On their backs were vermiculate patterns that were maps of the world in its becoming. Maps and mazes. Of a thing which could not be put back. Not be made right again. In the deep glens where they lived all things were older than man and they hummed of mystery. (*TR* 307)

While this crucial scene is read by Jay Ellis as a lamentation of "what is lost" (2008: 35) and by Edwards as a nostalgic pastoralism in the evocation of an "almost Emersonian sense of Nature as sacred text" (2008: 55), the discursive placement of this coda suggests otherwise. As it is situated not only at the end of the novel but also right after the father has died, I read this flashback not in the apocalyptic tradition of a warning as Ellis does[43] but as a statement on the irreversible nature of the post-eventual situation that cannot "be put back." Unlike the father's pastoral memory, "the perfect day of his childhood . . . the day to shape the days to come" (*TR* 12), toward the beginning of the novel, this coda functions differently. While the father's memory is replete with idyllic scenery, "straw hat[s]," (*TR* 11), "clear water," and "warm" decor (*TR* 12), this final image, for its lack of a clear focalizing agent lacks the subjective nostalgia that the father's reminiscence evokes. Although one could argue that the passage is narrated either by the dead father or by the son, which is attested by the "human" signifiers of the fairy-tale frame, in the direct addressing of the reader in the second-person singular or the haptic interaction between fish and human, the passage also implies a crucial anti-anthropocentric perspective. This is amplified by the map on the brook trout's back, which offers an alternative expression of this new ontology without relapsing to a similar form of anthropocentric construction as the "sacred idiom." The map, indeed, offers a different articulation of this ontology of inanimate beings in that it is structured in spatio-pictorial terms and not in a temporal mode of narrative. The spatiality of this structure, which is first presented as a human guide for orientation, is immediately complicated when it is described as an architecture that problematizes straightforward direction. Notably, the referent for the map remains unspecified as a "thing which could not be put back." While this thing could certainly be read as the ecological event that is irreversible, one may also read this "thing" as a synecdoche for the post-eventual order, which was already imminent in the situation before the event occurred but was simply overlooked, or could not be perceived. In this sense, the fact that the map is situated outside of the phenomenological apprehension of the fish is symptomatic of a general ignorance of these thing-structures by animate beings.

So if the alternative map on the fish's back is certainly a map that is still embodied by a living being, what Estes calls a "biocentric map" (2013: 213), this biocentrism is put into perspective in the perseverance of the "*things* [that] were older than man." Again, the novel correlates and distinguishes various existential temporalities. Just as before, the endurance of inanimate objects is contrasted with the evanescence of human, and generally biological, existence in the framework of the novel's event. By characterizing this enduring form of being as "all things," the novel's end thereby indicates not a lamenting glimpse at a world still in its becoming that is epitomized by the unperturbed animals. In fact, it not only radically de-anthropocentricizes the "world" as a planet "older" than man; even more so, it somewhat neutrally indicates a bigger picture in which brook trouts have equally perished like the father and, eventually, his son—another imagistic *memento mori*. Although this grand-scale temporality is cushioned in a rhetoric of evolutionary becoming, where the "once" conjures a simple but inevitable change of biological existences, the passage's clear delineation of a before ("once") and an after ("Not be made right again") situates this development in the context of the revolutionary eruption of an ecological event. The only future that is left is bestowed to the *things* that, like the water, are depicted as anthropomorphically humming, again a symbolic imagery of the celebratory mood that the event has begotten the inanimate.

Within the event's framework of progressively exiling its biocentric content, where "the last instance of a thing takes the class with it. Turns out the light and is gone. Look around you. Ever is a long time. But the boy knew what he knew. That ever is no time at all" (*TR* 28), the sense of temporality that the boy acknowledges redraws human time on earth as an ephemeral point that has passed. In contrast to a variety of readings of *The Road* that accentuate the perseverance of humankind even in the face of ultimate destruction, if viewed from the perspective of the event, the novel's quite radical message seems to draw a picture of a literally post-human world, a world without the possibility of human survival, neither in material nor in symbolic form. In fact, the post-animate world that is conjured leaves no redemption that was still a hope for T. S. Eliot's *The Wasteland*. If the absolute degeneration of Western culture was still recoverable in 1922 by an exoticist turn to a romanticized Asian alterity, the wasteland of *The Road* leaves no room for animate rejuvenation.

As a consequence, fidelity to the event consists, on the part of the earth's animate beings, in an affirmative act of self-sacrifice. Just as the last survivor of a biological class willingly "turns out the light and is gone," a faithful subject of the event not only names the event an ecological event that centers on a notion of inanimism; if truly faithful to this new situation, the subject also needs to embrace this quite nihilistic new present, which, however, is only nihilistic for animate beings. The subsequent section explores how the novel produces different kinds of subjects, with a primary focus on the constitution of a reactive subject, the father.

In the name of the father

After having elucidated what kind of event affects the novel's narrative and to what extent this new present brings an end to the anthropocentric and biocentric world, this section explores how the father's ignorance and betrayal of the ecological singularity in *The Road* results in his becoming a reactive subject. His distancing from the faithful subject of the mother as well as his adherence to the gone consumerist culture sacralizes the gone world; furthermore, his holding on to capitalist notions in respect to inanimate objects functionalizes these inanimate beings and denies their subjective status, while he more generally perpetuates a Promethean myth of "carrying the fire," which amplifies his perpetuation of human narrative as a cultural praxis that is supposed to antagonize the propositions of the event's non-narrative world.

For Badiou, the reactive subject is one of three possible subjective forms.[44] Next to the faithful subject, which acts in fidelity toward an event by adhering to and fulfilling the new present it proposes—a form that is examined in more detail in Chapters 4, 5, and 6—the event may also produce an obscure subject, as the subsequent chapter on Jess Walter's *The Zero* attests. If faithful subjects are the positive instantiation of this process of relating to an event—Badiou even calls them the "Good"—then the reactive and obscure subjectifications, according to his logic, are "Evil" (*E* 40–89). Yet, Badiou's distinction between Good and Evil, which seems somewhat dated after twentieth-century philosophy, reconceptualizes these terms within the logic of the event. Since an event not only initiates a new present but simultaneously presents what went unrepresented before, this emancipatory avail seems for Badiou justification enough to employ terms that have been problematized with Nietzsche at the latest.[45] For Badiou it is a distinction, as he writes in *Logics of Worlds*, between "those who incorporate themselves to the evental present (the new) and those who do not believe in it, who resist its call (the old)" (54). The reason for the existence of other than positive subjective forms—for why should ignorance of an event make one a subject?—lies in the already explicated inexorability of an event. If an event happens within a specific situation, it necessarily affects the beings within that situation. To this extent, Badiou observes that "unfortunately, one cannot simply 'renounce' a truth" (*E* 80) as nonexistent. An event necessarily requires you to position yourself in relation to it. Still, since the subjective procedure that is occasioned by an event is not entirely deterministic, the various ways in which a subject may relate to such an event lie in its hands.

In regard to the ecological event of *The Road*, the father chooses to negate "the evental trace and the thoroughgoing repression of everything that resembles the subjective form" (*LoW* 56). However, Badiou emphasizes that, while "it is really the 'no to the event', as the negation of its trace, which is the dominant instance . . . of the reactive subject-form" (*LoW* 55), it is not the act of ignoring an event, but simply resisting its call. A mere rejection of the event would imply that both father and son keep on living as they used to. But this is obviously not the case. According to Badiou:

> This view underestimates what I think we must term reactionary novelties. In order to resist the call of the new, it is still necessary to create arguments of resistance appropriate to the novelty itself. From this point of view, every reactive disposition is the contemporary of the present to which it reacts. Of course, it categorically refuses to incorporate itself to this present. It sees the body—like a conservative slave sees the army of Spartacus—and refuses to be one of its elements. But it is caught up in a subjective formalism that is not, and cannot be, the pure permanence of the old. (*LoW* 54)

As will be depicted in the following paragraphs, these mechanisms of creating "reactionary novelties" lie in the father's reinstatement of consumerist culture as well as the passing on of the Promethean fire, which represents both the perpetuation of a functionalized relation toward objects in terms of "culture" as well as the simple continuation of their existences as animate beings and arguably humans' most important practice of narration. This adherence to the pre-evental world is thus not a pure "permanence of the old" but a reactive adaptation of the old within the parameters of the new situation. Even in terms of this negative dimension, the reactive subject is thus also active, since it affirmatively produces a seemingly new present by denying the existence of the faithful subject's body. Yet, to reiterate it once more, I refrain from seeing this active disposition as a form of reagency, which I see more justified in the case of faithful subjects. The reactive subject of father and son thus "claims to produce something—and even, frequently under the cloak of modernity, to produce some kind of present." (*LoW* 56). Yet, as Badiou insists, it is "needless to say, [that] this present is not the affirmative and glorious present of the faithful subject." It is a measured present, a "negative present, a present 'a little less worse' than the past, if only because it resisted the catastrophic temptation which the reactive subject declares is contained in the event. We will call it an *extinguished* present." (*LoW* 56)

As counterintuitive as it might sound that father and son choose a "present 'a little less worse' than the past," since they inhabit a planet that has experienced a "world-consuming holocaust" (Schaub 2009: 155), this present seems, nevertheless, better to them than the ultimate wager that the mother as a faithful subject opts for.

The necessary juxtaposition between a faithful and a corrupted form of subjective procedure requires the primacy of a positive truth condition from and against which the reactive subject distances itself. Without a faithful subject of the event, the "reactive subject would be incapable of appearing" (*LoW* 57). The negativity of the reactive subject therefore not only addresses a moral sense of evil; it simultaneously implies the negative relation that it harbors to the faithful subject. What could be conceived as the reactive subject's activity within the post-evental situation, but which does not constitute a similar form of reagency as in the case of faithful subjects, incorporates the extinction of the new present and, at the same time, the suppression of the subjective body. Although "the body is held at the furthest distance from the (negative) declaration that founds the reactive subject" (*LoW* 56), this act of dissociation also assumes a more concrete form.

In this vein, I see the mother as a faithful subject who not only accepts the new propositions evoked by the event but who is simultaneously suppressed by the father both discursively and ethically. It seems to be part of the father's manipulative endeavor, which affects both his son and the reader—since "the reader is very much in the position of the boy" (2013: 206) as Estes notes—to other the mother's behavior and scapegoat her as an irresponsible and unrepresentable madwoman. Particularly because the mother appears to be an egoistic nihilist who abandons her family for the sake of personal redemption, reading her as a faithful subject who simply enacts the admittedly radical wager that the event proposes elucidates how an event may ultimately change a situation that can only be understood in terms of the situation. Regarding her act of suicide as irrational and cowardly necessarily fails to comprehend her position, because it views it from a perspective that has not experienced such an event or, as in the case of the father, actively attempts to oppose its propositions.[46] However, this also elucidates to what extent events contribute to human emancipation and reagency. The Road gives a highly provocative and complex variation on Badiou's theory by creating a faithful subject that is quite opposed to the common notion of it, which rests on a particularly anthropocentric understanding. Yet, if Badiou's notion of the emancipatory impetus that is essentially universal is thought through to its end, *The Road*'s inanimate subjects of water, dams, and detritus clearly seem an inevitable potentiality within this logic.[47]

As part of the inanimate subject, the mother's suicide manifests a faithful response to the ecological event. And, indeed, in the vein of a larger discursive practice that interconnects "nature" with the "female,"[48] one could also see the mother as a metaphorical manifestation of the animate earth, faithfully withdrawing into non-existence. Unlike the father and his son, whose ignorance and betrayal of the event renders them reactive subjects, the mother steps up to the singularity's proposition and actively decides upon her own death. Thereby the novel inverts Badiou's claim that the fidelity always implies a "'Keep going!' [Continuer!]" (*E* 52), since it may also demand the fatalistic cessation of life.

In one of the haphazard flashbacks, a time when the son has not yet been born, wife and husband discuss the implications of the new situation:

We're survivors he told her across the flame of the lamp.

Survivors? she said.

Yes.

What in God's name are you talking about? We're not survivors. We're the walking dead in a horror film.

I'm begging you.

I dont care. I dont care if you cry. It doesnt mean anything to me.

Please.

Stop it.

I am begging you. I'll do anything.

Such as what? I should have done it a long time ago. When there were three bullets in the gun instead of two. I was stupid. We've been over all of this. I didnt bring myself to this. I was brought. And now I'm done. I thought about not even telling you. That would probably have been best. You have two bullets and then what? You cant protect us. You say you would die for us but what good is that? I'd take him with me if it werent for you. You know I would. It's the right thing to do.

You're talking crazy.

No, I'm speaking the truth. Sooner or later they will catch us and they will kill us. They will rape me. They'll rape him. They are going to rape us and kill us and eat us and you wont face it. You'd rather wait for it to happen. But I cant. I cant. . . . We used to talk about death, she said. We dont any more. Why is that?

I dont know.

It's because it's here. There's nothing left to talk about.

I wouldnt leave you.

I dont care. It's meaningless. You can think of me as a faithless slut if you like. I've taken a new lover. He can give me what you cannot.

Death is not a lover.

Oh yes he is. (*TR* 57–58)

Compared to the dialogues between father and son, which are marked by reduced staccato language in terms of both quantity and quality, the mother is here represented as an extremely active character who refrains from simply adhering to her husband's opinions as the son's characteristically relenting "Okay" attests. In standing her ground against the father's begging, she insists on the futility of living after the event has occurred. In fact, she undermines the very concept of survival in demonizing themselves within a pop-cultural framework instead of accepting his Promethean rhetoric. The imminent repercussions of the event that leave no choice to those affected are furthermore expressed by the woman's passive inflection of having been brought to this as a result of the inexorability of the ecological event. In the face of the inevitable ramifications, the mother thus also acknowledges that there is no point in arguing about this new situation—she thus faces the father: "You have no argument because there is none," (*TR* 59) which cogently expresses the epistemological dimension of the event, leaving no other options; what the event, indeed, calls for is the unmitigated wager that it demands as its "truth." Her intention to commit suicide is therefore not a self-willed act of a human subject but part of the faithful truth-procedure of a subject of the event. Despite this passivity, her understanding that self-destruction is "the right thing to do" nevertheless offers her the slightest moment of reagency: though confronted with the devastating effects of the ecological event, she still has the power to decide on a self-willed death. Unlike her miniscule moment of reagency, the father, who is symbolically leaning over a lamp, wants to continue to live and repress the event's consequences. In remaining the passive "human animal" (*E* 10) that he is, his seemingly active decision to reject death manifests, however, a passive course of action, simply "wait[ing] for it to happen." In contrast to the mother who virtually becomes an "Immortal" (*E* 12) through her acceptance of the event, the father upholds his "animalistic substructure," personifying "the status of victim, of suffering beast, of emaciated, dying body" (*E* 11).

Since this passage again is not a neutral hindsight but focalized through the father's perspective, one should note his subjective presentation of the mother, whom he embeds in a discourse of madness and irrationality. He also characterizes her by a blunt lack of empathy, failure of responsibility, and even infidelity. This ascription of faithlessness is particularly telling, for it is, indeed, she who becomes not a "faithless slut" but a subject who acts in utter fidelity, albeit to a different set of conditions, since these parameters (family, love) have been essentially altered in the view of the singularity. Conceiving her as "crazy" thus attests to his comprehensive unwillingness to acknowledge the event and feeds into his ethical dissociation of her actions. Moreover, his negative depiction of her, which has specific manipulative effects on the reader, is equally conveyed on a discursive level. Not only is the mother narratively excluded from the text and makes only scarce appearances in the father's memories of her (her absence from the beginning of the novel could be viewed as another religious allusion to the relation between what Vanderheide terms the "filial dyad" [2008: 108]) but she is also repeatedly presented in a discourse of alterity. For instance, even before the mother's suicide has been narrated, she comes to haunt the father. In the father's dream, "his pale bride came to him," furthermore being described in a ghastly manner with "rib bones painted white" and wearing "a dress of gauze and her dark hair was carried up in combs of ivory, combs of shell. Her smile, her downturned eyes" (*TR* 17). After this description by the narrator, the novel presents a paragraph break that focalizes through the father: "He mistrusted all of that. He said the right dreams for a man in peril were dreams of peril and all else was the call of languor and of death." (*TR* 17).

The mother's return from the dead paints her spectral status in hauntingly dark images, with her livid color and naked, thin body as well the oxymoronic facial expression conjuring token ghost figures out of the most commonplace gothic tales. What is more, her aristocratic demeanor, being described as a "bride" who wears a mummy-like dress and a crown, juxtaposes various cultural fabrications of the spectral that through its conglomerate exaggeration point to their constructedness. The evocation of a haunting madwoman, whose resemblance to Charlotte Brontë's and Jean Rhy's Bertha Mason seems literally uncanny, draws on classical representations of the undead in order to cast a negative light on the mother.[49]

Additionally, the discursive alignment of this scene, where the already-dead mother returns before her actual narrated death, thus underscores the father's manipulative intention to dissociate himself from her and convince both son and reader of his reasons to do so. This discursive detachment is equally transported in the father's distrust of "all that." His overly rational stance that unmasks the unconscious return of his wife as the "wrong" kind of dream finds its way in the typographical representation of the text, where the dream of the dead mother and the father's reflections on it are depicted in two different textual segments.

The contrast that *The Road* opens up between two different fidelities toward the event offers, within the context of the theory of subjects of the event, a productive way of re-reading and questioning the novel's *a priori* positing of good and evil. Instead of relating the father's responsibility and determination to go on to a positive ethical conviction, while the mother is irrefutably portrayed as part of the ominous "bad guys," reading the novel under the lens of Badiou's theoretical approach offers a reversal of these stipulations. If the inevitable repercussions of the ecological event are taken into account, this ethical dialectics is turned upside down and thereby self-reflexively points to the text's narrative construction. Specifically the scenes in which the mother is represented address and complicate the ontological status of the narration, which is symptomatic for the father's status as a reactive subject. Not only does he thus manipulate the narration, both as an extradiegetic and as an intradiegetic agency that has severe consequences on the reception process of both reader and son; what is more, however, the novel's narrative situation, which appears to be neutral and objective, originating apparently in an extra-hetero-diegetic voice, is put to the test throughout the novel and makes one raise the question of the novel's fictional truth-value, an aspect that has been almost exclusively ignored within the research.[50] A consequence of conceiving the father as an unreliable narrator is inherently tied to his subjective status.[51] His attempts to ignore and betray the event, not in an exclusively nostalgic return to the past but in the creation of an "extinguished present" (*LoW* 56) that is amplified by his clinging to a consumerist way of life as well as by the symbolic insistence to keep "carrying the fire" (*TR* 87), make him, in fact, one of the "bad guys" (*TR* 80) and undermine his glorification as a "hero of the road" (Brontë 214), which much of the criticism of the novel supports.[52]

The father's continuous insistence on his own goodness thus appropriates his narrative sovereignty that proves to have certain effects in the addressees of his presentation. Both his son and the reader are thus subliminally deceived in being presented with a seemingly neutral, direct mediation of what is actually a subjective mediation of the father. In this sense, the father uses his narrative position to convince the recipients of his tales of his own inherent goodness, while portraying the mother in a fundamentally negative light. However, while the father thereby projects a specific form of extinguished present on the mother, this is part of a larger project in which he betrays the truth of the event that is, in fact, latent within himself. Badiou thus writes in *Ethics*:

> The denial of the Immortal in myself is something quite different from an abandonment, a cessation: I must always convince myself that the Immortal in question never existed, and thus rally to purpose, in the service of interests, is precisely its negation. For the Immortal, if I recognize its existence, calls on me to continue; it has the eternal power of the truths that induce it. Consequently, I must betray the becoming-subject in myself, I must become the enemy of that truth whose subject the "some-one" that I am (accompanied, perhaps, by others) composed. (79)

Besides the denial of the mother's subjective status, the father has to convince himself repeatedly of the shortcomings of this procedure, which, due to the universal appeal of the event, he could faithfully accept just as well. Simultaneously, the reactive procedure thus calls for a denial of this truth and its potential realization for oneself, as well as a betrayal of this present with all of its accompanying manifestations.

While the demonization of the faithful subject is a necessary result without which the father would have to admit the pressing grasp of the ecological event and thereby acknowledge his own mistaken path, he therefore cannot simply ignore the body that the mother personifies but must actively and repetitively antagonize this "some-one." Although the negative relation that requires the father to proactively become an "enemy of that truth" accounts for his status as an evil subject, the body of the faithful subject does not fail to confront him with his missed opportunity. As a matter of fact, "the form of the faithful subject nonetheless remains the unconscious of the reactive subject" (56), as Badiou observes in *Logics of Worlds*. One may glimpse this return of the repressed quite vividly in the mother's haunting return in the father's dreams.

However, in opposing this recurrent confrontation with the truth that the ecological event produces, he also applies various techniques of shutting out this new present, which equally follow a structure of repetition.[53] As a matter of fact, the father's reactive status could generally be viewed as enforcing repetitions to the extent that this embodies a literal *Wieder-holung*: his clinging to a consumerist culture retrieves the gone capitalist world of consumption, while his repetitive invocation of a Promethean theme of "carrying the fire" (*TR* 87) serves as a symbolic rite that negatively denies the new present while constructing an extinguished one that rests on the repetition and retrieval of the old order. Unlike the faithful subject's ongoing affirmation of the event's points, of which Danielewski's *Only Revolutions* is a prime example, the father could be said to perpetuate his reactive condition in a repetitive negativity, which finds neat expression in his anaphoric thought: "You will not face the truth. You will not" (*TR* 71).

A first aspect that subscribes to the father's reactive status, besides his dissociation from the fidelity of the mother, consists in his sacralization of the gone consumerist culture. Even though their evolutionary relapse to a status of gatherers is clearly conditional on the existential climate of the barren earth of the novel, which one could argue requires father and son to harvest the goods that are left, this does not account for their devout sacralization as well as functionalization of these goods. While they display an almost religious apotheosis toward specific "relics of our consumerist, technological society" (Estes 2013: 198), this does not indicate that they have accepted these inanimate objects within the egalitarian ontology that the ecological event has brought about.[54] Rather, their devotional attitude is only restricted to particular objects that serve their purpose. In a sense then, the father's relation to his surroundings reverberates with previous figures of McCarthy's work that dominate and exploit their environment; the father's functionalization of his environment, whether "natural" or "cultural," also harkens back to a larger American ethos in relation to the continent's environment that runs through the New World's colonial history. Additionally, if the conditions of the event are taken at face level, this mode of existence that perpetuates their life through the consumption of such products also rejects the inanimate environment by antagonizing its new present through their survival.

One of the most obvious remnants of late capitalist society is their "grocery cart," which in the beginning is described as containing "their plates and some cornmeal cakes in a plastic bag and a plastic bottle of syrup" (*TR* 3). As a vital "necessit[y]" (Estes 2013: 198) for their travels through the land, the shopping cart as "both physical and symbolic container" (Wilhelm 2008: 132) accommodates all the equipment that they need to survive; but it also, as the presence of plates indicates, literally carries a civilized cultural identity for them.[55] However, it is not merely a tragicomic signifier of their obstinate nostalgia for a time when the abundance of goods was still taken for granted, functioning "as a stark reminder of plenty" (2008: 132) as Wilhelm notes. What is more, the shopping cart additionally represents one instance of inanimate objects that are being functionalized by them to their needs of survival.[56] In this vein, when one of their shopping carts breaks down, they just leave it behind in the dirt and replace it with another one, which seems symptomatic for the postmodern culture of interchangeable mass production, whose waning they lament.

Although their repeated plundering of gas stations and supermarkets certainly follows the pragmatic logic of the textual world, according to which these sites are most likely to contain items for their survival, the impression that these locales of late capitalist society still function as sites of memory and nostalgic comfort cannot be totally put aside. A prominent and often commented-upon scene that attests to this nostalgia is marked by their discovery of a Coca-Cola tin. While prying the wasteland they discover one of the relics of consumerism, a supermarket, upon entering which they find the pinnacle of postmodernist culture.

For one thing, the father's devotional relation to the Coca-Cola can, sitting down in front of it as if in front of an altar, (*TR* 21) is again expressive of his functionalization of the inanimate objects of the world. Although he exhibits a certain reverence in front of the tin can, he instantaneously offers it to his son as a "treat," (*TR* 22) ready to be consumed. To this extent, it seems noteworthy that, while he continuously displays caution toward the foods they find, which is emblematized by the description of the "ancient runner beans and what looked to have once been apricots, long dried to wrinkled effigies of themselves," the soft drink is encountered with less skepticism. The explicit characterization of these goods within a temporal dimension of decay suggests the uselessness of those goods, which are juxtaposed with the seemingly endless shelf life of the Coca-Cola. Notably, it is the once organic fruit that is here described in the context of a simulated chain of signs, "effigies" that have lost touch with a referential source. In contrast, the Coca-Cola can is depicted as a unique and holy object of sacrality, the last of its kind.

It seems thus equally remarkable that the popular soft drink is endowed with a proper name. Since hardly any proper names make their way into the novel, with not even the two protagonists being identified, this straightforward reference to the epitome of consumer culture not only metonymically calls upon capitalist society but also marks the different situations that father and son inhabit. While the father may look at the can and recall a signifier that evokes the gone world, his son is unaware of its existence ("What is it?"). In contrast to DeLillo's *White Noise* where Jack Gladney listens to his daughter's somniloquist whispering of the ominous words "Toyota Celica" (1986: 155) that mark the child's full immersion within the capitalist semiotic system, *The Road*'s son has no direct knowledge of this particular world. In this sense, instead of merely being a last remnant of the pre-eventual situation—signifiers of a "culture of hyperabundance" (2013: 202), as Estes writes—the Coca-Cola can is used by the father in order to reinstate and memorialize the old world.[57] The reverential attitude they assume toward the soft drink—opening it with exaggerated care, sitting down as in prayer—is grounded in the fact that it is the last of its kind. Simultaneously, the can's sacred status is legitimized by its apparent ability to rejuvenate the lost order of postmodern consumption. In other words, the "sacred act" (Estes 2013: 200) that the consumption of the Coca-Cola can implies refers back to the situation prior to the event and projects this order within the changed post-eventual environment. The father cherishes little successes, like finding food or useful objects, because such "ameliorations are small novelties, [which] will bear out his perception that he is partaking in the new era, while wisely avoiding incorporating himself into it" (*LoW* 56). Particularly the father's insistence that the son drink the can on his own insinuates his intention to instill in him a similar desire for this gone world, as if attempting to convert him in a symbolic rite of initiation, which will be discussed in more detail later in this chapter.

Their consumerist behavior perpetuates a cultural milieu that was overhauled by the event and their concomitant relation to the inanimate objects of the new situation, which are also evident in another scavenging scene.[58] When coming across a gas station, the exploitive intentions they display toward these sites become particularly manifest. He goes through "the drawers but there was nothing there that he could use. Good half-inch drive sockets. A ratchet. He stood looking around the garage. A metal barrel full of trash. He went into the office. Dust and ash everywhere. . . . A metal desk, a cashregister. Some old automotive manuals, swollen and sodden" (*TR* 5). When he realizes that there is nothing to be taken, "he picked up the phone and dialed the number of his father's house in that long ago. The boy watched him. What are you doing? he said" (*TR* 5).

This scene neatly displays the father's utilitarian relation toward objects. By his distinguishing between "good" and useless objects, his anthropocentric assumptions do not take the objects for what they are in the post-eventual setting. This is heightened by the way his scavenging is represented. Through the oscillation between short sentences, as if taking stock of the haphazard objects that are covered in an egalitarian "dust and ash," and the phrases that show him in a reflective manner, considering the usefulness of these objects, the passage conveys the father's dexterous scanning of his surroundings. By means of the linguistic presentation of his gathering and the implicated process of sequestering good and bad objects, the excerpt thus again puts the reader in a similar position of having to sort through a pile of garbage and detect the potential use in this textual landscape of ruins. It, indeed, seems as if the father's skill of reading the meaningless wasteland that simply contains garbage in the light of a specific anthropocentric stance that lets him distinguish between what will and what will not contribute to his survival, reflects on the reading process itself. For the reader certainly sees in the father a figure who knows how to navigate the bleak and indistinguishable mass of abandoned remnants, which asserts his standing as a skillful survivor as well as a decipherer of his encoded (or even uncoded, meaningless) surroundings.

However, here the father's knowledge of reading his environment is undermined as he tries to call not simply his father but his house. Thereby he expresses another nostalgic longing for a particular place that is yet gone, again, in the spatially characterized time that has passed with the eruption of the event. Despite the constant rational and dexterous handling of the barren land, he succumbs to a nostalgic longing that is just one instance of his unreliable status, which even the boy notices.

Seemingly confused by his irrational lapse, they leave the gas station empty-handed. But the futility of their scavenging is immediately put right. Having left the gas station behind them, the father resorts to his human skills: "We're not thinking, he [the father] said. We have to go back." (*TR* 5) And sure enough, they get lucky and discover the very symbolic resource: "Oil for their little slutlamp to light the long gray dusks, the long gray dawns. You can read me a story, the boy said. Can't you, Papa? Yes, he said. I can" (*TR* 6).

After having exhibited an emotional negligence, the father instantaneously has to reassert his rationality, insisting that they have to use their minds and "think," as a manifestation of their cognitive superiority over the inanimate waste around them. Only through reason and pragmatic circumspection are they able to survive in this new situation. And, as a reward for their hardships, they retrieve a small portion of oil that proves essential for their survival.

What this passage additionally opens up is a tripartite constellation that directs the view to the inherent connection between consumption, cultural perpetuation, and narrative—all factors that underscore the father's reactive subjectivity as they are mechanisms of ritualistic repetition. Even though "together with his memory, the man's identity is eroding," (2010: 782) as de Bruyn notes, his attempts to antagonize his amnesia are marked by continuous forms of repetition.

First, by discursively interlinking the successful search for goods, and specifically an item that will further preserve their survival on this planet, with the son's desire for a story, the novel creates a nexus between a return to capitalist consumerism and narrative that insinuates their relation to human perseverance. In this sense, the continuation of their lives is not only underscored by their active engagement with the waste yard of their surroundings but is also perpetuated by their ostensibly unique ability to tell stories. In relying on this inherently anthropocentric praxis, they thus attempt to negate a world that literally leaves "no other tale to tell" (*TR* 32). Without the need for a perceiving subjectivity that aligns happenings into a causal order and thereby gives meaning to that sequence, the novel continuously showcases to what extent it rejects this essentially human form of cultural sustenance.

Second, this reinscription of the past into the present is framed in a more general project that shows again their dependence on the old world, particularly its technology, of which narrative is arguably one the most fundamental imprints.[59] Besides the obvious ecological reverberations of the last drops of fossil fuel they are using up, the importance of light, and specifically its "carrying," is a crucial theme in the novel and also relates consumption and narration to the father's status as a reactive subject. They open up another dimension of these modes of reiterating the maxims of the old world. While the semiotic of luminosity/light generally bears an explicit connection to the literary representation of events, as could be observed in the previous considerations of the religious connotations of *The Road*'s singularity and which is also manifested in *Against the Day*'s scientific events, the trope of fire assumes a different function in the novel that is highly polyvalent.

As is well documented in the criticism on the novel, the theme of "carrying the fire" harkens back to the ancient Greek myth of Prometheus.[60] In the tale of the titan who steals fire from Zeus, bequeaths it to men, and gets punished by being chained to a rock and visited daily by an eagle who feasts upon his liver, one may glimpse obvious echoes in *The Road*'s use of this myth. For as Daniel Luttrull shows in respect of Hesiod's *Prometheus*, the titan embodies "a twofold legacy of blessings and curses. He founds civilization with his gift of fire, but at the same time, his rash disregard for Zeus brings an avalanche of suffering upon both himself and the human race" (2010: 17). Viewed in an ecocritical context, this reading insinuates, once more, that the novel's catastrophe was initiated by human agency. By metaphorically transferring Prometheus's infringement of a divine order into a discourse of deep ecological disposition, man's usage of technology becomes a two-sided coin that accepts progress for utilitarian sacrifices. Whereas this could suggest an ecological critique of technology as the origin of environmental crisis, the father and son's continued maxim to "carry the fire" plays a crucial role for their self-proclaimed status as the "Good Guys" (*TR* 80), as Estes convincingly shows. For him, the "fact that the man and the boy have a positive relationship to technology and consumer society" (2013: 199) is inexorably related to their ostensible moral incandescence.[61] On this level, the novel might also insinuate an apologetics in that it distinguishes between a good and a bad form of technology that is intricately tied to the father's anthropocentric view. While the bow that wounds the father in the end constitutes a "primitive or degraded" (ibid.: 201) variety, his revolver is for him not only a necessary evil but literally an inevitable good that, in recalling an American Western subtext, symbolizes his martial control over his environment.

In order to avoid adopting this problematic dualism, according to which the Promethean transgression and, by extension, technology itself constitute a necessary evil that must be accepted for the ulterior advancement of human culture, I again want to stress that my reading of the novel's singularity does not see it as a man-made happening. As an ecological event, it does not harken back to a specifiable "human" or "natural" causation. All this notion accounts for is the implicit aftermath of its eruption, without the possibility of rationalizing its origins. Simply viewed from the standpoint of the truth that the event evokes, it is not their mere reliance on technological tools that, in my view, makes them indistinguishable from the "bad guys"; instead, their specific relation to both the objects of technology as well as the idea of technology as an inherent mode that sustains human existence infringe on the event's propositions.

What is more, particularly in the Romantic rewritings of the myth from Goethe to the Shelleys, Prometheus, because of his secular transgression of a divine law is considered the "ideal man: one who, like Satan, strains against seemingly unmovable boundaries and pits his ego against the world in the face of almost certain defeat, but who, unlike Satan, maintains his integrity throughout the struggle" (Luttrull 2010: 18). This humanist empowerment in the face of transcendentally inhibiting forces cogently accounts for the positive readings of the father as a prototypical instance of human perseverance. As Luttrull shows, the Nietzschean notion according to which Prometheus, in contrast to Eve, "is an analogue for active sin and masculine, Aryan progress" (2010: 18) may thus be glimpsed in his active struggle to substantiate human existence. As part of a larger project of subjective emancipation, the Promethean hypotext seems to humanistically stain McCarthy's novel as a work of anthropocentric perseverance.[62]

However, viewed in light of the theory of the subject of the event, the emancipatory undercurrent has to be reconsidered. Instead of viewing the Promethean transgression as a crucial defiance of divine law (which for Lotman would unmistakably be the narrative event), if read in relation to the ecological event, the father's "carrying of the fire" is seen as a symbolic rite that renders his *eventical* hubris a reactive act of betrayal. In the vein of the ecological event's rejection of animate life, the father's insistent motivation to carry the fire as a general metaphor for the rejection of the truth of the new present again instrumentalizes the inanimate substance of "fire" for his ulterior needs. As a substance that is tamed by human hands, its material dimension, which quite pragmatically keeps them warm and allows them to see, is moreover conveyed into a more symbolic function for them. The fire that they are carrying is, as the father clarifies to his son on his deathbed, "inside you" (*TR* 298). Despite the novel's emphasis on the anti-anthropocentric inclination of the element, father and son thus translate it into a signifier for human domination and survival. For fire is, in the beginning of the novel, one of the most concrete agents of the event's ramifications, wiping out all that is living: "Within a year there were fires on the ridges and deranged chanting. The screams of the murdered" (*TR* 33). "Everything," the father further reminisces, "was on fire" (*TR* 204). Yet, if its destructive force extinguishes all forms of animate beings in the ultimate aftermath of the event's eruption, with time's progress, fire's utter absence equally underscores the new propositions of the ecological event by indicating the futility of human existence. Toward the beginning of the novel, which is chronologically years after the event occurred, the father is "watching for any sign of a fire or a lamp. There was nothing. The lamp in the rocks on the side of the hill was little more than a mote of light and after a while they walked back. Everything too wet to make a fire" (*TR* 8). By instantaneously equating the absence of light with nothingness, the novel creates an environment to be viewed through an anthropocentric lens that denies the existence of beings outside of human perception. While their search for other signs of luminescence obviously implies their civilizational intention to look for other fire-carrying good guys, the passage's neutral observation that their surroundings do not invite the act of "making a fire" also suggests the new situation's utter hostility toward this form of technological praxis. Instead of implying that the event absolutely abandons the existence of fire, which would reject the being of an inanimate object, the excerpt stresses that what is rejected is the anthropocentric act of making a fire.

And, indeed, the father seems at times to acknowledge the event's propositions as when "in a drawer he found a candle. No way to light it. He put it in his pocket. He walked out in the gray light and stood and he saw for a brief moment the absolute truth of the world" (*TR* 138). It is in moments like these when the father acknowledges the "absolute truth" that there is no possibility of making fire, of continuing to carry it, of perpetuating their existence, and seems to glimpse the pointlessness of his errand so that he becomes aware of his reactivity and has to confront his own betrayal. But instead of conceding the event's truth, he relapses to the stubborn insistence on his mission. For his reactivity demands that he "must always convince [himself] that the Immortal in question never existed, and thus rally to purpose, in the service of interests, is precisely its negation" (*LoW* 80). Besides his recurrent acts of consumerism as well as the continuous quest for symbolic rites that circle around the motive of fire, which finds its apex when he recovers a flare gun (*TR* 257), his reactive creation of an extinguished present also translates its external materiality into an interior source of spiritual dimensions.

By internalizing the fire as an anthropocentric concept, the father actively adapts it and not only corrodes the boundary of inside/outside that technology as a discourse seems to construct, but additionally, he converts the inanimate substance into the epitome of human survival. This anthropocentric shift from fire being a part of the event's inanimistic subject to a reified human concept thus marks a recurrent taming that attests not only their ostensible moral innocence but also, in the same breath, their superior status within the post-eventual world of inanimate beings. Particularly through their ability to transform a pure multiple into a master metaphor for human progress and survival, it is the more general linguistic appropriation of their environment that extends the mere handling of fire on a practical basis. Put differently, the Promethean hypotext offers, in relation to *The Road*, a mediation on human language. By extending the reading of fire as "the first (mythical) technology" (Estes 2013: 199), it more abstractly also becomes a metaphor for language as such, which they are literally carrying inside them since all systems of writing have been abandoned and oral communication prevails. In this respect, the hubris that Prometheus performed consists in the fact that he endowed mankind with their sovereign ability to be linguistically autonomous. In detaching themselves from the sacred language, they enact a secular infringement that finds its blueprint in the Babylonian tower and points to the advent of linguistic emancipation and simultaneously to consequent confusions.

Nevertheless, if these are tales of emancipatory transgressions of a divine order by means of the secularization of human language, the Promethean overtones in *The Road* suggest the negative dimensions of this reflection on language. As part of the novel's inanimistic situation, it is not God's wrath that punishes the violation, thereby endowing a transcendental power with the might to discipline humanity, keeping them within their all-too human bounds; instead, the event's premises subliminally present the father with a truth that he himself chooses to discredit. One may thus see in the novel a counterpoint to the tradition of Promethean rewritings that all seem to suggest the titan's infringement to be itself an event that occasioned human emancipation from transcendental limitations. If then, from Hesiod over Aeschylus to Goethe and Shelley (both Percy and Mary), literature inquired into the Prometheus-event that changed roles between God and man, this author-god transposition also finds its way in *The Road*, without, however, suggesting a positive connotation of this turn of tables.

In contrast to Luttrull, then, for whom "the Prometheus myth becomes an ever more provocative call for rebellion against limitations and an exhortation for civilized humanity to realize their potential by breaking traditional boundaries," which transforms Prometheus from "an ambitious and conventionally virtuous hero pitted against a malevolent deity, to a tragic hero for whom hubris, traditionally a flaw, is now a strength: a vise to enlarge our moral horizons, a lens to focus us on the material world, and a spur to urge our race on" (2010: 19), I am skeptical about the merits of this liberal-humanist eulogy in the context of *The Road*.[63] In fact, even though it is not intended to do so, Luttrull's argument that "the most revolutionary way for him [the father] and his son to live is to observe society's traditional values" (ibid.: 25) attests their disregard of the event's new present. Unlike Luttrull's diagnosis of the novel's "ultimately hopeful Promethean vision" (ibid.: 25), I suggest an interconnection within the framework of the event and thereby see his Promethean overtones as inexorably tied up with his status as a reactive subject. This is obviously not to say that the Promethean transgression of divine law is a similarly negative infringement and thereby to defend the conservation of religious systems; to the contrary, the father, who is "a Prometheus type" (ibid.: 21), is declared evil solely because he betrays an event, not a theological imperative.

Similar to the endless recurrence of the eagle, who reminds Prometheus of his infringement, the novel's inanimistic environment thus continuously confronts the father with his hubris. It is this dialectics that the novel conjures, between a world without narrative and, following from this, semantic potential, and father and son's repeated attempts to instill their surroundings with human forms of narrative, that is investigated in the last part of this chapter. After having elucidated to what extent their Promethean carrying of the fire implies a more general project of human perseverance, I now focus on how the novel specifies this mythical "leitmotiv" (Estes 2013: 199) in relation to human language and narrative, which manifests a third aspect of the father's reactive project of repeating and thus perpetuating human existence that infringes upon the ecological event and its truth. This moreover illuminates how the son has to be viewed in a similar manner as his father.

It was previously observed that the novel's environment aspires to come up with an alternative mode of mediation that does not rely on an anthropocentric notion of language or narrative and is ultimately unsuccessful. Whereas the formulation of a "sacred idiom shorn of its referents" (*TR* 93) made advances in an anti-anthropocentric direction, it was only the concluding "maps and mazes" (*TR* 307) that suggested a cogent alternative through its spatial form that shifted the focus from the temporal and subjective dimensions of both human language and divine idiom. To some extent, one might, indeed, see the novel as a whole as testing out a narrative praxis that approximates the new present of a planet reigned by inanimate objects, which also distances *The Road* from McCarthy's previous novels.[64] It has thus been observed by Kunsa that the novel's linguistic style is markedly different from that of his other works (2009: 68). She is not alone in arguing that "*The Road*'s divergence from McCarthy's previous work is especially evident when the novel is contrasted with *Blood Meridian* because their styles and concomitant worldviews differ so strikingly" (ibid.: 58). Whereas *Blood Meridian*, set in mid-nineteenth-century America and inquiring into the myth of the continent's pastoral,[65] displays a "prose often allusive and baroque to the breaking point, prose frequently likened to that of William Faulkner," *The Road*'s style, "on the contrary, is pared down, elemental, a triumph over the dead echoes of the abyss and, alternately, over relentless ironic gesturing" (ibid.: 58). Not only does the novel's often short and hypotactically aligned sentences contrast with Blood Meridian's profuse narrative excesses, but also *The Road*'s lack of typographic markers, from quotation marks to haphazard inverted commas, as well as the absence of any paratextual information (chapter titles in *Blood Meridian* still take up more than half of the page), indicates this attempt to let the discursive presentation resemble the sobriety of the narrative's situation. Moreover, its lack of proper names, particularly the continuous play with the third-person pronoun "he"—all-too-often symbolically capitalized—complicates the clear identification of the characters. Unlike Kunsa, who argues that despite the occasional confusion of these pronouns, at times referring to the father, at others to the son, "the characters are clearly knowable and differentiable from one another by what they do" (ibid.: 61), I am hesitant about this clear separation. It seems, rather, to be part and parcel of the novel's narrative endeavor to create a "world" that is fundamentally indistinguishable, again being motivated by the event's egalitarian impetus, fashioning an ontology of objects that are "shorn of its referents" and, more crucially, from anthropocentric signifiers at all.

Even if one would problematize the narrative situation of the novel, pointing to the recurrent moments of indecision where it is not clear who narrates or focalizes the happenings, and ascribe the narrative authority to the father, the pressing implications of the event on his linguistic representation would be equally pervasive. In other words, if one assumed the novel to be narrated by the autodiegetic figure of the father—who nevertheless avoids the clear identification of a narrative I—instead of an extradiegetic agency, the spare prose only attests to the event's effects upon his narrative capabilities. Yet again, the father's acceptance of what one might call blank prose, lacking not only rhyming synthesis but also structural guidance and semantic reference, as a sign of the event is repeatedly counterfeited by acts in which he decidedly employs human language and particularly narrative that attest to his reactive subjectivity. In order to perpetuate his existence, he thus acknowledges that "language also has been returned to its rudiments and now must be re-imagined" (ibid.: 58).

Generally, the father's endeavor to prevail in the post-evental environment is symptomatically conveyed in his imperative to "make a list. Recite a litany. Remember" (*TR* 31). His conservative and conservational attempts are thus reflected in the form of this ethical imperative, structured just as such a "list," in three clusters of syntactically brief commandments.

In a further characteristic scene that consists of two consecutive narrative segments, the father displays to what extent he is eager to perpetuate narrative as a cogent praxis to counterpoint the inanimistic post-evental situation. Having arrived at the coast, he digs a hole in the sand in order for the son to keep warm. But the text itself comments on the symbolic dimension of this construction: "All of this like some ancient anointing. So be it. Evoke the forms. Where you've nothing else construct ceremonies out of the air and breathe upon them" (*TR* 78). As soon as the fire has gone out, the father again maintains his Promethean role and "blew the flames to life and piled on the wood." But he is not only a guardian of technology. He is also a watchman for his son: "He stood listening. The boy didnt stir. He sat beside him and stroked his pale and tangled hair. Golden chalice, good to house a god. Please dont tell me how the story ends" (*TR* 78).

Besides the recurrent religious undertones of the passage, explicitly terming his act an "anointing," the father interweaves this ritual praxis with the creation of narrative. In the face of the event's hostility toward animate beings, the father counteracts the "nothing else" with the symbolic evocation of forms that refer back to a pre-evental past. But again, he is not merely performing a nostalgic ceremony, but actively reinscribes these rites in his current situation, thereby "produc[ing] some kind of present" (*LoW* 56), a reactionary novelty. It is particularly noteworthy that he describes this act in relation to human respiration. Thereby, he not only addresses the vital necessity of these rites for their survival but also suggests an oral form of story-telling.

By phonologocentrically grounding his restorative intentions, he fashions himself as an author-god, whose very breath inhabits the potential of existential redemption.

After the narrative ellipsis, however, the novel immediately exhibits the utter evanescence of his attempts, the creeping cold and the absence of fire indicating this ephemeral quality. Faced with the impressionistically depicted list of inanimate objects, the father accentuates his status as an animate being, again showcasing his divine power in breathing "the flames to life." His ability to bring life and perpetuate it by the sole means of his uttered words thus also proves to have effects on his son. While asleep, the son is literally unconsciously initiated by the father's enacted symbolic rite. Taking advantage of the boy's helplessness, the father reflects on the boy's suitability to serve as a repository for his ulterior motives. Specifically, the father's reflection that the boy would be "good to house a god" once more exhibits his Manichaean sequestering of good and evil, here extending his anthropocentric criteria of usability and uselessness onto his son.[66]

This nexus between narrative and life is already established in analepsis when the mother explains that a "person who had no one would be well advised to cobble together some passable ghost[,]" to divinely "breathe it into being and coax it along with words of love" (*TR* 59) like the breath of God. What is more, she advises the father to "offer it each phantom crumb and shield it from harm with your body. As for me my only hope is for eternal nothingness and I hope it with all my heart" (*TR* 59).

Just before the mother leaves them to kill herself, she, paradoxically, introduces the father to this autopoetical praxis. Whereas she as a faithful subject craves death, she advises the father to generate a system of meaning that "passes" in a variety of ways. Nevertheless, the question of the ontological status of this flashback, the mother's evocation of another spectral rhetoric once again characterizes her in specific ways. What is more, and particularly important for the discussion of narrative and its relation to the father's survival, is the mother's equivalence of narration with a "passable ghost." Her suggestion to assume the role of God, who uses his breath in order to bestow life, hints at the creative and literally spiritual dimensions of this endeavor. Additionally, by viewing this ghastly figure as an act of narration, one can see this "passing" as clandestinely pretending to be what it is not. In this sense, the father's narrative manipulations pass as something else, without revealing his ulterior motives. It, therefore, again reflects on the process of reception, addressing the father's narrative attempts at subliminally coaxing both son and reader to assume his belief system.

The enduring character of this narrative praxis, viewed in this light, equally passes as a divine act of creation that seeks to antagonize the destructive features of the ecological event by posing its own set of rules. Moreover, by addressing the ontologically insecure status of such an act of narration that floats in between spheres of the animate and inanimate, the mother provides the father with a powerful praxis for his survival. Her spectral status therefore reflects on its disposition of oscillating between death and life, which neatly summarizes the reactive subject's rejection of the inanimate conditions of the event. To "cobble together some passable ghost" manifests therefore another, yet especially powerful, mechanism that lets the father reinstate his existence, averting the inanimate by contriving his own act of creation. What he creates is not merely a narrative of survival. He fundamentally employs this narrative in order to "coax" his son into believing that they have to continue to live. The ambiguity of what the "passable ghost" denotes, either a ritual practice or the son himself who needs to be taken care of, amounts to the same thing. It is the son, as both the recipient of the father's narrations and the very product of these narrations, who combines the father's attempt to negate the progressive death of the world. Through his acts of narration, and his reliance on late capitalist structures and the Promethean myth, he pursues to negate the event's new present and actively tries to offer his son an ostensibly new present. As Schaub puts it, "the father has the boy to serve as his ghost" (2009: 159), which Luttrull confirms in writing that "the man is a Prometheus type, and the boy is, in a sense, the fire the man carries down to the world" (2010: 21).

A last instantiation of the father's reactive reinscription of the past into the present marks the narrative entrapment of his son, where "the boy was all that stood between him and death" (*TR* 29). Besides his active suppression of the faithful body that the mother epitomizes, he concomitantly refrains from letting his son choose his own path of fidelity. He not only projects all of his hopes of survival onto his son but also actively denies him the possibility to act on his own. This suggests an additional facet of his reactive status that expresses his intention to "become the enemy of that truth" (*LoW* 80).

One of the most explicit scenes of such active inhibition manifests itself when the boy confronts the father with his desire to die. When the boy notes that he wished to be with his mom, the father repeatedly silences the boy: "You mustn't say that," "Don't say it. It's a bad thing to say" (*TR* 56–57).

The boy's wish to follow his mother and thereby become a faithful subject himself is vehemently thwarted by the father. By prohibiting the son to express his choice to act in fidelity to the event, the father instantaneously applies his Manichaean ethics that again tries to cast a literally "bad" light on the faithful subjective procedure. When the son admits the inevitability with which this affirmation of the truth of the event manifests itself, that he "can't help it," the father urges his son to cling onto life, without having any idea of how to go about this.

On a discursive level, one can also glimpse the father's subliminal forms of manipulation, slowly "coaxing" the son to adopt his stance when the son confronts him with the subjective status of the mother just before the flashback where they are "arguing the pros and cons of self destruction with the earnestness of philosophers chained to a madhouse wall" (*TR* 60). Placed right after the previously noted scene when the "clocks stopped at 1:17" (*TR* 54) and right before the mother breaks the matter of her intended suicide, the narrative alignment creates a specific effect in tangling up the chronological order of the diegetic happenings. Yet, the narrative leaps between flashbacks and the diegetic present inverse the linearity of the narrative's sequence. By framing the son's desire to follow his mother's path in between another flashback of the event, as well as the mother's ostensibly irrational behavior, the narration produces a particular effect on both son and reader. The repeated mediation of the event, after the first lines of the novel already introduced us to the singularity, with the particular notation of "1:17," could in this respect also offer another intertext that is symptomatic for the father's gambit. Read as a reference to Gen. 1:17, as noted previously, this passage suggests the singular eruption of a divine creative act; linking the passage to Ex. 1:17, however, offers a more appropriate context in relation to the father's reactive intention. Harkening back to the redemptive search of the Jewish people for the holy land, this reference relates not only to a prominent theme in American cultural history but also to the spatial "narrative quest" (Vanderheide 2008: 108) that father and son engage in. Ex. 1:17, which says: "The midwives, however, feared God and did not do what the king of Egypt had told them to do; they let the boys live," has specific reverberations within the father's reactivity. Without attempting to find clear parallels between the setting of the oppressed Jewish people and their relation to God or King, I want to stress the similar notion of rejecting a transcendental command. While I do not suggest that a King's order is, in any sense, comparable to the eruption of an event, one might still see the father as trying to undermine the radical truth that the novel's ecological event evoked by referring to an ostensibly analogous setting where the rejection of an order was the right thing to do. In other words, just as he evokes the Promethean hubris, the father calls upon another religious type that here serves his ulterior needs to question the status of the event, comparing it to an inherently different milieu. He thus seeks legitimation for his perseverance, his motivation to "let the boy live," in corrupting the ecological narrative in another form of repetition, returning to the typological structure of a biblical tale.

What is more, framing the son's craving for death not only in this biblical context but also just before the mother is unmasked as a suicidal madwoman discursively inhibits the son's liberty to choose. Through the narrative configuration, the son has no option but to believe his father's cunning that attempts to instill in him a similar motivation to keep "carrying the fire."

Besides the recurrent scenes in which the father confronts his son with an utterly questionable notion of good and evil that "tends to collapse upon closer scrutiny" (Estes 2013: 206) but which plays a crucial part in the son's Weltanschauung, Vanderheide has convincingly shown that the novel's idiosyncratic dialogues play their part in contributing to the father's conversion of his son. Vanderheide thus observes that "the ritualistic manner of the dialogue between father and son, which more often than not resembles the fixed form of a catechism in its repetitive question-and-answer format" (2008: 109), is, in fact, not dialogical in the sense of two equal partners of communication: "There is nothing dialogical about such dialogue. Such exchanges serve rather to establish and buffer a common understanding, a single point of view on the world shared by both interlocutors" (ibid.: 110). This ritualism, which for Vanderheide is manifest "both at the structural level in the narrative's ostentatiously paratactic syntax and at the thematic level through the thoughts, words and deeds of the characters" (ibid.: 109), is a clear indicator of the father's attempts to symbolically embed the son in his reactive relation to the event. A prime example of this catechistic style is marked by their discussion about the bad guys and their derived own goodness. As Badiou attests in *Ethics*, the father simply deduces his own moral authority by differentiating himself from a posited evil. "You wanted to know," the father confronts the boy, "what the bad guys looked like. Now you know. . . . My job is to take care of you. I was appointed to do that by God" (*TR* 81). When the son asks him whether they were "still the good guys," the father can merely insist upon their own goodness without the need for verification:

Yes. We're still the good guys.
And we always will be.
Yes. We always will be.
Okay. (*TR* 80–81)

Although aligned as in a dramatic text, the lack of quotation marks, as well as the repetitive echoes of the two dialogue partners, indicate to what extent this rather suggests a soliloquy that dialectically expresses one synthetic train of thought. In the reinforced epiphoras that stress the father's ethical worldview, one might again glimpse how he resorts to a paradigm of repetition in order to secure what is lost as well as to re-inscribe this old situation (here a Manichaean ethics) within the post-evental situation. The success of this structurally iterative act of conversion can be glimpsed in the son's characteristically relenting reply that expresses his skepticism toward his father's seemingly benevolent motivations but ultimately fails to fully dissent.

Despite the son's haphazard moments of skepticism of these deeds, epitomized by his loss of the gun (*TR* 247) as well as his refusal to listen to the man's stories any longer, since "those stories are not true" (*TR* 286), he nevertheless eventually yields to his schemes. Next to the first harbingers of the father's creation of an autopoetic system that the son embodies and which become manifest when the son becomes linguistically creative beyond the father's knowledge (*TR* 155, 170),[67] the apex of the boy's stepping up to the father's manipulations is when he ambivalently declares: "I am the one" (*TR* 277). In accepting his messianic status to redeem them, he has abandoned his wish to be with his mother and perpetuates what his father has instilled in him under the cloak of human perseverance and fatherly education.

In this vein, when the father dies at the end of the novel from his worsening medical condition—the symptoms of which tellingly suggest tuberculosis, "known until recently as 'consumption'" (Becker 2010: 48)—the son has assumed a reactivity that makes him perpetuate the system that his father held on to. In the case of the mother, the figure of spectrality was employed in order to accentuate her aberrational alterity and simultaneously conveyed the structural form of a return of the repressed faithful subject. Here, the creation of his own "passable ghost" (*TR* 59) that serves as a medium in between life and death manifests another decisive rejection of the event that is transferred from father to son. While the mother simply craves "eternal nothingness" (*TR* 59), the father attempts to defy such a clear separation between life and death. Not only does the son carry on the narration when the father dies and the capitalized impersonal pronoun "He" (*TR* 300) now shifts to the boy; additionally, the son's ritualistic consecration of the father is exhibited in his waking next to him for "three days" (*TR* 301). Most profoundly, however, the son actively keeps the father alive and, as another defiance of the evental *memento mori*, rejects the propositions of the event in sacralizing the dead father as a God-like figure—which, indeed, starkly contrasts with *Only Revolutions*'s amorous subject that faithfully creates such a narrative beyond death. So when the boy joins the ostensible "good guys," another religious community, he keeps alive the memory not only of his father but also of the subjective procedure he incorporated: "He tried to talk to God but the best thing was to talk to his father and he did talk to him and he didn't forget" (*TR* 306).

If viewed from the perspective of the concept of the subject of the event, I would agree with Kunsa's observation that "the child is carrying the fire of hope and righteousness from the old story toward the new one," (2009: 68) but I ascribe this to his reactive status that defies the propositions of the event. Kunsa goes on to argue that "the father gives his son language, and after the father's death, the son goes on to seek that still elusive New Jerusalem that waits somewhere beyond the pages of the novel" (ibid.: 69), but this celebratory reading, according to which he embodies an "Adamic figure, a messiah not unlike Christ himself" (ibid.: 65), a reading that pervades the criticism, is rendered questionable within the context of this study.

In conclusion, this chapter shows to what extent the novel's ecological event purports a new situation that is radically different from the novel's prior setting as well as from the reader's environment. In showing how, if thought from the perspective of the theory of the subject of the event, the father rejects this new situation that proffers the emancipation of inanimate beings, I have tried to make a case for this approach's radical claims, which are irrespective of a particular distinction between humans, animals, or objects, thereby indicating to what extent this scope is not a naive return to an inevitably anthropocentric undertaking. On a general level, *The Road* thereby engages in the American cultural history of apocalypse but critically dissociates itself from these narratives. In staging an ecological event, the book should not be aligned to the jeremiad tradition that uses apocalypse in order to change the relation between human and environment, one alleged function of ecological discourse.[68] If the book is said to be interested in an ecological project, reading it from the perspective of Badiou's notion of events, however, rather suggests that its reflection on a "world-less world" (Carlson 2007: 60) undermines the problematic rhetoric of ecoapocalypse and opts for an alternative mode of addressing ecological concerns. Through an entirely anti-anthropocentric and anti-biocentric environment, the novel moves beyond the various binaries that ecological discourse still maintains. Whereas for Buell or Garrard, ecoapocalypse has to be used with caution, since "only if we imagine that the planet has a future, after all, are we likely to take responsibility for it" (Garrard 2013: 105), *The Road* offers an intriguing alternative and, for some, a certainly negative modulation. If thought according to the event, McCarthy puts life into perspective, giving those entities a voice that are often neglected from the seemingly encompassing grasp of ecocriticism, without relapsing to an essentialist discourse of recognition (as the chapter on Beatty's *Slumberland* makes even more clear). His imagination of an event that produces an inanimate subject therefore also inquires into a metapoetical reflection: What is the role of narrative and, more concretely, of the novel in a world that abandons all forms of story-telling?

In combination with Badiou's ideas, *The Road* utters a radical anti-biocentric project and, by adhering to the unbiased notion of set theoretical mathematics that thinks beings as pure multiples, accounts for the problem of prioritizing between the various beings of the world. As a consequence, this theory offers an approach that, despite its alleged abstraction, proves circumspect applicability for fictional narratives and the events they evoke. Nevertheless, as this chapter also sought to make clear, this universal impetus is only universal in its potentiality. While the eruption of an event necessarily implies a reaction, the father's rejection of the ecological event emblematizes that the mere manifestation does not naturally result in a faithful subjective procedure but can just as well generate a reactivity. With this chapter, the theory of the subject of the event exemplified one possible relation to the event that diagnosed its corruption in the process of fidelity. Another aspect of such "Evil" phenomena, as the following chapter elucidates, may also be tracked in relation to the event. Jess Walter's *The Zero*, in this context, shows how a simulacra event may occasion a different form of subjective infidelity, the manifestation of obscure subjects.

"With us or against us"

The Obscure Subject in Jess Walter's
The Zero (2006)

8:48 AM, North Tower &
American Airlines 11.
9:03 AM, South Tower &
United Airlines 77.
—Let's roll.
3,030 go. $15 billion Airline bailout.
—civilization over.

Mark Z. Danielewski, Only Revolutions.

. . . as if they know already what's going to happen.
This . . . event.

Thomas Pynchon, Bleeding Edge.

Events bear a striking resemblance to apocalypse. Yet, as the previous chapter on McCarthy's *The Road* demonstrates, the concept of the event distances itself from religious, technological, and ecological apocalypse in distinct ways. Nevertheless, particularly because of the importance of apocalypticism in and for American culture, which seems to crave an imagination that counts on happenings that allegedly imply epistemological and ontological breakdowns, this chapter's analysis of Jess Walter's "9/11" novel *The Zero* shows why this existential need for events must be met with caution.[1] Since America displays a particular affinity to clean slates, being itself grounded on such singular ruptures that ostensibly ushered in a new world, it proves a specifically fertile environment for the theory of disruptive events that create subjects. However, this inherent disposition simultaneously requires caution, so as not to celebrate and exploit this narrative of fresh beginnings without reflecting upon its problematic consequences. Particularly in response to the terrorist attack of September 11, 2001, one may glimpse how the sociopolitical milieu of the United States displays "an obscure desire for catastrophe" (*E* 38) as a counterpoint to its unstable sense of self. Within the context of this study, it seems thus inevitable to talk about the happening that Jean Baudrillard has termed the "'mother' of all events" (2002: 4), to inquire into the role it played for the American nation and to delineate how fiction plays its part in unmasking the happening as a simulacra event.

While certain strands of American culture (and particularly literature), indeed, contextualize the attacks in an environment of absolute and traumatic change, by now, with enough historical distance to it, dissent against the master narrative of "9/11" (Hoth 2011: 14) has gained momentum. A plethora of critical responses to "9/11" questions to what extent it really was an "event,"[2] and whether the terms of "change," "unrepresentability," and "trauma" are appropriate to describe what happened.[3] Nevertheless, the initial response to the happening, be that in literature,[4] philosophy,[5] history,[6] or literary studies,[7] indeed established a powerful discourse that did not approve of objection. Notably, in this environment of ideological streamlining, even the arts were not able to critically reflect on the incident, readily mimicking the political rhetoric, according to which "9/11" incited a far-reaching geopolitical, social, economic, and cultural rupture that affected not only the United States but really disseminated from local site to global stage (Habermas in Borradori 2003: 28).[8]

While this chapter does not attempt to grapple either with the problematic political and historical issues or with matters of literary historical nature[9] by semantically, or aesthetically, charging the happenings of September 11 with more relevance than they deserve, it simultaneously cannot dodge the discussion. This is particularly due to the fact that the term "event," which is a foundational theoretical model of this study and an essential concept for the fiction that creates subjects of events, has become inflationary since and because of "9/11," as Hoth argues (2011: 11).[10] Despite the increased usage of the concept, critical responses either rely on an evental notion that is grounded in ordinary language use, or they exclusively propel negative analyses, opting for what Baudrillard terms the "zero hypothesis." This states that "September 11 merely constituted an accident or incident on the path to irreversible globalization" (2002: 51). One key factor for integrating the attacks within a paradigm of continuity, rather than marked by radical rupture, is manifested in its intertextual embeddedness. Especially because "9/11" was already premediated through fictional narratives,[11] it could neither halt the "uninterrupted profusion of banal images and a seamless flow of sham events" (ibid.: 27) nor evoke the "resurgence of the real" (ibid.: 28) as Baudrillard would have it. In other words, it does not manifest an order that was not already imminent in the situation prior to the "event." Badiou aligns himself to this rejection of 9/11 as event. Christopher Norris thus explains to what extent Badiou

> maintains that certain episodes commonly thought of as major, even epochal events—such as the collapse of soviet-type communism in 1989–91 or the 2001 attack on the Twin Towers in New York—should instead be viewed as the dramatic yet in many ways perfectly intelligible (if not predictable) outcome of developments already in train. (2009: 160–61)[12]

In its reliance on specific fictional as well as political structures,[13] narratives, and vocabularies operating in the mediation of "9/11," the happening's predictability makes it difficult to view it as a radical outburst of the new. Still, Baudrillard's rejection of the "zero hypothesis" reverberates in the discussion of the fictional potential in relating to "9/11." For Baudrillard, this negative stance is

> ultimately [a] despairing hypothesis, since something very extraordinary occurred there, and to deny it is to admit that henceforth nothing can ever constitute an event, that we are doomed to play out the flawless logic of global power capable of absorbing any resistance, any antagonism, and even strengthening itself by so doing—the terrorist act merely hastening the planetary ascendancy of a single power and a single way of thinking. (2002: 51)

Although this study shares Baudrillard's sympathy for a notion of a singular event that is able to shatter a global capitalist system, his embrace of a maximum hypothesis, which implies "the maximal gamble on the character of September 11 as event" (ibid.: 52), should be met with caution. Instead of generalizing and projecting one grand narrative that effaces other alternating ones, it seems more circumspect to judge case by case how fictional narratives depict, reflect on, and alter "9/11." In fact, in the vein of a larger metapoetical argument, it is particularly the power of narratives that undermines a mimetic notion of representation, which would yield "9/11" to discourses that are determined by political exploitation. In both the fictional and critical discussions of September 11, one might, indeed, detect a "resurgence of the real" to the extent that the "reality" of "9/11" as an event uncannily dominates how fictional narratives can talk about it.[14] As a consequence, I show that fiction may undermine other discourses that readily assumed the happening in a discourse of singularity. Next to Walter's *The Zero*, which is placed center stage in this chapter, it is specifically novels such as Danielewski's *Only Revolutions*,[15] Matt Ruff's *The Mirage*,[16] or Pynchon's *Against the Day* and *Bleeding Edge*[17] that offer a historiographical metafictionist rewriting of the happening and thereby serve as a political counterpoint to the much-preached about return of the real (and realistic). This chapter therefore shows how such self-reflexivity can also be employed as part of a critique. And this seems particularly important because, as Birgit Däwes observes, September 11 has "called into question the role of art and aesthetics in its processing" (2011: 3). Through its metafictional interrogation of the eventfulness of "9/11," the novel under discussion critically reflects on other discourses that instantaneously and dangerously instrumentalize the concept of the event for ulterior reasons. However, in contrast to other narratives that equally undermine the happening's status as an event, *The Zero* also explores the scope of subjective creations within this environment. Just as *The Road* produced an "evil" form of subject by showing how the father's ignorance of the event corrupted his fidelity, so does Jess Walter's novel delineate the becoming of an obscure subject that is engendered through its confusion of "9/11" with a genuine event. Its creation of a paralyzed and determined evil subject who adheres to a simulacra event thus not only reflexively criticizes the problematic appropriation of a "simulacrum of truth" (*E* 74) as part of what Žižek calls a "pseudo-postmodern game" (2002: 17); within the context of this study, the novel also sheds light on the subjective complications that may arise within the realm of the event, which proves to have very concrete ethical effects.

In the light of a concept of the event that this study suggests, *The Zero*'s representation of and reflection on "9/11" rejects its status as a maximum singularity. Yet, even though the novel undermines the happening as a genuine event, it nevertheless shows how the adherence to a simulacrum event also composes a subject, albeit an obscure one. Whereas the reactive subject of *The Road* ignores the existence of an event, obscure subjects are created by their confusion of what they take to be an event. Another manifestation of such subjective creations is constituted by bringing

> into being, and nam[ing], not the void of the earlier situation, but its plenitude—not the universality of that which is sustained, precisely, by no particular characteristic (no particular multiple), but the absolute particularity of a community, itself rooted in the characteristic of its soil, its blood, and its race. (*E* 73)[18]

Brian Remy, the novel's protagonist, in fact fulfills both criteria and becomes evil. Remy's evilness is constituted by his fidelity to a simulacrum event. Furthermore, he appropriates what is rather a political state of exception than a proper event, thereby sustaining his sovereign power. Instead of arriving at an absolute and universal idea of "Evil" derived through negative demarcation, the novel theorizes a different "ethic of truth" (*E* 40) that simultaneously eschews relativist as well as universalist "Ethics," which has been discussed to some extent in the theory chapter of this book.[19] Rejecting "9/11" as an event serves the localization of political responsibility not in an orientalist Other but holds up a mirror to the American nation itself. It shows, as Derrida writes, that "'terrorists' are not, in this context, 'others,' absolute others whom we, as 'Westerners' can no longer understand" (qtd. in Borradori 2003: 115).[20] However, instead of going beyond problematic Manicheanisms in relativist terms, blurring boundary lines between self and other, the novel opts for an intelligible understanding of evil that involves the relationship between subject and non-event.

By juxtaposing two seemingly different identities of the novel's protagonist Brian Remy (one visible in the text, the other clandestinely present in narrative gaps), the novel seems to suggest that "9/11" has occasioned a traumatizing rupture where we can literally "read" an ethically "correct" Brian Remy. Not only is the textualized Remy a hero of September 11; he also tries to counteract his other self that continuously acts in morally dubious ways. It becomes clear relatively early in the novel that the protagonist suffers from posttraumatic stress disorder that leads to dissociative episodes that remain blank in the text. This formal technique seems to suggest that Brian's identity is oscillating between his present good deeds and his questionable ones in the gaps. I want to undermine this interpretation by highlighting the interconnection of these two identities, offering a reading of Brian as a coherent obscure subject who has to be made responsible for his actions. Indeed, just as *Only Revolutions*'s circular form illuminated a literary appropriation of the repetitive and infinite level of reagency, so does *The Zero* give the concept of the obscure subject a particular narrative form. By implying textual blanks, the novel therefore articulates a literal take on the philosophical idea of an obscure subject by implementing this obscurity on its mode of representation.

Thereby, *The Zero* does not simply criticize political and mass media discourses in their immediate incorporation of "9/11" into an already existing system under the guise of rupture and change. In a similar vein as the chronomosaic of *Only Revolutions*, which involves the interrogation of various historical happenings as events, *Slumberland*'s reflection on the end of the Jim Crow era and the end of history, or *Against the Day*'s reflection on scientific happenings, *The Zero* makes the case "that not every 'novelty' is an event" (*E* 72). What is more, it argues that a subject may also be created by confusing an incident's status as an event. While *The Road* shows that fidelity "is never inevitable or necessary" (*E* 69), Jess Walter's novel suggests that events are rare occasions and not every terrorist attack as media happening implies a fundamental ontological rupture. In this context, a subject cannot be just a passive recipient, myopically clinging to every "novelty" that occurs. For it to become a faithful subject of the event and not an obscure one, the "human animal" has to be active, minutely examining the singularity and deciding upon its supplementary potential, as difficult and epistemologically problematic as that might be.

To this extent, *The Zero* exceeds the simple critique of "9/11" as a unique event, thereby resisting a mere "pseudo-postmodern game of reducing the WTC collapse to just another media spectacle," which for Žižek "is not the point" (2002: 17). Rather, the novel's point is to advise caution in relating to events, showing how a simulacrum event may also invoke a subject, as non-events may carry with them "all the formal traits of a truth" (*E* 74). By evoking tropes of trauma, unrepresentability, or change, "9/11," indeed, relies on various mechanisms that are integral parts of events. Indeed, it is not exclusively genuine events that evoke subjective procedures. A simulacra event might thus also engender "a universal nomination of the event, inducing the power of a radical break, but also the 'obligation' of a fidelity, and the promotion of a simulacrum of the subject" (*E* 74). What fundamentally distinguishes the faithful from the obscure subject, moreover, is that it "regulates its break with the situation not by the universality of the void, but by the closed particularity of an abstract set [ensemble]" (*E* 74). Instead of accepting the universality of human beings, America focused on its own narcissistic essence. Discarding the imminent potential that "9/11" as an event incorporated, Brian Remy is not empowered by his faithfulness to the new propositions that the event conjures. Instead, following an essentialist project, he is limited both diegetically and narratively. This chapter shows first how the novel questions the nomination of "9/11" as an event (continuity, taboo, trauma). Following from this, I argue that the novel creates an obscure subject, a subject that clings to a simulacrum event, is paralyzed by determining powers, and thus becomes evil, directing terror at everyone (*E* 77).

Re-presenting the present

Jess Walter's 2006 novel *The Zero*, set in the aftermath of the Twin Towers' collapse and telling the story of police officer Brian Remy, easily fits Birgit Däwes's "literary subgenre" of the 9/11 novel (2011: 6). Paratextually, the novel already evokes the images of September 11 on its cover, depicting two empty rectangles standing side by side.

However, unlike other novels, which simply incorporate the attacks into their diegesis as another of many narrative incidents (*Falling Man, Extemely Loud and Incredibly Close, Saturday,* etc.) in an all-too-uncritical way, *The Zero* self-reflexively engages with the event and particularly examines its eventness. This is achieved in a remarkably metafictional manner, which makes Däwes subsume the novel into her taxonomy of a Barthesian "writerly text," in which "representational challenges" are transformed into "semantic, structural or formal innovations, such as multiple perspectives, extensive allegories, non-linear forms of narration, visual elements, creative layouts, metafictional angles, and various other textual experiments" (2011: 21). For her, such texts are marked by "plot structures [that] are closely interwoven with a metanarrative inquiry into memory, historiography, and fiction" (2011: 359). In addition to these metafictional interrogations, *The Zero* also reflects on the nature of the event and thereby undermines a variety of tropes of the "9/11" maximum hypothesis.

Already the very beginning of the novel interweaves semantic clusters of continuity and change and thereby interrogates the happening's eventfulness:

> They burst into the sky, every bird in creation, angry and agitated, awakened by the same primary thought, erupting in a white feathered cloudburst, anxious and graceful, angling in ever-tightening circles toward the ground, drifting close enough to touch, and then close enough to see that it wasn't a flock of birds at all—it was paper. Burning scraps of paper. All the little birds were paper. Fluttering and circling and growing bigger, falling bits and frantic sheets, some smoking, corners scorched, flaring in the open air until there was nothing left but a fine black edge . . . and then gone, a hole and nothing but the faint memory of smoke. Behind the burning flock came a great wail and a moan as seething black unfurled, the world inside out, birds beating against a roiling sky and in that moment everything that wasn't smoke was paper. And it was beautiful. (*TZ* 3)

In employing tropes of blazing destruction, chaotic anxiety, and the suicidal iconography of falling that has entered what Hoth refers to as cultural knowledge (2011: 51), the novel's beginning metonymically evokes the attack on the Twin Towers. Coupled with specifically American narratives of religious connotations ("creation," "grace,"), the beginning furthermore situates the narrated in an explicit topological framework. The apocalyptic depiction that turns "the world inside out," which initially seems to be mediated through a heterodiegetic narrator, however, shifts in mid-sentence to a more subjective focal point. The mid-sentence correction of the phenomenological perception of floating animals into textual referents manifests a first harbinger of the narratological complexities that will become more prominent at a later point of this discussion, since they crucially relate to an analysis of the novel's representation of an obscure subject. What appears as an external mediator at the beginning of the text turns out to be the focalized through Brian, who seems to experience a cataclysmic event *in medias res*.

Over this metamorphosis, from bird to paper, another metaphorical layer hovers, induced through the anthropomorphic ascription of human outcries of anguish.

While one might read the implicit refusal to represent human death as a euphemistic surrogation, shunning brute abjection in favor of more palatable circumscriptions, the excerpt also hints at the unrepresentabilty of death, which dominated the televised mediation of "9/11" as well as the majority of fictional narratives, that will be discussed in more detail in the following paragraphs. Reversing the movements of news cameras on September 11, the narrative closes in "enough to see," so that the novel's beginning, on the one hand, reflects on the mechanisms of censorship surrounding the happening and, on the other, pronounces its poetic endeavor to examine its status as an event from close-up.

This is also implied in the passage's final line. The scene's beauty not only recalls Karlheinz Stockhausen's controversial remark that the happenings of September 11 were "the greatest work of art imaginable for the whole cosmos" (qtd. in Castle 2012: n.p.); more profoundly, the phrase also evokes the concept of aesthetic judgment, however, immediately distancing itself from Kant's notion of the sublime. Although the textual mediation of the happening is, like in the case of the apocalypse, marked by specific similarities, the novel questions any pretensions of sublimity, which could be viewed as bearing traces of an evental disposition. However, Brian Remy's description of the burning World Trade Center as beautiful rejects the scene's sublimity, which might indicate its eventfulness. While both the event and the sublime seem to imply a notion of epistemological rupture, *The Zero*'s beginning discards an equation of the attacks with a sublime manifestation. For in judging the happenings in terms of beauty, the passage insists that Remy perceives the spectacle not without form. For Kant, aesthetic judgments may be discriminated in sublime, "formless object[s]" and objects whose beauty "consist[s] in [their] being bounded" (1987: 98). If one could see a parallel between sublimity and an event, since both are marked by surpassing epistemological capacities, Remy's evaluation, however, undermines such a diagnosis. Instead of insisting on "9/11" as an experience that cannot be grasped within cogent parameters of cognition, the declaration that "it was beautiful" emphasizes that there exists a discernible and assessable form. As a consequence, being a manifestation of neither overwhelming mathematical nor of overpowering dynamical sublime, the novel distances itself from a particular aesthetic and ethical phenomenon that centers on a powerful notion of the subject.[21]

This is because, unlike the inciting of terror as a sublime "negative pleasure," the judgment of the destruction as a beautiful, "positive pleasure"

> carries with it directly a feeling of life's being furthered, and hence is compatible
> with charms and with an imagination at play. But the other liking (the feeling of
> the sublime) is a pleasure that arises only indirectly: it is produced by the feeling of
> a momentary inhibition of the vital forces followed immediately by an outpouring
> of them that is all the stronger. (ibid.: 98)

While Remy's description whitewashes any negative valorization that would incite terror and thus insists on a continuity of vital perpetuation, the rejection of the sublime simultaneously declines a rational subject. For one effect of the sublime is to assert the spectator's "superiority over nature" (ibid.: 120). If experiences of sublimity confirm the workings of reason by adding to every "unboundedness the thought of its totality" (ibid.: 98), thereby taming the seemingly overpowering magnitude or might of the outside world, *The Zero* in accordance with the subject of the event's antihumanist conception of subjectivity denies this stance. It is thus telling that the novel shies away from evoking the discourse of the sublime in relation to "9/11," as this would bridge the gap from aesthetics to morality, strengthening a humanist concept of the subject. *The Zero* eschews a notion of a rational, self-same subject whose "basis [is] merely within ourselves and in the way of thinking that introduces sublimity into our presentation of nature" (ibid.: 100). Sublimity as a concept exercising and practicing reason (ibid.: 98), in other words, is equally discarded for being grounded in the mastering of awe-inspiring outside forces, without acknowledging the disruptive dimensions of such influences.

The novel thus suggests that "9/11" was no event. Through its rejection of any similarities between the terrifying experience of the sublime and an event, the novel questions certain parallels between sublimity and eventness. Moreover, the beginning can also be read as suggesting that the discourse of the sublime is misapplied in the context of subjective creations. Despite certain parallels between the two phenomena, the experience of the sublime always involves a certain remoteness to the happening, whereas a subject of the event can only be evoked through proximity.[22] As Žižek observes in *The Ticklish Subject*: "Against this Kantian celebration of the sublime effect on passive observers, Badiou insists on the immanence of the Truth-Event: the Truth-Event is Truth in itself for its agents themselves, not for external observers" (1999: 161). This is particularly amplified by the passage's ontological status. Instead of getting a literally im-mediate depiction of an event, Remy's subjective experience turns out to be re-mediated. The seemingly direct presentation of the happenings is only a dream-like impression that Remy goes through when having attempted to commit suicide. In presenting Remy's state of consciousness, the novel only offers a secondary mediation, a representation in the guise of an immediate presence of an event. As in the case of the French Revolution as observed by Kant, the relation between subject and event requires a disposition of proximity, of full immersion and not the mere admiration "from a safe distance by passive observers" (Žižek 1999: 161).

The matter of mediation is, indeed, a persistent concern of the novel that raises doubts about the happening's pretensions to be a genuine event. The framing of the attacks in an aesthetic/poetic context, with the floating pages suggesting textual embededdness, hints from the very beginning at an intertextual premediation. The line "everything that wasn't smoke was paper" (*TZ* 3) insinuates in a constructivist manner that there exists no extra-medial reference, which would constitute the nature of a proper event, granted that the differentiation between paper and smoke implies a medial difference, where there also exists something beyond paper, that is, texts. This evocation of tropes of destruction suggests that the brute violence is beyond textual signification, part of an unrepresentable event. Still, one could also see the interdependence of paper and smoke as two different aggregate states of the same textual material.

What also adds to the parallelism of art and the attacks is the novel's continuous insistence on its performative character. Not only are Remy and his colleague Paul Guterak giving various celebrities tours into the restricted site of The Zero (*TZ* 12, 23), thereby perpetuating a quite eclectic form of disaster tourism. The sacralization of Ground Zero is also especially amplified by its theatrical description:

> At night, The Zero was lit like a stage. Or a surgery. It was quiet—not exactly peaceful, but a person could think. The work seemed less showy to Remy, the loss more personal, less produced than during the day, when everyone posed for photographers and TV cameras, when grief and anger became competitive sports. (*TZ* 36)

Despite the fact that Ground Zero appears to discard its put-on spatial identity of the day, which is clearly marked by a rhetoric of postindustrial simulation, its description as a space of performance insinuates that the site is affected by processes of enactment and re-enactment even at night. This ritualistic connotation is also suggested by its comparison with a medical operation. Clearly evoking the imagery of national wounding, *The Zero* stands as a spatial site that requires not only re-enactment but repeated care. Whether used for curative purposes or for dramatic practices, *The Zero* cannot totally abandon its performative character; all it accomplishes is a gradational lessening, being "less showy," "less produced."

The novel's questioning of "9/11" as an event is not only achieved through an emphasis on continuities preceding the attacks. It also depicts how the "Days After," the title of *The Zero*'s first chapter, are ultimately no different from the days before. By amplifying various attempts in which different discourses instantaneously aspire to transform "9/11" into a marketable good (*TZ* 26, 52, 150, 176, 184, 222, 284), integrating it into imperial structures of economic stratagems, the happening's singularity is called into question. What is more, the novel gives voice to the bereaved, who deny that anything changed on that day. For example, April, who has lost both her sister and her husband, explains:

> "It just surprises me, I guess. Afterward, I really thought that everything would change . . . I don't know . . . that we would be different. Stores would never open again . . . business shut down . . . lawyers quit their practices and run into the woods." She smiled wistfully. "I just assumed the newspaper would stop coming out. Instead . . ." She chewed a thumbnail. "This whole thing . . . it just became another section in the paper. Like movie reviews. Or the bridge column." (*TZ* 145)

What April, like Baudrillard, imagines to involve the end of the American postmodern Lebenswelt, global capitalism at its limits, society disintegrating by aspiring to hermitism, is instantly subsumed by democratic liberalism and its discourses. Instead of fundamentally changing the American situation, the happening is normalized and integrated in existing structures. 9/11, "this whole thing" becomes simply a part, a puzzle piece in the media's discursive architecture. April's boss, a real estate manager, accordingly observes that "the downtime is looking like nothing more than a blip" (*TZ* 162). Discussion of the seemingly apocalyptic event in a language of economic movements reveals how the happening is incorporated by a discourse that implies flexible, yet calculable prognoses.

In addition to insisting that the happening was predictable and did not manifest a singular rupture by highlighting structures that were already discernible before the attack happened, it also investigates another theme that is shared by events and "9/11": the issue of unrepresentability.

Presenting the unrepresentable

As part of the "9/11"/event equation, proponents of the maximum hypothesis have insisted that the attack obliterated any form of re-presentation. According to this argument, the sheer singularity of the attacks traumatized victims to such an extent that they were unable to use language in any meaningful way and, on a larger scale, implied the end of a whole discursive regime.[23] An epistemological caesura occurred, which rendered narrative or interpretative approximations futile. Randall summarizes this stance, according to which "'9/11' surpasses our contemporary language by the rapidity and unexpectedness of its traumatising images" (2011: 73). If this abyss between the Real and the Symbolic is, indeed, crucial for the workings of events and the creation of subjects, *The Zero* engages critically in this discussion and demarcates a distinction between the unrepresentable and the not to be represented. Sielke accordingly observes that the "rhetoric of the unrepresentable remains a risky business" (2010: 405), since it may be co-opted by a government in order to legitimate "changes of policies, violations of international conventions, and the war in Iraq by insisting on the rupture" (ibid.: 395).

It is particularly in dialogic communications that the novel highlights the problem of taboos. In a conversation between Brian Remy and his colleague Paul Guterak, both ponder the aftermath of September 11. Paul, who resembles the figure of a comic side-kick, reveals to Remy that the attacks have, as a matter of fact, improved his life:

> "See what I'm sayin' . . . " Paul wrestled with words. "I know . . . what you're saying," Remy said quietly. "And maybe you're right. But there are things we can't say now. Okay? You can't say you've never been this happy. Even if you think it, you can't say it. Everything is . . . there are things . . . we have to leave alone. We have to let 'em sit there, and don't say anything about 'em." "Like the scalp." (*TZ* 12)

This conversation is symptomatic of the subliminal political mechanisms that are guiding the rhetoric of unrepresentability. Guterak's reluctance to voice the forbidden is revealed not as an impossibility of communication but as a stratagem of political surveillance. Being happy about the attacks' aftermath is thereby strictly excluded from the "9/11" narrative, since it would not only undermine the story of cultural trauma and question the heroification of rescue workers but would also expose any cartography of evil by undermining the clear-cut responses toward the atrocious attacks. While Guterak is in a position of resisting this regulatory endeavor, exemplifying the bodily confrontation with language and its imposed limits, Remy has already internalized the controlling narrative of communicative impossibility. As a consequence, he is speaking "quietly," possibly fearing disciplinary measures if overheard. Moreover, he emblematizes the prohibition of verbalizing the improper by struggling with his words. Through his elliptical hesitations, one glimpses how he tries to express the fact that they are not allowed to express.

Guterak's humorous response additionally adds to the novel's critique of the rhetoric of unrepresentability and, as a consequence, lays bare its non-eventfulness. The scalp is representative of how the mediation of the attacks effaced the materiality and actuality of death. Being prohibited from mentioning the scalp, one of the few human remnants to be found at the site, thus feeds into what Petersen terms the "iconic-narrative" discourse on death, which supplements speaking about death:

> Indem er das Leid der Opfer medialisiert erfährt, braucht sich der Zuschauer nicht mehr selbst von der Erfahrung des Todes zu distanzieren, um sie ertragen zu können. Eine Distanzierung wird durch das Medium immer schon mitgeliefert. (215)[24]

The medial distance that Petersen addresses here could again be seen in the context of the sublime. Yet, whereas the sublime still implied an immediacy of experience, as remote as the observer may be located from the happening, the mediation of "9/11" implies another layer that hinders the direct confrontation between human and event. Particularly through its hypermediation, being constantly confronted with the ever-repeated images of the attacks, Brian finds himself inescapably immersed in mass media dissimulation:

> Remy felt a jolt of déjà vu, anticipating each muted image before it appeared, and it occurred to him that the news had become the wallpaper in his mind now, the endless loop playing in his head—banking wings, blooms of flame, white plumes becoming black and then gray, endless gray, geysers of gray, dust-covered gray stragglers with gray hands covering gray mouths running from gray shore-break, and the birds, white—endless breeds and flocks of memos and menus and correspondence fluttering silently and then disappearing in the ashen darkness. (*TZ* 9)

The interconnection of various stages of mediation, pre-mediation ("anticipating"), and re-mediation ("déjà vu") subscribes to Baudrillard's notion of hyper-reality, in which Remy has internalized the simulacra of September 11. In his mental architecture, the iconographic representations of "9/11" have assumed the position of a monotonous background decoration that serves as the substrate for his other mental processes. By blurring the mediated images with Brian's subjective recollections, the novel intratextually refers again to its beginning. Once more, *The Zero* here surrogates the depiction of death of animate people for inanimate objects. Furthermore, the depiction of colors expresses not only the actual genealogy of the happening. The causal enumeration of the plane crashing into the towers also reduces the representational complexity. While there are first "blooms of flame, white plumes" turn black until the monochromatic "gray" is spread over all objects of reference. But it is not only dust that materially covers lower Manhattan. Whereas the livid color could also indicate the static noise of corrupted media transmissions and would thus imply an end of mediation, the "gray" rather suggests a progressive form of medial taboo. Thereby, the passage hints at the avoidance of any explicit display of dead people, metonymically substituting them for abstract numbers of casualties, or non-human objects. As part and parcel of a political and medial program that co-opts the formula of traumatic unrepresentability as part of a grander ideology, the monochromatic gray assumes the function of white noise by drowning everything out in a subliminal way.

There is yet another dimension evident in the mentioning of the scalp that also contributes to the novel's questioning of "9/11" as an event. Using a specific trope of the violent confrontations between Native Americans and European colonizers, *The Zero* intertwines two historical moments of the United States. However, this is not simply a postmodern technique intended for ahistorical pastiche but rather projects two quite distinct milieus in order to emphasize possible connections. At one and the same time, the scalp indicates the brute violence of the attackers while also indicating a persistent narrative of American Imperialism: the scalp not only others the religious fanatics, who through their auto-immune suicide (Derrida in Borradori 2003: 94) even exceed the violence of Native Americans and thus manifest an unimaginable "savagery"; by echoing the colonial context of violent exploitation, appropriation, colonized resistance and revenge, the scalp frames the seemingly impossible to grasp and makes it intelligible as an unacceptable outburst of violence. Yet, it is one that has to be contextualized, since it is based on ideological motivations, which are indicative of complex, but predictable political mechanisms.

Having shown how the novel presents "9/11" as a non-event, I will now focus on how this may, nevertheless, produce a subject. In keeping faith with a simulacra event, Brian Remy becomes an obscure, evil subject and how this finds a unique expression in the novel's form.

Un-representing the obscure subject

In addition to the diegetic examination of "9/11" and the topic of its unrepresentability that is unmasked as a matter of taboo and censorship, *The Zero*'s formal implementation of the unrepresentable segues into the production of a subject that is faithful to a non-event. In addition to pointing to the constructed and imposed manner of failing to relate to the happening, the novel also transports the "unrepresentable" from the story-level to a structural framework, which fundamentally affects the protagonist. Like in so many "9/11" novels, *The Zero*'s protagonist is represented as severely traumatized. Yet, in contrast to most other books dealing with the aftermath of the attacks, it also incorporates signs of posttraumatic dissociation on the level of *discourse*. The narrative integrates textual voids, which halt the narrative often in mid-sentence. When the narrative continues, we often find Brian in a different place, without knowing how he got there, let alone what he did in the interim. It turns out that in these moments of dissociation, he commits ethically dubious deeds. Brian explains these blanks as such: "Okay. This was the problem. These gaps in his memory, or perhaps his life, a series of skips—long shredded tears, empty spaces where the explanations for the most basic things used to be" (*TZ* 5). As it turns out these "empty spaces" interlink his mnemonic blanks with textual voids in a self-conscious manner that epitomizes the construction and the representation of an obscure subject.

Thus, Brian's skips of consciousness are not simple surges of oblivion, like spaces between words of a continuous, meaningful sentence. This would be tantamount to mere paragraph breaks in conventional novels that serve as narrative ellipses. What is different about such narrative jumps in time and/or space is the fact that, in *The Zero*, they occur without forewarning and interrupt not only the reader's process of reception; more crucially, these textual gaps put Brian in a similar position, in which he has to put the pieces together in inquiring what happened in the meantime.

Equally so, I reject the interpretation of these blanks as an alternate identity, expressing the unstable and fluctuating construction of selves. By granting such a reading, one too easily yields to a relativist ethics, in which the conduction of evil actions may simply be accredited to a different identity, as in the case of Chuck Palahniuk's *Fight Club* (1996) or Bret Easton Ellis's *American Psycho* (1991). And, indeed, the novel formally suggests the dissociation between a present Brian, eager to live an ethically sound life, and the unrepresented parts of Brian's self, continuously engaging in morally questionable acts. Yet, I read Brian as a coherent obscure subject, which is evoked through his faithfulness to a simulacra event and makes him evil in relation to an affirmative ethics of truth.

This implies that only through Brian's fidelity to the non-event of "9/11" does he become evil. Seeing the non-event and his faithfulness to it as the source of a negative subjective composition does not emulate the rhetoric of a "loss of innocence" that has continuously circulated in the discourse on "9/11." Quite the opposite, by insisting that "9/11" is no event, the novel questions the singular dimensions of the happening that would result in a coercive pathological structure. This is not to say that the attack and the consequent loss of lives did not manifest a trauma for those affected by it. Rather, the novel distinguishes between trauma and event, in that the former is overpowering, while the other implies aspects of empowerment. As a consequence, *The Zero* stresses the subjective component of any faithful procedure. A subject of the event explicitly consists of two aspects and neither of them may be seen as the center of this procedure. Yielding the traumatic happening too much power over its "subjects" would simply locate the source of evil in a man-made terrorist ambush. The novel thus insists that the creation of evil is not a result of reacting to the horrible attack of the Twin Towers but essentially lies in the ways in which humans relate to a non-event. Put differently, it shifts the focus from the event to subjective fidelity, or rather infidelity.

To this extent, one might grasp the focus on the component of subjective fidelity specifically in the novel's structure. Formally, the novel's temporal order does not only reject the equivalence of the attacks with an event once more. Although the novel commences with the already mentioned subjective and haunting recollection of the attacks, the first sentence's evocation of tropes of theo-logocentric beginnings ("creation," "primary thought," "turning the world inside out") turns out, as I have already suggested, to be of a deferred nature. With the rejection of a beginning *ab ovo* *The Zero* again diminishes the happening's potential as an evental transformation of a given order. What is more, the setting *in medias res* narratively focuses on the examination of Brian becoming an obscure subject. Unlike *The Road*, *Against the Day*, *Only Revolutions*, and *Slumberland*, which produce faithful subjects of the event, *The Zero* excludes a constitutive aspect of faithful subjective creations from its diegesis. As part of its obscure subjective procedure, the novel transports this corrupted procedure on its formal representation.

However, the textual absence of the attacks from the narrative does not align itself with other narratives in which "the 'spectacle' itself remains mostly absent from explicit description," as Randall writes (2011: 8), because of fiction's mimetic impotence. Randall shows that the majority of novels dealing with "9/11," in fact, do not represent the attack. On a second metapoetical level, *The Zero* hence engages in the question of representation and its limits by addressing aesthetic questions. According to the proponents who see "9/11" as a genuine, yet unrepresentable event, one is led to believe that art and especially literature is unable to semiotically grasp the attacks and approach them semantically. Let alone that novels create a counternarrative—not one against terrorism, as DeLillo would have it, but a fictional re-invention of "9/11" as an event.[25] Randall summarizes this stance, according to which the "events transcend literary representation, their visual symbolism, immediacy and unprecedented historical significance (or rather their global reach on TV) rendering fictional reinterpretation unnecessary" (ibid.: 8). In the face of the visual, iconographic omnipresence of "9/11" as a televised narrative, I agree that fiction cannot help to represent the happenings, if it merely insists on its mimetic capabilities. Critics are thus eager to point out how the realist novel unsuccessfully grapples with the representation of the attacks.[26] By contrast, *The Zero* invests efforts in writing against allegations of unrepresentability by laying bare its own modes of representation. Especially because the rhetoric of unrepresentability "'prohibits criticism and innovation' and thus creates taboos and boundaries that threaten to shut down ideas and representations that are deemed to have, in some way, transgressed what can and cannot be said about a particular event" (ibid.: 16), it is crucial to engage in a political critique of these mechanisms. Besides addressing such taboos through its metafictional reflexivity, the novel's exclusion of the attacks implies its rejection of its eventness, rather than yielding to the unwritten law of not depicting the happening. Furthermore, this evasion occupies itself more with the subjective component of the subject of the event, to stress it once more. In contrast to Mark Z. Danielewski's *Only Revolutions*, *Slumberland*, or *Against the Day*, *The Zero* does not inspect the constitution of a faithful subject of the event but, rather, enters at a stage when the subject has already been produced. The novel setting in at the moment when Remy has already entered a process of fidelity, albeit to a simulacrum event, shows that modes of determination are already in progress. Tellingly, he thus exclaims at the beginning: "I am the police" (*TZ* 4). His identification with the executive branch of the state illustrates to what extent he has absorbed the government's stance to "9/11," substituting his singular identity for a collective institution without reflection. This transformation, from citizen to governmental dispositif is particularly striking, as it occurs at the moment just after Brian has attempted suicide. While this obviously evokes a discourse of traumatization and raises the question whether the cause of the psychological wounding was, in fact, self-inflicted, the dimension of biopolitics is even more eminent in the context of "9/11" and its status as an event. For if September 11 is supposed to manifest an event, and more concretely, a political one, this would result in a subjective procedure that would endow those faithful to it with a liberation from these disciplinary and/or controlling apparatuses. Instead, Brian's identification with the police rather suggests a strengthening of the society of control.

The oscillation between activity and passivity, choosing one's identity or it being imposed, also relates to the grander, epistemological dimensions of the novel. The combination of epistemological and ontological inquiries relates to Brian's status as an obscure subject. In his undertaking of gathering and collecting signs in order to arrive at a coherent notion of truth, both in relation to the happening of September 11 and in respect to his own self, Brian fruitlessly struggles for (re)agency. He fails to make sense of the traces he comes across in order to arrive at an understanding of a conspiracy related to the attack, just as he does not succeed in deciphering the textual blanks that point to a seemingly different form of his self. As an obscure subject, Brian is presented as lost not only within a network of determining powers of political discourses but also within his "other" self.

On one level, Brian's inquiry into signs as referents of a readable narrative that are supposed to help him in his mental confusion suggests the problems of interpretation that both Brian and the reader face. As a consequence, Brian functions as a detective in more than just one way. While he is a police detective in search of himself, he also literally embodies this figure's aptitude to read signs and interpret them to solve the riddle of March Selios, a paralegal who mysteriously seems to have escaped the collapse of the World Trade Center, thanks to inside information.

Framed in a larger project of hunting down terrorists, Brian gets appointed head of a new executive force of the "Documentation department," which gathers all the paper that was spread over the city after the Twin Towers' destruction. The Boss, a ridiculously patriotic caricature of New York City's mayor, explains the need for this:

> *There is nothing so important as recovering the record of our commerce, the proof of our place in the world, of the resilience of our economy, of our jobs, of our lives. If we do not make a fundamental accounting of what was lost, if we do not gather up the paper and put it all back, then the forces aligned against us have already won. They've. Already. Won. (TZ 19)*

Paradoxically, The Boss sees the collection of material paper as the appropriate means of resisting the decline of a postindustrial, immaterial economy. Again, the novel caricatures responses to September 11.[27] Through the relational discrepancy between the loss of lives and the gathering of paper as an adequate response, *The Zero* ridicules political narratives, which obstinately seek to come up with productive means to counter the terrorists' goals.

However, one might go even further and insist on another, more problematic dimension of Remy's appointment as a gatherer of documents. In this vein, it is the constitution of an archive that is seen as crucial for the protection and perpetuation of an essentialist national discourse. In gathering economic documents, Brian becomes an *archon* who does not merely archive material but effectively inhabits a position of power, albeit, only at the cost of subjecting others. Derrida observes how the *archons* "are first of all the documents' guardians. They do not only ensure the physical security of what is deposited and of the substrate. They are also accorded the hermeneutic right and competence. They have the power to interpret the archives" (1998: 2). By establishing a fixed spatial site, The Boss insists on the topo-nomological necessity (ibid.: 3) of securing "proof of [their] place in the world." The architectonic accumulation of knowledge, the "*gathering together* [*of*] *signs*," which "aims to coordinate a single corpus, in a system of synchrony in which all the elements articulate the unity of an ideal configuration" (ibid.: 3), is part of political processes of power that aim to found an essentialist topography. The endeavor to gain power over knowledge is thus motivated by the mastering of discourse, inhabiting the right of determining not only the place of the documents, but also the interpretative sovereignty, which concomitantly implies the cartographic production and legitimation of friend-enemy oppositions.

In mistaking "9/11" as an event, Brian may seem empowered. Even though "9/11," as depicted in *The Zero*, does not constitute an event, it nevertheless implies "all the formal traits of a truth" (*E* 74). This means that the happening simulates various mechanisms that are also eminent in genuine events. Especially through its dissimulation of trauma, unrepresentability, and singularity, "9/11" passes as an event. As a consequence, it also evokes the "'obligation' of a fidelity" (*E* 74). However, Brian's faithfulness to this simulacrum, which makes him a "*simulacrum of the subject*" (*E* 74) differs from the faithfulness of subjects of events. It is his exclusion of those "who are arbitrarily declared not to belong to the communitarian substance whose promotion and domination the simulacrum event is designed to assure" (*E* 74) that renders him an obscure subject. In contrast to faithful subjective formations, "fidelity to the simulacrum . . . has as its content war and massacre. These are not here means to an end: they make up the very real [*tout le réel*] of such a fidelity" (*E* 74). On the one hand, the universal appeal of unique events is forfeited. Its potential to be recognized without distinction of class, race, or gender, is substituted in the process of becoming an obscure subject by a lethal commitment: "What is addressed 'to everyone'" in this case, writes Badiou, "is death" (*E* 74). On the other hand, the propositions of events cannot result in the stressing of one particular multiple at the cost of others. In seeing the "American" set being addressed by the event, the obscure Brian chooses to extinguish other multiples that do not conform with this one. Brian could therefore be seen as becoming *evil* in the sense of Giorgio Agamben's notion of the sovereign, even though he does not employ this semantically laden word.[28]

Agamben shows how sovereign power and its declaration of a state of emergency have always been contingent upon the exclusive inclusion of a *homo sacer*.[29] In Agamben's extension of biopolitics, the sovereign only establishes his power by constituting a sacred man, a being that has been deprived of its political life (*bios*) and is reduced to a more fundamental form of living (*zoē*), what Agamben calls "bare life." As a sovereign, Brian "separate[s] *zoē* and *bios* in another man and . . . isolate[s] in him something like a bare life that may be killed" (Agamben 1998: 42).

Remy takes on the status of a sovereign in assuming 9/11 to mark a state of exception. He is thus not merely an inversed paperboy, gathering rather than distributing information, since the "Liberty and Recovery Act mandates the recovery and filing of documents. It doesn't specifically limit [them] to those documents recovered that day" (*TZ* 209). Nor does it limit Brian and his dubious colleague Markham to recovering textual objects that are supposed to resolve the mystery around March Selios. In extending Brian's power over documents, the Liberty and Recovery Act, as a legitimization of a state of exception, allows him to go after some "undocumented aliens" (*TZ* 113), which supposedly form a terrorist cell. Through his compliance to the simulacrum truth that "9/11" propels, Brian acts as an obscure subject by identifying and bringing down enemies of the American nation. Both Brian and his cruel colleague Markham do not shy away from employing various questionable means in order to deny the universality that "9/11" as a genuine event would have implied. They stress "the absolute particularity of a community," namely that of American citizens, which manifests itself in the arbitrary construction of a "Muslim" alterity.[30] The naming, construction, and exploitation of the "Muslim" Other echoes the consignation of the "Jews" in the Third Reich, as Badiou elaborates. In this sense, "the name 'Jew' was a political creation of the Nazis, without any pre-existing referent. It is a name whose meaning no one can share with the Nazis, a meaning that presumes the simulacrum and fidelity to the simulacrum" (*E* 75). Without overstressing any analogy between Nazism and "9/11," *The Zero* amplifies the construction of a Muslim set, which originates in both cases from the fidelity to a simulacrum event.[31] In this vein, Brian becomes an evil obscure subject in depriving Muslims of their political status and turning them into *homines sacri*.

One example of this exhibition of individual sovereignty manifests itself when Brian, in attempting to obtain more intelligence on the sleeper cell, anonymously threatens the Muslim shopkeeper Mahoud. In one of the novel's blanks, he sends him a note that says "Go home, camel-fucker. We know where you live" (*TZ* 111). The note's distinction between home and his place of living neatly exemplifies the process of turning Mahoud into "bare life." For Mahoud, whose "son is in the American army" (*TZ* 111), is here deprived of his status as a citizen of the United States. In being stripped of his national status, Mahoud undergoes a process of "denaturalization and denational-ization" (Agamben 1998: 132) in which he is told to go back home, to his *oikos*, which Agamben shows used to be the residence of "bare life" (*zoē*) (ibid.:

2). Through an essentialist dislocation, Mahoud loses his American citizenship and with it a loss of rights, while Brian is able to legitimate his dubious deeds. Brian's sovereignty, which is only guaranteed by excluding Mahoud from political life, becomes even more emblematic, for next to the note the envelope contains a pig's ear. In addition to the obvious reference to Muslim stereotyping, against which Mahoud protests, "I am Pakistani not Arab!" (*TZ* 112), the pig's ear underscores the process of political metamorphosis. In alluding to the semantical and sociological ambivalence of sacredness,[32] simultaneously implying absolute sacrality and ultimate taboo, the pig's ear marks this ambivalence, hovering in a "no-man's-land between the impure and the sacred" (Smith in Agamben 1998: 76). It therefore constitutes a material artifact that not only confronts Mahoud with cultural homogenization but also serves as a metaphor for Brian's sovereign constitution of a *homo sacer*. Within the state of exception that 9/11 seems to entail, people such as Mahoud are turned into "bare life," which legitimizes their harassment without consequences, since the figure of the *homo sacer* is according to Roman law "the one whom the people have judged on account of a crime. It is not permitted to sacrifice this man, yet he who kills him will not be condemned for homicide" (Festus qtd. in Agamben 1998: 71). Only within the state of exception can it thus be legitimized to turn people into sacred beings that may be killed without penal ramifications. Brian assumes this lethal sovereign position and transforms the merely biopolitical dimension directed at Mahoud into thanatopolitical measures.

Whereas the blackmailing of Mahoud remains, at least in the beginning, rather harmless, Brian and Markham also hunt down other ostensible members of the cell with more severity. At the end of Chapter 1, Brian and Markham take a trip to a vessel in "International waters" (*TZ* 131) to meet the incarcerated Assan, an ex-boyfriend of March's. Upon arriving at the cell in which Assan is kept captive,

Remy gasped.

There, on the bar, a man was perched like a trophy, hanging forward, his arms tied behind his back and slung on the bar so that it held him by the armpits, his feet against the wall dangling a few inches from the floor. The man was wearing nothing but a pair of tight red briefs and one white sock. It was cold and clammy in the room and his thick chest hair was wet and matted. A bucket of water sat below his feet. His shoulders and clavicles rose to points well above his head, which hung limply, bushy black hair dripping wet. (*TZ* 133)

The passage obviously echoes the United States' political crimes, especially as manifested in the heterotopic locales of Guantanamo or Abu Ghraib. Here the constitution of a *homo sacer* manifests itself even more expressively. In taking the state of exception on a literal basis, they *take* Assan *outside* ("*ex-capere*" [Agamben 1998: 18]) of national jurisdiction. While navigating in a deterritorialized space that is exterior to the American nation, the inclusive exclusion of this sovereign act is, however, hinted at with the place of his incarceration. Assan's confinement on a ship, which metaphorically evokes the American nation, returns this extra-national act of sovereignty to its constitutive basis[33]: the nation's sovereignty is guaranteed by declaring a state of exception and its concomitant creation of "bare life."

This "bare life" comes to the fore through the scene's vivid imagery. Not only is the power relation between the incarcerated Assan and his abductors manifested through his comparison to an object of competition. His naked body that bears the marks of torture, his Christ-like position, and the insistence on his animalistic pelage clearly indicate a very literal notion of life returned to its basic form.

What is more, the passage also conveys Remy's ethical position in-between. Remy, who continuously strives to be the good cop by resisting both the cruelties that bad cop Markham practices as well as his own undepicted deeds, is here depicted in a remarkably ambivalent manner, which represents his status as an evil obscure subject. The juxtaposition of Remy gasping with the following description of the torture scene conflates his apparent expression of incredulity and terror with a rather neutral and objective rendition. Through the use of a simile that compares the maltreated subject with a "trophy," or the list-like asyndeton that describes "his arms" and "his feet" as well as his present apparel, the vivid *histoire* of this scene is presented in a detached language, merely presenting it in a mimetic fashion. Despite the lucid content of the passage, its presentation seems marked by a constative and almost value-free tone. Although it could be ascribed to a heterodiegetic narrator, the discursive placement of the scene immediately after the narrative depicted Remy in a position of phenomenological reception rather indicates free indirect discourse. With Remy as the focalizing agent, the clash of his perceptible rejection with the imperceptible neutrality with which he apprehends the scene shows the dubious nature of his pretension to ethical integrity. Indeed, this narratological stratagem is revealing for Brian Remy as a coherent evil subject. Despite the discursive attempts of the text to neatly differentiate between a presented, textualized Brian Remy and his "blank" ethically corrupted alternate identity, this passage adamantly makes clear how these two identities cannot be sequestered as part of the deconstruction of a unified concept of the self. The novel thus shows that the separation between the Brian who writes his other half a note saying "Don't Hurt Anyone" is, in fact, the same person who responds: "Grow up" (*TZ* 90).

Remy's entanglement within this problematic mode of fidelity becomes equally apparent when the captive, Assan, inquires: "Are you some kind of police?" to which Markham responds: "No. We're no kind of police. . . . I'm a lawyer. . . . He's a lawyer. The guys you were playin' with before? Lawyers. Captain of the ship is a lawyer. Hell, everyone in America is a lawyer, Assan" (*TZ* 134–35). The transformation from police to politics indicates, once more, the relation between sovereignty and *homo sacer* and points to the interconnection of law and violence: "The sovereign is the point of indistinction between violence and law, the threshold on which violence passes over into law and law passes over into violence" (Agamben 1998: 32). Legitimized through the state of exception, the novel suggests that American citizens are endowed with a new juridical function, which very much resembles Foucault's notion of a society of control. However, the symmetric dispersal of power over a nation's subject here relies on the state of exception and its simultaneous creation of *homines sacri*. American citizens as lawyers thereby assume "the legal power to suspend the validity of the law, [which] legally places [them] outside of the law" (ibid.: 15). As sovereign lawyers, Brian and Markham stand concomitantly inside and outside of the law. By adhering to the principle of the state of exception, the ostensible event of "9/11," they suspend the law and ascertain their power. In the context of modern biopolitics, where sovereignty has passed "into a more ambiguous terrain in which the physician and the sovereign seem to exchange roles" (ibid.: 143), *The Zero* exemplifies how the adherence to an ostensible "truth" leads to a form of democratic totalitarianism.

Since Brian has already entered a process of fidelity at the beginning of the novel, he cannot extricate himself from the simulacrum event's operations. This is amplified by Brian's reaction to Assan's torture. Although Markham is the enunciator as well as the executor of the new form of law, Brian simply watches as if paralyzed: "Remy felt the boat lurch and then fall back. His mouth tasted like salt and bile. He tried to say something, but there was nothing" (*TZ* 135). At the mercy of the boat's motions, which metonymically represents the American nation, Brian feels repulsed, which attests to his inability to act. While his futile attempt at protest again harks back to the matter of taboos, it is here even more pronounced how his linguistic inability is turned into an ontological one. Not only is there nothing to say; there virtually is nothing, which describes his ethical determination when faced with a lack of alternatives.

The doubleness of his ethical demeanor is also underlined when he attempts to help Assan and tries to get him off the ship. During their escape from the place of torture, however, Assan delivers important information on the whereabouts of another member of the ostensible cell, after which the rescue boat returns him to "the ship they had just left" (*TZ* 139). Remy's ulterior intentions are once more unmasked in their questionable nature: "Remy rubbed his eyes. He would have liked to be more surprised. He watched as Assan was pulled up, banging against the ship, and then finally slipped over its side onto the deck like a huge fish" (*TZ* 140). While he formerly struggled more aggressively against the crimes literally conducted in his name, Brian now submits: "He leaned back, closed his eyes and listened to the waves lapping against the side of the boat, and even though he wished as hard as he could, for once, time was still" (*TZ* 140). This moment of epiphanic realization is accentuated by the exceptionality of his wish fulfillment. Being marked by discrepancy ("even though"), the idiosyncratic phrasing of his "wish[ing] as hard as he could" for temporal paralysis is granted unexpectedly as it supplants his former wish for action. Only when he craves a standstill, a lack of agency, does his wish come true. In Brian adopting the motions of the boat, the end of Part 1 marks the apex of his acceptance that resistance is impossible: "He had convinced himself that that [*sic*!] if he just abandoned himself to this skidding, lurching life, without questioning it, things would turn out okay. Once you started down a road, what good did it do to question the road?" (*TZ* 180–81). Although a subject may choose how to respond to an event, there is no question of responding or not. Once Brian has entered a process of fidelity, the novel illustrates the irreversibility of that course.

Paralysis and determination thus define Remy in his epistemological quest for truth. Not only is this truth found in the narrative thread of locating the terrorist cell via the location of March Selios. As should have become clear, the Oedipal adventure also interrogates the signs of Brian's self/selves. In the vein of novels such as Pynchon's *The Crying of Lot 49*, Auster's *New York Trilogy*, or Michael Chabon's *The Yiddish Policemen's Union*, *The Zero*'s "quest for meaning and truth" (Däwes 2011: 359) also stresses the ontological aspects of such a search.[34] Still, unlike the determined characters in other detective novels, Brian's limitation, to stress it once again, springs from his fidelity to "9/11." In contrast to other texts that also play with the instability of a coherent self, arguing for the simultaneity of different, often mutually exclusive identities, such as Ellis's *American Psycho*, Kathy Acker's *Empire of the Senseless*, or Palahniuk's *Fight Club*, *The Zero* interlinks the creation of a supplementary identity with the manifestation of an obscure subject. Yet, the novel does not merely distinguish itself from other novels that engage in the subversion of fixed identities by grounding the creation of a supplementary identity in an event, although a simulated one. *The Zero* further bases its argument for subjective determination and lack of (re)agency not in the fluctuation of performative roles but in the specific misguided fidelity of a character and the consequent responsibilities that it has to assume toward its actions.

By the same token, one might also read the hermeneutic analogy of both Brian and the reader attempting to fill the ellipses between narrative segments as an ontological statement on Brian's identity. Both are attempting to connect the presented with the unpresented. In reading Brian as an obscure subject, one might thus negate the novel's discursive representation as insinuating the dissociation of two separate identities. Instead of explaining his identitarian dispersal as a pathological, yet rationalizable, state, (Brian's psychiatrist thus observes: "Hallucinatory images. . . . What you're describing is textbook PTSD. Visions. Stress-induced delusions. Dissociative episodes" [*TZ* 194]); reading him as a subject faithful to a simulacrum offers important insights into his ethical responsibilities. The novel's narrative representation, not textualizing one part of Brian committed to evil, while the other tries in vain to resist such motivations, should prevent us from falling prey to the pitfall of ethical relativism latent in a notion of unfixed identities. The ascription of ethically problematic actions to an unrepresentable other identity is in this respect no different in its oppositional thinking than a geopolitical axis of evil. In this context, Remy asks his Muslim informant Jaguar whether he was working for them. He retorts:

> "Us?" He [Jaguar] laughed. "I'm sorry, but your idea of us tends to be a little bit fluid, my friend. *Either you're with us or . . . what?* You switch sides indiscriminately . . . arm your enemies and wonder why you get shot with your own guns. I'm sorry, but history doesn't break into your little four-year election cycles. *Are you with us?*" (*TZ* 291)

The fluidity that Jaguar addresses not only pertains to the construction of an evil alterity in political processes but also reflects Brian's oppositional thinking in terms of his own identity. After first insisting vehemently on the distinction between himself and evil Brian through his attempts "to do the right things, to make something out of this mess" (*TZ* 212), he has to concede not only evil Brian's determining reign over him but ultimately that they are part of the same obscure subject.

Brian's attempts "to open his good eye" makes him realize that "it was bandaged shut along with the bad one" (*TZ* 264). Brian's lapses of memory function not as an unrepresented and unrepresentable alter ego, which proves to determine the "present," textualized and readable Brian. Rather, it shows that the novel's narrative dissociation between a "good" Brian and an evil one are part of the same obscure subject whose assemblage, however, requires readerly connection. This is not to argue for a metaphysical, coherent subject. The only coherence that this argument insists on is a post-evental obscure subjectivity. Brian only achieves an obscure identity in the first place when confronted with the pseudo-event. In this vein, *The Zero*'s textual blanks articulate Badiou's concept of the obscure subject by giving it a particular formal articulation. By integrating narrative gaps, the novel could be seen as formally adopting the philosophical concept of such an evil subject, showing a specifically literary take on this idea by letting the text be interrupted by literally "obscure" passages, that is, segments that fail to be seen clearly. Through this, the novel also reflects on the effects of the happening on Brian's eyes/Is in a similar manner as *The Road* and *Against the Day* evoke a semantics of light and darkness in their mediation of events and the consequences they have on their subjects, while *The Zero* renders this in a distinctly formal manner.

Whereas the novel inquires into the opposition between American and Muslims and locates evil in a realm in-between, with neither of the poles being totally innocent, that Derrida points to, a more crucial emphasis lies in the precise, anti-deconstructive ascription of evil to a form of subjective faithfulness. It emphasizes Badiou's endeavor to arrive at a notion of Evil that is defined neither in solely negative terms, as an absence of the good, nor as a "consensual self-evidence" (*E* 58). Rather than insisting on the omnipresence of evil in the world, the novel pursues a cogent understanding of evil as a particular form of fidelity. Just as Eshelman attests for Badiou's *Ethics*, *The Zero* thus "stresses unified truth, goodness, agency, and consistency rather than victimization and the absolutizing of evil" (2011: n.p.). However, even though the novel shares the critique of victimization and radical evil, it does so without commencing at "the starting point of the Good" (*E* 60). It is crucial to note that for Badiou, the Good is primary: "Without consideration of the Good, and thus of truths, there remains only the cruel innocence of life, which is beneath Good *and beneath Evil*" (*E* 60). This does not mean that there exists a metaphysical and universal concept of "the Good" but that any "Good" has to be viewed as situation-specific and always in the light of the manifestation of an event. This implies that there has to be a potentiality of Goodness in the first place, that is, the manifestation of "9/11" as a genuine event, which carries within itself an "ethical consistency" (*E* 48), producing faithful subjects. While "9/11" is thus undermined in its potential to create a faithful subject of the event in the context of Walter's novel, the next three chapters inquire into more "positive" subjective procedures. The following analyses investigate amorous, artistic, scientific, and political subjective processes that keep faith in the events that occur and thereby acquire reagency.

"Let us go then, you and I"

The Amorous Subject in Mark Z. Danielewski's
Only Revolutions (2006)

*"Tell a girl: 'I love you.' No trouble with
two-thirds of that, it's a closed circuit.
Just you and she. But that nasty four-letter
word in the middle, that's the one you have
to look out for. Ambiguity. Redundance.
Irrelevance, even. Leakage. All this is noise . . ."*

Thomas Pynchon, "Entropy."

—We're without agency . . .

Mark Z. Danielewski, *Only Revolutions*.

While the previous chapters inquired into how the theory of the subject of the event may occasion unsuccessful subjective procedures—when a subject fails to enter into a process of positive fidelity (reactivity) or a mere happening is confused for an event (obscurity)—the last three chapters of this study explore the scope of properly faithful relations between individuals and their experience of genuine events, which endows them with reagency. If the events (or their simulation) were present from the very beginning in the previous two novels and affected their entire diegetic world, the following three chapters, at times, require more of the detective work that was intimated in the introduction to this book. Like in a crime novel, the analysis of events in these texts calls for an in-depth investigation of that which the texts themselves seek to exclude. Through its formal and diegetic construction of particular situations, a novel may posit a given order that negates the eruption of an event. By undermining linearity, or conjuring an encyclopedic narrative that aspires to include everything, a work of fiction may seek to construct a textual order that undermines the contingent and revolutionary manifestation of an event and therefore reject the creation of a subject. However, the ephemeral and seemingly trivial occurrence of two individuals meeting and falling in love may precisely undermine this entire logic and create an emphatic event.

Yet another reason for this microscopic search for events lies in the fact that *Only Revolutions*, *Slumberland*, and *Against the Day* all juxtapose a multitude of other happenings that might fit the generic understanding of "event" and therefore reflect on the epistemologically overwhelming input of having to decide among a variety of competing events. Whereas *Slumberland* and *Against the Day*, therefore, explore the scope of the possibility of political events that are interrelated with other truth procedures (aesthetic and scientific, respectively), Mark Z. Danielewski's *Only Revolutions* stays within the parameters of what Badiou calls the truth procedure that comes to unravel when two individuals fall in love.

To be sure, by connecting the construction of a subject of the event to the condition of love, one attracts mockery, particularly because love has become increasingly undermined as a conservative bourgeois myth within the twentieth century (and even before that). Just as the alienating processes in T. S. Eliot's *The Lovesong of J. Alfred Prufrock* have fundamentally negative implications for the relationship between the lyrical "I" and the absent "you" that serves as the title of this chapter, so does Saul from Pynchon's early short story "Entropy" intimate the ultimate "ambiguity" (2000: 90) of love as an authentic experience between two individuals. I argue in this chapter that *Only Revolutions* is not only aware of this tradition of conferring love a status of "irrelevance" (ibid.: 90), as Saul puts it, but that it also tries to construct an ethical and aesthetic counterpoint to these arguments by evoking an amorous subject of the event that is granted reagency. In essence, Eliot's, Pynchon's and Danielewski's reflections on love all share an occupation with the relation between the "I" and the "you." However, only Danielewski's novel implicates an evental disruption that offers a movement beyond these individualistic paradigms.

By substituting the primacy of the "I" and its relation to a "you" with a capitalized "US," *Only Revolutions* goes beyond the first-person and second-person singular and fashions a first-person plural subject of the event. Yet, while the fact that the novel is a story about love has been noted by a variety of critics, none has inquired into how this might be related to a process of two individuals becoming an amorous subject of the event.[1] This is particularly due to the novel's idiosyncratic presentation, which apparently results in what Mark B. Hansen sees as the novel's "evacuation of any character content or individuality" (2011: 190). In contrast to the often all-too-quick degradation of such formally virtuous works of fiction as having no political or ethical import, this chapter shows that the novel's form is part and parcel of the creation of a subject of the event.[2] Indeed, the novel mediates upon the rejection of mere self-absorbed textual play as solipsistic consequences of a pathological narcissism by making this an integral part of the process of how an amorous subject of the event is being created. In other words, I argue that while the novel starts out as conjuring a seemingly self-contained system that centers on one and only one individual, this textual solipsism is interrupted by the manifestation of a narrative event. The immersion in what I read in reference to Lacan's mirror stage, which is given a particular form in the novel, is disrupted by Badiou's notion of an event. If Lacan perceives the relation between the sexes impossible, reading the novel under the lens of Badiou shows how this impossibility is employed for the construction of a subject of the event. This event, marked by the encounter between the two homodiegetic narrators Sam and Hailey, initiates a processual truth procedure that abandons their respective solipsisms and progressively constructs a subject of love. However, before it can be inferred how this event's representation initiates a "*new* way of being" (*E* 41), it first needs to be analyzed in terms of how far the initial situations of the two narrators both diegetically and formally attempt to suppress the possibility of such an event. While the novel employs various structural and typographical notions of circularity that undermine movements of change, since they conflate any distinction between a before and an after, reading the novel as formulating an event that initiates a process of subjective constitution injects a specific form of temporality and makes possible a revolution. In first showing how the novel stresses circularity both in form and in content, I argue that these narcissistic and apparently hermetic worlds cannot construct a world on the foundation of an "other."[3] With the novel's heightened emphasis on narrative, formal, and linguistic ideas of solipsism, this proves to be the condition for an event to occur, which cannot be precisely anticipated from the respective limited perspectives of the narrators and consequently disrupts their worlds, moving them beyond the narcissistic reveries of the Lacanian mirror stage. Instead of trying to psychologize Hailey and Sam, I show how the novel's form literally mirrors such a subjective pathology and how through the narrative's singular event an empowered eventual subject emerges that substitutes the self-centered, narcissistic, aggressive characters and form at the beginning of the novel. Essentially, *Only Revolutions* stages the development from two unabashedly solipsist individuals into a subject that keeps faith to an event, through which they transcend their limited subjectivity at the beginning of the novel.

Yet, this empowerment is not a form of autonomous agency, grounded in the self-willed capability of a humanist subject. Sam's and Hailey's capability for reagency is contingent upon the manifestation of an event. My reading of the novel thus opposes Hayles's argument of a regression of their power: "Both protagonists start out at their respective beginnings perceiving themselves as supernaturally empowered and in charge; then, as they open themselves to the other, they begin to experience vulnerability as their growing love for the other gives a hostage to fortune" (2011: 174). In contrast, this chapter intimates that only by being faithful to the event of their encounter do they acquire reagency. This form of empowerment is specifically dependent on the loosening of a solipsistic form of domination and power that concomitantly admits vulnerability as part of participation in an infinite subjective procedure, which therefore goes beyond the finite constraints of a subject that Badiou insists upon.

Finally, *Only Revolutions* is a specifically noteworthy instance within the theory of the subject of the event, since, unlike the two previous novels discuss, it shows that an event does not have to be a cataclysmic form of destruction. "Starting out from something that is simply an encounter, a trifle," writes Badiou, "you learn that you can experience the world on the basis of difference and not only in terms of identity" (*IpoL* 16). The "quite banal fact" (*IpoL* 41) of the amorous encounter might not seem as singular as the collapse of a national emblem, the invention of a new scientific world view, the creation of a work of art, or the apocalyptic catastrophe that wipes out humanity; nevertheless, it is even more pertinent for creations of subjects within an everyday context of life, since "love is the truth procedure that, as compared with art, science or politics, although not necessarily the most common, is the most often proposed" (*C* 181). Particularly because of this typicality, I want to suggest that *Only Revolutions* could, indeed, be regarded as the most typical love story of world literature.[4]

Turning and turning in the widening gyre

Upon a first look, Mark Z. Danielewski's *Only Revolutions* seems to draw extensively on postmodernist themes and practices by playing with form, which, crucially, undermines notions of linearity and change. The novel's disregard of the conventional notions of form is foremost evoked by its parallel structure, with the two autodiegetic narrators Sam and Hailey recounting their stories from the two ends of the book, meeting in the exact middle on pages 180/181, only to distance themselves from each other once more.[5] Moreover, the text's penchant for circular themes and forms might be traced in its accentuation of the letters O and numbers 0 in green and gold, respectively, in Sam's and Hailey's narratives, or in each page's total of 360 words (180 in the chronomosaic[6] in the center of each double page and 180 in Sam's and Hailey's narratives). The publisher's suggestion to alternate "between Sam & Hailey, reading eight pages at a time," as the dust jacket informs the reader, evokes the topos of circularity even on a level of reception, since one literally has to turn the book around in a semi-circle in rhythmical intervals. Such obvious play with form has led critics to stress the novel's postmodern character: for example, Dirk van Hulle claims that Danielewski's book is "a case of neo-experimental récupération," (2011: 137) because of its formal idiosyncrasies that, in Hansen's words, are "pseudo-Oulipean" (2011: 190). According to Philip Leonard, the novel purports a "Möbius band-like non-linearity" (2010: 46).[7] It quickly becomes obvious to what extent the novel's visual representation and seemingly inexhaustible aestheticization of recurring markers of circularity are part and parcel of a specific agenda of rejecting what proves essential for processes of evental subject formation. The novel's structure is literally anti-narrative, in the sense that it avoids a clear progression and relation between two incidents, since the application of causal relations is undermined by deconstructing any form of teleology. This seems to problematize the very idea of the subject of the event that requires the differentiation between a before and an after.

Only Revolutions's amplification of circular, atemporal motives is also palpable on a level of content. At the beginning of both narratives, the stress on continuities and flux is expressed through the initial declaration on Hailey's side: "Samsara! Samarra!" (H1). Mentioning Samara, the Buddhist and Hinduist implication in a continuity of metempsychotic wanderings, at the very beginning of the narrative sets the scene for a particular worldview. In thematically translating the formal emphasis on circularity, this holism crucially questions the notion of pure and singular new beginnings. In other words, in the very first word of the novel, Hailey immediately undermines the very concept of a beginning. This is also conveyed by "Samarra," a first paronomasia that conjoins an Iraqi city—intertextually referring to Somerset Maugham's coining of "having an appointment in Samarra" that indicates the inevitability of death—with the spiraling motion of a samara, which self-referentially points to the reader's activity of reading the novel. Not only do these references again employ tropes of circularity and physical revolution in their semantic content, but they also suggest the fusion of these terms in the homonymic duplicity of the word and thereby metapoetically reflect upon the double-structure of the novel itself. Additionally, the chronomosaic on Hailey's part of the novel begins without beginning: "—to screaming./—he's gone." (H1). Like the commencement of Hailey's narrative, the chronomosaic refuses to position a beginning, or even a concrete enunciator, to most of its items, starting in mid-sentence and creating a tapestry of communicative threads. In the historical context of November 22, 1963, it becomes clear that the third-person singular refers to President Kennedy, whose assassination is euphemistically alluded to. By juxtaposing two antagonistic experiences of time on the very first page of the novel (birth-death), the beginning of Hailey's narrative abounds with such themes that seek to undermine the disposition of a linear movement and, rather, stresses circular revolutions.

This is also evident in Sam's beginning. Sam, who commences his story with the symbolic ejaculation "Haloes! Haleskarth!" (S1) similarly attempts to fuse beginnings and ends, death and life. Not only is the book's circular motif again implied in the first word, but the manner of its enunciation also reverberates with religious ideas of negating death. By referring to an act of canonization, Sam undermines the finality of death and refers to a religious form of resurrection in his first word, his expressive quality conveying a form of ritualistic performance. The "halo" therefore intimates a geometrical figure of circularity that mirrors the book's structure while simultaneously evoking the semantic layer of sanctity that characterizes the narrator in specific ways, as will be elaborated in the following paragraphs. Yet, Sam's mentioning of "Haleskarth!" (S1) is equally telling. Tellingly, "haleskarth" is an extinct word that means to be "free from injury" (*OED* 2010: 30). Once more, the novel's very first line coalesces antagonistic forms of temporality, here manifested in a word that doubles this oxymoronic fusion by, on the one hand, offering a compound of two incompatible integrities and, on the other, playing with the word's ejection from pragmatic usage and its meaning to oppose any kind of decay.

The novel's incessant reflection on death and the almost obstinate rejection thereof is furthermore highlighted in the repeated phrase "I can walk away from anything" (S1/H1). In contrast to the chronomosaic's continual reference to death, as in "Calcutta cyclone/ 20,300 go" (S2), Sam and Hailey proclaim themselves to be exempt from this human limitation. Whereas the historical column paints the casualties in a euphemistic language and at the same time reevaluates the utter teleology of death in a vocabulary of casual movement, Sam's and Hailey's ability to escape anything, particularly death, characterizes them as being more than human. Tied to this rejection of finality and the celebration of flux is also, as Pöhlmann has pointed out, the novel's language, particularly its temporal inflection. Both Sam's and Hailey's narratives as well as the chronomosaic are expressed in the present tense. In this respect, Pöhlmann argues that "the present tense emphasizes . . . potential: nothing is settled, nothing is determined, everything is possible, and yet everything is always happening in the present moment (not 'always will happen again' or 'has already happened')" (2009: 68). While this temporal presence chooses potential over necessity, I would argue that it is also symptomatic of two solipsistic individuals who try to be blind to the progression of time. The two "near-demiurges," as Hayles calls them (2011: 172), who claim to be "allways sixteen" (S|H167) and even claim that they "are the time" (H241), seek to fashion themselves as individuals who each stand above the "human" order of things. Indeed, while the book as a whole emphasizes notions of circularity, this seems to me to be inherently connected to the ways in which the narrator-protagonists characterize and perceive themselves. By employing linguistic, narrative, and formal tropes that reject any clear form of linearity, the novel not only constructs a holistic and immanent ontology outside of which nothing can be thought but also shows this to be linked to the psychological apparatus of Sam and Hailey as unabashed solipsists. Put differently, I contend that the novel's abundant play with circularity and revolutions is not merely a formal experimentation for its own sake but, rather, creates an intricate nexus between form and content. The revolutions that the novel's beginnings evoke, hence, not only intimate a thought-image for an immanent sphere that each Sam and Hailey resemble in their failure to acknowledge anything besides themselves but they also suggest a spatial constellation that reflects their subjective idea of order according to which everything only revolves around them.

Beyond the looking glass

Before the novel's amorous event and its consequential (subjective) aftermath can be analyzed, it is necessary to establish and demarcate what initial situation(s) are posited. The narrator-protagonists present themselves and are presented as narcissistic solipsists and accordingly fabricate a specific form of subjectivity and world-making through which a backdrop is created that seems to preclude the possibility of a stance outside of this paradigm. But since an event implies the overcoming of perceived impossibilities, *Only Revolutions*'s diegetic and formal aspirations to construct an immanent order that merely revolves around two individualist I's make the manifestation of an event even more disruptive. Hailey's and Sam's situations are, hence, being infringed upon by an event that opens up a world that goes beyond the mere contemplation of an individual order. If every event brings to the fore a being that was not perceived within the situation prior to its eruption, the "singular multiple" (*BE* 99) fixed by the "evental site" (*BE* 175), this is in *Only Revolutions*'s case the respective narrator on the other side of each page. While each page typographically includes the other, Sam initially does not properly discern Hailey, while Hailey fails to acknowledge Sam, despite the obvious "inclusion" of the other in their respective first words. The amorous event therefore shatters their various solipsistic orientations and makes them receptive to the presence of another being apart from themselves.

For Badiou, the process of love always "involves a separation or disjuncture based on the simple difference between two people and their infinite subjectivities" (*IpoL* 27). The basis for the possibility of an event to occur in the condition of love thus implies a fundamental moment of difference between two individuals, which could not find a more appropriate realization than in the novel's double structure. Through the quantitative discrepancy between Sam's narrative (S1) and Hailey's inversion (H360) and between Hailey's narrative (H1) and Sam's mirroring (S360), the novel typographically enacts the superiority of one narrative and the consequent marginalization of the other. Having the effect of a textual mirror refracting rather than reflecting also informs a reading of Hailey and Sam's self-fashioning that has severe limitations. As a visual resonance of psychoanalytic concepts, *Only Revolutions* absorbs the Lacanian notion of the mirror stage and its relation to narcissism, aggressivity, and love, in constituting its characters in a narcissistic way. Yet, instead of offering a psychoanalytical reading of the novel, I argue that these concepts elucidate how Hailey and Sam are constructed and how this undermines an autonomous and self-determined subject. Furthermore, the motivation to form an identity based on themselves is later superseded by a subject grounded on the evental eruption of a different alternative, a glance beyond the self-obsessed looking glass.

At the beginning of the novel, the two narrator-protagonists are represented as narcissistic individuals fostering aggressive acts of destruction and ultimately incapable of love for someone other than themselves. In this sense, *Only Revolutions* epitomizes Lacan's notion of subjectivity as situated in the mirror stage and thus opposed to "any philosophy directly issuing from the Cogito" (1977: 1). This is intimated most clearly by the visual representation of the novel, which literally mirrors each text in a "contrasting size (un relief de stature) that fixes it and in a symmetry that inverts it" (ibid.: 3).

Through its mere presentation, the novel not only gives this psychoanalytical concept a literary and literarily visual manifestation but also subscribes to Lacan's critique of the humanist subject as a self-contained autonomous foundation. The fiction of the subject as a rational identity is here intricately conveyed through the representation of both Sam and Hailey as "being born" on the text's first page and already inherently embedded in the realm of text. While the mirror stage for Lacan still emphasizes a specific visual disposition of the child seeing its own image, *Only Revolutions* translates this subjective stage in an entirely textual paradigm.

Sam's and Hailey's assertion that they are "allmighty sixteen" (H|S1) without further classification also places them within the formative stage between six and eighteen months (Lacan 1977: 2), in which subjective constitution takes place. Yet, as Dylan Evans is eager to point out, Lacan conceives the mirror stage as a more complex concept than being merely temporally limited to the formative stage of child development. Rather, "the mirror stage represents a fundamental aspect of the structure of subjectivity" that is formally "permanent" (Evans 1996: 115). Hailey's and Sam's continuous insistence on their agelessness attests to their incapacity to think outside of an epistemological framework that is not situated in the mirror stage. In other words, they cannot imagine a mode of being that would not be grounded on their own subjectivities, which atemporally fashions their narcissisms, thereby stipulating a specific modus that disallows the belonging of everything beyond their respective selves. What adds to this contextualization in the psychoanalytical framework of ego formation, moreover, is that Hailey and Sam have no history. Other than what the diegetic coordinates of their narratives provide, no information is given on their lives before their appearance on the mountain in the first pages of the novel. Hayles comments on this rootlessness when writing that "Sam and Hailey have no kin—no parents, siblings or extended family. To all appearances, they are *sui generis*" (2011: 169). In this sense, it is only when perceiving the self as other in the refracted text that they acquire a notion of their selves as existent in the first place.

According to Lacan, a child's notion of *je* is only constituted through the identification with the specular *moi* in the mirror, which resonates in the beginning of *Only Revolutions* in profound ways. Sam's I in the first pages of the novel hence depends on the distancing toward an alterity, conveyed in the second-person singular pronoun enunciated by Hailey. "By *you*," Hailey mourns on the mirrored other side of the page, "ever sixteen, this World's preserved./ By *you*, this World has everything left to lose" (H360, my emphasis). The "you" here functions as a mark of identification with oneself in the mirror that is at the same time not oneself. Hailey's mirrored, indeed, echoed "you" functions in this context as the *objet (petit) a*, "which isn't another at all, since it is essentially coupled with the ego, in a relationship which is always reflexive, interchangeable" (Lacan 1988: 321). Like the child who looks into the looking glass and grasps its identity by the identification with its image, Sam identifies with the textually mirrored you that also reflects his first-person singular.

The individualist quality of the existence that they embrace is, furthermore, transported in their use of language. The incessant creation of neologisms and the excessive play with words, as well as the instability of various objects of reference indicate to what extent their use of language is not intended for communication but rather for denomination and appropriation. As a latent critique of a normative notion of language, their "creative spellings, in which the words inscribed on the page differentially achieve enriched meaning through their relation with the 'correct' spellings" (Hayles 2011: 173) are irrespective of the essential social function of language. By approximating, yet not fully arriving at, a Wittgensteinian notion of a private language, their stance toward language is grounded in the mere self-obsessed game with oneself and does not serve as a pragmatic means of communicating with others.

The relation between the ego and its counterpart then brings forth modes of aggressivity. Lacan's notion of the infant perceiving its specular image as a whole and thereby realizing its own bodily lack, which results in aggressivity, is not triggered in the novel because the "wholeness of the image threatens the subject with fragmentation" (Evans 1996: 115). In fact, the novel modulates Lacan's mirror stage to the extent that the unity of the body that the child perceives in the mirror is absent, whereas the "motor unco-ordination of the neo-natal months" (1977: 4) is inverted by Sam's and Hailey's movements of walking, leaping, and jumping (H|S1). In contrast to the inception of aggressivity in the child who realizes that its real body is inferior to its specular image, in *Only Revolutions* Sam and Hailey showcase a bodily control that suggests their egos to be superior to their specular refractions.

The destructive drives of both Sam and Hailey, rather, seem to be engendered by the very absence of their bodies in the opposite narrative. At the end of the novel that mirrors the novel's first pages, the respective other narrator-protagonists find themselves in "Solitude" (S360). In the mirrored text that Sam's first page shares with Hailey's final page, Sam is absent, and vice versa. It is their death and their nonexistence in the refracted specular text that inspires the extreme "aggressivity it [the child] releases in any relation to the other" (Lacan 1977: 7). While the specular image of the other in Lacan's mirror stage is, nevertheless, connected with the self, *Only Revolutions*'s textual mirror does not contain the individual as other but merely as its residues as mediated by a radical alterity, what Lacan would call "the big Other" (Evans 1996: 116). The symbolic immersion of this Other being "both another subject, in his absolute alterity and unassimilable uniqueness, and also the symbolic order which mediates the relationship with that other object" (ibid.: 133) is expressed in the presence of the other narrator in the opposite text, who symbolically holds the dead remains of the other in a protective maternal gesture.[8]

Aggressivity, as executed through acts of aggression, is thus not caused by the threat of bodily "disintegration and fragmentation" (ibid.: 6) but because of a cognitive lack. Put differently, the novel rearticulates the workings of the mirror image in its formative function and pinpoints the source of aggressivity in the deficiency not of a bodily but of a cognitive, ontological capability. While Lacan conceptualizes the development of the ego and the concomitant structure of aggressivity as triggered by the infant's perception of its synthetic body in the mirror and the fragmentation of its real counterpart, *Only Revolutions* suggests that Sam's and Hailey's narcissism and aggressivity are evoked by their inability to conceive of a difference in identifying with someone other than their selves. Confronted with the lone other narrator at the end of their journeys, Sam and Hailey fall prey to *méconnaissance*, since they misunderstand the refracted image for themselves, which allows them to glimpse an understanding of themselves (*me-connaissance*); their subjective constitution that relies on an order *outside* of their internal egos is further heightened by the very absence of their own selves in the narrative future that is represented on the mirrored other side of the page. Being confronted with their upcoming deaths that become apparent at the literal other side of the novel makes them resort to modes of aggression to compensate for this apparent attack on their seeming subjective sovereignty.

A first manifestation thereof can be traced in their exclamation that "Everyone loves/ the Dream but I kill it" and in their wish to "devastate|destroy the World" (S|H1). In the novel's ambivalent capitalization of nouns, there is no clear interpretation of which dream they are referring to. Still, the relentless distancing from an imaginary good, be that national myth or individual fantasy, enacted by a pubescent demonstration of power, paints a clear picture of the restricted relation between their selves and others. One might even see their desire to destroy the prevalent concept of psychoanalytic discourse as a futile attempt to become autonomous in naively seeking to counteract the determinative grasp of the unconscious.

A key aspect that conveys their aggressive domination of other beings can be grasped in their anthropocentric relation to "nature." Like the father in *The Road*, they display a particular attitude toward their environment that is marked by taming and nominal domination. Tamarack Pines, for example, "sway scared" (H1) when faced with Hailey's self-described power, whereas "Almond Willows/ slope and smile [her] comfort:/ —You're beyond all that./ Tag Alders along with Grass: —Beyond every grasp" (H2). As perceived from the highly unreliable, since it is narcissistic, and thus haughty point of view of Hailey, all other organisms are represented as inferior to her reign.

Equally so, Sam observes: "Golden Bears bow at my knee:/ —Go ahead Lieutenant General./ Take it all./ American Beavers allso chitter/ scared. Bowing. Fawning too" (S1). Gestures of courtly demeanor and promotions to military functionaries indicate to what extent Sam adopts hierarchical structures of domination and exploitation in order to guarantee his own position. "My destruction," he boasts, "is/the ultimate Peace" (S6). In fashioning himself as the superior agent of a militaristic or aristocratic kind, he characterizes himself in specific ways that revolve around aggression.

Their entrapment in the typographic mirror stage as well as their aggressive tendencies interconnect with Hailey and Sam's narcissism, not exclusively in the Lacanian notion of its dialectic "erotic-aggressive character" (Evans 1996: 120), but in a more general sense of a solipsistic relation to the world. On a linguistic level, the narcissistic mode of being is conveyed through the profuse referencing of the first person-singular pronoun: "*I* can walk away," "*I* kill it," "*I* leap free," "*I*'ll destroy," "Why don't *I* have any shoes?" (H1, my emphases); "*I* can walk away," "*I* kill it," "*I* jump free," "*I*'ll devastate," "Why don't *I* have a hat?" (S1, my emphases). From a quantitative perspective, both narrators celebrate their own selves as the center of the universe.

On a topological level, the pivotal *place* of the I is, moreover, transported in spatial correspondences. Not only does Sam discursively (and pop-culturally) appropriate space: "This land is my land" (S2), he also denies the existence of anything beyond that specific territory: "I will sacrifice nothing./ For there are no countries./ Except me. And there is only/ one boundary. Me" (S3). Through Sam's encompassing inclusiveness, implying spatial borders only if they are connected to the *objet (petit) a*, he assumes a geographic space that resembles nationalist narratives that cannot conceive of anything beyond their territorial rims. Indeed, this topology offers a spatial imagery of how a particular situation fails to account for anything that lies beyond its epistemic order. In mimicking nationalist narratives, Sam's epistemic geography emphasizes the predominance of his own subjective territory, which undermines the sovereignty of other areas beyond that jurisdiction. He even denies the existence of other spaces beyond his egocentric boundary, which represents a cogent account of how a particular situation denies the existence of anything outside of its own episteme, especially events. Yet, particularly because Sam and Hailey cannot account for the existence of anything beyond their subjective perimeter, this offers a fertile soil upon which the contingent eruption of an event breeds, even though this alone is not enough of a reason for an event to occur.

The excessive and dominating nature that marks the relationship between the two narrators and their surroundings can thus be grasped in their attempts at naming everything under their subjective paradigm. By simply taxonomically enlisting a myriad of animals and plants without acknowledging these beings' own sovereign existence, Hailey and Sam enact a colonialist practice of cataloging their "natural" environment in order to inscribe their own subjectivity on their surroundings. Whereas the father in *The Road* perpetuates the anthropological dominant of controlling the environment, Hailey and Sam do enact their subjective dominance without relating this to an event.

While they are thus not a form of a reactive subject—they are, in fact, no subject at this point—it is noteworthy that they assume an individualistic dominating role of ordering their environment, which for Badiou is usually executed by a state apparatus, religion, or political ideology. To this extent, the novel seems to suggest that a specific individual manner of approaching the world can also foster problematic ramifications in respect of recognizing other forms of being.

The manner in which Hailey and Sam catalog their environments, however, follows a particular pattern. The insistent distinction between apparently female and male spheres of life, therefore, also stresses the incongruity between the two characters and their narratives, thereby pointing to the radical disjunction between "two presentative positions" (*C* 183). Following specific evolutionary stereotypes of gender roles, Hailey, the gatherer, is counting and thus collecting the botanical multiplicity from "Atlas Mountain Cedars," "Trembling Aspens," to "Tamarack Pines" (H1), over "Mistletoes," "Shepherd's Purse," (H319) or, finally, "Silver Birch" (H320). Likewise, hunter Sam makes lists of a zoological variety that explodes a specific geographical localization, ranging from American "Bald eagles," "Golden Bears," to "American Beavers" (S1) over "even Siberian Tigers/ . . . , Giraffes, Gibbons and African/ Elephants" (S51). Remarkably, the biological differentiation between flora and fauna is stable and until the end does not permit categorical transgressions.

This embeddedness in a specific form of subjectivity that is founded on narcissism and excludes anything beyond this particular situation entraps the two narrators in a merely self-absorbed structure that denies the existence of beings that are not themselves, or related to their modes of perception. More importantly, however, narcissism as a key aspect of the formation of the ego harbors problems for the autonomy of subjects. Anastasios Gaitanidis observes that already Freud's

> discovery that the ego is formed through the dynamics of narcissism renders the autonomy of the ego in relation to the id problematic, forcing subsequent psychoanalytic theorists to demand either the (absolute or relative) restoration or the complete abolition of this autonomy. (2007: 13)

Gaitanidis goes on to show how Lacan's notion of narcissism, particularly in his concept of the mirror stage, followed the latter option, refusing "to see [the ego] as an autonomous agent that has its own independent origins and sources of energy and can thus produce objective knowledge of itself and outside reality" (ibid.: 21).

The novel makes a similar case in delineating the limitations of the narcissist protagonists. Both of their pretensions to autonomous empowerment, be it through the act of collecting, naming, and classifying apparently inferior species in a gesture that recalls an Enlightenment spirit, or through the various destructive threats of annihilation, ultimately cannot guarantee them the status of sovereign subjects. Despite their desire to safeguard and constitute their power and liberty, "allmighty" and "free" (S1) become empty adjectives describing two individuals that remain within the constraints of oppressive and alienating structures. Such restrictions manifest themselves early in the novel, thereby coinciding with and compromising the two characters' vainglorious outbursts. Sam, quixotically sitting on a pony, soon finds his means of transportation entrapped by a "CRONE" (S5) who with a lasso inhibits his movements:

> —Free him now, I brash.
> Ready to burn HER, turn HER,
> blow HER to ash.
> But allso amused.
> I calmly approach.
> SHE tightens the ropes
> until Horse groans.
> Then abruptly
> both are gone.
> A long tear quits me, tumbles by
> my strife and on the dry paths
> lashes my earth with life. (S5)

The narrative here implements a character that complicates Sam's omnipotence and deprives him of his ability to progress. Given the magical allusions of this episode as well as the placement of the crone at the beginning of Sam's trip, one might read this passage as inciting a particular literary form. With regard to Vladimir Propp's morphology of the fairy tale, the crone's actantial function to foment and endow Sam with the necessary tools for starting his adventure is thus doubly negated.[9] Not only is Sam's self-sufficient autonomy called into question through the mere fact of his having to rely on a different person to begin his adventure, but the magical helper also denies him his advance. The crone, indeed, leaves him stuck within the bounds of over-determined paralysis. In undermining a structuralist categorization of literary artifacts, the novel shows how Sam fails to overcome the structural boundaries that the text sets up, which could also be read in relation to Jurij Lotman's notion of events being topological transgressions. If an event for Lotman implies the breach of a semantic order (1977: 238), *Only Revolutions* leaves Sam remaining stuck within his own epistemic terrain and thereby confounds this particular theory of events. In criticizing this narratological notion of events, Sam is bound for deceleration until he comes to a standstill. He is "calmly approaching" and "tumbling," which contrasts with his initial movements of jumping, rebounding (S1), and spinning (S5), the kinetic energetic level having almost hit rock bottom. Just six pages into the novel, Sam hence remarks "that's the end" (S6) and accepts that he by himself is not able to initiate a course of happenings (or even events) that would secure and construct any freedom of action. As a kind of last resort, Sam decides to enact his destructive abilities. He "elect[s] to kiss/the World way" (S6). For him, it, indeed, wouldn't "take much./ That's it. Pitiliess. Kneel. Kiss Had,/ Horse, Mountain & All./ A byebye. By this" (S6).

However, just before fulfilling the lethal kiss of death, transforming a bodily gesture of empathy into an egotistic *coup de grace*, he is stopped by Hailey's first occurrence in his world.

While Sam is contained by narratological, or structural, limitations, Hailey falls prey to bodily oppression, becoming the victim of sexual violence. Right after the exhibition of her megalomaniac abilities, Hailey meets "a MOUSTACHED/TOOTHER" with whom she soon finds herself intimately engaged: "Wanna get down?" she is being asked. And soon enough she "just lie[s] down and let[s] HIM./ And when HE goes [she] go[es] too./ A round tear slips past, slides/from [her] life" (H5).

Despite Hailey's verbal resistance, she gives in to the rural boy's seduction and engages sexually with him. Remarkably, Hailey again employs the euphemism of "going" that here describes the moment of the farmer boy's ejaculation but simultaneously refers to the imminent connotation of death that is also applied in the chronomosaic. While on the first page she still insisted upon her invincibility, being able "to walk away from anything" (H1), she here has to concede her mortality after all. It becomes obvious that regardless of her apparent consent to this sexual encounter, she is severely traumatized by this act of physiological violence. Merely a couple of lines after having arrogantly declared that she is "the World which/ The Mountain descends from/ and [she] laugh[s] because it tickles" (H4), Hailey has to acknowledge her utter lack of power. In fact, her way of mediating the sexual encounter can be read as obscuring her utter helplessness. Not only is the change from dialogue to an interior point of perception and the concomitant shift from a direct to a more indirect mediation of the diegetic happenings telling for her narrative intervention as a means of securing her apparent power, but the anaphoric repetition of her consensual interaction and the boy's climax also convey the impression of hesitant insecurity, as she relapses to linguistic repetitions when at a loss of words.

In line with her protective impulses, Hailey's response to her lack of power is even more pronounced than Sam's episode of impotence, even though they reach the same conclusion of seeking retaliation. "O what dour, repugnant thing/just rolled over" her, she reflects (H6).

> So easily misused?
> Flowers from my curls so rudely
> removed? Time to just
> waste this fucker.
> No worries.
> —But what about Generosity?
> Clover & Snowberries shummy.
> My obliteration is
> the ultimate Gift.
> Over with a snap. A slap.
> —But there's so much more to meet,
> whine twines of Matrimony Vine.
> I don't give a shit. I'll nevernomore
> the World with a smooch.
> Blissfully too. Torridly cruel.
> Tiptoe and kiss The Mountain,

Trees, RudeRoot & All
byebye. Hot. (H6)

While briefly exhibiting incredulity because of the deprivation of her virginity, Hailey instantaneously craves revenge, which not even the botanical pleas for altruism may forestall and she prepares for total annihilation. On the brink of her "EndAll/ Smacker," however, Sam, "an imbecile," appears with his "Green Eyes with flecks of Gold" (H7), the inversion of Hailey's "Gold Eyes with flecks of Green" (H7), which marks a genuine event and substantially shatters their respective solipsist worldviews.

I have shown to what extent both narratives are similar in their characterizations that concentrate on their protagonists' respective "infinite subjectivities" (*IpoL* 27). Yet, situating them within psychoanalytic mechanisms, which casts doubts about their capacity for reagency, is only an initial state. Unlike Lacan's insistence that "the only reality that needs to be acknowledged . . . is that what motivates us to embark on this journey from insufficiency to anticipation—that is, our desire to deny our fragmentation and recover a sense of wholeness—can never be found" (Gaitanindis 2007: 22), the novel embarks on a different project. *Only Revolutions* orchestrates a process that abandons this structure of passivity and determinism. Through the novel's visual and diegetic juxtaposition of "two different interpretive stances" (*IpoL* 27–28) that despite their resemblances seem so intent on their own selves, a disjuncture presents itself that seems, indeed, irreconcilable. The novel could thus make no better point of what Badiou describes as such: "Love contains an initial element that separates, dislocates and differentiates. You have *Two*. Love involves Two" (*IpoL* 28). At the hand of this radical difference that juxtaposes two incompatible subjective paradigms that could not be more antagonistic, it, indeed, seems tempting to conclude that Hailey and Sam do not grant love a possibility. For Badiou, however, "love isn't a possibility, but rather the overcoming of something that might appear to be impossible. Something exists that had no reason to, which was never offered to you as a possibility" (*IpoL* 68). Overcoming the impossibility of sharing a world is precisely what is made possible by an event and thus creates *Only Revolutions*'s amorous subject of the event that shatters the limitations of the narcissistic look in the mirror.

The history of love

Before analyzing the genuine event that allows the creation of the subject of the event, it is pertinent to examine the novel's status of events in general. The reason for this is that the novel aligns Hailey's and Sam's narratives with a system that is conventionally understood to be the discourse of events par excellence: history. This juxtaposition of "historical" events and "literary" events is specifically important for any discussion of subjects of events. Most of the novels under analysis, therefore, reflect upon the ontological status of "real" and "fictional" events and ask how an event such as a scientific revolution, for instance, may be represented in a text. However, this goes further than a mere metafictional awareness of practices of how history is being written. While historiographic metafiction would stress the inexorably constructed quality of every historical event, these novels also question the status of historical happenings as events without forfeiting the existence of events *tout court*. Instead of merely pondering upon the discursive reality of history, these novels rather mobilize their poietical potential and create authentic events within their aesthetic perimeters. The juxtaposition of an excessive mass of happenings and the singular eruption of a genuine event for Hailey and Sam therefore comments on the epistemological uncertainties for individuals to decide which event is a genuine event. What is more, this also stresses that there can be no general history of events but that they always have to be related to the situations that they affect.

Like *Slumberland* and *Against the Day*, *Only Revolutions* critically reflects upon the nature of "historical" events and its mediation by juxtaposing other ostensible "events" that, nevertheless, fail to fulfill their singular promise for various reasons. In comparison to Against the Day, which incorporates a variety of events and a multitude of subject creations, *Only Revolutions* focuses, in much the same way as *The Road*, *Slumberland*, and *The Zero*, on one event only and its potential to constitute reagency. Whereas *The Road* evoked a discourse of religious and ecological apocalypse to differentiate its notion of an ecological event and *The Zero* distanced its event from notions of trauma and sublimity, *Only Revolutions* reflects on history and its writing as to how this discourse and this discursive practice relates to and constructs events. In arguing that there is a radical difference between the status of events in the chronomosaic and Hailey's and Sam's narratives, the novel's juxtaposition of these two textual genres serves to contrastively refine a working concept of the event, while other happenings are unmasked, within the novel, as mere historical data.[10] Instead of seeing the two textual segments, one "factual" and "objective," the other "fictional" and "subjective" as semantically dependent, I argue that the relation between the two textual segments serves simply to collocate and, thus, discriminate different understandings of events. This reading reinterprets Hansen's argument that

> the historical sidebar functions by furnishing a shared "objective" context that facilitates the concretisation of the double-barrelled narrative. Insofar as this context serves as a selectional matrix for according meaning to the narrative, it cannot remain extrinsic to the narrative, but is in fact so profoundly intertwined with it as to render dubious any attempt to demarcate the objectively historical from the intimately personal. (2011: 183)

For Hansen, the chronomosaic functions as a hermeneutic balustrade that situates and contextualizes the subjective narratives of Hailey and Sam by means of semantic interconnection. While I would agree that there are connections between the two textual segments, it seems less fruitful to analyze to what extent the novel undermines the binary assemblage by pointing to "potential correspondences between narrative and history" (ibid.: 183).[11] Rather, the visual and narrative contrast proves to highlight medial and conceptual differences that are related to fundamentally different conceptualizations of events.[12] In respect of the two different classes of happenings, one historical and objective, the other personal and subjective, the novel insists on the conceptual difference that only allows the latter to implement a genuine event. As a form of list, the chronomosaic at one and the same time adheres to and extends its generic principles and therefore fails to mediate events. Put simply, although the history gutter is placed at the center of each double page, it "is not about events but facts" (Pöhlmann 2009: 72), while Sam's and Hailey's narratives, which seem to be mere annotations to the processes of a larger history, witness an authentic event.

A first distinction in respect to the event between the chronomosaic and Hailey's and Sam's narratives is a simple quantitative observation. Singular—as will be depicted in the following—in the latter, excessive in the former, the historical columns are filled with a profuse mass of "raw material" that approximates what Michel Foucault conceives in *The Archeology of Knowledge* as a general history, made up of "dispersed events—decisions, accidents, initiatives, discoveries" (1972: 8). Ranging from fairly conventionalized happenings that have entered historiographic discourse such as major military conflicts from the Civil War (S1), over the First World War (S66) and the Second World War (S160) to the first (H218) and second Gulf War (H280), the chronomosaic also notes happenings with arguably less impact, for instance, diverse athletic competitions. The chronological collocation of factual happenings irrespective of their ostensible historiographic importance and geographical origin could be read as an attempt to furnish a global general history that is apparently blind to national, ethnic, gender, or class distinctions.[13] In its encyclopedic endeavor to list more or less discursively established historical "facts," the history gutter obviously reflects upon the process of its production. However, what stands out in respect of the eventual status of the diverse items is the chronomosaic's inability to communicate the singularity latent in the concept of the event as suggested within this study. Particularly the spatial and textual structure of what I choose to read as a list forsakes a singular notion of events and, rather, depicts the overwhelming profusion of mass-"events," thereby reflecting upon the epistemological problems of deciding upon the "reality" of an event and distinguishing it from mere "facts." As Badiou notes in *Infinite Thought* in respect to political events:

> It is a matter of knowing which singular political orientation to call upon; that is, which ones are worth our trying to seize the thought specific to them. . . . This is not an easy job in today's confused and chaotic world, when Capital seems to triumph on the basis of its own weaknesses, and when *what is* fuses miserably with *what can be*. (56)

Only Revolutions stages this "confused and chaotic world" by juxtaposing Hailey's and Sam's narratives with the chronomosaic, which is presented in a particular form that forfeits its discussion of events. The construction of an infinite catalog, whose pretension to completeness (Mainberger 2003: 5) is transported through its encyclopedic scope, renders indistinct the various items' exceptionality and assimilates them within a ubiquitously generic assemblage. Regardless of the vertical presentation, which is an obvious visual feature of most lists, they create, according to Mainberger, a horizontal semantic plane that undermines any hierarchical differences. Through typographic presentation, the list's items are being equated in a temporal, spatial, and semantic synchronicity. For Mainberger, it is the typographic presentation, the structural parallelism, (ibid.: 9) that synchronizes the depicted items and undermines any qualitative distinction between, for instance, "8:48 AM, North Tower &/ American Airlines 11./ 9:03 Am, South Tower &/ United Airlines 175." (S277) and "Beckham's kick" (S277).[14] What follows from the chronomosaic's specific use of the list is the liquidation of a unique concept of the event, since the singularity of each event is lost in the mosaic's emphasis on plurality and the consequent lack of distinction.

However, while lists take part in what Mainberger calls "enumerative games" (ibid.: 7), *Only Revolutions*'s list does not adhere to the conventional rules of such enumerations: "Sie alle konstituieren, organisieren und präsentieren jeweils eine Vielheit wovon auch immer, dabei zeigen sie die einzelnen Elemente dieser Pluralität als einzelne wie auch als zugehörig zu einem Ensemble" (ibid.: 7) (They all constitute, organize and present a plurality of whatever kind; in this they show the single elements of that plurality as individual constituents as well as the entire ensemble. [My translation]). Unlike Mainberger's general demarcation of the operative principles of enumerations, the chronomosaic is marked by disorganization and heterogeneity, what Umberto Eco calls an "excessive list" (2009: 254) that runs counter to the customary taxonomic and structuring endeavor of lists. This form of excess is for Mainberger a contagious, yet integral, aspect that affects the relation between the signifying constituents and its constitutive signified (2003: 8–9).[15] The mere and undifferentiated mass that Mainberger sees as deferring a stable identity of the list's referential object is, in the case of *Only Revolutions*, not exclusively a quantitative aspect. Next to the heterogeneous conglomeration of factual happenings from different discursive realms that explode the temporal denominator that is supposed to order them, the linguistic modes of the chronomosaic's bulletins also add to the shattering of consistency.

The history gutter is constituted by three linguistic clusters. First, it contains descriptive enumerations of proper names that may include people, topological sites, and historico-political happenings. A second complex are seemingly verbatim scraps of conversation, typographically marked by italicization and introduced through an em-dash. Proper names in conjunction with verbs of movement make up the last cluster of statements that incorporate the already mentioned euphemisms of death, but are also simple declarations of spatial movement. As a result of these different linguistic registers, the chronomosaic is opting for dispersal not only in terms of content but also through the incongruity of its form of mediation. Mainberger observes: "Zum Aufzählen gehört das Wiederholen—nicht der einzelnen Elemente, aber der Operation" (ibid.: 9) (To enumerate, one has to repeat—not the individual elements, but the operation of enumeration [My translation]). Although heterogeneity might be a principal factor of lists in terms of content, morphologic differences have to adhere to a discursive paradigm in order to secure a referential ensemble that does not buckle. The chronomosaic palpably contests this stability by relying on discrepant modes of mediating its happenings. However, mere divergence in presentation does not automatically imply incongruity and discordance between the mediated elements. Are there other ways of recovering the relation between the different forms of mediation that would render the history gutter's items unique events involved in processes of subjective creations?

Even though the appearance of various proper names could be read as instances of naming events, an essential part of reagency, this has to be viewed critically within the chronomosaic. Declarative in manner, the proper names are, however, deindividualized, decontextualized, and detemporalized by dismissing verbs, adjectives, adverbs, conjunctions, articles etc. Since "the chronological entries are written in epigrammatic style," they are, as Hayles observes, "merely gesturing towards the events they reference" (2011: 165). By lacking a particularizing article the happenings lose their specificity and thus become interchangeable as in a paradigmatic chain of signifiers: empty gestures without a concrete relation to a genuine event.

Moreover, the absence of verbs, adjectives, adverbs or conjunctions for forming a sentence that is not purely nominal forfeits both elaborated contextualization and repercussions of the happenings (as for instance, having a proper sentence: "The 'Fugitive Slave Laws' (S1) are introduced, a step backwards for African-American emancipation"). Since any subjective creation is dependent on the processuality of its unfolding and thus necessarily requires not only the nomination of a historical "event" but also inevitably implies a subjective process that relates to this rupture, the chronomosaic's decontextualized plethora of mere incidents supports neither the reading of these items to be events nor the construction of any form of subjective process. Devoid of any further explications, the proper nouns might, furthermore, either suggest the obviousness of its content without the need for elaboration, or simply perform an act of documentation. Both alternatives result in the non-eventfulness of the chronomosaic's items, since the event, in the first case, explicitly requires more elaboration, as it radically opposes its unproblematic integration within a specific situation, whereas evental fidelity, in the second case, implies more than merely stating a name. How these aspects are actualized differently to the effect of creating a subject of the event will be explored in the following paragraphs in respect to Sam's and Hailey's faithfulness to their amorous encounter.

In fact, the relation between the list's different constituents is at best eclectic. There exists no reciprocal relationship between the declarative documentations and the subjective traces of speech, which would insinuate processes of subjective fidelity. Thus, the omission of connectives between the various items, with punctuation marks and line breaks sequestering segments and isolating them from each other, as well as the distinct graphic depiction of proper name and speech acts, typographically questions the connection between the respective units. In their textual and semantic confinement, it is difficult to corroborate a sufficient relationship between the happenings and the fragmentary snippets of conversation: too disparate are the terms demarcating happenings and the subjective utterances to arrive at a cogent interconnection.

As a consequence, the chronomosaic's ostensible events have to be viewed critically. Within the diegetic and discursive framework of the novel, the happenings listed in the chronomosaic remain "objective" events, that is, incidents without relation to a subject and, thus, cannot be viewed as events in the first place.[16] Following Badiou, these happenings accordingly forfeit their eventfulness and evaporate without having acquired their event-identity, since this would require the fundamental work of the subject and its reagency. The novel does not lay out a definite relation between the multiplicity of happenings in the chronomosaic and any individuals that would become faithful subjects of these events.

That the history gutter refrains from articulating a notion of the event as proposed by this study, however, neither automatically implies that it is without function and "blur[s] by" (Danielewski 2012: n.p.) nor that it is simply a form of excessive list for its own self-referential sake (Eco 2009: 250). Instead, its textual presence is essential for a contrastive purpose. In the novel's penchant for symmetries and juxtapositions, one could grasp the chronomosaic's use as an *ex negativo* sharpening of the evental definition of Sam's and Hailey's narrative. In a larger metapoetical framework, *Only Revolutions* might additionally proffer a genre-specific stance in relation to reagency. Suggesting that events, as required for subject creations, cannot be adequately nominated in historical narratives, the novel makes a case for the novel as a unique form of narrative in respect to its potential for subject creations. In responding to postmodern eradications of such differences, the novel suggests an essential distinction in their respective involvement with subjective processes. It is particularly the novel, which has a close relation to events and subjects, that may propel something *new* and thereby fulfill its etymological origin. While the chronomosaic certainly contains happenings that might have the potential to be events in other contexts, the way it represents them within the framework of the novel fails to attain this quality. In this sense, I would not read Sam's and Hailey's narratives like Pöhlmann, who argues that they are a "historical rewriting" (2009: 73) but as an evental narrativization. I will come back to the relation between event and narrative in *Only Revolutions* at the end of this chapter, since it involves part of Sam's and Hailey's reagency and counteracts the finitude of their subjective procedure.

You—could not—

Although *Only Revolutions* does not integrate genuine events in its chronomosaic, the encounter between Sam and Hailey marks a unique event that ushers in a process of fidelity. However, given the novel's encyclopedic aspirations and stress of novelistic form, it becomes, indeed, the question of how the singular and contingent disruption of the two narcissistic narrative orders that fail to include anything outside of their individual subjective perimeters might be represented within the constraints of the book as a medium. While I argue that the novel's event, as an amorous event, manifests itself in the encounter between Sam and Hailey right after their initial solipsistic reveries, a simple analysis of this diegetical event would not do justice to *Only Revolutions*'s paramount awareness of form. In drawing on Emily Dickinson's prominent use of the em-dash, this part elucidates how the novel deals with the representation of a phenomenon that cannot readily be absorbed by the current order of things or be expressed by the language of a situation that seeks to deny its existence.

If, for Badiou, the event that opens up the possibility of an amorous subjectivity always commences with an encounter between two individuals (*IpoL* 28), *Only Revolutions* gives expression to this quite trivial postulation on a level of content. After Hailey and Sam have each experienced their fundamental powerlessness when confronted with various modes of structural determination and sexual exploitation, they meet the other. Just before the two narrator-protagonists let loose their world-ending wrath in response to the experienced moments of impotence, they are literally interrupted by the appearance of the other. The nature of this interruption is particularly important for the coincidence between their first encounter and the singular, contingent and disruptive nature of the event as the novel articulates it: "Only before my lips/can afflict—" (S7); "Only before my EndAll/Smacker can land—" (H7).

In a similar manner as in *The Road*, the novel represents an event in just one sentence, which neatly transports the evasiveness of this phenomenon. By mimicking the narratorial shock that the encounter with the other inspires, *Only Revolutions* does not go at length in describing the incredulous happening. Indeed, while one reason for the minimalist representation might lie in the fact that it cannot be described with the present linguistic means, since every event is "abnormal" (*BE* 175) and "the name cannot be drawn from the multiples presented in the situation, but rather from unpresented multiples" (Feltham 2008: 103), another reason lies in both narrators' active resistance to accept anything that would corrupt their narcissistic worldview.

For the first time in the novel (and scarcely afterward), both autodiegetic narrators are thus literally at a loss for words. While the textual sign that intercepts their destructive performance is also used when indicating speech in the chronomosaic as well as Hailey's and Sam's narratives, a crucial difference is the position of the em-dash. At the beginning of verbal communication, the em-dash stands either as a paratextual indicator for a separate manner of mediation, or, in the case of the history gutter, exemplifies the mosaic slicing of speech elements, grammatically severing the subject of communication. In contrast, its position at the end of the line, clearly identifying an elliptical hesitation, has to be viewed differently. In this vein, the linguistic interruption is not merely interjecting the physical attempt of destruction; nor does it simply make Sam and Hailey halt their narration only to continue it as an enjambment in the following line. In the trivial sign of the em-dash, one can detect the convergence of various intriguing factors that epitomize the event in *Only Revolutions*.

In regard to the novel's circumspect penchant for typographical idiosyncrasies, one cannot grant the placement of the dash minor relevancy, especially since it coalesces with the first time Hailey and Sam meet each other. Since the novel is highly aware of literary historical antecedents,[17] I read the dash as a reference to an American literary forerunner, whose "graphocentric poetics" (Crumbley 1997: 1) also involves the strategic placement of dashes.[18] It is thus helpful to compare the various functional resemblances between Emily Dickinson's "signature 'dashes'" (ibid.: 1) and Sam's and Hailey's dashes. While there are certain similarities in the specific employment of a graphic, non-verbal sign, I stress a particular employment of the dash in *Only Revolutions* since it has to be seen as inexorably related to the depiction of the event in the novel.

A first commonality in the function of the dash in Dickinson's poetry and Danielewski's novel is what Calvin Bedient argues in respect of Dickinson: the dashes are "placing obstacles in the way of what Roland Barthes calls unrolling the text" (1990: 820). In stark contrast to the Whitmanesque free verse, Dickinson's "pauses" (Lindberg-Seyersted 1976: 31) undermine the potentiality of language and highlight its enunciative boundaries (ibid.: xx).[19] The distinction between linguistic profusion and reduction is critical for the detection and analysis of the event. Particularly through the novel's linguistic style that resembles Whitman's ongoing incantation and is even extended through the onomatopoetic play with sounds as well as the omnipresent formation of neologisms, the appearance of the dash manifests a narrative hindrance.

This has to be viewed in stark distinction to the novel's representation that is aligned in verse. While McHale argues that *Only Revolutions*'s play with what he perceives in reference to Rachael Blau DuPlessis as a lyrical segmentivity,[20] the typographic interruptions can still be read in an ongoing flow. The employment of run-on-lines or punctuations accordingly enhances interpretative possibilities, creating a simultaneity of semantic layers, but does not interrupt the flow of reading in the same manner as the evental em-dash. In this vein, the placement of the em-dash at the particular point of Hailey's and Sam's first encounter functions as a narrative means to highlight a distinct moment in disturbing the otherwise unabridged flow of language that epitomizes their perceptual and hermeneutic breakdown.

In this sense, the em-dash typifies more than merely a pause in the narrative flow but resembles what in Dickinson are perceived as "instruments of linguistic disruption" (Mitchell 1999: 181). Here it becomes obvious to what extent the dash not only serves as a sign of interruption but implies a more radical token of disruption. If Bedient has argued that Dickinson's "begrudging yet obtrusive dashes seem an appropriately reluctant mark, snapping linearity over and over in an agitated unwillingness to proceed" (1990: 820), the novel's critique of linearity is even heightened, given that its formal and diegetic narcissistic circularity already questions such forms of progression. Although each protagonist instantaneously proceeds in his or her narcissistic relation to the world by simplifying and integrating the other in a discourse of alterity—be that pathological idiocy ("An imbecile" [H7]) or gender-specific prematurity ("Giggles." [S7])—the breaking point that is situated in the aposiopesis is a first portent of the momentous aftermath that will affect their respective situations. More than a simple enunciative hesitation, I see implicit in the em-dash the confrontation of the two narrators and their encompassing narcissism with a rupture that assumes the status of an ontological and epistemological gap.

Following from this, the dashes in Sam's and Hailey's narratives resist being seen as a connective, as has been argued for some dashes in Emily Dickinson.[21] In the case of Hailey and Sam, this works differently. From the point of view of their respective all-dominating situations, each is not able to account for the other, and anything that she/he embodies. For Hailey, the appearance of Sam, and vice versa, implies the substantiation of a singular phenomenon that cannot be understood by either of the two in terms of his or her respective cognitive, phenomenal, or linguistic interpretation of the world. The dash has, therefore, the status of a radical absence and cannot function as a bridging device that enunciates the continuity of their narratives. It is, as Crumbley attests for such graphocentric moments in Dickinson's poetry, the "disrupting [of] conventional thought patterns" (1997: 2). *Only Revolutions* thus adapts the dash to non-linguistically convey something that "doesn't enter into the immediate order of things" (*IpoL* 28) by, indeed, interjecting a highly *textual* marker that is explicitly not a paratextual sign or a phonocentric mode of articulation.

In this context, "the paradox of an evental-site is that it can only be recognized on the basis of what it does not present in the situation in which it is presented" (*BE* 192) is given literary expression in a novel whose formal virtuosity apparently includes all kinds of typographic idiosyncrasies. As contradictory as this statement might appear, *Only Revolutions* helps to grasp the intricacies of this argument. If one reads the em-dash as a reference to the Derridean *sous rature*, a means of criticizing logocentric assumptions that is aware of the hermetic inescapability of language, it is revealing that the crossing out here effaces nothing.[22] By marking the location of the singular multiple of the evental site, both narratives express the shattering experience to their present-state narcissism in referring to the nothing of the void. This blind spot of their re-presentations, the categorical structuring of the regime of what exists, exhibits and resolves the paradoxical undertaking of presenting that which in-exists. Exactly because neither of them is able to acknowledge what lies beyond his or her apparently all-inclusive scope, "the only representable figure of the concept of the event is the staging of its undecidability" (*BE* 194). By this, the presentation of the event as the transcendence of the present horizon of what is and of what can be thought does not walk into the trap of discursive immanence. In referring to an originary void, which consists of an infinite repertoire of possibilities, and not a problematic and always différential logos, the event thus safekeeps its potential for processes of change that do not remain bound within determining structures. To be sure, this is not a wholehearted transcendence but, rather, what Badiou terms in *Ethics* an "*immanent break*":

> "Immanent" because a truth proceeds *in* the situation, and nowhere else—there is no heaven of truths. "Break" because what enables the truth-procedure—the event—meant nothing according to the prevailing language and established knowledge of the situation. (42–43)

Since the acknowledgment of the prospective change of their ontological situation is impossible for the narcissistic egos that put their own manners of perceiving the world at the center of things, they are thrown back to a moment of indecision. Inability to decide determines the narrative confrontation of each with the other, since the prefiguration of a possible mode of action is abdicated by the event's very unprecedented nature. Similarly, the radicality of the event, and this makes the encounter in the novel a proper event, at first denies them successful reaction because there are no interpretive stances that would account for the "*new* way of being" (*E* 41) that is raised by this phenomenon. After all, since it "is an event that can't be predicted or calculated in terms of the world's laws" (*IpoL* 31), the novel's use of a typographic, non-phonocentric means makes palpable this quite abstract disposition of events.

For Badiou, "that which is purely hazardous, and which cannot be inferred from the situation" (*BE* 193) is what constitutes the absolutely contingent nature of the event and *Only Revolutions*'s use of the em-dash is a particularly intricate adaptation of this notion in a literary framework. While the em-dash is, indeed, "hazardous" in the sense that it bears the danger of disrupting the whole textual order, its appearance and status as an event are not as momentous as the ecological cataclysm in *The Road* or the terrorist attack in *The Zero*.

Nevertheless, it is precisely this triviality in which the encounter is cushioned that marks its unpredictability and radicality. It seems accidental, in this sense, that the climactic narrative prospect of annihilation is prevented by the mere appearance of a giggling girl and an apparently mentally disadvantaged boy. If this manner of presenting the novel's event suggests an impoverished conception of the event, since the triviality of its genesis forfeits the pretension of singularity, the generic procedure of love, as Badiou remarks, thrives on this ostensible banality. The amorous encounter implies "an apparently insignificant act, but one that is a really radical event in life at a micro-level, bears universal meaning in the way it persists and endures" (*IpoL* 41). As insignificant as an amorous encounter might seem from an outside perspective, for those involved it marks a singular manifestation. This obviously renders a quite quotidian conception of the event. However, I argue that in contrast to Heidegger's single event, it is particularly the realm of love, which undermines the elitism of events in Badiou's theory. While the "rarity" of genuine political, scientific, and artistic events may imply that some humans never experience an event, the condition of love seems to democratize these phenomena, since they indeed may happen to anybody. At the same time, Badiou is eager to offer an emphatic notion of love, which distances itself from other, idealist or skepticist conceptions thereof, which will be analyzed in the following part.

Keep going!

After having inquired into how the novel represents such a singular and abnormal phenomenon like an event within the textual constraints of a book, I further elaborate on how *Only Revolutions*'s evocation of a contingent event is crucially different from other conceptions of love and thereby manifests a particular case of a subjective process that is endowed with reagency.

Specifically "duration" and "persistence" (*IpoL* 41) are two key aspects that define the event in the realm of love and further concretize the amorous generic condition. The durative dimension of Sam's and Hailey's encounter simultaneously distances its understanding of love from what Badiou labels the "fusional," the "oblative," or the "superstructural" or "illusory" conception (*C* 181–82). While the first conception concentrates everything on the encounter and sacralizes the event, the second offers one individual to the other as in a religious context, whereas the last rejects the existence of love in the first place.

In opposition to the "fusional" conception, which Badiou also calls the Romantic orientation, the subjective procedure of genuine love implies a fundamental moment of endurance: "By 'endure'," Badiou does not simply mean "that love lasts, that love is forever or always" (*IpoL* 33). In this sense, the temporal dimension of the amorous procedure is a necessary caveat against "a romantic conception of love that in a way absorbs love in the encounter" (*IpoL* 30), which proves "existentially seriously lacking" (*IpoL* 31). Like *Against the Day*, *Only Revolutions* thus implements the manifestations of change, that is, the fidelity of the subject, over a course of time and not as an instantaneous eruption, since "love cannot be reduced to the first encounter" (*IpoL* 31). While certainly depending on the momentous eruption of an event, the constitution of a subject necessarily requires continuously and critically *re*engaging with its propositions, instead of simply zeroing in on the encounter.

The ramifications of the event on Sam's and Hailey's narratives has, therefore, to be analyzed as an unfolding process that has its evental origin in their first encounter but resists being reduced to an exact moment in time in terms of its unfolding. Especially when juxtaposed to the chronomosaic, which is defined by its temporal specificity, having to order its happenings always under the exact date of one particular day, Hailey's and Sam's narratives exemplify how their event has to be unraveled over time. As a consequence, the novel insists that "love is not that which from a Two taken as structurally given creates a One of ecstasy. . . . The ecstatic One can be inferred to be beyond the Two only as a *suppression of the multiple*" (*C* 181). This stance toward love assumes that love creates a unified subject from two different individuals. Such a "disaster of monism" (*C* 181) does not prove fertile for the creation of an amorous reagent, since it concentrates its energies solely on the moment of the encounter and all too quickly obliterates the two different standpoints in merging them into one homogeneous monad. For the romantic stance toward love,

> something happens that is in the nature of a miracle, an existential intensity, an encounter leading to meltdown. But when things happen that way, we aren't witnessing a "Two scene" but a "One scene." It is the meltdown concept of love: the two lovers met and something like a heroic act for One was enacted against the world. In Romantic mythology we can see how this point of fusion very often leads to death. There is a close and profound link between love and death, the highest point of which no doubt is Richard Wagner's Tristan and Isolde, because love is consumed in the ineffable, exceptional moment of the encounter, after which it is impossible to go back to a world that remains external to the relationship. (*IpoL* 30–31)

Romantic love, for Badiou, clearly invests all of its efforts in merging two individuals into a singular subject that is self-identical. It is particularly striking that Badiou sees Tristan and Isolde as a paragon for this conception of love, as *Only Revolutions*'s dusk jacket opens up a similar reference: "They were with us before Tristan & Isolde. And long after too." I will elaborate on why I see the love story of Hailey and Sam to be different from both Tristan and Isolde, and Romeo and Juliet (another paratext that both Badiou and *Only Revolutions* cite) and thus serves as the most typical love story in world literature at the end of this chapter.[23]

As both narratives refuse to grant the encounter the equivocation of "a heroic act for One," the novel simultaneously decentralizes the event's instantaneous impact and denies a mere unification of two individuals by abandoning their inherent differences. The rejection of viewing love to be a "'communion', namely, an experience in which I forget myself on behalf of the other" (*IpoL* 24), finds expression in the inherent typographic and diegetic differences that mark both narratives. While both mediations of the event start out the same ("Only before my" [S|H1]), they crucially emphasize their different and differing experiences of the event. While a "fusion" or "communion" would suggest that both narratives would literally mirror each other, *Only Revolutions* emphasizes the diegetic and typographic differences even after the event has occurred and thereby distances itself from these conceptions of love.

Because of the triviality under which the event comes to pass in their narratives as well as the consequent relapse to already established structures of cognition, *Only Revolutions*, moreover, circumnavigates an "obstinate sacralizing of the encounter" (*C* 181), without surrendering the potential that it encompasses as a generic truth procedure. Instead of sacralizing the event, Sam and Hailey, rather, invest their efforts in the consequent process of fidelity. Just as Badiou is more "interested in issues of duration and process, and not only [in] starting-points" (*IpoL* 29), so does the novel emphasize the event but concomitantly refrain from putting too much stress on it. As a negotiation of the theory of the subject of the event, *Only Revolutions*'s conception of love does start in an event but cannot be reduced to it.

Equally so, the novel rejects corroborating the conception of love that Badiou calls the oblative one. "Love does not involve prostrating the Same before the alter [*sic*!] of the Other," as Badiou explains. Whereas the Romantic stance toward love is rejected by the novel right away, since each immediately tries to distance himself or herself from the other and not perpetuate a kitsch idea of love at first sight, they flirt with an interesting inversion of the conception of love as a unilateral relationship of religious dimensions. Rather than offering himself or herself to the other, each, indeed, pursues seeing the other as a sacrifice to his or her narcissistic reign.

Still infatuated with their egocentric ways of relating to the world, both clearly aspire to the less vexing way that would subsist in a simple incorporation of the other in their respective worlds, in like manner as the diverse animals that they have typified and subjugated. Hailey thus observes right after their encounter that Sam "rears back before his/Queen,/shrill screaking [her] leap/On his knees. Elbows./Paralyzed. After all [she is] his cry's/redemptions" (H7).

Earlier confrontations with plants were described in similar anthropocentric patterns of hierarchical domination. Once again Hailey positions herself as the female sovereign, although her assumed authority now renders another human being inferior, linguistically forcing him in a reverential position and thereby denying Sam an equal status. For her Sam is merely an item, which may indifferently be absorbed in her attempt to catalog the world according to her subjective paradigm. As Badiou stresses, this implies not a proper fidelity, since "if I want to be *really* faithful to it, I must completely rework my ordinary way of 'living' my situation" (*E* 42). In contrast, Hailey initially merely absorbs Sam into her current narcissistic worldview and thereby fails to construct a new way of "living." She accordingly understands her relation to Sam as one marked by disparate investments, implying sacred forms of worship. To a similar extent Sam offers Hailey: "—*Okay, you can be my slave*" (H9). In the subjective relation between the one and the other there still dominates his or her own possessive first-person singular pronoun that relates to the other as a "you" but goes no further than that.

A third form of interconnecting the I and the you manifests itself in "the 'superstructural' or 'illusory' conception of love, so dear to the pessimistic tradition of French moralists" (*C* 182), which could also be seen in the prefatory quote by Pynchon or in Eliot's poem. By this Badiou implies "the conception for which love is only ever an ornamental semblance via which the real of sex passes" (*C* 182). He identifies this pessimistic view with psychoanalytical thinking, which, for him, holds that "love doesn't really exist and is merely camouflaging desire. Desire is the only thing that really exists. According to this vision, love is merely something the imagination constructs to give veneer to sexual desire" (*IpoL* 34). Badiou summarizes his notion of Lacan's stance toward the topic:

> The fact that you are naked and pressing against the other is an image, an imaginary representation. What is real is that pleasure takes you a long way away, very far from the other. What is real is narcissistic, what binds is imaginary. So there is no such thing as a sexual relationship, concludes Lacan. (*IpoL* 18)

However, in referring to Lacan's thesis of the impossibility of a sexual relation,[24] Badiou insists that love takes on the position of an evental phenomenon that supplements the impossibility of a sexual connection in a similar manner as the event in the novel overcomes the narcissistic dominant that guides both narrators' relation to the world. Although it might seem impossible for something as "ambivalent" as love to exist and easier to discredit it as a mere "four-letter word" (Pynchon 2000: 90), an event, nevertheless, has the potential of making that impossibility possible. Indeed, the overpowering momentum of an event not only accounts for the overdetermination one feels when in love but it also rejects the positing of a sovereign subject that may rationally decide upon engaging with someone else.

Yet, the novel similarly elucidates the disjunctive qualities of sex, which separates rather than unites (*IpoL* 18). This is amplified by one of the novel's frequent moments of narrative divergence between the two parallax views. What for Sam was "perhaps too long" (S47), for Hailey proves "too short, allready out" (H47). While the novel continuously dwells on such moments of relating a diegetic happening from two disparate perspectives, it seems as if the rendering of their sexual intimacy that is marked by distance and misapprehension is particularly telling. During the act of lovemaking, Hailey, moreover, observes: "Magnificent tits. Gripped. Until/missing. Misaligned, mistiming" (H47). Hailey's marveling at her own bodily splendor emphasizes to what extent she prefers to concentrate on herself and her own pleasure. Furthermore, the negative prefix "mis-" that characterizes the following words reveals how she judges Sam's lack of expertise, being a virgin (H45), in terms of a normative divergence.

In the same vein, Sam solely focuses on his own desire. Just before ejaculation "Sam releases from" (H47) Hailey: "I release with a jerk torrents/of me" (S47). Not only is the description of his sperm a metonymy of himself that again paints a clear picture of his narcissism but his doubtful credo of chastity: "—I'll always only come outside" (S48) could also be interpreted as a sign of dissociation. When at a later point in the narratives, Hailey reveals to Sam that she "can't ever come" (S72), the carnal incapability additionally undermines the possibility of their sexual connection.

Yet, although "Lacan reminds us, that in sex, each individual is to a large extent on their own" (*IpoL* 18) sex also contributes to some degree to the experience of love in *Only Revolutions*. "Surrendering your body," Badiou observes, "taking your clothes off, being naked for the other, rehearsing those hallowed gestures, renouncing all embarrassment, shouting, all this involvement of the body is evidence of a surrender to love" (*IpoL* 35–36). To this extent, sex is not exclusively "a relationship with yourself via the mediation of the other" (*IpoL* 19). Despite the insistences on their own pleasure, Hailey's and Sam's first sexual encounter also brings them together, not only physically, but also linguistically and, thus, as an amorous subject. For the first time both refer to themselves as "US" (H|S48), which obviously also evokes a grander national narrative. However, in the context of the change in their relating to the world, the capitalized first-person plural seems more pertinent in its apparently paradoxical combination of a singular I in a collective we. It thereby grammatically approximates the creation of one subject out of two individuals without giving in to a fusional conception of their being.

Whereas romantic love, oblative love, and illusory love are discarded as cogent conceptions of love, sex cannot simply be regarded as a negative fulfillment of narcissistic pleasure. Rather, Hailey's and Sam's ample sexual adventures oscillate between self-centered satisfaction and an amorous fidelity. An exemplary moment for this juxtaposition involves Sam's endeavor to switch sexual partners and experiment with group sex. In accord with the separating dimension of sexual pleasure, Sam is "leaving [Hailey] out of that/circle, just sitting allone" (H93). Although Sam is still on the verge of accepting the amorous encounter and still, if tangentially, clings to the consummation of his subjective desires, he is yet overshadowed by the implications of the event. "O my. What am I doing," Sam reflects and soon tries to revert his actions. He "dart[s] appalled/ from their groaning engorging. And/then one tear falls. Two. Tears still/streaking her cheeks when [he] sweep[s]/her up with [his] weeping arms" (S 93) For the first time since the beginning of the book, he abandons his egoism and even apologizes to her (S94): "I'm so sorry. I'm sorry sorry./And she: —I'm sorry sorry./I'm so sorry" (94).

Gone are both the greedy modes of feasting, gorging, and engorging, for the sake of short-sighted pleasure, as well as the prior inability to empathize with the other. Sam's changed attitude toward Hailey, and ultimately toward himself, is thus inscribed in the mere act of asking forgiveness, and also in the linguistic interconnection of Hailey's tears that he seeks to comfort in his "weeping arms." In a sense, he corporeally internalizes what she externalizes. Although they here abandon their sexual intentions, sex, even though occurring less often in their stories, is not abandoned completely in replacement for an incorporeal, abstract notion of love. Instead, sex is much more assumed as an integral part of love.[25] While they are eager to deny the manifestation of an event and simply try to perpetuate their narcissisms, their sexual relationship forestalls their becoming a reactive subject, which denies the truth of their encounter but slowly unravels their amorous fidelity. The ambivalence of sex, as both a disjunctive and inter-subjective practice, however, also proves to change within the course of the novel.

Toward the end of the book, they engage in a last bodily encounter. While all around them an enigmatic apocalyptic process lets animals, plants, and humans perish, they lie down, "until O suddenly O," Hailey reaches a climax: "I'm becoming—" (H313).[26] If Sam reproduces these happenings as Hailey "coming" (S313), it is Hailey's formulation of an ontological process that refrains from the unidirectional implications of "coming" that would also link it to the ever present and semantically loaded "going." Hailey does not simply come, in the sense of arriving at a specific temporal or ecstatic ejaculation; her movement is pointed in two directions, from herself to Sam and the other way around: she is in the process of becoming a subject, with their sex being a marker of this ongoing act. She never can be said to *be* a subject but always has to reaffirm her fidelity to the encounter, which continuously confirms her status as a subject.

This symbolic approach is amplified by Sam's "roaring admission: —I won't pull out" (H314). Again, one can read his statement on the level of sexual intercourse, thereby substituting his prior declaration of orgasmic privacy to being with Hailey, which can be seen as an answer to the decreasing forms of life in their environment, finally choosing procreation in the face of omnipresent death. On a second level, his resistance to pull out might also be situated in a more general context of acting in fidelity toward their being as a "couple."[27] Sam accepts the ramifications that the event brings about, becomes a subject faithful to their encounter in his adherence to their radically altered being.

Their mutual declarations of love (H|S315) attest to this commitment. In Badiou's words, the declaration of love assumes a crucial position within the post-evental process of fidelity:

> I must tell the other that something that commits me took place, at least as I see it. In a word: I love you. If "I love you" isn't simply a ploy to sleep with somebody, which can be the case. If it isn't a ploy, what is it? What's being said there? It isn't at all easy to say "I love you." That small sentence is usually thought to be completely meaningless and banal. Moreover, people sometimes prefer to use other more poetic, less commonplace words to say "I love you." But what they are always saying is: I shall extract something else from what was mere chance. I'm going to extract something that will persist, a commitment, a fidelity. . . . [Fidelity] means precisely that transition from random encounter to a construction that is resilient, as if it had been necessary. (*IpoL* 43–44)

In a similar manner as Pynchon's Saul argues in the epigraph of this chapter, Badiou stresses the seeming banality and difficulty of this phrase. This difficulty with this stereotypical phrase could be said to translate in the novel in the fact that they only confess their love at a very late stage in the novel, as if to hesitate from pronouncing their love in an explicit manner. However, a more important reason for the rather late declaration of love is also due to the processual taking hold of the event's ramifications. Even though both attempt to negate the truth of the event that prescribes the constitution of a subject that is faithful to the creation of a world based on difference rather than sameness (*IpoL* 39), they eventually are slowly but surely engaging in this process and abandoning their respective solipsisms. In fact, while the event can be localized quite straightforwardly in the em-dash, the progressive acceptance of their amorous truth is more fuzzy.

Yet, in order to trace this transition whereby the encounter is transformed into a construction of a truth—a "truth is quite simply the truth about Two" (*IpoL* 38)—the book offers a particularly important passage that illuminates the transition that manifests the construction of a "world other than through a solitary consciousness" (*IpoL* 39). Although "Sam and Hailey always claim they remain unchanged" (van Hullen 135), the evental manifestation initiates the relentless progression "*—from me to you*" (S|H56), which is contingent on the abandoning of the me, "*— for you from me*" (H|S64) that takes up speed over the course of the novel. However, while there are a variety of instances that contribute to this process and add to a continuous decrease in emphasizing their own respective selves, that it is "not I/ Allways" (S49), I want to concentrate on the novel's pivotal scene both typographically and narratively as this marks a crucial moment that elucidates the construction of a process of truth and the concomitant manifestations of reagency.

On pages 180/181, the precise middle of the book, Hailey and Sam typographically meet. By this point of the story, they have abandoned their road trip across America and since "low on fuel" (H138) are forced to become sedentary and "get a job" (S144). This episode assumes one of the various critical tests to their love. On the one hand, staying put and surrendering their penchant for velocity and movement is a challenge to their nomadic existence that utterly resists being bound to one particular place. Moreover, their yielding to the logic of Capital undermines their being together: "All work. The JustGettingBy/cycle of surviving. Where shifts/must shift, drifting US apart" (S169). As a latent critique of modern work life, the specialization of work spheres separates them for the sake of profit. Employers' harassment and customers' appropriation as well as Hailey's economic self-offering as a consumptive good vehemently strain their relationship: "—Over here Missy, these steadies motion./ —I'm only yours, Hailey grins./ —For now./ —Forever! Each raucously adds,/ suddenly flatulent" (S153). Yet, faithful to their love, such instances of corruption do not diminish their determination to remain together. On a rare occasion of "a tossandturn of bedding" (S177), the narrative substitutes the prevalence of their free direct discourse with a dialogic communication. They engage in an extended conversation, which narratively indicates to what extent they have approached and face each other on an equal level.

—How's life?
—Taking forever.

—Let'S dance?
—And take forever with US?
—Yes.
—Let's go.
—We're so poor.
—We'll work it out.
—I want you just this way. To never have to go away.
From you. From US. Allways kissing, adored.
the rest. And smiling. To hold you when we're
happy, we're lazy. Sad. When you're stubborn.
When you're brave. When you're mad. When you're
scorned. But allways beside me and my moods.
—That's too easy.
—Then be difficult. (S177)

Already here, their fidelity, not only to the other, but to the post-evental "US" as a new form of subjectivity takes positive and negative implications into account. Particularly the demand to "be difficult" subscribes to the indifferent persistence of their love that is certainly not "*easy*." Love, for both of them, is not merely defined by positive experiences but encompasses a whole spectrum. Sam's ultimate declaration of love also implies negative factors: "I want to let you go. Betray US./Give US Torment, Deaths and Futures./Then curl up with you through/Reunions, Abuses and Departures./Too when you arrive. When you're allone./When I go. When I'm allone. But/allways beside you wherever we roam" (S178).

In taking into account fundamentally negative ramifications, it becomes clear to what extent their having become a subject of their love is not only a comprehensive endeavor that remains indifferent to obstacles but which also proves to be irreversible. Even at the hand of ostensible avalanches that would undermine and ultimately put their love to the test, they cannot think outside of this new subjectivity that adheres to the event. In this sense, while it was, prior to the event, impossible to grasp the possibility of transcending their respective solipsisms, it is now the new form of relating to the world that is faithful to their encounter, which is "impossible to dismiss" (S179):

—To be apart of this?
—Whirls of ours.
. . .
—But who all chases US?
—Only US. —And outlaws US?
—US. —How?
—By something wide which feels close.
Open but feels closed. Lying weirdly
across US. Between US. Where we're
closest, where we touch, where we're one.
Somehow continuing on separately. (S179)

What prior to the event was dominated by the "I" has now been supplemented by the event and thus substituted for "Whirls of ours." Once again, the novel uses a circular motive although it now revolves around a "we." Upon being asked what possible threat there is to this new way of being, they respond that there is "Only US," that this new subjectivity cannot be grasped even by an exterior juridical litigation. Despite the fact that they make it sound as if the manifestation of an event and the consequent faithfulness is irreversible, they simply reject any possibility of "unfaithfulness" (*IT* 141) as forsaking one's fidelity, as *Against the Day*'s character Kit elucidates. Instead, for them, there is "*Only US*," since this assertion actively affirms their encounter. It is not the incorruptible and stable nature of an event that they address, but they continuously reaffirm their status as a subject of an event. The *point* where they "touch" and are "one" is narratively situated in the following pages, the novel's material center, which I identify as one crucial "point" that perpetuates their amorous subjectivity. "A point," is for Badiou

> a particular moment around which an event establishes itself, where it must be re-played in some way, as if it were returning in a changed, displaced form, but one forcing you "to declare afresh." A point, in effect, comes when the consequences of a construction of truth ... suddenly compel you to opt for a radical choice, as if you were back at the beginning, when you accepted and declared the event. (*IpoL* 50)

Only Revolutions once more shows how such theoretical concepts might be appropriated within literature by giving Badiou's notion of a point a particular formal implementation at the exact middle of the book. Not only are Sam and Hailey therefore "back at the beginning" but so is the reader who notices the unmistakable differences between the first pages and the present ones.

For the first time the novel here concedes the two narratives typographic equality: both narratives count 18 lines, the size of the font is the same, green and gold coloration appears on both sides. With the exception of the chronomosaic, the pages are, furthermore, not merely refracting each other, as is the case in the remaining 358 pages, but mirroring each other in exact identity. Especially when compared to the novel's two first pages, the contrast seems eminent. There, both narrators showcase destructive intentions toward "the Dream" (H|S1). Now they exclaim: "—Everyone dreams the Dream/but you are it" (S|H180). Affirmation replaces negation. While the initial stance is motivated by the narcissistic attempt to highlight the distinction between collective and individual, in the new situation each distances himself or herself from everyone in the realization of the other. If one goes as far as assuming "the Dream" to be their love, the hiatus between aspiration and fulfillment hinges on their actualization of this event. They do not dream the dream, they have become it. Within this new inter-subjective situation, they realize that the "—I won't help being" (H|S180). Perceiving the world from a single point of view has become a redundant pattern, even an irrelevant one.

With the essential help of their "HONEY," a recurrent ambivalent resource that they consume, they are "sticking [themselves] together," indeed "sticking US to the World"

(S|H180). By using the viscous resource that is produced synergetically by animals and plants, they enact the new ontological situation "'according to' the event" (*E* 41) by having "separate[d] out within the set of presented multiples, those which depend upon an event" (*BE* 232). The "US," that has prior to the event been an indiscernible multiple, is thus not merely a grammatical mode of enunciation but an entire subjective paradigm that could not have existed within their respective solipsistic perceptions. The "US" could, in other words, be seen as the name of the event that was unfathomable before their encounter. Remarkably, this process of fidelity toward the event is executed by adding the supplementary term "to" the world. In contrast to the beginning, where the world was always only imaginable within the phenomenological framework of their respective selves, where the world stuck to them, their faithfulness not merely supplements the "US" as the evental site that failed to be presented in the situation before the event. Rather than a mere addition, the "US" radically reshapes the world that was unable to grasp it. Only through the actual process of, first, giving a "supernumary name" (*BE* 396) to the post-evental situation, and second, integrating this new ontological paradigm do they actualize the event, which results in a changed world. They, indeed, "invent a new way of being and acting in the situation" (*E* 42). At the textual "point" of the middle of the book, they therefore display their fidelity in asserting the "point" of the event: as if returned to the beginning of the novel, they "declare [it] afresh" (*IpoL* 50).

The reiterated declaration of their love is needed since the ontologically complex character "CHANGING HOPE" seeks once more to drive them apart by confronting them with the inevitable need to decide: "—Everlasting Whims & Everlasting Loss./ Against Horrors passing with Love's passing./ Between Them you must choose" (H|S 180). Once again, Hailey and Sam face the devastatingly negative implications of their love. Indeed, HOPE undermines the very concept of choice, as the presented options are really two sides of the same coin. As a result, Hailey and Sam retort: "—Choice then is allways Them?" (S|H181). As in the beginning, the ability to choose autonomously is called into question. They realize the forsaken nature of their alternatives and surrender the possibility of decision to a superstructural agent, a "*Them.*"

However, Sam and Hailey have never been agents. Their reagency consists in the acceptance of the pressing consequences of their new situation and the "radical choice" (*IpoL* 50) they are compelled to declare is only dependent on the event and not a general humanist value. In other words, their choice is not contingent upon a binary set of options but, rather, becomes the act of choosing in the first place. Once more they accept their new world unconditionally, which also includes essentially negative aspects. Thereby they reassert the imperatives that the event forced upon them. Still, it is not exclusively a moment of passivity that makes them subjects of an event. Their reagency, rather, combines the contingent emergence of the event with the decisive fidelity toward its consequential propositions. Aware of their newly acquired subject-hood, they exclaim: "Here's to deciding./—So glad./—Allready welling up./—Laughter won't ever stop me./—I can't help bleeding./—Everyone dreams the Dream/but we are it" (H|S 181).

Faced with the "radical choice, as if [they] were back at the beginning, when [they] accepted and declared the event" (*IpoL* 50), they embrace the inescapability of having become "the Dream," even at the cost of mortality, since the price they have to pay for their amorous fidelity proves detrimental to their agelessness. What Badiou conceives as the lovers entering a new form of temporality (*IpoL* 33) finds expression in *Only Revolutions* through Sam and Hailey starting to "bleed." While this is again a pertinent marker that distinguishes their pretensions to be invincible at the beginning of the novel and the now acquired mortality, it also displays to what extent a subject of the event is no "über-subject" (*IT* 131). While the event is eternal, since it is a set that expands infinitely, which *Slumberland* helps to grasp in the following chapter, Badiou is eager to insist that "a truth alone is infinite yet the subject is not coextensive with it" (*BE* 395). Interestingly then, while the narcissistic narrator-protagonists at the beginning of the novel maintain that they are immune to death, their fidelity to their encounter has made them vulnerable. However, *Only Revolutions* not merely translates this condition on a literary level but goes beyond Badiou's ideas of the relation between the infinite event and the finite subject. While the novel also subscribes to Badiou's notion of a minimally collective subject of the event in the case of love, it also uses this disposition to show a literary modulation of his idea of subjective finitude.

I could never walk away from you

On one level, the novel complies with Badiou's assertion that the finite subject cannot outlive the event. This becomes already obvious when Sam's and Hailey's moment of utter synchrony lasts only so long: "—Somehow now, here, we're one, while allready/ somewhere nearer we go on apart" (S|H182). Reflecting metafictionally on the physicality of the book itself, this statement involves not merely the separation of their narratives. Rather, this can also be viewed in the light of the curious ontological status of being one and two at the same time. "The lovers as such," writes Badiou, "enter into the composition of one loving subject, who exceeds them both" (*E* 43). The ultimate aftermath of their having become a single subject that simultaneously is more than just the sum of its parts relates to an idea of the subject that is radically opposed to its ordinary equivalence with an "individual."

However, the observation that "Our/ time together waning./ And both of US dismayed by/ why this is so" (S185) not only addresses the physicality of the book that necessarily involves their separation in terms of pages but is also indicative of a miraculous process that has started to unravel and which implies their physical weakening. In each of the respective narratives, the narrator becomes literally faint because of the consequences evoked by the encounter, which is again insinuated on a typographical level: their respective narrative amount on the page decreases; their font size fades. Moreover, flora and fauna are graphically ceasing from the text. Everything "all around [them] keeps dying" (H268). Becoming aware of their devitalization, they decide to quit their jobs and return to the place where they started their journey and first encountered each other, which is physically a return to the beginning of the book.

On the way back to the Mountain, they intend to get married (H239) in order to counteract the process of their weakening, since this would be another "point" that might potentially reaffirm their fidelity to the event (*IpoL* 51). However, their aspirations to symbolically sanction their love fail at first. "THE FRAIL DISTRICT CLERK" refuses to marry them, running them through the entire bureaucratic process. "First there's an application./Second there are tests. There's/certification. And above all, there's the Law./You're both unfit. You even have ID?/Sam: —No./—What about you?/ Me: —No./—Then no. That's the way it goes. It's protocol" (H256).

The clerk's use of bureaucratic language neatly conveys how they fail to fit the legal regulations of becoming married, since their fidelity toward the event cannot be understood from an outside perspective of "applications," "tests," "certification[s]," and "protocol[s]." Next to the fact that the irrational wager that constitutes any fidelity to an event and particularly that of an amorous procedure is a clear counterpoint to these rational modes of cataloging, it is also a question of perspective. Since any event can only be perceived from the situation it affects, the clerk is unable to account for their love and to serve as a juridical medium to sanction their fidelity.

Yet, the clerk's refusal to marry them also addresses their complex ontological status of being one and two at the same time. Lacking an official, and, more importantly, a single identity, they cannot be wed, since this inevitably implies the bond between two individuals. The clerk addresses Sam and Hailey as separate individuals and cannot grasp their having become a single subject. In Badiou's terminology, they might be represented by the state in terms of distinct individuals, but fail to belong properly as a subject of love, since the "law" that is positioned "above all" lacks the means to recognize them as properly belonging to the situation, a political dimension of Badiou's theory that is elaborated upon in the following chapter on *Slumberland*.

Although each eventually succeeds in pledging to be faithful to the other, they continuously become weaker until ultimately one of them dies. Despite this pessimistic end to their story, there are three domains, which testify to their obtained reagency since having become a subject, that negotiate Badiou's notion of an amorous subject that goes beyond its finite constraints. Essentially, *Only Revolutions* follows up on the double-status of the amorous subject that is more than the sum of its parts and uses this to inquire into the possibility of an infinite fidelity to the event of love.

On a diegetic level, their attained reagency lets them discard their worst enemy. For the third time in the novel, "there's the CREEP" (H274). Having made two appearances already, the Creep persistently attempts to bind the two, slow them down and, ultimately, separate them. The Creep's function as the primary "antagonistic force" (Pöhlmann 2009: 65) to the two protagonists can be grasped already in his graphic accentuation, having the color purple that also paints the date of the chronomosaic, as well as the book's classification as a novel (ibid.: 66). His exact mixture between Sam's green and Hailey's gold, his telling name that opposes their relation to speed, and his use of "rationality" (ibid.: 69) are further indicators of his antithetical role. In an earlier confrontation, Hailey gets to experience "THE CREEP's fingernails," which are "digging sharp [her] scalp, turning [her] from Sam, with a terrifying plan" (H82). Only by employing a fairy-tale con, they "trip/ THE CREEP backwards" (H87) and are, for now, able to escape.

Yet, the Creep is not gone for long. He is "Still. Stalking" (H273). One more time, the novel stresses contrasts through juxtaposition and lets the appearances of the Creep coincide in the double pages. If the Creep was characterized by his ability to entrap Hailey and Sam when they have not fully embraced their love in a former confrontation, his attempts "to tie [them] down" (H275) are now brushed away by them without effort. "Sam just takes away the trap:/—We're free" (H276). The Creep is thus readily discarded and has lost his structurally antagonistic role. He no longer assumes a threat to their love, since they have engaged in a powerful process that, within the novel, can only find an end in themselves: "Selfishness, not any rival, is love's enemy. One could could say: my love's main enemy, the one I must defeat, is not the other, it is myself, the 'myself' that prefers identity to difference" (*IpoL* 60). In conformity with their new subjectivity, the Creep's role changes as well. When they were still separate characters not fully committed to their love, he presented a danger to them individually. Yet now, he is no enemy any more. Empowered by the evental ramifications, they can shift the discernment of an exterior source of corruption to the positive identity of their new situation. In other words, their reagency amounts to the realization that the real obstacles for sustaining their amorous encounter have always to be directed at their own actions, which allows them to liberate themselves from one of the novel's most insistent antagonistic forces.

On a second level, their reagency becomes evident through the respective death of the other and how they react accordingly. If there is a range of moments of parallax discrepancy that yields two entirely different accounts of things, it is particularly their mediation of the various deaths of the other that are specifically contradictory. Upon having "reach[ed] the [mountain's] top where cottony air threatens blizzards" (H321), they get separated. Hailey trips and falls into a cliff; Sam gets stung by a bee and bolts. When Hailey returns unharmed to the top, she finds Sam: "No! There though, still on top, across this frigid top,/ just ahead of me. O no. Lying among that arc of heavy/ boulders" (H327). Hailey is found by Sam in a similar posture in his narrative. In their respective accounts, they have to admit that the other is "Impossibly still. Just gone. Dead" (S328). It seems as if all their efforts to elude death were in vain and that this marks the end of their subjective process.

Indeed, the contingent nature of how they die in the respective narratives seems to mirror the haphazardness of their initial encounter. However, as unmotivated as their respective deaths come to unfold, I would deny it the status of an event or that it results in their abandonment of their subjective process. Granted, each reacts to the death of the other in a rhetoric that approximates eventfulness as well as in modes of action that would signify the "renunciation" (*IT* 142) of their fidelity. Sam, for instance, laments Hailey's death as such: "unbound without contentment, leaving me/ lost, too on my own" (S330). Hailey equally comments that she is "now undone, tied/ to Love no more. To Liberty no more" (H340). Particularly through the return of the singular point of perceiving the world ("me"), the lack of dialogic communication, that marks the dissolution of their bond of "Love," it appears as if the unpredictability of death reverses their amorous subjectivity and results in the relapse to their prior situation that they inhabited alone. What attests to this is the return to aggressive intentions that is mediated in a monologic manner, which recalls the narcissistic beginning of the novel:

> I am the fury at last
> no hope will prevent. Not even this ravaging cold,
> tossed along by blizzardy groans, Open,
> will help. Wipe it all out. Because
> I've no hand to kiss, fondle, hold.
> How uncomplete I am. Neglected. Missing and
> unmissed
> . . . Where rancor's
> touch stayed by frozen slush refrains from
> releasing all I miss so much: his mayhem,
> his closeness, his warmth. Unguarded. Struck.
> . . .
> And just that simply, on my behalf,
> I come around. Because I'm blazing.
> Because I am too soon.
> Because without him I am
> only revolutions of ruin.
> The harvest of War reaps only the seeds of War.
> And I'm now just for sowing.
> Here's how my agony frees.
> Annihilate everyone of course. Because I'm disdained
> & unsafe. And I'll take jeers away with castrations & rape,
> murders & feers not even the dead will escape.
> Surrounding the Scoundrels, Relevants, Culpables and
> Tamed. Resolved. Annihilating their tolerances.
> . . .
> And every town will burn.
> I'll hunt the Strong. And the Lucky. Skulls splashed.
> Rolled. Limbs hacked. Tossed to creek beds.
> Along every road.
> Cities swept loose by fire.
> And for those who beg and plead,
> Organizations and Outstanding Citizens, I'll gnaw
> through their teeth.
> And every nation will burn. (H345–48)

Hailey's pre-apocalyptic soliloquy parallels the aggressive threats from the beginning of the novel. However, in comparison to her attempts to "nevernomore/ the World with a smooch" (H6) in response to sexual violence, the fury she seeks to unleash in order to redeem Sam is more versatile and picturesque in its deliverance. While her hatred was directed to a single object in the former setting, her "uncompleteness" now occasions the eradication of a multifaceted variety of beings implying detailed descriptions of violence. Equally so, the initial threat to destroy the world was in the beginning merely a juvenile boast in response to the limitation of her own individual being. In contrast, she now mobilizes her energies to take revenge on Sam's death. In its all-inclusive scope, Hailey simultaneously recalls and negates Whitman's democratic aspirations and enumerates for the sake of effacement, not affirmation.[28] Her self-description as "only revolutions of ruin" coupled with the climactic final sentence suggests, indeed, that the loss of Sam reverses her new subjective mode, eradicating the "US."

Yet, as before, Hailey does not live up to her promises. Like Sam, who realizes that he is "someway still/ pushed by that unslackening pang beyond any cure" (S330), an apt description of their amorous encounter, she acknowledges that she is "allways stung by him/ and ever after" (H343). While their abandonment of the event is certainly an option, they actively deny this possibility and maintain their faithfulness that again prevents cataclysm. Rather than seeing their deaths as another event that disrupts their ontological situation, they integrate the loss of the other as another point of their amorous fidelity. Faced with the ultimate reason to abandon one's fidelity in the condition of love, they, indeed, "keep going!" (*E* 91). Their decision to save the world becomes part of their fidelity to the other, as showcased by Sam:

> For her
> the World turns and to blow it away
> would forfeit all the World allready Loves of her.
> . . .
> How here without, she still somehow,
> over with, comforts now what I'd obliterate.
> And she's just chillin on the snow.
> She exists for more. More exists for her.
> And I cannot destroy more.
> For I cannot destroy her. Ever. (S355)

In keeping faith with their love, Sam decides that any form of destruction would "forfeit all the World," that is, it would contradict, even abandon, the imperatives of the event. Although Hailey is not among the living any more, she remains present "somehow" and protects the world from the afterlife. In fact, the existence of her body manifests a trace that, in conformity with his eventual faithfulness, must not be infringed upon. This active decision of letting the world live implies another facet of their reagency. Both the denial of the other's absolute nonexistence and the consequent act of preservation take their origin in the event and could only be fulfilled through their fidelity to its conditions. Faced with fundamentally negative conditions, they nevertheless succeed in substantiating their love. In an affirmative act, they perpetuate rather than surrender and once more rectify their status as a subject that can even exist when the other is gone. By actively resisting death, they become what Badiou calls an "immortal animal" (*E* 10–12):

> We are dealing with an animal whose resistance, unlike that of a horse, lies not in his fragile body but in his stubborn determination to remain what he is—that is

to say, precisely something other than a victim, other than a being-for-death, and thus: something other than a mortal being. (*E* 11–12)

Paradoxically, they only achieve this immortal status through their mortality. Nevertheless, *Only Revolutions*'s seemingly contradictory formal alignment that concomitantly narrates the death of their respective partners as well as their survival gives a complex account of this duality of being mortal "animal" and "immortal" subject at the same time.

This defiance of endings percolates into the last aspect of Hailey's and Sam's reagency. For one thing, they break with their relation to the natural world and soften the rigid distinction between animals and plants. While Sam thus lets loose "explosions of Aster, Yarrow, Buttercups and Clover" (S357), Hailey observes "Crickets, Coyotes, Beavers, while Golden Bears range and Bald Eagles rise" (H357) over Sam's dead body. Confronted with the vanishing of their respective biospheres, they embrace what the novel hitherto ascribed explicitly to the narrative of the other. The rejuvenating act (Pöhlmann 2009: 65), therefore, revitalizes the narrative as such, as is transported through the depiction of the font, as well as by energetic verbs of movements that are a counterpoint to their respective lethal immobility.

As a consequence of their world-affirming mode of action, they also conserve the other as when Sam chooses to "let ice blossoms vine her hair" (S355). To counteract bodily decay by encapsulating the other in ice is not all. Both antagonize death in the enshrining of the other in terms of more symbolic means:

By him now. My only role. And for that freedom,
spread my polar chill, reaching even the warmest climes,
a warning upon the back of every life
that would by harming Sam's play, ever wayward
around this animal streak of orbit & wind,
awaken among these cataracts of belligerent ice
me.
And my Justice.
At once.
The Vengeance of my awful loss set
free upon this crowded land. An old terror
violent for the delirium of
ends.
But those who would protect him, frightened
by such Beauty & Savage Presence to do more,
my cool cries will kiss their tender foreheads
and my tears will kiss their gentle cheeks,
and then if the Kindness of their Love, which only
Loving ever binds, spills my ear, for a while I might
slip down and play among his foals so green. (H358–59)

Evidently, we now enter sacred spheres. Each of them becomes a guardian whose protective role consists simultaneously in negative caution as well as in affirmative benevolence for those who either choose to reject or partake in the deification of their dead bodies. Conjuring such ritualistic connotations, creating a discursive field through the semantic cluster of "Justice," "Vengeance," "Beauty & Savage Presence," the kissing of foreheads, or the "Kindness of their Love" unmistakably incites the field of religion. However skeptically one might relate to the allusion to such a discourse, it seems as if both of them showcase their maximum level of empowerment in the creation of such a myth.[29] Indeed, just as Badiou insists that his notion of fidelity is not a religious concept but "refers directly to the amorous relationship" (*BE* 232), so does *Only Revolutions* elucidate that, despite the ritualistic connotations that have a particular context in religious traditions, it is first and foremost a practice of an amorous subjective condition.

I would, indeed, argue that an essential part of their reagency lets them leave behind the formal rigidity of the book itself by creating such a mythical narrative. Only through their creation of a particular story are they enabled to abandon, as Hansen argues, "the constraints of the historical world and the constraints of the book as form" (2011: 190). And I would specify, only by being faithful to their amorous encounter are they able to create a story that does not merely revolve around themselves individually in a circular loop that is indifferent toward the lapse of time. Unlike the chronomosaic of Hailey's side that remains blank from the year 2006 on—the year when the novel was published—their symbolic act of having made themselves the protagonists of a story of love attests to the mortal constraints of every subject of love while concomitantly undermining this temporality by establishing a narrative that is projected into the future and again tries to circumnavigate the finitude of this subjective procedure. While they do not *transcend* the circularity of the book as such, they leave behind this form of circularity as it is fostered by the two narcissistic individuals of the first pages.

This starkly opposes the ritual of self-adulation at the beginning of the novel. Faithful to the event despite the death of the other, their myth stands as an archetype of their amorous fidelity. Sam thus ends his narrative but simultaneously begins a new story:

> By you, ever sixteen, this World's preserved.
> By you, this World has everything left to lose.
> And I, your sentry of ice, shall allways protect
> what your Joy so dangerously resumes.
> I'll destroy no World
> so long it keeps turning with flurry & gush,
> petals & stems bending and lush,
> and allways our hushes returning anew.
> Everyone betrays the Dream
> but who cares for it? O Hailey no,
> I could never walk away from you. (S360)

Especially the last sentences reduce the somewhat ideological nature of their created myth. Although their story is supposed to stand as a paragon for love, it does not assume to be a prescriptive "Dream." What they experience is something expressly subjective. In this sense, they do not care to what extent others are truthful to a generalized "Dream" of love. In the last sentence, Sam again insists that the myth they created is an individual myth with no pretensions to being normative. As the most individual form of an "*ethic-of*" (*E* 28), *Only Revolutions* suggests that there can be no general Ethics, particularly in the condition of love, while this, nevertheless, offers a microscopic ethics that is solely dependent on the two individuals who are concerned with their amorous encounter. If the amorous event does not administer a general ethical imperative for all humankind, it crucially affects those within this particular situation and forces them to position themselves to it.

Nevertheless, by having translated an intradiegetic event into an extradiegetic story of love, the novel gives the idea of reagency a particular literary form. The transversal of a mere intratextual "trifle" (*IpoL* 16) to a story of love through a mise-en-abyme feat elucidates the repetitive and extensional quality of reagency in the novel. By making the act of reading the book *again*, Sam and Hailey make sure that their amorous generic condition is extended from the intratextual incident to a poetological gesture that is closely linked to their reagency. They translate the "keep going" (*E* 91) to a level of reception by urging the reader to start from the beginning and to read the novel again, which makes their intention to maintain their amorous fidelity percolate out of the apparently hermetic limitations of the book. Thereby, the novel mobilizes its formal structure and shows that the initial motives of circularity that stressed the inability of indicating change and thinking beyond the immanence of their respective narcissisms undergo a fundamental revision. In the context of the radical defiance of the finitude of the subject of love, *Only Revolutions* rejects the very concept of an ending, since the reader's arrival at page 360 only means that he or she may now flip the book over once more and start at the beginning, which creates an infinite process of reception and, at the same moment, keeps them and their story alive.

In conclusion, this is also what differentiates the novel from other love stories to the extent that one might speculate how far the novel can be seen as the most typical love story of world literature. As Badiou argues, there are

> many stories or novels [that] focus on cases where Two are particularly marked out, when the two lovers don't belong to the same class, group, clan or country. Romeo and Juliet is clearly the outstanding allegory for this particular disjuncture because this Two belong to enemy camps. (*IpoL* 28–29)

While *Only Revolutions*, like *Romeo and Juliet* or *Tristan and Isolde*, starts out with a similar structural opposition, what differentiates the novel from the other two canonical texts is not only its unprecedented typographical and linguistic execution of the initial disjuncture that is required for the event of love to happen. Most strikingly, *Only Revolution's* unyielding perpetuation of the amorous fidelity differentiates it from other conventional love stories. Unlike such stories, the novel does not proffer a romantic or oblative conception of love. Rather than simply "re-enacting the archetypal tale of Romeo and Juliet" (Hayles 165), Sam and Hailey decide to invest efforts in the perpetuation of their love that even implies being existentially apart from the other. Unlike Juliet and Isolde, their inability to "walk away from" the other does not result in self-sacrifice. In accepting what for others might only be a trifle, they become a subject of the event in affirming love as their only revolution.

"You'll never be passé"

The Aesthetico-Political Subject in Paul Beatty's
Slumberland (2008)

Is there something to be gained
by establishing distance from blackness?

Paul C. Taylor, "Post-Black, Old Black."

Was there some battle everybody was fighting,
and he had missed it?

Richard Wright, *Native Son.*

Although the political dimensions of the subject of the event have been latent throughout the previous chapters—from McCarthy's ecocritical dimension to Walter's interrogation of the biopolitical mechanisms after "9/11"—the following two chapters take the political more into focus, without reducing these works merely to their political import. In fact, by conjoining politics with other "conditions," these novels interrogate the political in quite different terms than what Badiou has in mind. Whereas *Against the Day*'s evocation of a scientific event that makes modes of resistance possible elucidates how Pynchon unmasks the necessarily political aspects of seemingly apolitical and even antipolitical spheres and thereby undermines the disciplinary separations of modernity, Paul Beatty's *Slumberland* engages in arguably one of the most pressing political concerns of and in the United States. In this sense, the novel extends what W. E. B. Du Bois in 1903 argued was the problem of the twentieth century (2007: 3) into the new millennium and thereby offers an intricate response to Kenneth Warren's much discussed question that also bears the title of his book: *What was African American literature?* Next to pointing to the actuality of racism in the contemporary age, the novel inquires into the ways of how to answer such acts of discrimination and, inherently connected to this, how to achieve emancipation, both political and aesthetic.[1]

Granted that this has always been a concern throughout the heterogeneous literary production of African Americans[2]—from Frederick Douglass's slave narrative (1845) to Richard Wright's existentialist *Native Son* (1940), Ralph Ellison's virtuous *Invisible Man* (1952) over Toni Morrison's *The Bluest Eye* (1970), or Percival Everett's *Erasure* (2001) and Colson Whitehead's *Apex Hides the Hurt* (2006)—the manner in which Beatty's

2008 book reflects on the color line offers, as this chapter argues, a crucially different answer than other so-called Black Artists.[3] It does not rely explicitly on a notion of "blackness" that refers to racial or national essentialisms and it, simultaneously, rejects the recent discourse of post-blackness.[4] *Slumberland* opts for a different alternative by evoking a subject that through its resurrection of a political event, allows its faithful followers to be aesthetically productive and thereby gain political *and* aesthetic reagency.

While *The Road* offers a reactive subject that clings to the situation before the event, *The Zero* depicts an obscure subject faithful to a simulacra event, and *Only Revolutions* and *Against the Day* exemplify the production of subjective fidelities, *Slumberland* sheds light on a nuance of faithful subjective procedures that Badiou only introduces in *Logics of Worlds*.[5] If all other subjects experience the imminent eruption of an event (or its simulation) in the diegetic present, the autodiegetic narrator of Beatty's novel reinvigorates an event that has ostensibly been forgotten. This resurrective practice is crucially different from the faithful procedure in *Only Revolutions* or *Against the Day* since it focuses on a bygone temporality rather than the evocation of what Badiou calls a "present" (*LoW* 51). While the novel's protagonist eventually helps to bring such a new temporality into being, this is only evoked by his continuous reflection on time, specifically the peculiar dimension that he calls the "day before yesterday" (*SL* 13). Through his engagement with this ontologically complex modality of the past and with the help of jazz musician Charles Stone, Sowell W. Ferguson (a.k.a DJ Darky) becomes a faithful subject by resurrecting the eternal truth of human equality that for Badiou started with the "Spartacus" event.[6] This event expresses both the non-naturality of slavery (*LoW* 65) and, more generally, "the maxim of emancipation in the present tense" (*LoW* 63). Still, in contrast to Badiou's often quite polemical reflections on political fidelity, which always seem to hinge on "trouble and disorder" (*IT* 55), both *Slumberland* and *Against the Day* contemplate different, not always violent but, nevertheless, revolutionary forms of political fidelity.[7] Although both novels are equally concerned with the political, by which I mean political emancipation, they offer alternatives to Badiou's notion of a "revolutionary politics" (*C* 147).[8]

Despite these modifications, *Slumberland* exemplifies the political fidelity of resurrecting an event. Thereby, it extends Badiou's brief comments upon this subtype of fidelity and shows that events and the truths they evoke are not merely tenuous phenomena of only temporal validity; rather, such "long sequences of truth" (*IT* 140) may propel propositions that persevere throughout time. As Badiou phrases it: "Of no truth can it be said, under the pretext that its historical world has disintegrated, that it is lost forever" (*LoW* 66). Without a doubt, this sounds somewhat suspicious given Badiou's Marxist background, which makes his political vision appear to be part of a classical historical materialism.[9] However, while Marx's fulfillment of a classless society reverberates at some points in Badiou's writing, he also stresses the inevitable infinity of this process because of his set theoretical denial of any teleological utopia.[10] Indeed, the eternal appeal of events denies any form of finality and, as this chapter makes clear, rather focuses on the iterative practice that again and again makes one a subject of an event.

That truths are eternal and universal does not mean that specificities of cultural and historical nature are being overlooked. Badiou's notion of an evental eternity should not be viewed as professing an essentialist idealism that posits unchangeable transcendentals, because the mode of resurrecting an event does account for the particular settings in which it is brought to bear. In this context, Badiou observes that "a resurrection presupposes a new world, which generates the context of a new event, a new trace, a new body—in short, a truth procedure under whose rule the occulted fragment places itself after having been extracted from its occultation" (*LoW* 65). By resurrecting a bygone event, the subject is not equally resurrected but reinscribes itself anew at the hand of a new situation that counteracts the forces that tried to bring an end to this particular event either by denying it or, as *Slumberland* depicts, by normalizing it. In contrast to the extinguished present that *The Road*'s father seeks to create by ostensibly creating a nostalgic "present," the faithful subject's resurrection relates to a genuine event and adjusts it to the particularities of its present situation of oppression.

The adaptable perseverance of this eternal subjective procedure is thus hinted at when Badiou observes that "the subject whose name is 'Spartacus' travels from world to world though the centuries" (*LoW* 65). Just like a traveler who changes with the places he visits, the subjective body also answers to the specificities it encounters, appreciating and integrating the historical and spatial givens of its surroundings. While Badiou mentions three site-specific instantiations of the Spartacus event, "Ancient Spartacus [Spartacus's revolt], black Spartacus [the Toussaint-Louverture Haitian revolution 1796], red Spartacus [Karl Liebknecht and Rosa Luxemburg's communist insurrection in 1919]" (*LoW* 65), Beatty's *Slumberland* invigorates a new fidelity, making the case that this event is far from being irrelevant to the present age. Indeed, its inherently political avail to emancipate those who face (racial) inequalities is not transferred into contemporary America simply in order to point its finger at the unabating racist problems of the United States.[11] More intricately, the novel's projection of the problem of the color line as a genuine national, that is, American, problem is extended in that its protagonist travels to the divided Germany of the late 1980s and early 1990s to work at the eponymous Slumberland bar. If, then, "there is nothing particularly radical in insisting that race continues to matter in U.S. social life" (2011: 93), as Warren provocatively observes, *Slumberland* surpasses this antiracial critique by showing the transnational implications of America's racial other as well as by giving a politico-aesthetic answer to these modes of repression.[12] For in order to find the mysterious jazz musician Charles Stone, who is supposed to ratify Sowell's almost perfect beat (*SL* 33), he ventures on a "quest" (*SL* 25) to Berlin to find the ingenious recluse. *Slumberland* thereby literally translates racist problems from the United States to a Germany that has supposedly cleaned up its historical deeds, which is neatly conveyed in one of the narrator's repetitive spatio-temporal conflations. Sowell describes Berlin as "a clean city," even "antiseptic" (*SL* 11). "This is not the hermetic sterility of a private Swiss hospital," he goes on to describe Berlin, "but the damp Mop & Go slickness of a late-night supermarket aisle that leaves [him] wondering what historical spills have just been tidied up." (*SL* 11) The process of wiping away the historical stains of the past is here described as a problematic project because of its unsustainable mechanism of positing literally "antiseptic" clean slates. The imagery of the supermarket, moreover, is a first harbinger of the historical parallels the novel continuously draws between America and Germany and its political problems.[13] Despite or particularly because of the transnational marks of racial repression and discrimination, in a first step I read *Slumberland* within the tradition of African American narratives of emancipation. After inquiring into the novel's interrogation of the continuity of racist discourses within the allegedly liberal environment surrounding the 1990s—the heyday of liberal democracy, multiculturalism, and respect for the other—I go on to show how this political interrogation is tied up with a critique of two prominent historico-political happenings of the twentieth century. By undermining the eventness of both the end of history as amplified by the fall of the Berlin Wall as well as the event of black emancipation after the Jim Crow segregation, I then investigate in a second part how the novel offers an alternative event that inhabits the potential of human emancipation.[14] In this vein, the novel again displays the difficulty of choosing what happening constitutes an event and what is merely a historical incident. This difficulty amounts to

> knowing which singular political orientation to call upon; that is, which ones are worth our trying to seize the thought specific to them. . . . This is not an easy job in today's confused and chaotic world, when Capital seems to triumph on the basis of its own weaknesses, and when *what is* fuses miserably with *what can be*. (*IT* 56)

By distinguishing the current order of things ("*what is*") from the possible intrusion of "*what can be*," *Slumberland* addresses a key concern of American literature and literature as such. If political emancipation is a key concern for the so-called African American literature, the second part of this chapter inquires into an inherently connected dimension of this political project: aesthetic emancipation. By bridging the gap from purely political to aesthetic issues, I conclude by arguing that the novel's resurrection of a political event leads to the creation of an aesthetic event. While Badiou insists on the strict separation of the four generic procedures (science, art, politics, love), *Slumberland* makes a remarkable case for showing how particularly African American literature is incessantly invested in the interplay of these two spheres, that is, art and politics. It should become clear that within this literary tradition, politics and aesthetics are two inseparable concerns that are mutually interdependent and cross-fertilize.[15]

From identity politics to evental politics

In reading Beatty's *Slumberland* in the tradition of African American narratives of emancipation, I neither suggest that the novel is historically out-of-date, engaging in a process that has lost sight of the political reality "at a time when the grounds for asserting black identity and black solidarity are ever more tenuous" (Warren 2011: 110),[16] nor do I want to ascribe to the novel a particular "black" essence that would simplify an African American work of art as having to be political per se, what Walter Benjamin has called in a not altogether different context, a *"tendency"* (1970: n.p.).[17] Instead, I insist that the novel is highly aware of this tradition and explicitly refers to the history of African American emancipation as a process—what I want to suggest is a fidelity— crucial even today. In agreement to some extent with Warren's diagnosis that post–Jim Crow black literature has no collective political project that it can refer to, *Slumberland* seeks to point to the importance of this project, without being nostalgic or positing an essentialist "black" collective. What is more, despite the various modes of parody, pastiche, and cultural mixing that the book offers—a "baroque/brat-rap/mash-up ontario" (*SL* 23), as DJ Darky calls it himself—it still positions itself self-reflexively (but positions itself, nevertheless) within this literary tradition.[18] As opposed to reading the novel as a metafictional critique of black art, what has recently been suggested to be "post-black,"[19] interpreting the novel within the scope of the theory of the subject of the event offers a way to circumnavigate an essentialist "black" identity, political or aesthetic, without losing sight of these political and aesthetic concerns.

Although the conditions for writing and living during the times of slavery have obviously radically changed in *Slumberland*'s textual present, the novel, nevertheless, highlights that processes of racial stereotyping, oppression, and violence have simply been rechanneled. To be sure, modes of oppression that black citizens experience have changed from a physical, overt, and legal level to more subliminal ways of a psychological and structural kind, which, nevertheless, leads to the death of one of the novel's characters, who commits suicide after persistent racial discrimination.[20] Additionally, they have transferred from a concrete national jurisdiction to a global level that runs hand in hand with America's imperial undertakings. With the spread of liberal democracy into post-war Germany, the novel suggests, America has installed its political system and, hand in hand, its social narratives of racial discrimination. Through its spread of popular cultural discourses, through medial and institutional channels such as the "ivory-covered," "cultural trading post" of the *Amerikahaus* (*SL* 57), Germany was able to adopt a political system as well as its latent sociocultural undercurrents, which DJ Darky has to confront in the textual present of the late 1980s.

He thus faces straightforward stereotyping when arriving in Germany that is induced by Western Germany's extreme exposure to American economic and popular culture.[21] Commenting on his first encounters with Germans, Sowell observes that they continuously liken him to black characters of American TV culture: "*Du siehst aus wie* . . . , and then I go home and look up Urkel, Homey the Clown, and Dave Chapelle on the Internet" (*SL* 5). Besides the obvious lack of cultural sensitivity that the Germans display—not only confronting Sowell in German but also literally trying to translate him into their native language, trying to typify him in a neo-colonial gesture—one also glimpses the stereotypical inability of white people to tell the difference between individuals of other ethnic groups, since the Germans cannot distinguish among black people and view them as a homogenous undifferentiated mass. [22] Yet, it is even more pressing to realize that the characters that Sowell is compared to are exclusively minstrel characters that all assume an inferior role within the cast of their various shows. Although comedian Dave Chapelle and Homey D. Clown from *In Living Color* certainly embody subversive potential in undermining the history of black-face, Steve Urkel's overly exaggerated clumsy character in *Family Matters* is marked by specific black stereotypes. Next to Urkel's recurrent slapstick gags that suggest a lack of bodily control that amounts to what Eric Lott termed "physical burlesque" (1992: 28), which are followed by a (stereo-)typical catchphrase "Did I do that?," Homey equally conforms to specific comedy stock figures with his repetitive vernacular one liner "I don't think so—Homey don't play that."[23] Although certainly working at the margins of subversion and affirmation, the manner in which Sowell is confronted with these stock figures perpetuates specific discourses of homogenization. By unmistakably being embedded in a discourse of racial stereotyping, whether positive or negative, the German audience clearly lacks the historical consciousness of handling such complex characters. In his "father's generation," DJ Darky reflects, "there were only four niggers he could look like: Jackie Robinson, Bill 'Bojangles' Robinson, Louis Armstrong, and Uncle Ben, the thick-lipped man in the chef's hat on the box of instant rice. Today every black male looks like someone. Some athlete, singer, or celluloid simpleton" (*SL* 6).

Sowell is obviously deeply ironic in his take on the current American racial situation and how it disseminates into cultural production and reception. While the mid-twentieth century still had a token collection of male African Americans in the most prominent cultural spheres, the narrator lampoons the current social milieu. As a matter of fact, the revolutionary potential that Sowell, in a blend of nostalgia and satire, sees latent in the pre–Civil Right era has now succumbed to a renewed sense of minstrelsy and subordination.

In spite of the ostensible end of the Jim Crow era and the emancipation of African Americans—"The Negro is now officially human," (*SL* 3) as Sowell again ironically remarks—*Slumberland* emphatically stresses that political emancipation is not a singular process that can be marked with a specific historical point in time, like the abolition of slavery, or the Civil Rights Movement. For it would be utterly naïve to conceive of a complex social, cultural, and political problem as being solvable within a single act of rebellion. Whereas Badiou's political reflections are often exemplified by the event of the French Revolution, which intricately grounds the political dimensions of his set theoretical approach, *Slumberland,* rather, examines a political process that equally rests on the manifestation of an event but is invested in a more strenuous and necessarily lengthy process. Instead of implying that emancipation is thus an either-or quality—either you are emancipated and free or not—the novel conceives of it as a prolonged political fidelity that requires reiterated affirmation. If a political event such as the French Revolution thus points to the social inequality between those represented by the State—what Badiou sees as the set theoretical operation of inclusion—and those actually belonging to it, such political events as the emancipation of African Americans cannot be said to be resolved through a similarly singular happening.[24] In contrast to the French Revolution, which brought about an imminent change in the relation between the inclusion and the belonging of French citizens (before the Revolution they were merely part of the State, represented as a subset, whereas afterward they truly belonged to the situation by essentially changing that situation, at least for some time), African

American emancipation equally refers to the event of human equality but relies more thoroughly on the repetitive subjective affirmation of its points. In other words, the event that proposes the egalitarian belonging of excluded or even included members profoundly relies on a subject and its ongoing struggle for "a radically egalitarian and universalist outlook" (2009: 91). Just as Sam and Hailey need to continuously reaffirm their love, so does the subject of African American emancipation need to stick to the event in order to fully bring about social and political (and, one might add, aesthetic) belonging. Crucially, the event therefore does not simply try to include the excluded middle but aspires to a deeper level of social equality.[25] As *Slumberland* insists, the mere inclusion into society is utterly problematic because of its conception of a pre-existent unity of society into which an aberrant multiple has to be integrated.[26] With Badiou, one has to view such processes in which previously excluded minorities make their way "into" society as fundamentally changing the entire social system. What the politically emancipatory undercurrents of the subject of the event imply is therefore not an integration into society, where excluded identities become part of a larger social body; the political condition, rather, necessitates that such multiples become an element of this body, entirely changing its political physique.

As a consequence, *Slumberland* makes the case that because of the mere inclusion of African Americans into society, the event of emancipation has been co-opted by the state and thus been normalized, as Badiou calls it (*BE* 176). Instead of rigorously taking the propositions of equality at face value, American society merely added the multiple of African Americans as an essentialist group into the already existent homogenous melting pot. This then could be seen as diametrically opposed to the government's endeavor to make an event out of a non-event in the case of Walter's *The Zero*. In contrast, *Slumberland* shows how an event may also be normalized, readily co-opted by the state of the situation in order to prevent the creation of a subjective procedure that would crucially initiate change.

In this vein, Sowell highlights that social inclusion by no means stops racist discrimination, which is best described in his incredibly dense and allusive opening remarks of the narrative:

> You would think they'd be used to me by now. I mean, don't they know that after fourteen hundred years the charade of blackness is over? That we blacks, the once eternally hip, the people who were as right now as Greenwich Mean Time, are, as of today, as yesterday as stone tools, the velocipede, and the paper straw all rolled into one? The Negro is now officially human. Everyone, even the British, says so. It doesn't matter whether anyone truly believes it; we are as mediocre and mundane as the rest of the species. The restless souls of our dead are now free to be who they really are underneath that modern primitive patina. Josephine Baker can take the bone out of her nose, her knock-kneed skeleton back to its original allotment of 206. The lovelorn ghost of Langston Hughes can set down his Montblanc fountain pen (a gift) and open his mouth wide. . . . The revolutionaries among us can lay down the guns. The war is over. . . . The battle cry of even the bravest among us is no longer "I'll see you in hell!" but "I'll see you in court." So if you're still upset with

history, get a lawyer on the phone and try to collect workmen's comp for slavery. Blackness is passé and I for one couldn't be happier, because now I'm free to go to the tanning salon if I want to, and I want to. (*SL* 3–4)

Absolute emancipation, so the overall message goes, is still a long way ahead, if it can be achieved at all.[27] The humorous and deeply ironic beginning of the novel playfully juxtaposes a before and after of African American emancipation, particularly the Civil Rights Movement, and depicts its effects on the political and social status of black people. In drawing a qualitative distinction between the present and the times before blackness became "passé," Sowell comments, tongue-in-cheek, on the new situation that the event of emancipation has brought about. After centuries of violent exploitation, African Americans have now ostensibly been accepted in the midst of society, being as average as every other citizen. The need for violent revolution has accordingly become redundant, which relegates to the museum the tools for insurrection as well as politically motivated, "populist" poetry. Amiri Baraka's machine gunners may well step back. There is no need to die anymore, as Claude McKay had it; one simply goes to court now. While the narrator certainly criticizes the contemporary status of passivity that comes close to what Badiou terms the occultation of the event of emancipation (*LoW* 66) and which makes sense of the novel's trance-like title, he equally opts for a different political alternative than violent means, which will be analyzed more thoroughly in the second part of this chapter.

Through the manifest ironic tone of the passage, which is conveyed through the emulation of a rather euphemistic rhetoric that literally whitewashes the actual reality of African American emancipation, Sowell clearly undermines his own message. This is, furthermore, amplified by the collocation of seemingly incongruent semantic fields and grammatical categories—black people, indeed, being likened to obsolete instruments of human civilization and (white) culture. What the passage thus points to through its ambivalent irony is the radical gap between African American inclusion and their belonging. Sowell emphasizes this social discrepancy through his recurrent formulations of unfulfilled conditions, indicating the asymmetrical relation between what is and what should be. It is, in other words, a difference between being and appearing, which already the very first line of the novel expresses with its comment on the unactualized state of affairs ("You would think"), that black is obviously not "passé," an unmistakable and critical wink at post-race arguments.[28] This chasm is further elaborated when the narrator refers to the British "saying so," nodding to the colonial past of the late empire and simultaneously marking the distinction to a political reality, where nobody really "believes" it. The contrast between being and appearing, which is also glimpsed in the disparity of Baker and Hughes's performances that unravel a deeper core that the surface covered like a "patina," hints at the difference between sociopolitical inclusion and belonging. If postmodernist theories of representation would argue that there is no core that can be reached beyond the surface performances of African American citizens, I suggest a different reading that discerns a more fundamental level of sociopolitical belonging instead of mere recognition.[29] Without returning to an essentialist conception of a black identity that can be discovered and, as Sowell has it, that can now be lived since emancipation has opened society to black people, I locate this "common cause" that not only makes possible political emancipation but also creates a collective that is indifferent to qualitative denominators in an event. Instead of creating a group identity based on phenotype, language, or "culture," the novel proffers a notion of collectivity that holds together in the various fidelities to the event of emancipation, irrespective of race, class, gender, etc. Emphatically, the novel substitutes identity politics for evental politics. In taking root in an event, "all identities [are] in a sense absorbed by the movement, but the movement itself [is] not reducible to any one of them" (*TRoH* 78). Since the universal appeal of an event is "indifferent to differences" (*E* 27), identity politics' insistence on differences is forestalled and the ethics of recognition substituted for an ethics of truth. By creating a basis for collective political action, which, nevertheless, may imply different forms, the event suggests a political constitution that moves beyond racial or national essentialisms, "affirm[ing] the generic, universal and never identitarian character of any political truth" (*TRoH* 77), as will be depicted in the next part.[30]

However, being history, the event that bears the trace that would enable the formation of a subjective body whose fidelity consists in the active rejection of racism and the furthering of an egalitarian society is epistemologically inaccessible. It is, as Sowell continuously emphasizes, "yesterday." However, this is not merely another self-reflexive reverie on the impossibility of knowing and writing the past. Rather, it is part and parcel of a subjective process that is, nevertheless, more complicated than the other subjective procedures that this study looks at.

As has been mentioned in the previous chapters, the premise for the creation of a subject of the event requires face-to-face contact with an event. The novel's present, however, lacks such an event. This is particularly striking because of the book's setting during the time of the fall of the Berlin Wall, which is often read as the epitome of the Western democratic project. Like the other novels discussed in this project, *Slumberland* integrates other major historical happenings but, just as *Only Revolutions* or *Against the Day* do, rejects the evental status of these incidents. In doing so, it metonymically undermines the discourse of the end of history as the purported end for the need for an emancipatory politics (*C* 147).[31] The critique of seeing the fall of the Berlin Wall as a political event is thus embedded in the novel's critique of the end of the Jim Crow era,[32] as both narratives attempt to construct simulacra events in order to obscure the need for an ongoing fidelity to the event of emancipation.

Toward the middle of the novel, almost in passing, Sowell asks a bystander about what he retroactively will call "the fateful one," October 3, 1990: "Where did all these people come from? Was there a soccer game?" (*SL* 112). By comparing one of the most influential German social and political happenings after the Second World War, which additionally represents a first symbolic act that led to the alleged end of history, to a soccer game, Sowell undermines its eventness. Just as *Only Revolutions*'s chronomosaic allocates "9/11" with sports "events," *Slumberland* reflects on the linguistic usage of the concept "event" and crafts a terminological and ontological differentiation. More than a mere sign of myopic historical disinterest in and ignorance of world affairs, Sowell has no knowledge of the Wall—he even claims: "the Berlin wall was not a part of my lexicon" (*SL* 113)—which results in his failure to conceive of the happening as a political event. In this manner, the Wall's collapse simply does not constitute an event for him, since, despite the political similarities between East Germans and blacks, he does not count himself to this particular situation. In fact, this event not only fails to pertain to Sowell but also, more fundamentally, does not amount to be a genuine event in the first place. On both an individual and a collective level, the professed change of this fateful day falls short of materializing. "After the Berlin Wall fell . . .," Sowell notes, "nothing really much changed for me" (*SL* 120). "My world," he continues, "was the new Germany—same as it ever was" (*SL* 135).

This continuity is also manifested when, as part of his artistic endeavor, he tries to record the sounds of this momentous day to make them part of his phonographic work of art:

I took out my minirecorder and taped the sounds of freedom. Cars horns blared. A woman slammed a pickax into the Wall, grew tired, and then began to spit at the bricks. Chanting. Clapping. People said, "Wunderbar!" whenever a reporter shoved a microphone in their faces. Cameras clicked. Singing. Flashbulbs popped. A beer-hammered young man, too inebriated to lift his head, vomited his first Big Mac onto his first pair of Air Jordans. His boys teased him about wasting a month's pay on sneakers that didn't even last him a day. All in all, freedom sounded a lot like a Kiss concert. (*SL* 119)

As before, Sowell's comparison of the Wall's fall to an "event" of mass culture raises doubts about its genuine status and again addresses the ubiquitous profanity of the term "event" in postmodern times. By the same token, the juxtaposition of the emancipatory "sounds of freedom" that are depicted in the staccato-like apposition of brief acoustic impressions with the instantaneous dissemination of capitalist globalization merges two antithetical images and suggests the doubtful nature of this ostensible "freedom." By indicating that the confrontation with "liberty" amounts to the incorporation of Eastern Germans into the grasp of global capitalism and results in the full bodily immersion into a system of exchange, *Slumberland* insinuates a re-reading of this symbolic happening and its status as an event. With the very moment the Wall falls, so the novel suggests, capitalism starts to wrap its tentacles around the last outposts of commercialization, which is neatly transported by the culinary incorporation as well as the textile envelopment of the body of the Eastern German. In very much the same manner as Pynchon's *Gravity's Rainbow*, *Slumberland* casts doubts on the liberatory potential of the United States' interaction with Germany and addresses modes of continuity in the progressive spread of a biopolitical world order.

Through the novel's radical critique of the discourse of the end of history that champions the assertion of liberal democracy as a teleological endpoint, *Slumberland* criticizes the American capitalist system, its globalizing aspirations, as well as its ideological profession of an end of politics because of the consensual affirmation of democracy. While the novel is certainly not the first to do so, it, nevertheless, stands out in critically contemplating the spread of democracy as it is transmitted in the ideological narratives with their eschatological undercurrents. Nevertheless, the novel does not stop at a mere critique of such political schisms, undermining the evental status of a seemingly fateful historical happening that seeks to paint a euphemistic picture of the obsolescence of an emancipatory politics as a result of having reached the teleological endpoint of a historical dialectics. It essentially moves beyond a simple critique of history and its writing by criticizing the discursive mechanisms that nominate an event for ulterior reasons and simultaneously offers a cogent alternative. While *The Zero* unmasks the political effects that are engendered by this obscure nomination of a simulacra event, *Slumberland* goes on to refer to a different and, as one might add, a proper event that bears the potential for political and aesthetic emancipation.

However, the fall of the Wall, which could be compared to the simulation of an event such as September 11, 2001 [33] also brings about change even though it is not the singular change that a non-ontological singularity encompasses. Sowell admits that "Germany changed," reminds him "of the Reconstruction period of American history, complete with scalawags, carpetbaggers, lynch mobs, and the woefully lynched" (*SL* 134). Sowell, indeed, sees a variety of parallels, since Germany now "had every manifestation of the post-1865 Union save Negro senators and decent peanut butter," including "minstrel shows—tuxedoed Schauspieler in blackface acting out Showboat and literally whistling Dixie," as well as "requisite whining editorials warning the public that assimilation was a dream, that the inherently lazy and shiftless East Germans would never be productive citizens. There were East Germans passing for West Germans" (*SL* 134). Here it becomes obvious to what extent Beatty's "juxtaposition of the Wall and the color line" (Blausteim 2010: 730) is a more complex undertaking that does not create simple historical parallels between the United States and Germany. For the obvious analogy that one might draw between freed slaves and freed Eastern Germans is problematized to a large degree within this passage. Despite the similarities between the separation of the American nation and the German nation that has come to an end, Sowell creates various doublings that resist being resolved entirely. The passage's historical evocation of the Reconstruction era's two groups of "scalawags" and "carpetbaggers" therefore suggests a more complex analogy, where East Germans are compared to the Southern population and the American North is projected onto Western Germany. Through this conceptual shift, surrogating the relation between the white and the black population for a North-South emphasis, the novel undermines the binary between a degenerated South and its morally superior North through its comparison to the present German situation. In fact, through Sowell's emphasis on the continuing, albeit institutionally relocated, forms of racist practices, one might read his spatio-temporal displacement as a general questioning of the status of the American nation's struggle for emancipation. Black emancipation, Sowell intimates, was only a minor aim of the post-Civil War period that has not been fully actualized but, rather, transferred to its cultural unconscious.

If Sowell earlier denied that the Wall has brought about any sort of change, his creation of this historical resonance intimates that the alleged emancipatory progress that the Civil War and the abolition of slavery allegedly furthered simply redirected modes of repression to different social practices that are equally latent in reunified Germany. This change for the worse in respect of social equality becomes manifest when Doris, Sowell's one-time lover, derogatorily calls journalist David Levin an "old Jew," which makes Sowell indulge in a crucial reflection on the Wall. Her racist rant, indeed, makes him "miss the Wall," since before the wall came down "no one calld [him] *Neger* to [his] face or said *Jew* as a pejorative" (*SL* 138). Although the demolition of the Wall appears to be a synechdochal and symbolic image for the dissipation of racist thinking, the narrator suggests the contrary. Only with the absolute dissemination of liberal democracy and the freedom of speech have racist tendencies started to become expressible again within German society. Crucially, this return of the repressed makes itself felt in the entirety of society, which the novel highlights in that Doris—clearly one of the more liberal characters in the novel—articulates this pejorative. Again, Sowell pessimistically notes that particularly through the exposure to "American cop shows" (*SL* 138) as a metonymical format that embodies America's cultural imaginary (proffering racist stereotypes, requiring repetitive and continuous reception) does Germany refurbish its racist attitudes. It thus seems remarkable that his answer to this rejuvenated environment of social discrimination is to rebuild the Wall. Although Sowell clearly ties this wish to a rhetoric of nostalgia, comparing it East and West Germany's romantic craving for an idyllic past, his inquiry into the past distances itself from a nostalgic return in crucial ways. Through Sowell's inquiry into a specific temporal nature, one may grasp both his receptiveness toward a political event that bears the potential of emancipation as well as his concomitant critical reflection on a recent discourse within African American studies that is intricately tied to these issues.

Sowell's obsessions with a different temporal past are deeply related to his continuous reflections on time and can be seen as participating in his attempt of resurrecting the event of emancipation. Wishing for the Wall to return is part and parcel of a larger reflection on temporality that begins in the very first chapter of the novel. In tune with Sowell's initial musings on the pastness of the black man—employing terms such as "Once-eternally," "Greenwichtime," "as of today, as of yesterday" (*SL* 3)—one of his recurrent narratorial reflections makes Sowell reveal his preoccupation with the "day before yesterday."

> Most languages have a word for the day before yesterday. *Anteayer* in Spanish. *Vorgestern* in German. There is no word for it in English. It's a language that tries to keep the past simple and perfect, free of the subjunctive blurring of memory and mood. I take out a pen, tapping the end impatiently on a bar napkin as I try to think of a English word for "the day before yesterday." I consider myself to be a political-linguistic refugee, come to Germany seeking asylum in a country where I don't have to hear people say "nonplussed" when they mean "nonchalant" or have to listen to a military spokesperson euphemistically refer to a helicopter's crashing into a mountainside as a "hard landing.". . . Listening to America these days is like listening to the fallen King Lear using his royal gibberish to turn field mice and shadows into real enemies. America is always composing empty phrases like

"keeping it real," "intelligent design," "hip-hop generation," and "first responders" as a way to disguise the emptiness and the mundanity. (*SL* 13)

If reunified Germany's dreamwork relies on the recovery of a bygone past that is to substitute the present in a gesture of rejection, Sowell inquires into a more complex form of the past that is not finished yet. For him, the "day before yesterday" amounts not simply to an active engagement with one's past but, indeed, to a project to move beyond the burden of history by stressing an unexpressed and unrealized potential. This amounts to something different than a postcolonial form of reinscription but which, rather, attempts to leave "yesterday" behind while concomitantly reaching for a time before "yesterday." If, for example, Salman Rushdie's strategies of resistance stay within the textual perimeters of history, necessarily working from within, Sowell *simultaneously* strives to emancipate himself from history/yesterday while and through seeking to access a reference point that lies beyond this history of oppression. Equally so, this investment in the past is also to be distinguished from Kenneth Warren's argument that contemporary African American literature aestheticizes "the recovery of lost stories" (2011: 102). For *Slumberland* does not try to make "the past present to us by any representational means necessary" (ibid.: 103) but inquires into the pastness of it without letting this paralyze those living in the present, thanks to the resurrective trace of an event.

In order to reject the simplicity and perfection (as both a qualitative modality and a temporal one) of the past, Sowell becomes a literal "*refugee*," not merely attempting to escape the past through emigration but turning again into a "fugitive" and thus confronting it actively. This becomes especially evident in Sowell's political-linguistic creativity. His response to the lack of a proper term for a more complex modality of historical awareness has to be viewed as both a general reflection on the relation between history and language, and his personal epistemological inability to reach that passed/past event. In stark opposition to what he sees as an American proclivity for euphemistic signifiers without referents, Sowell's intention to create a new, unadorned temporal concept aims to fill a cultural void and even to move beyond the present situation, its literal "mundanity," by exploring a way beyond the burdens of history. Yet, if his linguistic suggestions—"*penultidiem . . . prepretoday . . . yonyesterday . . . Retrohence*" (*SL* 15)—are symptomatic of his unrelenting obsession with trying to access a specific temporality beyond history, they ultimately remain unsuccessful, mere shots into the dark.

Sowell's attempt to move not beyond but *before* the past can be seen as an intriguing and, in fact, proleptic comment on a recent discourse in African American studies[34] that tries to "posterize" (Taylor 2007: 626) this cultural domain in the face of postmodern developments.[35] *Slumberland* engages in this debate by ironically commenting on Kenneth Warren's much-disputed argument that African American literature should be historicized as a cultural project that merely extends from post-emancipation until the end of the Jim Crow era (2011: 1).[36] More generally, however, the novel engages in the overarching discourse of "post-blackness" in an extremely critical way. For one thing, the novel addresses Warren's thesis that radically contextualizes African

American literature as a specific politico-cultural project. In doing so, Warren seeks to question African American studies' transhistorical, even ahistorical, detachment from the reality of American history (ibid.: 9) and ascribes to African American literature a specific and collective political project of engaging with Jim Crow segregation.[37] Warren argues that with the waning of segregation as a de jure reality, this literature's "instrumental and indexical" (ibid.: 10) aspirations were fulfilled, which led to the disintegration of a collective aesthetic-political enterprise.[38]

Commenting on this discourse, the novel evokes this debate by designating its narrator-protagonist with a crucial telling name: Ferguson W. Sowell not only bears "a pun on 'soul'" (Blaustein 2010: 726), thereby pointing to the Civil Rights era but also refers to what Warren sees as the beginning of African American literature, namely the 1896 "U.S. Supreme Court's decision in *Plessy v. Ferguson*" (2011: 1). By bearing Warren's starting point and endpoint of this particular literary and political project in his name, from the Ferguson trial to the end of the Soul era,[39] Sowell literally bears the marks of this political endeavor on his identity. Yet, instead of affirming Warren's arguments about a specific, limited historical and aesthetic period, *Slumberland*, rather, evokes this discourse in order to satirize it. Sowell as a figure of the *post*–Jim Crow era identifies himself, or rather is identified, in the context of the political struggle against segregation. Even more pessimistically, he cannot move beyond this historical period, which fundamentally haunts him as it writes itself on his body and thereby determines his identity. In other words, *Slumberland* undermines the possibility of "posterizing" blackness, as Taylor dubs it, by evoking this allegedly limited and redundant African American identity in the present. To a similar extent, the persistence of the African American political struggle is highlighted by Sowell's pseudonym that he assumes: DJ Darky. In spite of the dynamic and ostensibly liberatory play of identities that performance studies suggest, it seems symptomatic that even when Sowell tries to escape his historical past, he is determined by his racial identity (which is stressed even more so when he receives an anonymous letter with his Germanized name "Schallplattenunterhalter Dunkelmann" [*SL* 41], which again ascribes to him a racial identity from an outside position, tellingly a Stasi agent). Besides the narrator's satirical mocking of the past tense of blackness (*SL* 3), his name also indicates the inevitability of the narrative that is supposed to be left behind. However, while post-blackness and "Post-soul faces similar problems as postmodernism and postcolonialism" (2007: 630–31), as Taylor rightly observes, the novel does not contend itself to stop its critique of race in a hybrid deconstruction of the term, undermining it within its own discursive rules. Just as postmodernism, poststructuralism, or postcolonialism can always only critique the system it seeks to abolish from within its own perimeters, using its own weapons so to speak, one may wonder to what extent the posterizing of blackness is a cogent political and aesthetic form of emancipation. The novel, therefore, critically rejects the argument that "Post-blackness is blackness emancipated from its historical burdens and empowered by self-knowledge—the knowledge that race-thinking has helped create the world with which critical race theory and liberatory notions of blackness have to contend" (ibid.: 639), opting for a different alternative.

To this extent, *Slumberland* critically reflects upon the possibility of moving beyond blackness as a specific historical category, pointing to the problematic impulse of this discourse that, on the one hand, borrows the postmodernist skepticism toward grand narratives (race) but, on the other hand, simultaneously relapses to the metanarrative of the end (of history, politics, race). What is more, in the face of the striking need for an emancipatory politics, Sowell's resurrection of an event amplifies that emancipation is an eternal project that can never become "passé" but requires continuous reaffirmation, irrespective of skin color, gender, or class belonging. The novel "replace[s] an identitarian object and separating names with a real presentation of generic power such as its significance has been disclosed to us by the event" (*TRoH* 81).

Crucially, however, this resurrection is intimated in the novel through the very traversal that is hinted at in Sowell's name. From the political inception of the Ferguson trial to the aesthetic reverberations of the Soul era, *Slumberland* shifts the exclusively political focus of both Warren's historical delimitation as well as Badiou's truth procedures. For while Badiou stresses the specificity of a revolutionary politics, *or* a groundbreaking aesthetics, the novel stresses that a project of emancipation may also thrive on the cross-fertilization of political and aesthetic practices. In the next part of this chapter, I analyze Sowell's artistic "quest" (*SL* 25) and show how it is inevitably caught up in political strata. Moreover, I depict how this is related to a resurrective practice that will occasion political emancipation through the new creation of an aesthetic event that, in turn, bears political repercussions.

Art and propaganda

The event of emancipation, as has been observed, is "yesterday" and beyond Sowell's reach. Yet, through his artistic endeavor, trying to compose the "perfect beat" (*SL* 33), he is led to follow the trace of the mysterious jazz musician Charles Stone, who urges him to resurrect the political event of emancipation. Through Stone, Sowell comes to understand the political dimensions of his art and, ultimately, is able to generate an aesthetic event himself. While there is no direct confrontation in the novel between Sowell and what could be seen as the political event of emancipation, no immediate epiphanic revelation as in the case of Sam and Hailey in *Only Revolutions* or Yashmeen and Kit in *Against the Day*, *Slumberland* personifies the non-ontological singularity in Stone, who is diegetically and discursively depicted as a contingent, unidentifiable, and contagious trace of a larger political fidelity that is transcribed into aesthetic realms.

Slumberland's evocation of an artistic practice that leads to the resurrection of a political event could thus be seen as relapsing to a traditional fulcrum of African American political emancipation that Warren conceives in terms of its indexical and instrumental nature. Warren makes the case that African American literature saw its literary merits primarily in its political avail, on the one hand, being an instrument for political emancipation and, on the other, indicating "racial progress, integrity, or ability" (2011: 10). While I see *Slumberland* as being crucially concerned with political emancipation (and less so with this literature's indexical function) and therefore still consider it an African American novel according to Warren's definition, it crucially expands this dialectic in the light of a more intricate structure. In contrast to Warren's subordination of literary practices to political ones, Sowell's confrontation with the dialectics between politics and aesthetics is structured differently. Starting out to create a pure apolitical work of art, which is a purported mark of post-black aesthetic freedom,[40] his artistic confrontation with Stone makes him realize the need for the political resurrection of the event of emancipation. Following from this, both Sowell and Stone acquire their reagency in producing an aesthetic event that again bears political ramifications, having gone full circle.

In the beginning of the novel's chronology, Sowell's aesthetic practices of creating a perfect beat are more concerned with a *l'art pour l'art* mentality. Although he is retrospectively aware of the political milieu of his entering musical school—"The white students were placed in an advanced mathematics class at the university; we Negro boys, and the lone girl, were given instruments and sent to the Wilmer Jessop Academy of Music" (*SL* 21)—he initially embodies the apolitical tendencies that some ascribe to the so-called post-black Hip Hop generation.[41] Indeed, Sowell's alleged apolitical aspirations, which are influenced by postmodernist techniques of ahistorical pastiche, already become evident when he mixes "a version of Handel's *Messiah* composed entirely of elements from the Beastie Boys' *Licensed to Ill* album [sic!]" (*SL* 23). In contrast to a modernist aesthetics, what Eliot perceived as Joyce's mythical method, Sowell does not need an archetypal guide in order to structure his chaotic present. His sampling reappropriates Händel's baroque choral works by inversing a source-text and original dichotomy, rendering the religious opera profane through its contact with popular culture.

A further crucial exemplification of Darky's aesthetics is manifest in his explanation that his perfect beat is to be "a timeless piece of art, you know, like the Mona Lisa of music" (*SL* 35). His emphasis on the beat's timelessness is especially striking, for it not only counteracts the necessarily temporal dimension of a beat that essentially is based on repetition, rhythm, and timing; by invoking da Vinci's painting, he also refers to one of the best known and clearly least revolutionary works of art, both aesthetically and politically. Moreover, his intention to create a work that "transcends mood and time" (*SL* 29) conflicts with his other reflections on temporality. Nevertheless, his somewhat naïve aspirations in his idealist process of production, seeking to create a work of art that bears the potential for transcendence for both his listeners and himself, immediately reminds him of the necessarily spatio-temporal grounding of any process of reception.

Thus, when Sowell plays his "sonic Mona Lisa" (*SL* 29) to his fellow DJs, the novel instantaneously addresses the pertinent political avail of his creation. The narrative juxtaposes their listening to his beat with a somewhat unmotivated dialogue about their drinking German beer, which they toast "To the Rheinheitsgebot [sic!]" (*SL* 30). Besides the obvious racial reference to the German tradition of brewing beer according to a legislated "pure" norm, the narrative collocation also addresses the ostensible purity of Sowell's music. While he overtly stresses the "impurity" in aesthetic respects concerning the inter- as well as extra-musical references he allocates in his beat,[42] he obstinately denies the political dimension that it conveys.

Confronted with his fellow DJs' responses to his beat, which reminds them of "the code of Hammurabi, the Declaration of DJ Independence, the Constitution," Sowell retorts that their "Constitution metaphor is too political. You're making it seem like my music is propaganda." (*SL* 35) A clear nod to W. E. B. Du Bois's "Criteria of Negro Art"— "all Art is propaganda and ever must be, despite the wailing of the *purist*" (2000: 22, my emphasis)—Sowell is confronted with the inevitable politics of his art, the domains being "unseparated and inseparable" (ibid.: 18), as Du Bois has observed. However, whereas Du Bois situates art merely as an instrumental and indexical discourse that is supposed to "compel recognition" (ibid.: 23), *Slumberland* complicates this secondary status of art and opts for a more powerful understanding of the interrelation of these spheres.

By comparing his perfect beat to various legal documents, his fellow DJs draw a genealogy that likens Sowell's beat to a 4,000-year-old history of the most prominent artifacts of, on the one hand, emancipatory progress and, simultaneously, the exclusion of the enslaved in this political order. For both the Babylonian code of Hammurabi and the American Declaration of Independence constituted a crucial legal advancement in respect of laying the groundwork for a more egalitarian society, be it in the former's guiding principle of the *lex talionis*, the eye-for-eye maxim that introduced a penal code that to some degree leveled the differences between the polity's inhabitants,[43] or the latter's rejection of a monarchic order, similar to the French Revolution. Still, it goes without saying that the alleged equality that these legal codes professed omitted specific multiples from its legislation.

It is in this decisive moment of the narrative that the novel introduces Charles Stone. Right at the brink of Sowell's rejection of the political dimensions of art, he is told that his beat needs the *ratification* of Charles Stone, which is similarly alluded to by the narrative's innuendo about prominent political documents of modernity such as the "Magna Carta" or the "musicalized Equal Rights Amendment" (*SL* 35–36). This use of a political legislative concept seems particularly striking because it again intermingles these spheres. Even more so, by ascribing a political function to the aesthetic realm, and particularly to Stone, it echoes the mechanisms of political representation. In this manner, Sowell's beat only becomes official, just as African Americans have become part of the political body, if a superior representative apparatus ratifies its existence. Because of Stone's politico-aesthetic capacity, one might assume that Stone's position in the art world is analogous to that of the state in the political body. If so, Stone would be endowed with a superiority that casts doubts about Sowell's ability to obtain the political or aesthetic powers to produce art by himself. In other words, Sowell would depend upon Stone for his act of ratification/representation within the art world just as the African Americans rely on the state to acknowledge their inclusion.

However, the manner in which the narrative represents Stone undermines his status as an aesthetic sovereign who holds the puppet strings in his hand. As an individual exempt from the aesthetic *and* political order because of his revolutionary avail and because of his textual evasiveness, Stone is, rather, encoded with particular characteristics that make me read him as bearing the trace of the event that Sowell resurrects. In this sense, there is a dependence that marks the relationship between the two, but it is not a power relation that would subject the one to the other. Instead, by viewing Stone as carrying the trace of the event, I suggest that Sowell is only dependent on the reclusive Jazz musician as a subject is dependent on the event for its manifestation. To this extent, I argue that Stone bears the trace of the event upon him, rather than being a personification of it, to the effect that in the end the novel makes them both create an aesthetic event.

While Stone is certainly not an event himself, he does bear the marks of some of its properties.[44] First, Stone is introduced in the narrative through his aesthetic and political evasiveness. "Background information," Sowell observes, "was scarce"; he cites *The Jazz Encyclopedia*: "**Stone, Charles**—b. 4/7/1933, Los Angeles, California. A well-respected musician proficient in the improvisational techniques of the free-jazz movement of whom little is known." (*SL* 37) The other only extant account of him is a "redacted copy of a brief FBI file," which is depicted in typewriter font and bears various erasures:

Dear Mr. Hoover,

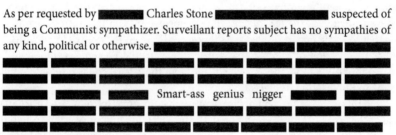

As per requested by ■■■■■ Charles Stone ■■■■■■■■■■■ suspected of being a Communist sympathizer. Surveillant reports subject has no sympathies of any kind, political or otherwise. ■■■■■■■■■■■■■■■
■■■■■■■■■■■■■■■
■■■■■■■■■■■■■■■
■■■ ■■ ■■ Smart-ass genius nigger ■■■ ■■
■■■■■■■■■■■■■■■
■■■■■■■■■■■■■■■
Stay American, Baby!
Buddy Rich. (*SL* 38)

The typographic characterization of Stone, in an aesthetic and a political attempt to contain his persona, is symptomatic of his resistance to be grasped in acts of discursive containment. In a strikingly similar manner as in the case of an event, both the encyclopedia's taxonomic attempt at grasping the aesthetic phenomena that Stone embodies, and the FBI's controlling apparatus, which interrogates him for potential political affinities, remain unsuccessful in arriving at a particular definition of Stone. Quantitatively ("little is known") and qualitatively ("no sympathies of any kind, political or otherwise"), Stone evades these modes of representation, which is further highlighted by the black eradications that mark the letter to Hoover. By typographically stressing the specificities of the respective medium of containment, the novel points to two powerful discursive practices—of the encyclopedic archive and the letter as part of the McCarthy *dispositif*—which, nevertheless, fail to account for him to the full extent. Just as an event of art cannot be readily incorporated into the existing order of aesthetic knowledge and the political forms of representation fail to account for aberrant multiples in more than a mere re-presentative manner of individuals such as "Charles Stone," so does Stone evade both discourses. Only within the parameters of human groups of political orientation ("Communist") or race ("nigger") does the state acknowledge these existences.

Stone's evasiveness is amplified in the nickname that Sowell and his colleagues bestow on him. His name, "the Schwa," implies that his music as well as his person are "like the indeterminate vowel," namely "unstressed, upside-down, and backward. Indefinable, but you know it when you hear it. For us the Schwa is the ultimate break beat. The boom bip" (*SL* 36). In this, Sowell and his fellow DJs substitute the concreteness, even the physicality in his original name, for a nickname that carries with it various resonances to an event. Just two consonants away from a concrete racial identity, Stone is likened to the linguistic concept of indefiniteness per se. Like the event's "indeterminate," "upside-down" potential, Stone defies the movements of categorization within the system of linguistic systematization itself. As before, Stone undermines the discursive paradigms of systemic attempts of trying to contain him, approximations of definition being permitted only so far. Moreover, the Schwa's linguistic sign ə also plays on the notion of the event, translating it from set theoretical diction (ex) into a linguistic one by highlighting the literally "upside-down" implications on a typographical level. Another indicator of the Schwa's likeness to an event is contained in Darky's emphasis that for them he "is the ultimate break beat." As Tricia Rose explains, "break beats are points of rupture in their former contexts, points at which the thematic elements of a musical piece are suspended and the underlying rhythms brought center stage" (1994: 250). *Rupture* is the key word here. As a musical analogue for the radically disruptive energies of an event, *Slumberland*'s characterization of Stone as the "*ultimate* break beat" employs an acoustic phenomenon that translates these philosophical ideas into the field of art.

A final aspect that emphasizes the Schwa's proximity to an event is the effect that his music has on those who hear it. In tune with Sowell's description of his music as "anarchy" (*SL* 97), the former's art transports a life-changing, contagious impetus. Once in Germany, Sowell engages on a "tri-forked" path of "three life-altering gigs . . . only to find out that all roads lead to the Schwa" (*SL* 172). Besides a gig at the "Department of Ancient American Studies," which no one attends except for a "pretty, vaguely Mediterranean-looking woman" (*SL* 181) who turns out to be the cleaning lady, Sowell also plays Stone's music for two somewhat diametrically opposed crowds. First, he plays the Schwa's version of the "Horst Wessel song" (*SL* 176) to a Neo-Nazi audience:

> As the Schwa's band turned the anthem inside out he [Thorsten, one of the Neo-Nazis] sat there holding his head as if he had a headache. I imagine Adolf Hitler had the same expression on his face when he witnessed Jesse Owens pull away from his vaunted supermen in a blazing mastery of muscle. . . . The Schwa was doing to National Socialism what Warhol had done to the Campbell's soup can. A few partygoers blubbered nostalgically in their drinks, but most stood at a slouching attention, unsure if the bop rendition of the song was an honorific tribute or an insult. (*SL* 176)

Through the radical and specifically political appropriation of one of the most revered cultural artifacts of the Third Reich, Stone literally turns the anthem inside out. He not only inverses the musical original and adapts it for his subversive needs. Even more so, he turns the anthem as a symbolic discourse of nationalist essentialism on its head and undermines the blood and soil ideology of such cultural products. The comparison that is drawn between his appropriation and Warhol's pop-art stresses this aesthetics of serial repetition and decontextualization and, once more, investigates a critique of American cultural discourse by hinting at its subliminal racist codes, which are conveyed in his analogy between fascism and capitalism.

The profound effect of Stone's remix of the Wessel song on the fascist audience is heightened when Darky plays another of the Schwa's songs to a camp of Afro-Germans who gather to try to "construct an identity from historical scratch" (*SL* 179). If his music proved to create a specific unease in the racist xenophobes, pointing to their unstable racial beliefs,[45] the repercussions here are more tangible and constructive. At the annual camp meeting at the "Black Forest" of what the narrator terms the "W. E. B. Du Bois's Talented Tenth" (*SL* 177), Sowell confronts two generations of rootless "nonstandard people" (*SL* 180) with the Schwa's music. One group is made up of "second- and third-generation descendants of French colonial soldiers who occupied the Rhineland after World War I," with typically German names like "Maximilian, Bertolt, Uschi, Axel, Effi, and Detlef," a "noble effort to make them, if not more German looking, then German sounding" (*SL* 178). The second group was "younger and hipper," the "offspring of the black American Cold War occupiers. Their fathers mantelpiece Polaroids, their namesakes jazz legends and Blaxploitation antiheroes. Miles, Billie, Dexter, Superfly, Shaft, and Buck and the Preacher" (*SL* 178). In the spatial separation that the volleyball court, where both groups stand face-to-face with each other, one grasps that the generational gulf that is sketched between the two generations of Afro-Germans seems to account for two distinct communities of these mongrels whose separation is intimated by their names. However, Sowell undermines the distinction between these generations framing them in a game metaphor that crucially relies on interaction. By the same token, in the vein of the event's universal appeal, the Schwa's music affects them regardless of their generational affiliation:

"What is happening? Nordica asked. . . . I need to know what is happening to me. Why do I feel so unsecure? Afraid, and yet not frightened." The room mumbled with agreement. Overcome with German inquisitiveness and black paranoia, these sons and daughters of Hegel and Queen Nefertiti wanted an answer. I wanted to tell them that the Schwa's music leans heavily on semitone, that tiny musical interval that's a half step between harmony and noise, for a reason. He wants to show us that the best parts of life are temporal semitone, those nanoseconds between ecstasy and panic that if we could we'd string together in sensate harmony. If only we could be Wile E. Coyote walking on air for those precious few moments before the bittersweet realization he's walking on air. I didn't say any of that because I didn't know the German word for semitone or if my audience knew who Bugs

Bunny was. I simply said, "What is happening is that you've been turnt out, baby."
The Schwa turns us all out sooner or later. (*SL* 181)

The contagious effect of Stone's music creates specific affects in the Afro-German group. While Nordica's attempts to come to terms with her response to this music echoes a feeling of sublimity that distinguishes between positive and negative fear, a dimension that was already analyzed in more detail in Chapter 3 of this book, the inexorable repercussions of listening to his music are particularly portentous in Sowell's observation of its potential to make them "turnt out." As "*turned out*" is "one of those ignoble black-American idioms" (*SL* 179) that carries the meaning of "turning good people bad, being 'normal' and then becoming addi[c]ted to drugs or becoming a prostitute" as the *Urban Dictionary* clarifies, this negative ramification is telling for the Schwa's aesthetic potency.

First, by employing a vernacular idiomatic, which is crucially exempt from "standard" English dictionaries, Sowell tries to account for Stone's effect by relapsing to a particular, unofficial linguistic repository. This becomes especially clear when Sowell notes that, unlike his other attempts to come up with new words for the fictional "*Kensington-Merriwether Dictionary of Standard American English*" (*SL* 14), he would not sell this neologism to the "*Kensington-Merriwether* for a million dollars" (*SL* 179). Just like Stone evaded the discursive regulations of the *Jazz Encylopedia*, Sowell rejects the textual containment of this phenomena, since this would imply a restriction of its potential.

However, Sowell's notion of being "turnt out" is not simply an insistence on cultural specificities that relies on an essentialist notion of black urban culture. It, rather, uses the linguistic capabilities of African American vernacular creativity, which offers an explicitly non-encyclopedic way of accounting for Stone's phenomenon. For while the inception of this absolutely contagious sensation, literally making those who hear it addicted to its propositions, is based in African American urban culture, its viral potential does not discriminate between such groups. Sowell's remark that "the Schwa turns *us all* out sooner or later" on the one hand insinuates the inexorability of his aesthetic appeal. On the other hand, it addresses the universality of its reach. The "us" that the narrator refers to makes no distinction between generational groups, skin color, gender, or even, as became clear at the hand of the Neo-Nazis, political orientation.

Indefiniteness, evasiveness, rupture, contagion. The way in which the novel presents the reclusive musician, on both a diegetic and a discursive level, draws heavily on the notion of a singular event. In this, *Slumberland* gives expression to another facet of events, showing that they do not always have to imply a violent physical eruption, as in the case of *The Road*, or a psychological meltdown, as in *Only Revolutions*, but may also be inscribed on an individual who bears its trace.[46] What is more, if the other events that this study investigates always imply the construction of a new present, the Schwa's connection to a resurrective practice suggests a different temporal vector. Since he bears the trace of an event that is past, he archives its potential in a look beyond yesterday. Sowell thus comments that "to many, the Schwa, like Muddy Waters, Mance

Lipscomb, and Ötzi the five-thousand-year-old iceman found in an Alpine glacier, was a well-preserved mummy, a music primitive seemingly unspoiled by commercialism and modernity" (*SL* 212). Specifically Sowell's description of Stone's preservation hints at his referring back to a past beyond the past. In his being compared to two modes of conservation, I maintain that Stone embodies not simply a nostalgically imbrued figure of anticapitalist counter-modernity but, rather, suggests a premodern figuration of the eternal perseverance of the event of emancipation that, like the Ötzi's or Tutenchamun's rediscovery, are proof of a layer of sediment of more ancient times. In other words, Sowell's desire to access the day before yesterday is encapsulated in Stone, who bears the trace of the event.

Still, if the novel is explicit about the extensional dimension of the effects of Stone's music, it is less clear about stating what particular qualitative repercussions it generates. In fact, while all admit that Stone affects their being, the novel remains more clandestine about the actual propositions that his music elicits, if he should, indeed, bear the trace of an event. By the same token, Sowell initially fails to grasp the political repercussions of his music. In line with his apolitical inclination, Sowell thus intends to relate to the Schwa on a purely aesthetic basis, which is highlighted by his consideration to explain his music in purely musicological terms to the Afro-Germans ("I wanted to tell them that the Schwa's music leans heavily on semitone, that tiny musical interval that's a half step between harmony and noise, for a reason" (*SL* 181). His rationalization of Stone's music, dissecting its architecture and even digging for an authorial intention ("He wants to show us"), simply ascribes to it an aesthetic value, without considering the political implications. In a sense, the novel thereby investigates to what extent a fidelity toward an event does not have to be instantaneous (as in the case of *Only Revolutions*) and may also progress from a "misreading" of it, a wrong interpretation of its implications to a proper faithfulness. Sowell's initial inability to grasp the political reverberations of Sowell's music, a reminder of the event of African American emancipation, thereby inverses Kit Traverse's fidelity in *Against the Day*, which moves from a genuine fidelity to a relapse to the pre-evental scientific world. If Badiou is less uncompromising in such conversions,[47] *Slumberland* explores the scope of how a subject may reconsider its fidelity to an event.

To be sure, the Schwa's political motivations should become clear to Sowell upon their first meeting. Not only does he turn out to be "the crazy-looking black guy who asked for donations to rebuild the Wall" (*SL* 148), which embodies a seemingly nostalgic response to the various cravings of East and West Germans who resent reunification. But when the musician finally consents to perform at the Slumberland bar, the political innuendos of his performance cannot be denied. Looking for an appropriate instrument on which to play, Stone takes a "paperback book from his jacket pocket and clear[s] his throat":

> The Schwa ruffled the pages of the book over his pant seam, and the resulting
> sound rivaled that of the best Max Roach brushwork. I nearly fainted. He lifted the
> book to his mouth and played chapter seven like a diatonic harmonica; blowing

and drawing on the pages like leaves of grass in the hands of Pan. Who knew a signet paperback was in the key of D? For the more percussive sounds he rapped the spine on his elbow, thumb drummed page corners, pizzicatoed the preface, flutter tongued the denouement, and bariolaged the blurbs.

Brothers, will you meet me.
John Brown's body lies a-mouldering in
the grave;
John Brown's body lies a-mouldering in
the grave;
John Brown's body lies a-mouldering in
the grave;
His soul's marching on! (SL 165–66)

When Stone appropriates the materiality of the book, which happens to be Faulkner's acoustically engaging *The Sound and the Fury* (and which obviously does not contain a Chapter 7), the hour of Pan has struck. Like the hybrid mythical creature Pan, the Schwa's musical recitation creates, again, a concrete sensation. If it is not *panic* that Sowell incites, one might read Sowell's evocation of this ancient figure as suggesting the universal appeal that his music conveys in the prefix of building a collectivity (as in *pan*-Africanism, for instance). Moreover, the harmony that Stone transports through his harmonica is also referred to by the botanical metaphor of an egalitarian society that Whitman so famously sketched out. Sowell's amazement at the acoustic dimensions of literature once more diverts his attention to the political innuendo that it may emit, if only handled correctly. By using the entirety of the book, Stone indeed points to the musicality of the medium beyond its diegetic content. Equally so, he stresses a comprehensive methodological approach that grounds a work of art in its physical and social context and does not merely indulge in the withdrawn reveries of its content.

Most striking in Stone's performance, however, is his verbal recital of the popular tune "John Brown's Body," which "was first sung at Fort Warren" on "12 May 1861" and "quickly became a Union favorite" (Nudelman 2001: 639). The ambivalent figure of abolitionist John Brown assumes a crucial role in the nation's history but particularly relates to its past as a slave country, with arguably the most important literary reflections by W. E. B. Du Bois, Langston Hughes, and Ralph Ellison.[48] If it is true, as Robert McParland argues, that the John Brown resurrection constitutes "one of the most controversial incidents in American history" (2010: 115), this poses the question of how and to what ends Stone integrates this nationalist tune in his performance. In fact, while Stone's integration of this outspokenly political happening again suggests the political nature of his art, it more pertinently addresses a specific historico-political past that attunes to Sowell's eventual resurrection and critically reflects on Brown's incorporation into both a Southern discourse of civil disobedience and a Northern narrative of religious martyrdom. Brown, who led a civil insurrection that was intended to spark a slave rebellion at Harpers Ferry in 1859 but was ultimately stifled by Robert E. Lee and ended in Brown's execution, could thus also be regarded as being part of the subjective body that constituted the slave rebellions that Badiou sees as relating to the Spartacus event.[49]

Remarkably, however, Brown was immediately incorporated for the ulterior motives of both the American South and North. While part of the South's resentment to his act was obviously due to his attempt to free the foundational source of their social, political, and economic order, one might also see another reason for their animosity in the quality of his political act—a violent act of revolution.[50] The outrageousness of Brown's attempted coup thus lies in his violent means, appropriating the prerogative of the white Southern population and directing them against themselves. Yet, even though Stone refers to Brown's revolutionary fidelity, the musician crucially does not call to arms. Indeed, Stone and Sowell's work of art substitutes a revolutionary politics for a revolutionary aesthetics, disintegrating the rigid distinction between these two spheres. Thereby, *Slumberland* goes beyond the classical Marxist understanding of the artist that imposes on him the task of furthering political awareness in order to bring about the proletarian revolution.[51] While there are similarities to the Marxist notion of the artist in respect of his political responsibility, *Slumberland* relies not simply on the class struggle but on a more fundamental notion of human equality, irrespective of socioeconomic position. What is more, the relation between content and form, which is a fundamental issue of Marxist literary criticism, does not make Sowell and Stone suggest a political message that serves as propaganda.[52] More fundamentally, they, rather, inquire into Benjamin's notion of being political by revolutionizing the very form of their art. In this respect, one could see *Slumberland*'s aesthetics equally as writing against the principles of some Marxist notions of what art is supposed to do, particularly through its negation of social realism by modernist and postmodernist techniques such as collage, anachronisms, unreliability of narration, and fusion of high and low culture, among others.

Finally, if one agrees with Eagleton that "the narrative Marxism has to deliver is the story of the struggles of men and women to free themselves from certain forms of exploitation and oppression" (Eagleton 2002: xii), both Badiou and Beatty undermine the autonomous agency that the people embody "themselves," since they are dependent on an event.

Still, in reflecting on both Badiou's and Brown's calls for action, Stone interrogates a different form of political fidelity, emphasizing the commemorative dimension of such a procedure, which consequently does not have to be grounded on blood. Nor is it based on soil. Sowell hence equally integrates Brown into his musical work of art by criticizing how he was put to the uses of furthering nationalist essentialisms or religious ideologies. While the one side regarded him "as a murderer and a lunatic" (McParland 2010: 115) because of his disobedience to current sociopolitical norms, he was equally assumed by the North within a Christian narrative of sacrifice, which is inherently connected to the religious grounding of the American nation: "In the North," observes McParland, "he was a redeemer" (ibid.: 115). Despite Brown's unmistakable configuration of a political subjective procedure that seeks to act in fidelity to the event of black emancipation, he is instantaneously co-opted by regulative mechanisms that seek to undermine this revolutionary potential either by casting it in a negative light or by integrating his radical act into a larger narrative of national constitution.[53] For instead of him functioning as an emblem of civil equality, "his death [represents] one of the founding moments in the development of a Northern nationalism based on the affective power of self-sacrifice" (2001: 641), as Franny Nudelman observes. Nudelman further notes:

> Offering a secular rendition of Christ's burial and resurrection, "John Brown's Body" puts religion to work in the service of war-time nationalism. Opening with the graphic "John Brown's body lies a-mouldering in the grave," the song proceeds to describe the transformation of Brown's corpse; he becomes a foot soldier in "the army of the Lord" and finally a martyr. As Brown's body decays, his spirit is reborn and, in turn, donates new life to the army and the nation it serves. (ibid.: 640)

Once more, *Slumberland* reflects on the complex relation between an event, or in this case a subject's relation to an event, and the manner in which the state assimilates these happenings. While the North tried to divert the emancipatory and revolutionary impetus for its nationalist claims, which goes hand in hand with the transformation of Brown's body as a political signifier into a religious symbol,[54] Stone refers to Brown to crucially different ends. In the vein of an evental politics, Stone relies on the bodily remnant of Brown not as an essentialist formation of a racial or national group identity but, rather, fashions a subjective *body* that avoids any essentialist groundings, which can be grasped by the sole fact that John Brown had WASP origins.[55] As Badiou observes in respect of historical riots, the "identitarian object" is destroyed to the extent that "it is no longer identity that counts, but non-identity" (*TRoH* 93–94). If one might interject that Sowell equally appropriates Brown's body and "John Brown's body" as a symbolic act to create a group identity, this ritualistic recitation emphasizes the *ad hoc* nature of this identity. Not only does this political procedure refer to a genuine truth of human equality that Brown sought to participate in, even if unsuccessful and in somewhat problematic terms; the constitution of a subjective identity also disavows the seemingly *a priori* givenness of an essentialist belonging, emphasizing, rather, the necessarily repetitive quality of this praxis. Put differently, while the militaristic tune aspires to fashion a collective by positing an "American" essence, Stone's use of "John Brown's body" calls for political fidelity that doubly denies the positing of a logocentric narrative of origins, which guides the constitution of modern nation-states. By referring to an event that is absolutely contingent and necessarily emancipatory (pointing to the excess of inclusion over belonging), Stone's call for a political fidelity distinguishes itself from the constructed and ostracizing mechanisms of a nation. Moreover, because of the fact that the event that Stone wishes to resurrect is epistemologically beyond grasp, his summons to a subjective procedure doubly evades the reference to an origin and, rather, highlights the structure of repeating one's fidelity, which takes a quite different spin in the case of a resurrection.

As in the case of Sam and Hailey's recurrent assertion of the points of the event, so does Stone insist on the inexorably iterative character of any fidelity. To recapitulate, for Badiou,

> [a] point is a particular moment around which an event establishes itself, where it must be re-played in some way, as if it were returning in a changed, displaced form, but one forcing you "to declare afresh." A point, in effect, comes when the consequences of a construction of truth . . . suddenly compels you to opt for a radical choice, as if you were back at the beginning, when you accepted and declared the event. (*IpoL* 50)

However, whereas the matter of reaffirming the event anew relates in the case of Sam and Hailey to the eruption of an event that they experienced face-to-face, Stone's literal "replaying" in a "changed, displaced form" that asks those faithful to it to declare it "afresh" differs essentially because of the ontic absence of this political event in their lived present. In a sense, one could argue that Stone's fidelity, to disseminate the need for a return to the political event of emancipation, relies heavily on repetition. Whereas Sam and Hailey simply reaffirm the points that mark their fidelity, Stone has to create a sensibility by repeating the truth of emancipation that is, as an act of resurrection, doubly strenuous, since he has to shake those in the literal Slumberland out of their apolitical reveries by pointing to a political event that is out of reach.

Without going into a media-specific analysis of music, *Slumberland* makes a case that it is especially the structural specificities of a song such as "John Brown's body" that transport specific aesthetic sensibilities of Badiou's philosophical notion. As a song, it not only aestheticizes the purely political implications but also stresses the repetitive character of subjective faithfulness. The threefold repetition of "John Brown's body lies a-mouldering in the grave" employs the musical inclination to repetition in order to shed light on a political subjective procedure. One could thus read this repetitive summoning as being snatched from its militaristic use and, rather insinuating a different form of ritual, for example, a subjective faithfulness to a political event.

This ritualistic undercurrent similarly avoids the religious context that Nudelman has observed to be part of the iconization of John Brown as a figure of Biblical self-sacrifice for a larger cause. If the concept of the event bears close parallels to biblical apocalypse, the notion of resurrection equally echoes Christ's death as well as his return from the dead.[56] In a similar manner as *The Road* distances itself from a religious understanding of the event, so does Stone's resurrective intimation, incorporating a symbolic marker of a subjective fidelity to the event of emancipation into his song, give a secular take on the notion of resurrection. For if the return from the dead implies in the case of Jesus the manifestation of a sacred might, Brown's resurrection, which is tantamount to the resurrection of the political event, is fundamentally a human and, particularly, subjective feat.[57] Put differently, whereas Jesus ascended to heaven because of a transcendental manifestation, the reaffirmation of the event of emancipation requires the faithful assertion and, indeed, the excavation of this forgotten truth.

Yet, the spectrality that Brown's body articulates, a living corpse so to speak, attests to this notion of unfinished business and attunes to the notion of resurrecting a bygone event.[58] Particularly through the metaphysical disintegration of "body" and "soul," Stone's reference to "John Brown's body" evokes the semantic reverberation of a ghostly figure that returns to haunt those surviving, facing them with a project that still awaits fulfillment. In a similar vein, this structure of return is perfectly conveyed in the presentation and content of the song, which indicates the need for resurrecting a political truth that "lies a-mouldering in the grave." The manner in which Stone references the particular part of the song that juxtaposes the dead-alive, body-soul, ephemeral-eternal dichotomies neatly conveys his wake-up call, highlighting the repeated attempt to leave Brown's body to the grave in the repetition of this line thrice. Against the commemorative implications of "John Brown's body," Stone decontextualizes and uses only a fragment of the song (decidedly avoiding the chorus "Glory, glory, hallelujah") in order to counteract the stupefying effect of the militaristic appropriation of John Brown. Next to the mass-mobilizing impetus for a national cause,[59] "John Brown's body" could also be said to have the reverse effect and through its commemoration merely channels the need for political action into political paralysis that is transported by the reiterated stress on the pastness of Brown's political intention, being buried at the site of social exclusion.[60] Still, acting against this lulling repetition of the allegedly finished business symptomized by Brown's location in the grave, the perseverance of his "soul," which could be read as an analog for the still unrealized truth of emancipation, is still alive and kicking. By extracting "John Brown's body" from Southern processes of occulting the truth of black emancipation as well as by a discourse of nationalist or religious ideology, Stone alters the commemorative dimension of the song in order to stress the need for resurrecting what John Brown assumed to be a political event some 130 years ago. The persistent quality with which Brown's soul marches on and calls for the formation of a new subjective body is reflected in the event of human equality's reluctance to be relegated to the grave, as a specific site of ritualized closure.

Despite Stone's straightforward insistence upon the return to the political event, Sowell is still not entirely convinced "to fulfill [his] part in the resurrection of the black man" (*SL* 121). What Sowell does agree to is to perform together with Stone in order to recreate "a wall of sound" (*SL* 191) that is supposed to replace the Berlin Wall. In fact, although Sowell approves of their joint performance on an aesthetic basis, their duet will not only help to resurrect the event of emancipation but will also create a new, aesthetic event. In this vein, Sowell promotes their (to him) apolitical "BLACK PASSÉ TOUR—BUILDING WALLS, TEARING DOWN BRIDGES" (*SL* 209), which inverses the multiculturalist stance of ethical cosmopolitanism and, rather, "celebrate[s] the city's resegregation" (*SL* 211). Despite the apparent nostalgic, even regressive undercurrent of their project, Sowell stresses his intention to move beyond blackness and create the utopia of a post-racial society.

Nevertheless, both are eager to point out the fundamental ambivalence of the wall: "They'd [the audience] have to figure out for themselves if the wall of sound was confinement, exclusion, or protection" (*SL* 198). While this is a crucial remark, since it rejects the unequivocal interpretation of a nostalgic return to the time before reunification, viewed in the light of the theory of the subject of the event, it also addresses the various relations that an event may occasion. Although an event always demands a form of fidelity, the work of art that they are about to produce, which not only serves as a resurrection of the political event of emancipation but also "presupposes a new world, which generates the context of a new event, a new trace, a new body" (*LoW* 65), does not prescribe in what manner they react: they essentially "have to figure out for themselves" how they relate to it. If "confinement" could thus be said to relate to a reactive subjective procedure, which nostalgically craves the return of the wall for its ability to separate East and West Germany, those desiring "exclusion" certainly relate to the respective side in a manner that might be viewed in the light of an obscure fidelity, excluding those they do not see as part of their social order. The event would thus grant "protection" to those who act in faith to its propositions, if only by forming a collective that sustains a common purpose, which becomes evident in their project.

> In the treeless places where the Wall's footprint had been erased by progress in the form of condominiums or vacant lots that would soon be turned into condos, there was no shortage of local artists who were willing to fill in the blanks. For instance, Steffi Rödl strung a clothesline made of barbed wire across the trash-strewn vacant lot that sat behind a row of apartment houses on Stallschreiberstrasse. Using wooden clothespins, she hung a twelve-foot-high curtain of shiny charcoal-gray silk that billowed majestically in the wind, a brilliantine representation of the Berlin Wall aired out like so much dirty laundry. In Potsdamer Platz, where the Wall had been eradicated by commercialism and skyscrapers, in lieu of radios— which would never have been heard over the din of downtown traffic—Michael Harnisch projected a musical stave across the white limestone base of the Sony Center. A computer instantly annotated the music and projected the notes onto the wall, the concert's score running through downtown Berlin like a ticker tape opera. Using the Brandenburg Gate as a backdrop, Uwe Okulaja lined up a bank of high-powered green and red lights that, like a giant equalizer, shot a pulsing LED readout 250 meters into the night sky. There were other installations: a dancing fountain, an oscilloscope, and pushcarts where you could rent a set of those chintzy museum headphones and take a sonic tour of the new Berlin Wall. (*SL* 205–06)

For one thing, note the spatial dimensions of their aesthetic project. In appropriating the capitalist-encroached places that gentrify and sterilize the city, Sowell, Stone, and other artists convert urban space into an aesthetic project, thereby creating what Badiou calls "a new site" (*TRoH* 23). Through various installations, the group of artists thereby unshackles the stability of the privatized public sphere by transforming it into an ambient work of art that affects the entire city. This spatial transfiguration is specifically interesting, for it approximates what Badiou understands as the evental impetus in art, which he defines as a crucial interrogation of form.[61] For him, an aesthetic event always breaks the "tension between the intensity of the sensible and the tranquility of form" (*LoW* 73), meaning that it allows for a new formal aesthetics to be considered as an aesthetics at all.[62] What formerly appeared to be "formless is grasped as form" (*LoW* 73). Especially through their transformation of a given spatial order, an order that is so ostensibly self-evident, accessible, and unquestionable as the public sphere, they change the perception of Berlin and its inhabitants by unraveling a sensibility that could not be perceived before. Yet again, the evental impetus does not bring about a transcendental revelation that remained beyond the epistemological grasp of Berlin's inhabitants but, crucially, works from an immanent perspective, being installed "among existing streets." Although they give the Wall a new form, it required the impetus of an event to make them able to construe this new sense of formalization. Even so, by constructing a new site, "which is nevertheless internal to the general localization that is a world," they aspire to "real change" (*TRoH* 57).

By the same token, I would argue that it is the process of resurrecting the political event of emancipation that allows them to interrogate this new aesthetic form, which clearly runs against Badiou's line of argument. For his notion of the aesthetic event's "affirmative idea of the split is when something which was in the negation, part of the formalist impossibility, becomes [an] affirmative possibility" (2004: n.p.) can equally be related to political matters. The political art that Rödl, Harnisch, Okulaja, and others perform thus takes its cue from the social "negation" and assumes giving a form to this lack of political belonging on an aesthetic level. The materiality of Steffi Rödl's cloth thereby simultaneously serves to cover and highlight the "blank," "vacant" spaces beyond the resident's environment of living. Her clothesline thereby gives form to a particular capitalist negligence by destabilizing the literal concreteness of the Wall, juxtaposing various semantic layers (the cloth as "dirty laundry" suggesting labor exploitation, its "barbed wire" hinting at socioeconomic and national borders) that give the political a different aesthetic form, even a form at all. Indeed, against Blaustein's argument that "the Schwa might just as easily be Baraka's archetypal revolutionary, or, in Ralph Ellison's contrary characterization of beboppers, 'the least political of men'," (2010: 734) I read the novel as emphasizing the profound political motivations of both Stone and Sowell as well as other artists involved in this project. To an extent, one could see them as being Benjamin's revolutionary artists who perceive that there is a "decisive difference between merely transmitting the apparatus of production and transforming it" (1970: n.p.). Their political tendency only fulfills itself through their revolutionary inquiry into form. As Terry Eagleton summarizes: "It is not just a question of pushing a revolutionary 'message' through existing media; it is a question of revolutionizing the media themselves" (2002: 57).

Even more so do Michael Harnisch and Uwe Okulaja's installations conceptualize a new form. By making visible the music that Stone and Sowell are about to perform, they create a new aesthetic sensibility for what has before only been conceived in auditory ways. Being able to experience the sonic wall as in a guided tour, these artists profoundly destabilize the fixed space of the museum and disseminate the kinesthetic experience of art (and politics) around the lived environment of the city's inhabitants. To this extent, despite their pretensions to simply create "a wall of sound" (*SL* 191), they fundamentally inquire into the semiotics of form and make visible what was before invisible.[63] This then obviously participates in Stone's political project of resurrecting the event of emancipation, which similarly hinges on the making visible of the invisible. However, the pivotal moment, in both aesthetic and political terms, only arrives when Stone and Sowell perform their work of art together.

Here it must be noted that it seems misleading to see them as individually creating an aesthetic event themselves, since this runs against the grain of the event's conceptual framework of being fundamentally contingent and particularly pre-subjective. Instead of endowing the two musicians and the other artists who contribute to the wall of sound with a Romantic notion of authorship, an "idealistic conception of invention" (2005: 11), as Badiou writes in *Handbook of Inaesthetics*, I, rather, argue that they are only able to create an aesthetic event because of their resurrection of a political event. Politics and aesthetics, the novel shows, cannot be thought apart from each other and only become manifest in the wake of an event. Once Stone is successful in pointing to the forgotten event of emancipation, a subjective process is under way that does not merely rejuvenate the "old" event but fundamentally creates a new one. This conforms to Badiou's notion of resurrection that concomitantly creates a new present as well as fights the processes that try to negate the validity of this subjective procedure (end of history, end of politics, end of Jim Crow): "With regard to every genuine present, one can rightfully hope that a new present, by activating de-occultation, will make that present's lost radiance appear at the salvific surface of a body" (*LoW* 66). Thereby, the novel complicates the notion of artistic events, which for Badiou are not works of art itself (2005: 12) but, rather, subjective processes, and his reflections on the creation of a new event through the process of resurrection. In this vein, *Slumberland* appreciates the inter-conditional transfers of such a mode of resurrection, where a resuscitated political event may affect aesthetic fidelity, which again creates a revolutionary work of art that is fundamentally political. "In the final analysis," writes Badiou, "the pertinent unit for a thinking of art as an immanent and singular truth is thus neither the work nor the author, but rather the artistic configuration initiated by an eventual rupture (which in general renders a prior configuration obsolete)" (ibid.: 12). What *Slumberland* points to, thereby extending Badiou's conceptual framework, is that this newly distributed form of sensibility, to borrow Rancière's expression, is necessarily aesthetic *and* political.

It is, then, only when Stone and Sowell play together—Stone and Sowell as materialism and idealism conjoined, if you will[64]—that Sowell realizes the political dimensions of his music. This is intimated already when at the beginning of their performance, Stone plays by himself and Sowell offers once more another of his comparisons that tries to grasp Stone's performance. "The Schwa's music," Sowell notes, "shatters time," makes one travel in time: "If there is such a thing as a vehicle for time travel it's music" (*SL* 224).

Besides once more likening Stone's music to a literally shattering experience, Sowell here returns to his obsession with temporality. If his account seems contradictory, since it conflates a freeze-frame disposition of time with the fluctuations latent in time travel, one might see both modalities as being part of the phenomenon of the resurrection of the event that Sowell progressively comes to understand. While Stone's music thus implies a radical break that renders time out of joint, this singularity is immediately followed by Sowell's return to the event of emancipation through the musical qualities that surpass scientific speculations. Sowell's recurrent nods to lowbrow aesthetics here make him cite Robert Zemeckis's 1985 pop-cultural classic *Back to the Future,* which cogently insinuates the temporal oxymoron that he engages with. For it is not a linear vector that Sowell embarks on, either into the past (nostalgia) or into the future (utopia); he crucially returns to the past and its forgotten event in order to effect a different future.

Like the other novels discussed in this study, a clear decision of when the event occurs, or when a subject acknowledges its existence remains necessarily fuzzy. It would be simplifying in respect of both Badiou's theory and the literature under consideration to insist on a singular textual marker that represents such moments. *Slumberland,* thus, likewise insists on the processual nature of a becoming subject that, nevertheless, inspires absolute change. Put differently, if an event is always a singular point, then the relation a subject assumes to it may evolve over time.

Moreover, while the novel criticizes the alleged "events" of the end of Jim Crow legislation or the fall of the Berlin Wall and relates to the textually absent event of emancipation, one could read Stone's and Sowell's performance as approximating a genuine diegetic event, which, in turn, only appears because of Sowell's embrace of the political fidelity. Within the ongoing conversion of Sowell to the event of emancipation, which is even further complicated by the retrospective, post-evental narrative situation, I would argue that the time in between Stone's solo and the musical performance they engage in together approximates an event. Indeed, while Sowell once more employs a rhetoric of disruption—"sensibilities were scattered" and he is afflicted with "PTSD" (*SL* 225)—to describe the effect of Stone's music, it is only when he plays his "timeless work of art" (*SL* 35) to the audience and Stone joins his beat that he is ultimately struck by the resurrective impetus:

> He was switching up the tempo. Segueing from a frenzied fortissimo to a languid legato by quoting from "Lift Every Voice and Sing," the Negro national anthem. . . . Musical mason that he was, the Schwa erected a series of African-American landmarks upon the foundation I had laid down. The contrapuntal effect of our discordant architectural styles meshed together wonderfully. (*SL* 228)

Throughout the novel, *Slumberland* stresses the temporal dispositions that are interconnected to the resurrection of the event. While the "tempo" certainly relates to the speed with which Stone accompanies Sowell's DJing, it could again be said to connect to notions of tempo-rality, with the jazz musician radically changing time ("switching up" implying a radical change in mood, as the *Urban Dictionary* explains). In this vein, Stone perfectly adapts to Sowell's "foundation" and integrates, once more, specific landmarks that refer to the event of emancipation. Although Stone here insistently tries to confront Sowell with his political responsibility, which he tries to achieve through the "legato" blending of their apparently "contrapuntal" "architectural styles," Sowell still struggles with this proposition. Although he does not deny the "tune's genius," in his "mental landscape where blackness [was] passé, his quoting the Negro national anthem was a blatant violation of the zoning laws. By constructing a new black Berlin Wall in both [Sowell's] head and the city, he was asking [him] to improvise" (*SL* 228). Sowell "was daring [him] to be 'black.' But blackness is and forever will be passé and [Sowell] held [his] compositional ground, hit [his] presets, and leaned on [his] turntables, furiously scratching the coda" (*SL* 228). Particularly through the juxtaposition of Sowell's insistence on the present tense ("is") of his post-black "mental landscape" with the past tense ("was") of Stone's apparently political transgression, Sowell constructs a psychic geography that fortifies his persuasion to remain apolitical and to refrain from letting an essentialist black identity be imposed on him. By Stone playing the "Negro national anthem" over Sowell's allegedly timeless piece, the DJ is clearly put out of his comfort zone. However, instead of viewing this as an act of creating a stable "black" identification, I would, rather, suggest that this is part and parcel of Stone's attempts at resurrecting a more general political fidelity. Remarkably then, while the music that Stone played always had an undeniable effect on Sowell, it is only when they duet that he appreciates the full effect of the jazz musician's intentions. Nevertheless, because of Sowell's unremitting insistence on the pastness of black identity—which seems for him to be tantamount to political activity—he responds by playing "*I shall not be moved/Like a tree that's planted by the water/I shall not be moved*" (*SL* 229). The comic effect of this is obvious. While Sowell intends the content of this archetypal song of black emancipation to give voice to his reluctance to acquiesce to the political obligations that Stone raises, he is ultimately "forced to relent to [his] racial and turntable obstinacy" (*SL* 229) by his own integration of what could be seen less as an essentialized African American than a song of political protest for emancipation, from his ostensibly pure aesthetic conviction. In Sowell's "beat parfait complete," he addresses the crowd with the telling words: "remember, 'All art is propaganda'" (*SL* 229). This symbolic conclusion of their performance marks Sowell's affirmation of the political nature of his art, which goes hand in hand with his resurrection of the political event. Not only does the verb of commemoration indicate his own act of returning to this event; it also manifests an imperative for those attending to adhere to the truth of emancipation. Next to the affirmation of Du Bois's dictum, Sowell and Stone's art is not simply a propagandistic cog in a political machinery. "Propaganda" could thus be conceived in its original sense of a "congregation for propagation of the faith," (*OED* 1993: 2378) with "propagating" (*OED* 1993: 2378) implying the "spread and promot[ion]" obviously not of a religious faith but of a political truth.

Having stepped up to the political debt of the event of emancipation, Stone and Sowell have thus created a new aesthetic event. Yet, their authority over this new form of what was hitherto in-form is inevitably tied to their resurrection of the political event. In other words, their aesthetic reagency, the ability to create a revolutionary work of art, is fundamentally dependent on their fidelity to the event of emancipation. Only through this are they endowed with the creative potency of fashioning "a new world, which generates the context of a new event, a new trace, a new body" (*LoW* 65).

To be sure, the manner in which they create this new event, which serves as an aesthetic reminder of the political event of emancipation, is equally so hardly a conscious act of self-willed creation. This is stressed not only by Sowell's far-from-active posture—"I gave myself up to the current. Surrendered to the sound, waiting, praying, for the next eddy of cacophony to pick me up, smash my head against the rocks, and put an end to my misery" (*SL* 22)—but also by Stone's apparent signs of confusion when he hears Stone's beat: "Even though he'd been expecting a miracle, he wasn't quite ready for the thoroughness of the boom. His hands shook. He was faltering, unsure of himself" (*SL* 228). Through this obvious destabilization of their authority over their creative act, aesthetic production in the context of the subject of the event's reagency crucially distances itself from Romantic authorship. Besides the fact that they *collectively* create this work of art and do not rely on an individual myth of aesthetic agency, they can only produce art, revolutionary art that is, because of the impetus of the political event.

To this extent, Sowell steps up to his fidelity when in a last conversation with Stone, he asks him what he was thinking about in his last solo. Stone responds:

> "I was thinking about the phrase on the banner, 'Black Passé.' How being passé is freedom. You can do what you want. No demands. No expectations. The only person I have to please is myself." "You'll never be passé. 'Shit, you keep spinning like that and neither will you.' 'I don't know about that. To be passé you have to have been happening at some point in time, and I never was nor never will be happening.'" (*SL* 230)

This last dialogue ties up a variety of issues that were discussed in relation to temporality, politics, and aesthetics throughout this chapter. In Stone's pondering on the possibility of (negative) freedom, one might well read *Slumberland*'s general stance toward the discourse of "posterizing" (Taylor 2007: 626) blackness. Against Kenneth Warren's plea for the pastness of African American literature, and with it the coherence of African American political struggle, the novel proffers the validity of this political project in the contemporary age (be that the novel's diegetic present of the late twentieth century or its publication in the first decade of the twenty-first). Read in the light of Badiou's notion of events and subjects, the disciplinary turn away from "blackness" might be understandable from an anti-essentialist point of view, but it also bears the danger of solipsism, with the only person accountable for one's actions being oneself. Against this relativist notion of freedom, *Slumberland* makes strong the importance of an *ethics-of*. "Ethics does not exist," as Badiou once more so provocatively insists. "There is only the ethic-of (of politics, of love, of science, of art)" (*E* 28). While the event of political emancipation certainly does not grant "freedom" and necessarily imposes "demands" and "expectations" that have to be met in order to sustain their subjective status and to deny another occultation of this truth, Sowell realizes that this political dimension is not a limitation but an enrichment of his aesthetic endeavors.[65] Importantly, however, the novel expands the singular referential realm, which through the manifestation of an event may engender ethical behavior by marking the relation between political fidelity and aesthetic productivity. In this sense, Stone addresses the interconnection between these spheres and their ethical import when he tells Sowell to "keep [it] spinning." Put differently, through Sowell's fidelity, which needs to "keep" going in order to reaffirm on a regular basis the political truth of human emancipation, his aesthetic practice serves as a valiant form that reinscribes the revolutionary potential of politics into art. If Badiou thus conceives the only real politics as a revolutionary politics, *Slumberland* suggests that the only real art is revolutionary art, in terms of both its form and its content.[66]

This also plays out on a structural level of the novel itself. Formally, the novel integrates this in its narrative order, as the autodiegetic narrator Sowell retells his "quest" (*SL* 25) in retrospect. Although this narrative perspective is an important means within African American literature, with Douglass and Ellison certainly as the two seminal instances where autodiegetic perspective is employed to stress literary and political self-legitimation, in the case of *Slumberland*, Sowell does not recount and thereby legitimate his *life* but focuses on his processual acceptance of the event. As was already observed in the previous chapters, an event cannot be anticipated, which implies that the teleological expectations of the quest narrative seem amiss in the context of the subject of the event. A subject cannot perceive itself to be on a linear voyage to self-realization, enlightenment, emancipation, etc., since it cannot fathom the event that is radically outside of its epistemological and ontological vocabulary. In the light of the narrative structure that Bernard W. Bell sees as the quintessence of African American writing (1990: 1142–43), the quest that Sowell embarks on implies a different register than the tradition of this literary practice, for he employs this narrative form to serve the purpose of retelling his resurrection of the political event and its inspiration of aesthetic productivity. Indeed, *Slumberland* as a whole could thus be said to assume another pointal reaffirmation of the event that not only recounts his becoming of a subject but also serves the means of itself being a fictional artifact that strives to keep this event "spinning." While quest narratives thus seem to hinge on the constitution of a subject, Sowell continues his political fidelity by making his autodiegetic narrative a testament to the event. In the vein of the impurity of his aesthetic endeavor, he, indeed, now gives the musical event a concrete narrative form in a literary work of fiction, which begins, like a scratched record, in the diegetic present after the event to recount his "part in the resurrection of the black man" (*SL* 121), only to arrive at the end of the narrative again at the recollections of the narrating I, the post-evental textual now. Only because of the event, one could argue, does he tell his story; only in keeping this political truth alive does he create a narrative.

Although at the end of the novel Sowell concedes in retrospect that his "perfect beat has had a far less reverberatory effect" (*SL* 233) than he expected, the impact on his constitution of a subject faithful to a political event and the consequent empowerment that lets him constitute a genuine work of art should not be underestimated. Not only has he himself realized the political responsibilities of emancipation, but he has also created a work of art that serves as a new, though context-specific, installment of this event. Without aspiring to any authoritative and originary, "ingenius" (Badiou 2005: 11) *invention*, he nevertheless has "inscribe[d] into the textual body that bears the trace of the new an entire reactivation, an entire updating to the present" (*LoW* 66).

To sum up, *Slumberland*'s interrogation into the practice of resurrecting a political event reaffirms this political truth in the realm of art, which can obviously be read on both a diegetic and a meta-level for the novel itself, by combining and critically inflecting the two modes of temporality that Kenneth Warren sees as indicative of "black" literature. While his notion of African American literature, that is, literature of the Jim Crow era, is constituted by a proleptic impetus, trying to imagine a future that has not been actualized, he sees post-Jim Crow "black" literature as being retrospective.[67] *Slumberland* combines both modes in its persistent reflections on temporality, which is symptomatically conveyed when Stone declares, "You'll never be passé." In contrast to Warren's insistence that in order "to understand both past and present, we have to put the past behind us" (2011: 84), Sowell inquires into the way in which a resurrection of a political event (a past beyond the past) offers ethical potential. By resurrecting a "passed" political event, the novel writes against historical overdetermination and aestheticizes the possibility of a *future simple* that is marked by, if not simplicity or stability, a subjective future, nevertheless.

"There is nothing to compare it to now"

The Scientific-Political Subjects in Thomas Pynchon's
Against the Day (2006)

*Most people's lives have ups and downs that are relatively gradual, a sinuous
curve with first derivatives at every point. They're the ones who never get struck by
lightning. No real idea of cataclysm at all. But the ones who do get hit experience a
singular point, a discontinuity in the curve of life—do you know what the time rate
of change is at a cusp? Infinity, that's what! A-and right across the point, it's minus
infinity! How's that for sudden change, eh? Infinite miles per hour changing to the
same speed in reverse, all in the gnat's ass or red cunt hair of the Δt across the point.
That's getting hit by lightning, folks.*

. . .

It will look like the world you left, but it'll be different.

Thomas Pynchon, Gravity's Rainbow.

The essence of mathematics *is its freedom.*

Georg Cantor, "Über unendliche, lineare Punktmannigfaltigkeiten V."

Thomas Pynchon's novels have gained a reputation, which has even evolved to a critical
commonplace, of being fictions about other worlds. By projecting alternative worlds,
to paraphrase Oedipa Maas's famous reflection in *The Crying of Lot 49*, Pynchon's
novels fundamentally question the monadic "given" world without abandoning the
interconnections of "possible" worlds with "actual" ones. His 2006 *Against the Day* equally
subscribes to this ontological mode of metafiction[1] when it already mentions in the blurb:
"Maybe it's not the world, but with a minor adjustment or two it's what the world might
be." However, while the novel, very much like Pynchon's other novels, reflects on worlds,
their making, and offers different ones, I argue that *Against the Day* distances itself from its
predecessors by engaging in the production of alternative events. Despite the projection
of different, often counter-factual worlds, this chapter shows that Pynchon's sixth novel
fundamentally inquires into the question that Badiou formulates as such: "How are we to
be faithful to changing the world *within the world itself?*" (*TRoH* 67).

Within the context of this study, *Against the Day* differs from the other novels
discussed since it integrates a variety of events, and consequently, a range of subjects
of events within its diegesis, instead of merely focusing on one such manifestation

as in the case of *Only Revolutions* and *Slumberland*.[2] While it is a particular concern of the last three novels to juxtapose a variety of "historical" happenings with the genuine eruption of an event, *Against the Day* incorporates not merely a range of other historical incidents, which are no events, but also sets side by side a panoply of events. The depiction of the mysterious Tunguska event, the celebration of the Haymarket bombing, or a dynamite explosion that proves to catapult Lew Basnight into a world that "didn't seem like Colorado anymore" (*AtD* 185) is not simply a rewriting of hegemonic historiography but proves to entail a poetic program of producing and reflecting upon events and subjects. Moreover, in contrast to Danielewski's novel, which produces a subject of love that consistently reinscribes its subjecthood by repetitiously affirming the points of the event, *Against the Day* elucidates that fidelity to an event is not to be taken for granted. Although Kit Traverse's fidelity to the Quaternionist event makes him abandon his familial, economic, and scientific dependences, this form of reagency is forfeited when he turns his back to the event and thus results in "unfaithfulness to the event" (*IT* 140), the abandonment of a fidelity. The analysis of Kit's shifting fidelity thereby exhibits to what extent fidelity to an event implies an ongoing process of affirmation, even when confronted with "moments of crisis" (*E* 78).

In contrast, although equally confronted with inherent scientific doubts, Yashmeen Halfcourt evolves to a sustained scientific-political subject who extends the evental propositions of the Riemann event onto other spheres that are seemingly lying outside of this truth condition. Like *Slumberland*, *Against the Day* therefore creates an "inter-conditional" scientific-political subject, if only the development is inversed: if Sowell resurrects a political event that makes him partake in an aesthetic one, Yashmeen's scientific fidelity percolates into political terrain complicating Badiou's argument that "science and politics are completely different thinkings" (*IT* 61).[3] By creating a collective subjective procedure, Yashmeen exemplifies a form of fidelity that adapts "theoretical" scientific insights to the "real" axis of politics.[4]

Upon first glance, Pynchon might not seem the first choice when it comes to notions of subjects, events, and/or agency. For the characters of his previous novels do not exactly come off well in this respect. Particularly his epochal *Gravity's Rainbow* figures prominently in questioning the concept of a rational, self-same subject that has the ability to act without regard of determining outside forces, as was illustrated in the introduction. Tyrone Slothrop thus permanently loses his identity and as a consequence forgets his mission in the Germany of the Second World War. The apex of this critique of a humanist notion of characters that affects their literary representation and their ostensible function within narratives manifests itself in the protagonist's dispersal and consequent disappearance from the novel. The only moment of possibility, the Δt that marks an infinitesimal singular point between two moments of decision, reverses what Timothy Melley calls Slothrop's "incorporation" by literally ex-corporating him in a Christ-like form of transcendence, becoming "a cross himself, a crossroads, a living intersection" (Pynchon 2006a: 637).[5]

What seems even more questionable within the scope of this chapter is that I argue that *Against the Day* creates a scientific subject of the event. On the one hand, this seems counterintuitive, since Pynchon's use of science and scientific discourses generally is interconnected with human determination and seemingly attests to his allegiance to "King Ludd" (1984: 40).[6] Slothrop's disappearance is thus inherently connected to his determination by scientific discourses, which also makes itself felt on a linguistic level. His "scattering" that is closely tied to the mathematical concept Δt uses scientific terms that fundamentally undermine his status as a humanist subject.[7]

In contrast, this chapter shows that mathematics, "one of the most crucial ways of imagining worlds in *Against the Day*" (Pöhlmann 2010: 25) is not on the same grounds as chemistry and physics in *Gravity's Rainbow* or (para)geography and astronomy in *Mason & Dixon*.[8] While "the novel uses concepts of the mathematical imagination to pursue that purpose [of imagining another world] and to comment on its own fictional strategies in the process" (2010: 25), I want to extend Pöhlmann's reading in illustrating how a scientific-political subject of the event comes to the fore by relating to these scientific discourses.[9] In arguing that science, mathematical Quaternionism, and Riemannian geometry to be exact, generates a truth procedure in which some of the novel's characters become subjects endowed with reagency thus clearly steers against Pynchon's earlier work.[10] Yet, this chapter is neither specifically interested in juxtaposing the different notions of subjects in Pynchon's oeuvre, nor in sketching a particular change within these works. By focusing on *Against the Day*, I, rather, emphasize the fact that Pynchon's works should not be pigeonholed into one existing formulaic set. In compliance with a variety of critics' assertions that, in Heinz Ickstadt's words, the novel is "notably different from any of its predecessors" (2008: 218),[11] I want to add to these observations by analyzing its creation of a scientific-political subject of the event that cannot be detected to a similar extent in his prior novels. While the political impetus of more tangible forms of resistance, particularly Anarchist dynamiters, has been analyzed in some respects,[12] I argue that even the apparently innocuous and inconspicuous scientists Kit and Yashmeen are ordained with the political power to antagonize the given system, a concern that runs through Pynchon's entire oeuvre.

What is more, my claim that *Against the Day* not only creates a scientific subject of the event, but that this realm is also and fundamentally affected by political concerns, is, just as in the case of *Slumberland*, running against Badiou's notion of separate generic truth procedures.[13] *Against the Day*'s diegetic world(s) equally depict a hybrid entanglement of science and politics, thereby counteracting the separation of these spheres. In fact, Yashmeen's active reformulation of a scientific truth condition into a political one crucially extends Badiou's subjective conception by highlighting the impermanence of a fidelity without relapsing to a betrayal of the event, as in the case of Kit. She rather exemplifies a subject that remains faithful to the event only by poaching the generic hermeticism that Badiou formulates.

Before examining the conflation of two generic procedures that are executed by a Quaternionist and a Riemannian scientific-political subject of the event, it is necessary to briefly sketch the novel's setting, as this elucidates its historical milieu for scientific and political events. *Against the Day*'s hybrid interconnection of sacred and profane discourses suggests a specific view of modernity and relates to the epistemological and ontological crisis that its characters have to face. Despite the perseverance of uncertain foundations, what Georg Lukács has called the "transcendental homelessness" of modernity, Pynchon, nevertheless, mobilizes the poietic abilities of literature and offers two cogent subjective processes. If Kit and Yashmeen are confronted with the loss of transcendental structures, the "*immanent* break" (*E* 42) of scientific events endows them with moments of empowerment. By overlapping the singular character of the Quaternionist event that is a genuine scientific event with an inescapable political dimension, the second part of this chapter shows how Kit acquires reagency in the face of increasing mechanisms of exploitation, alienation, and exclusion. The focus of the last part of this chapter rests on Yashmeen Halfcourt who equally becomes a scientific-political subject of the event, however, with radically different trajectories, more sustained and sustainable.

The sacred, the profane, and the sciences

Against the Day abounds with different and competing scientific discourses. Still, I argue that Quaternionism and Riemannian geometry present not simply scientific discourses among many others but two proper scientific events. While such discourses, as for instance, Ætherism or alchemy, also evoke tropes of scientific subjectivity and generate the prominent Pynchonian theme of unfulfilled possibilities, of "roads not taken," they do not constitute an event in my reading of the novel. Although the novel delineates the hybrid interconnection between sacred and profane discourses, of religion and science,[14] I only see the scientific procedure of Quaternionism and Riemannian geometry as inhabiting the potential for its followers to become subjects of events and thereby to transcend such structures. While they are not allowed transcendence into entirely different worlds, mathematical or religious, those faithful to scientific events achieve instants of reagency, moments of grace.

The novel's setting at the turn of the century, spanning the time between the Chicago World's Fair in 1893 and the years just after the first World War, evokes a time of radical economical, sociological, cultural, and, particularly, scientific change and, following from this, crisis.[15] In this period's formulation of groundbreaking scientific discoveries, the novel incorporates scientists such as Albert Einstein, or Nikola Tesla,[16] and visits the ivory towers of scientific groundwork, particularly Göttingen, Cambridge, and Yale. In a similar vein as the novel's predecessors, *Against the Day* offers a rhizomatic web of different, often mutually exclusive, scientific discourses and depicts a genealogy of modern Western knowledge production.

A crucial theme that amplifies the novel's transitionality, in which paradigmatic shifts fundamentally affect the transcendental foundations of the world's inhabitants, constitutes the "luminiferous Æther" (*AtD* 58).[17] *Against the Day*'s discussion of the ontological status of the Æther thus propels its adherents into an epistemological crisis that is closely related to modern processes of secularization. While structures of sacrality are still very prominent in the novel's depiction of the sciences, this is not merely a return to pre-secular times. Instead, the deep connection between science and religion not only questions the concept of modernity as an era of disciplinary dissociation; more fundamentally, the novel points to the structural similarities between religion and science and exhibits the epistemological crises of its adherents at the turn of the century. This state of uncertainty will be taken up by the scientific event of Quaternionism and Riemannian geometry, which endows Kit Traverse and Yashmeen Halfcourt with new structures of meaning and, ultimately, reagency.

One of the novel's characters, Merle Rideout, who is scientifically indebted to photography and amalgamation, embodies this epistemological fluctuation between spheres of the sacred and the profane. Particularly at the hand of the novel's discussion of the Æther, one can grasp the epistemological and ontological crises that the novel positions itself in. The question of the existence of the Æther is for Merle "closer to religion than science" (*AtD* 58). In the vein of modernity's untying of the Gordian knot, as Bruno Latour phrases it (1993: 3), Merle positivistically dissociates himself from the metaphysical problem that the Æther presents. Although a self-proclaimed scientist, Merle incorporates the capitalist, Weberian paradigm, which establishes a difference between "the practical side of things" (*AtD* 58) and uselessness, basing existence on a material, if not to say materialist, foundation: "Exists, doesn't exist," the narrator focalizes through Merle, "what's it got to do with the price of turnips basically." (*AtD* 58). On the one hand, he contemplates the Æther's hypothetical existence that echoes the experimental research that the Case institute conducts (and where the Michelson-Morley experiment produces evidence for the Æther's inexistence), sharing the binary orientation of logical deduction; on the other hand, he discards the very basis of this deduction in the same breath by conflating an ontological problem of existence with an even more "basic" concern: survival. Moreover, as a concept with "too many unknowables," the Æther's close associations to "divinity" (de Bourcier 2012: 123) make Merle apply Occam's razor as he seems to reject it as an epistemologically inaccessible problem in the first place. Remarkably, however, Merle does not entirely abandon the Æther, since he positions it only "closer to religion than science," thereby projecting a plane on which proximities and distances are relational, rather than absolute.

This *Gretchenfrage*, the question of religion, proves to be closely connected to scientific questions in the context of the Æther. At Cleveland, where the Michelson-Morley experiment is to be conducted, Professor Heino Vanderjuice tells Merle in his "lecture-hall style":

> You're quite right, of course, the Æther has always been a religious question. Some don't believe in it, some do, neither will convince the other, it's all faith at the moment. Lord Salisbury said it was only a noun for the verb "to undulate." Sir Oliver Lodge defined it as "one continuous substance filling all space, which can vibrate light . . . be sheared into positive and negative electricity," and so on in a lengthy list, almost like the Apostles' Creed. It certainly depends on a belief in the waviness of light—if light were particulate, it could just go blasting through empty space with no need for any Æther to carry it. Indeed one finds in the devout Ætherist a propensity of character ever toward the continuous as against the discrete. Not to mention a vast patience with all those tiny whirlpools the theory has come to require. (*AtD* 58)

Like Merle's topological projection, which does not entirely dissociate the discourse of religion from that of science, Vanderjuice equally argues for the proximity of both fields by employing such terms as "faith," "belief," or "devotion." Although his first sentence seems to suggest a genealogy in the discourse of the Æther as it was transported from religious substance to scientific concept (de Bourcier 2012: 127), he stresses that its sacred structure has persisted despite the change of historical or social constellations. Especially his emphasis that "it's all faith at the moment" depicts a cultural milieu that rests on discursive and disciplinary hybridity rather than distinction. This is also transported by the professor's referencing of Robert Gascoyne-Cecil, Lord Salisbury's linguistic approximation of the concept. Next to the physical properties of moving in wavelike motions, lacking as a consequence any linear and reliable system of reference, Vanderjuice approaches the Æther's persistent fluctuations from a discursive angle. The Æther's physical flexibility is thereby paralleled by its linguistic adaptability, in which it may change syntagmas with ease. Instead of simply drawing a paradigmatic and thus semantic parallel between Æther and the noun "undulation," Salisbury's cross-syntagmatic relations exhibit "nineteenth-century descriptions of the Æther as an 'elastic solid'" (ibid.: 125) also on a linguistic level. In fact, the Æther's configuration as a medium that conveys light, as de Bourcier observes (ibid.: 125), equally permeates into the realm of language, where it mediates itself between apparently distinct words ("Æther" and "to undulate") and creates new semantic connections.

Whereas Sir Oliver Lodge's definition is represented more in the context of physicist terminology, Vanderjuice's comment on the structural paradigm of the scientist's approach that resembles a religious dogma again makes the Æther serve the function of an "interdisciplinary" medium. Note also the passage's dramatic irony. For the reader's advanced state of knowledge will discern the "belief in the waviness of light" to be antiquated with the advent of quantum mechanics. Since our current state of knowledge claims that light is both wavelike and particular, the Ætherists' own "particular" hypothesis will turn out to be at least partly wrong. Nevertheless, light's double ontological status, simultaneously wave and particle, does not entirely reject the beliefs of the "devout Ætherists," since they are at least partially right.

The Ætherists' subjective crisis is hinted at, on the one hand, through the "vast patience with all those tiny whirlpools the theory has come to require," where the imagery of a vortex evokes existential confusion and even hazard through a literal death by water; on a more general level, epistemological insecurities are addressed by means of the Æther and its status as a concept in between scientific and religious discourse. Through the accumulating evidence of the Æther's nonexistence, the Ætherists are even deprived of a metaphysical sphere in the realm of science, which fails to offer them a new narrative, which may structure their world.

The epistemological uncertainties that the novel's (scientific) characters experience are amplified when Vanderjuice goes on to say that everyone "wander[s] at the present moment through a sort of vorticalist twilight, holding up the lantern of the Maxwell Field Equations and squinting to find our way" (*AtD* 58). For Vanderjuice, this new experiment "could be the giant arc-lamp [they] need to light [their] way into the coming century" (*AtD* 58–59). Once more, Vanderjuice draws a different picture of modernity and frames this in explicit, and even literally photo-graphic, language, which in the novel is an important imagery that is connected to the manifestation of events.[18] Despite the century-old project of the Enlightenment, the turn of the century is still situated in a "vorticalist twilight." The transitionality of this state indicates again the subjective confusion, as if positioned in a vortex, and conjures a metaphorical zone in between day and night. This photo-logy is extended by the probing motions of the scientific community, where a theoretical, electro-magnetic formula assumes the function of epistemic illumination. Remarkably, Vanderjuice describes these attempts not as directed from an inside to a sovereign, enlightened outside position, but merely as *a* way.

Moreover, the act of "squinting" seems especially peculiar. On the one hand, this ocular gesture implies that the "twilight" is turning from night to day, thereby indicating a teleological narrative of increasing civilization or even a theological progression as in the case of *Genesis*, which was analyzed in respect to *The Road*. Yet, since this natural process evolves steadily, repetitiously, and, thus, with foreboding, the protective reflex seems more likely to be related to a contingently erupting surge of light that the lantern may unravel. The squinting could therefore be seen as a general disposition that some of the novel's characters assume and which relates to the singular manifestation of a scientific event. In contrast to a subliminally creeping form of "enlightenment," the passage here renders science as a generic condition conceptually distinct from a "natural" form of knowledge acquirement, which is perpetually in becoming. In breaking with Pynchon's prior scope of scientific evolution, *Against the Day* engages in a different form of scientific insight. Equally so, as distinct from the rational subjective "Enlightenment," *Against the Day* shows that this act of subjective empowerment is not grounded in the humanist foundation of an autonomous subject. Subjects of events are only "enlightened" by the manifestation of an event.

Some sciences, Pynchon implies, enable their devotees with certain forms of epistemological, and the consequent ontological, insights. Such a condition that is marked by singular revelations may blind those affected by it and thereby fundamentally alter their "eyes" in a double sense. The cautionary impetus that guides the scientific pioneers could, however, also be read as a form of skepticism toward a new form of epistemic disclosure, an incredulity that will be analyzed in more detail at a later part of this chapter.

In this sense, the discourse on the Æther functions as a joint at which epistemic inquiries are substantiated in the interface between religion and science. Instead of a secularized modernity, *Against the Day* shows that science not merely substitutes religion but effectively borrows and adapts some of its epistemological and ontological modes of operation. While Quaternionism shares a similar indebtedness to the sacred, which will be depicted in the following, Ætherism's status as a generic condition is problematized when Merle's scientific compatriot Roswell Bounce observes:

It's like these cults who believe the world will end on such and such a day, . . . they get rid of all their earthly possessions and head off in a group for some mountaintop and wait, and then the end of the world doesn't happen. The world keeps going on.

What a disappointment! Everybody has to troop back down the mountain with their spiritual tails dragging, except for one or two incurably grinning idiots who see it as a chance to start a new life, fresh, without encumbrances, to be reborn, in fact. . . . So with this Michelson-Morley result. We've all had a lot of faith invested. Now it looks like the Æther, whether it's moving or standing still, just doesn't exist. What do we do now? (*AtD* 62–63)

The "cult" that Roswell likens to Ætherism bears close relations to particular forms of Protestantism. Ætherists awaiting a groundbreaking event that will end the world reverberates the Puritan notion of apocalypse, a theme even more prominent in *The Road*. Roswell's comparison between the religiously and scientifically devoted, who uncritically move in military motions and are metamorphosed into tail-bearing animals—their spirituality resembling a biological atavism—again shows to what extent these realms are more alike than they wish to admit. However, both fields here fail to live up to their posited hypotheses and the resulting movements of transcendence fail to materialize. Neither spiritual promise of redemption, nor scientific faithfulness, which was shattered as the Æther proved to be no truth at all, provides them with helpful structures. The continuation of the world, which Roswell ironically mourns, thus implies that, on the one hand, both parties in vain awaited, even expected, an event. However, since events are fundamentally non-ontological and absolutely contingent, they cannot be predicted. On the other, it becomes equally clear to what extent the refutation of such expectations and the deprivation of structuring narratives ("election" "Æther") leave them in a state of paralysis, not knowing what to do.

Against the Day conjures a diegetical world that is historically defined by epistemological insecurities. The novel exhibits these concerns through the clashing discourses of science and religion, showing not only that these fields share certain mechanisms and structures but also that both cannot supply their adherents with cogent forms of "ethical" imperatives. While both discourses, science and religion, struggle for the best explanation of the world, *Against the Day*, in very much the same vein as its predecessors, depicts the persistent inaptitude of their aspirations. Although the specific belief in Ætherism does not endow its followers with a sovereign position of knowledge, other scientific revelations mark an event, since they endow its subjects with a new ontological mode of perceiving the world coupled with a particular "*ethic-of* (of politics, of love, of science, of art)" (*E* 28).

Scientific forks in the road

In respect to the Æther, *Against the Day* exemplifies that science does not simply figure as a disenchanting discourse that cleanses knowledge from metaphysical elements but also adapts the structure of religious practices. This implies that *Against the Day*'s depiction of scientific knowledge is not just a (better) substitute for religious knowledge. Instead, the novel shows how both rely on similar notions of "transcendence."

In contrast, Quaternionism and Riemannian geometry are depicted as inhabiting an evental disposition by distancing themselves from a notion of epistemological or ontological transcendence. In other words, the scientific branches not only constitute an event (mathematical ones), but they also evoke subjective fidelities. Yet, added to the epistemological uncertainties that the novel's characters experience, they concomitantly suffer from existential insecurities. Particularly the Quaternionists get increasingly excluded from the scientific community because of their methodological idiosyncrasies as well as their defiance of the preexisting social order.

What adds to the novel's emphasis on transitionality in which both scientific and religious discourses grapple with the epistemological foundations of the world is the increasing economization of these disciplines. A paradigmatic example for the way in which capitalism appears as the metanarrative that fundamentally affects and decides upon the existence of other discourses is the juxtaposition of chemistry and alchemy. Rather than a simple setting side by side, in order that these discourses "los[e] their oppositeness" (50) as *Gravity's Rainbow* puts it, the scientific milieu that the novel conjures addresses a more fundamental issue of evolution/historicity. Merle Rideout, in a conversation with miner-anarchist Webb Traverse thus notes: if you look at the history, modern chemistry only starts coming in to replace alchemy around the same time capitalism really gets going. Strange, eh? "Maybe capitalism decided it didn't need the old magic anymore." (*AtD* 79). Capitalism's active position that Webb here addresses represents a crucial theme in the novel's discussion of science and its technological adaptations. According to Webb, capitalism does not merely constitute another narrative on an equal footing with chemistry or alchemy but assumes a sovereign position from which it is anthropomorphically depicted as choosing the practices that best fit and perpetuate its mechanisms. Along these lines, Merle even equates capitalism with evolutionary biology as a grand narrative that selects those discourses most adapted to its surroundings. As in a process of natural selection, the struggle for survival between competing discourses is integrated into an economic principle. Faced with the apparently disenchanted socioeconomic order of modernity, alchemy is ejected from existence because of its metaphysical nature, with chemistry being a more appropriate science to replace the "old magic" and which culminates in *Gravity's Rainbow*'s Imipolex G, a material that covers the outer shell of the V-2.

Even more so, the topic of evolution also relates to the structure of events. For the scientific discourses that constitute an event within the diegesis of *Against the Day* are not to be situated within a creeping process of evolutionary becoming but manifest a singular rupture. If Pynchon emphasizes the former process of change in becoming in his "Is it O.K. to be a Luddite?," *Against the Day* extends this evolutionary ontology by evental singularities. For whereas such scientific developments as the Industrial Revolution are "far from being revolutionary," since they are "less conclusive, more like an accelerated passage in a long evolution," (1984: 40), specifically Quaternionism and Riemannian geometry manifest an ontological scission that remains unprecedented.

Such clashes of scientific discourses that are embedded in a Darwinian "struggle for survival" also characterize Quaternionism, as it tries to prevail in the light of the upcoming discipline of Vectorism. While chemistry has, in the historical setting of the novel, already discarded its otherworldly opponent, the Quaternionist question at the turn of the century is not entirely settled.[19]

A first explicit mentioning of Quaternionism in the novel immediately frames the discipline in relation to Vectorism and the continuing debate between these two mathematical theories.[20] At a meeting of the "Transnoctial Discussion Group," debaters from the two respective camps begin to argue over "tonight's announced topic [, which] was 'The Nature of Expeditions'":

> "We learned once how to break horses and ride them for long distances, with oceangoing ships we left flat surfaces and went into Riemann space, we crossed solid land and deep seas, and colonized what we found," said Dr. Vormance. "Now we have taken the first few wingbeats of what will allow us to begin colonizing the Sky. Somewhere in it, God dwells in His Heavenly City. How far into that unmapped wilderness shall we journey before we find Him? Will He withdraw before our advance, continue to withdraw into the Infinite? Will He send back to us divine Agents, to help, to deceive, to turn us away? Will we leave settlements in the Sky, along our invasion routes, or will we choose to be wanderers, striking camp each morning, content with nothing short of Zion? And what of colonizing additional dimensions beyond the third? Colonize Time. Why not?"
>
> "Because, sir," objected Dr. Templeton Blope, of the University of the Outer Hebrides, "—we are limited to three."
>
> "Quaternionist talk," shouted his collegial nemesis Hastings Throyle. "Everything, carnal and spiritual, invested in the given three dimensions—for what use, as your Professor Tate famously asked, are any more than three?"
>
> "Ever so frightfully sorry. The given world, in case you hadn't noticed. Planet Earth."
>
> "Which not so long ago was believed to be a plane surface." So forth. A recurring argument. (*AtD* 131)

Next to the recurring intersection of religion and science, epitomized by the interrogative grounding of scientific developments at the mercy of a sacred agency ("Will He…?") that depicts, once more, the accompanying epistemological insecurities and the craving for structural institutions, the passage also gives a neat summary of the difference between Quaternionism and Vectorism. Specifically their divergent take on space is highlighted by this passage. While both disciplines could be said to transcend Euclidean geometry, they do this on quite different grounds. Vectorism extends the three axes of a traditional, Cartesian x, y, z coordinate system by adding multiple axes "beyond the third." Setting out from a container-like model in which three dimensions mark an absolute, Newtonian space, Vectorism adds dimensions to these three in order to calculate in multiple dimensions.

Although the Blope claims that Quaternionism is "limited to three" axes, they also extend the Euclidean ones in making them complex axes. To this extent, Quaternionism does not simply add further axes to the existing xyz system but calculates with four aces, three complex ones and a real one. This is expressed in Quaternionism's representative formula "$i^2 = j^2 = k^2 = ijk = -1$" (*AtD* 561). Its complex axes i, j, and k, are simultaneously made up of real and imaginary parts.[21] A complex number z thus consists of a real number a and an imaginary number bi: $z = a + bi$. The imaginary component can also be grasped in the Quaternionist formula, where the equation $i^2 = -1$ amounts to the same as $i = \sqrt{-1}$. Since the prevalent notion of mathematics in which the novel is set dictated that one must not take the square root of negative numbers since the result is not part of the system of real numbers, imaginary numbers could not be thought on the same terms as, for instance, rational or natural numbers. Here it becomes clear to what extent Quaternionism's use of four dimensions counterintuitive, even systemic prohibition, was not taken well by mathematicians and how it approximates an evental status of scientific hubris.[22]

In emulating Pynchon's incorporation of historical scientific discourses, we may thus well be led to Michael J. Crowe's illuminating *A History of Vector Analysis* from 1967, which certainly served as a plausible source text for some of *Against the Day*'s scientific contexts and helps to grasp the novel's adaptation of this event. For one thing, Crowe cites Sir William Rowan Hamilton himself, who comments on the subversive potential of imaginary numbers:

> In the THEORY OF SINGLE NUMBERS, the symbol $\sqrt{-1}$ is absurd, and denotes an IMPOSSIBLE EXTRACTION, or a merely IMAGINARY NUMBER; but in the THEORY OF COUPLES, the same symbol $\sqrt{-1}$ is significant, and denotes a POSSIBLE EXTRACTION, or a REAL COUPLE.... (Hamilton in Crowe 1967: 25)

Hamilton here addresses what I mean by Quaternionism's ontological and epistemological intrusion into the existing mathematical order (if one may speak of one singular mathematical order in the first place.) It is thus especially its transgressive tendency, going beyond a "theory of single numbers" that does not allow, nor can it even imagine, the possibility of a number such as $\sqrt{-1}$.[23] Hamilton stresses the alterity of this "symbol" (note that it is merely a symbol, not a consistent number) and if it has to be accounted for as a number, then it is only by adding the ontological description of its imaginary nature.

While Pynchon is known for integrating mathematical symbols in his fiction, be it the later to be discussed Δt, or $\int$, to name but the two most prominent ones, *Against the Day* emphasizes the $\sqrt{-1}$ to depict the non-ontological impetus in a textual manner. If *Only Revolutions* equally made use of its typographic potential to give expression to that which lacks any representative quality, Pynchon goes outside of the linguistic constraints of literature and integrates a mathematical symbol that for him conveys this friction. By employing an impossible number that, nevertheless, can be thought according to the Quaternionist propositions, the novel inquires into the nature of language by pointing to that which goes beyond it. Against the poststructuralist claim of the immanence of texts, *Against the Day* offers a realist and dynamic outlook that emphasizes the existence of beings beyond language. The essential question of how to epistemologically grasp an event that exceeds our present capacities to know it is thereby answered by building on the interconnection between mathematics and literature. Not only does the novel thereby reject language as the ultimate horizon of reality, which denies the existence of beings outside of this realm, but the novel also crucially rejects the Two Cultures debate by emphasizing the mathematical input for fictional universes. However, Pynchon simultaneously avoids a reverential attitude toward the sciences— for this would certainly break with his Luddite persuasion. Particularly Quaternionism, which, as Engelhardt has shown, bears close connections to the creation of fictional worlds (2013: 214), offers itself in *Against the Day* as endowing the literary a means of going beyond itself. The very *aporia* of finding ways of representing an absolutely non-ontological rupture is, therefore, not a natural science that seeks a mimetic relation to the world. In investigating theoretical mathematics at the turn of the century, *Against the Day* employs this discipline's crisis because of a lack of any ontological referential system and thereby points to equal epistemological problems.

Yet, whereas Hamilton here still paints a picture of parallel coexistences, a theory of single numbers on the one side, and a theory of couples on the other, the novel's depiction of Quaternionism as a scientific event expands this by rendering the event and its new propositions viral. Indeed, the isomorphism that is also typographically highlighted in the passage announces part of Hamilton's fidelity to the Quaternionist event, integrating the propositions of Quaternionism next to the accepted prior situation. However, this is not simply a literal bilocation of two scientific systems where each takes on its own independent existence: just as the two systemic fields are interconnected by a semi-colon, so does Quaternionism as a genuine event start to percolate into other disciplines and radically change their working premises. Although Hamilton was not the first to consider the reality of complex numbers,[24] it is his subjective fidelity that made it a proper truth procedure, as will be depicted in the following part. With the help of this scientific event, Hamilton transformed Euclidean space into a complex plane with four axes (hence the name "quaternion").[25]

Such "anti-mathematical" characteristics certainly emphasize to what extent Quaternions imply an evental disposition. Their sheer disruptive potential in that they "broke bonds set by centuries of mathematical thought" (Crowe 1967: 30–31) amounts to a manifestation of singularity that defied the predominant situation of mathematics. Its formulation of seemingly paradoxical hypotheses that not only oppose the current state of mathematical knowledge but to some extent even contradict its very being makes Quaternionism a genuine scientific event.

This non-ontological appeal that Quaternionism embodies is thus hinted at when a Quaternionist gets asked the ontological question: "Yes but what is a Quaternion?" upon which he replies: "What 'is' a Quaternion? Ha, hahahaha!" (*AtD* 538). What is here cushioned in a humorous context harbors at least three possible interpretations that relate to Quaternionism's status as an event. First, the Quaternionist seems to laugh at the question because of the addressee's lack of knowledge, which would manifest the workings of a power relation, but also suggest the radical chasm of knowledge between those within the Quaternion community and those excluded. Only if faithful to the Quaternion event is one able to discern the "truth" of its condition. Those exterior to the situation that is affected by the event have no means to grasp its ramifications. In a Freudian context of a discrepancy of effort,[26] the laughter could also be explained through the uneconomic impossibility of explaining what Quaternions actually are, since this literally implies an impossible feat. Within the economic context that guides the practicality and, thus, the perseverance of scientific discourses in the novel, Quaternionism is relegated to a position in which it can only be laughed at, since it fundamentally undermines the workings of the capitalist order. Third, the Quaternionists' response might indicate a sense of uncertainty that correlates to their existential insecurity that will be elaborated on in the following part. In this reading, the Quaternionists' response is guided by a nervous gesture of insecurity, since Quaternionists are excluded from the social order because of their controversial scientific propositions.

Because of its radical rethinking of the existing mathematical system, Quaternionism may also be viewed as an event, since the Quaternions constitute an evental site. As a singular multiple that was not acknowledged prior to the eruption of the event, its supplementation to mathematical systems occasions the fundamental change of this system. In contrast to other, merely evolutionary changes within scientific discourses, Quaternionism marks what Thomas Kuhn termed a scientific revolution.[27]

Besides the historical reality of the scientific practice, Pynchon's novel employs its alterity in order to show how it affected not only the discourse of theoretical mathematics but also that of its actual subjective followers and thereby segues into political dimensions. While Quaternionism, according to Crowe, was "epoch making, for quaternions were the first well-known consistent and significant number system which did not obey the laws of ordinary arithmetic" (30), this is not the place to enquire into its position within the history of science.[28] In focusing on its literary, narrative, and political function, Quaternionism in *Against the Day* equally embodies evental dispositions and occasions subjective fidelities.

In this vein, the novel also insists on the incisive manifestation of an event that fundamentally influences those who grant it existence. At one of the "irregularly spaced World Conventions" (*AtD* 526) at Ostend, the Quaternionists celebrate "the anniversary of Hamilton's 1843 discovery of the Quaternions (or, as a disciple might say, theirs of him)" (*AtD* 560). Note that the Quaternionists commemorate Hamilton's act of "discover[ing] . . . the Quaternions" and not Hamilton as a scientific genius himself. As a matter of fact, their subjective fidelity to the Quaternionist event is not only accentuated by celebrating the day of Hamilton's discovery (and not, for instance, of his birth); they even insist on a realist notion of the world, in which Quaternions are not invented by a subjective construction, but, on the contrary, seem to exist beyond any human epistemology. The anthropomorphic quaternions simply used him as a medium to manifest their ontological reality. Instead of a cult of personality, the Quaternionists assume the day of the scientific event as a ritual marker, in which Hamilton simply figures as a mediating device that made possible the Quaternion's manifestation.[29]

While this might be read as a commonplace of scientific authorship, according to which "a scientist qua scientist is, literally, a nonauthor" (Biagioli in Benesch 2009: 5),[30] it more fundamentally relates to the passive position that the evental subject assumes when confronted with an event. In fact, this is specifically highlighted by the narrative depiction of Hamilton's experience of the Quaternionist event, which is retold by one of the Quaterionists:

> "We all know the story. It is a Monday morning in Dublin, Hamilton and his wife, Maria Bayley Hamilton, are walking by the canalside across from Trinity College, where Hamilton is to preside at a council meeting. Maria is chatting pleasantly, Hamilton is nodding now and then and murmuring 'Yes, dear,' when suddenly as they approach Brougham Bridge he cries out and pulls a knife from his pocket— Mrs. H. starts violently but regains her composure, it is only a penknife—as Hamilton runs over to the bridge and carves on the stone $i^2 = j^2 = k^2 = ijk = -1$," the assembly here murmuring along, as to a revered anthem, "and it is in this Pentecostal moment that the Quaternions descend, to take up their earthly residence among the thoughts of men." (*AtD* 560–61)

The account of Hamilton's confrontation with Quaternionism attests the arbitrary eruption of an event. Taking a walk with his wife, and not, for example, studying in his office, Hamilton is struck by the contingent illumination of the Quaternions. Again, Quaternions are represented as more than a human contrivance. In this, the passage also insists on the agency of Quaternions as an animate entity that almost consciously decides to inhabit human thought. By employing a religious register once more, Quaternions are compared to the manifestation of the Holy Spirit. However, rather than undermining Quaternionism as a scientific discourse that abounds with religious metaphysics, the passage could also be interpreted as an attempt to show the evental analogies between the Christ event and the Quaternionist event.[31] Whereas the convergence of science and religion in other instances emphasized a ritualistic habitus (creeds, devotion, election), Quaternionism is compared to a religious theme only in that both mark an event.

Moreover, Hamilton's passive position is emphasized by his submissive demeanor toward his wife. As if paralyzed by Maria's constant gossiping, he conforms to husband-wife stereotypes, until he is struck by the event. Notably, his passivity is now abandoned and his subjective constitution makes him author the Quaternionist formula. Particularly through his use of a "penknife," Hamilton's process of writing and, thus, giving a name to the event is augmented as an even more material form of inscription. His engraving thus literally makes Quaternions appear as set in stone, which, on the one hand, seems ironic because of their peculiar ontological status, but, on the other, only fortifies Hamilton's belief in the truth of the event. While the process of writing on stone certainly evokes religious innuendos, Hamilton could also be said to adapt the literally complex ontology of the Quaternions by carving them on the material body of the earth.

Additionally, the inscription in the bridge gives the Quaternionist event a very concrete locality, which would not have been as stable if simply documented in a book. By emphasizing the local specificity of this mathematical event, Hamilton decides against distributing and disseminating his ideas through writing systems among the mathematical community and stresses the place-boundedness of this event. Despite these attempts, Hamilton's formula, which functions as the name of the event, might be dependent on its progenitor for being articulated. Nevertheless, his attempts at containing it spatially are undermined when the formula spreads to affect others who pledge their fidelity to this event. Not only has the event thus been narrativized into a communal story of origins that its subjects "all know"; what is more, the formula has left its material place at Brougham Bridge and evolved to a narrative, "a revered anthem" that holds the collective Quaternionist subject together.

Yet another aspect of Hamilton's passivity might be grasped in comparing the passage's presentation with the actual document of Hamilton's "discovery." For, in contrast to Hamilton's letter to his son Archibald H. Hamilton in 1865, which clearly served as the source for Pynchon's adaptation, *Against the Day* delineates the event in quite different terms.

> But on the 16th day of the same month [October 1843]—which happened to be a Monday, and a Council day of the Royal Irish Academy—I was walking in to attend and preside, and your mother was walking with me, along the Royal Canal, to which she had perhaps driven; and although she talked with me now and then, yet an *under-current* of thought was going on in my mind, which gave at last a *result*, whereof it is not too much to say that I felt *at once* the importance. An *electric* circuit seemed to *close*; and a spark flashed forth, the herald (as I *foresaw, immediately*) of many long years to come of definitely directed thought and work, by myself if spared, and at all events on the part of *others*, if I should even be allowed to live long enough distinctly to communicate the discovery. Nor could I resist the impulse—unphilosophical as it may have been—to cut with a knife on a stone of Brougham Bridge, as we passed it, the fundamental forumale with the symbols, i, j, k; namely
>
> $$i^2 = j^2 = k^2 = ijk = -1,$$
>
> which contains the Solution of the Problem, but of course, as an inscription, has long since mouldered away. (Hamilton in Crowe 1967: 29)

Most notably, from a narratological perspective, Pynchon does not adapt the homodiegtic stance of Hamilton's letter but doubly mediates the event in the third person, thereby creating a certain distance between Hamilton and his discovery. Although authorship might be unconventional in scientific practices, Hamilton's first-person letter claims a more conscious and "subjective" form of revelation. Note that he is here immersed in a mathematical problem, while his wife's talking is simply a background noise that, if compared to Pynchon's depiction of Maria's "pleasant chatting" clearly emphasizes *Against the Day*'s critique of the masculine assertion of authorship that Hamilton constructs in his letter. Whereas *Against the Day* contrasts the manifestation of the event with the quotidian situation of a wife-husband conversation that highlights the unexpected eruption in a more pronounced context of contingency, Hamilton's letter, rather, illustrates the continuity of his self-determined reflections. This is amplified by his claim that he "*foresaw, immediately*" the consequences of his discovery without acknowledging the overpowering impetus that an event implies. Hamilton, instead, fashions himself as an autonomous scientific genius that self-consciously closed the "electric circuit" delivering the "*Solution*" to his "*Problem.*"

Unlike this Romantic myth of scientific authorship, *Against the Day* depicts Hamilton as inhabiting a passive position in the face of the event. The novel thus rejects his status as a sovereign humanist subject that actively creates Quaternionism. Nevertheless, as a *subject of the event* the novel shows that he attains a degree of empowerment in his authoring of the Quaternion formula that creates the foundation for other subjective procedures. Indeed, while Hamilton could have simply rejected his "illumination" as unfounded non-sense, or have adapted the formula in other spheres, he specifically translated the scientific event into a truth condition that harbored profoundly new insights.

Still, the construction of a faithful scientific subject does not constitute a naive process of emancipation for its subjective community that endows them with new "ethical structures," which help them to acquire orientation. Because of Quaternionism's subversive impetus, they are confronted by various mechanisms of exclusion.

Whereas the interdisciplinary friction between chemistry and alchemy proved to rest on capitalism's notion of usability, the clash between Vectorism and Quaternionism can be viewed from a different angle. Although there exist similar structures of capitalist incorporation, which is hinted at in Prof. Vormace's Vectorist subscription to a "colonizing" (*AtD* 131) enterprise that echoes the Turnerian frontier spirit, the two scientific convictions may also relate to two different subjective procedures toward a scientific event. Instead of elaborating to what extent Vectorism could be seen as a reactive procedure that denies the existence of a Quaternionist event, I will focus on an instantiation of the Quaternionist subject of the event who converses from Vectorism to Quaterionism and as a consequence becomes a faithful subject of the event. However, Kit does not remain faithful to the event and will ultimately turn his back on his fidelity, thereby metamorphosing into a reactive subject that ignores the truths that the Quaternionist event elicits.

Nevertheless, the confrontation between Vectorism and Quaternionism does need some elaboration, for the novel assumes this antagonism to depict the Quaternionists as an excluded middle within capitalist modes of production. Instead of viewing the empowerment of subjective fidelities to an event as a transcendence of antagonistic forces, *Against the Day* thereby shows how the very praxis of keeping faith in an event does rarely lead to a utopic notion of liberty but often implies radical ramifications. Quaternionists not only struggle with foundations of knowledge but their very being in the world becomes increasingly jeopardized, only because, as I would argue, they themselves unshackle the ontological stabilities of the world. Put differently, a subject of the event is far from attaining a fully emancipated status of absolute liberty; the fundamentally hazardous nature of expressing one's fidelity to an event, which could be discerned in Sam and Hailey's seemingly losing their invincibility in *Only Revolutions*, results in *Against the Day* in those being faithful to the event falling victim to modes of exclusion and oppression. The Quaternionist's precarious existence, as a singular multiple itself, combines the merely scientific appeal of the Quaternionist event and traverses into political waters. The narrator thus goes on to explain that

"Quaternionism in this era still enjoyed the light and warmth of a cheerful noontide" whereas "rival systems might be acknowledged now and then, . . . but those of the Hamiltonian faith felt an immunity to ever being superseded, children imagining they would live forever" (*AtD* 131–32).

Although they are here "still" accepted as an alternate narrative, their childlike naivety is soon unmasked in its existential uncertainty. Once more, an evolutionary biologist framework guides the description of another scientific discourse and expresses the volatility of the Quaternion's right to exist. The projection of a discourse on biological life upon scientific discourses, however, also addresses the material struggle for survival of its human followers. The novel's use of metaphors of light pinpoints the evanescent nature of "this era" that is on the brink of changing into more existentially threatening terrain. Like biological organisms, the adherents to the scientific event may absorb energy ("light" and "warmth"), but the "cheerful noontide" implies at the same time the inescapable advent of less procreative times. The life of Quaternionists, as a scientific species and "their great struggle for existence" (*AtD* 531), is, in other words, about to become severely endangered. Somewhat later in the novel, this change is already more tangible. At Ostend, the scientific milieu has altered fundamentally. Since the "Quaternion Wars," of the 1890s, "true Quaternionists, if not defeated outright then at best having come to feel irrelevant," (*AtD* 526) are progressively expelled from the centers of knowledge formation. They "could be found these days wandering the world, dispersed, under the yellow skies of Tasmania, out in the American desert, up in the Alpine wastes of Switzerland, gathering furtively in border-town hotels, at luncheons in rented parlors, in hotel lobbies . . . they were eyed suspiciously by waiters" (*AtD* 526). Now, they had "fallen from grace" and came "to embody, for the established scientific religion, a subversive, indeed heretical, faith for whom proscription and exile were too good" (*AtD* 526).

The shift from "bothered acknowledgment" to a full-fledged scientific war does not merely pertain to an academic debate but has palpable ramifications for the "Hamiltonian devotees." Through the Vectorist hostility, Quaternionists have to leave not only the institutional setting but even national territory. The juxtaposition of the Vectorist "home" and the Quaternionist diaspora transports the spatial logic of this scientific quarrel. For the "transatlantic" scope of this pogrom-like expulsion only leaves the Quaternionists limited points of refuge. Being forced to surrender sedentary lives, they opt for the transitional spaces of deserts and wastelands, only temporarily stopping at places in the periphery. The nature of their existence, oscillating between physical "defeat" and less violent "irrelevance" thus marks their systematic exclusion from the social order. Here the political context of the Quaternionist fidelity becomes apparent. In contrast to Badiou's theory, the singularity of a multiple that makes possible an event is here oscillating between a scientific singularity and a political one. Whereas the singularity, that is the discrepancy between being included in a system of thought and properly belonging to this system, in Quaternionism as a scientific procedure exists, on the one side, in their stressing of imaginary numbers, the subject of this event becomes, on the other, itself a singular multiple in a political sense. Only through their fidelity toward the "irrational" tenets of Quaternionist mathematics do they become excluded from the institutional and the political/social order. The development from a merely scientific idiosyncrasy to a societal aberration leads to various processes of othering. Disciplinary derision is thus extended by symmetrically dispersed mechanisms of surveillance, with the deviant being "eyed suspiciously by waiters." Once again framed in religious language, the scientific paradigm of Vectorism is equated to a dominant narrative that co-opts activities of expulsion that have resounding historical precursors.

Particularly striking is the almost parenthetical insertion in which the narrator comes to the fore and asks ". . . yes but what choices, if any, remained?" In the context of the very bleak reality of the Quaternionist displacement, this lack of choices attests the absence of agency. Yet, as will be shown in the upcoming part, even at the hand of such coercive structures, the inability to choose, viewed in the light of an evental fidelity, will empower some of the Quaternionist subjects of the event and elucidates my notion of reagency.

This crisis of existence becomes even more evident in a conversation of those present at Ostend, considering "their great struggle for existence" (*AtD* 531), a "*Kampf ums Dasein*" which they had lost (*AtD* 533). Or, as one of the Quaternionists remarks:

> Of course we lost. Anarchists always lose out, while the Gibbs-Heaviside Bolsheviks, their eyes ever upon the long-term, grimly pursued their aims, protected inside their belief that they are the inevitable future, the *xyz* people, the party of a single Established Coordinate System, present everywhere in the Universe, governing absolutely. We were only the *ijk* lot, drifters who set up their working tents for as long as the problem might demand, then struck camp again and moved on, always ad hoc and local, what do you expect?
>
> Actually Quaternions failed because they perverted what the Vectorists thought they know of God's intention—that space be simple, three-dimensional, and real, and if there must be a fourth term, an imaginary, that it be assigned to Time. But Quaternions came in and turned that all end for end, defining the axes of space as imaginary and leaving Time to be the *real* term, and a scalar as well—simply inadmissible. Of course the Vectorists went to war. Nothing they knew of Time allowed it to be that simple, any more than they could allow space to be compromised by impossible numbers, earthly space they had fought over uncounted generations to penetrate, to occupy, to defend. (*AtD* 533–34)

Some of the Quaternionists here attest the hopelessness and even irreversibility of their situation: they have become an absolute other. By addressing their "struggle for existence" in German, the passage not only refers to Josiah Willard Gibbs's letter to Thomas Craig where he writes that he "believe[s] that a *Kampf ums Dasein* . . . is just commencing between the different methods and notations of multiple algebra, especially between the ideas of Grassman & of Hamilton" (qtd. in Crowe 1967: 182) and thereby intertextually inserts another "authentic" document. In this way, one of the conversationists also seems to foreshadow the social Darwinist appropriation of evolutionary biology that will lead to the apex of biopolitics in the Third Reich. But this transformation of scientific research into political exclusion, which makes the Hamiltonians into a religious community destined for escape, is not merely restricted to a religious, or even racist setting.

For the Quaternionists, indeed, figure as a group that combines various identities of the excluded. As a consequence, their entire ontological mode of existence is being questioned. They assume their object of analysis and become "imaginary existence[s]," "Ghosts. Ghosts," or "the Jews of mathematics" (*AtD* 533). The analogy goes even further, because now they are even forced to wander "out here in [their] diaspora—some destined for the past, others the future, even a few able to set out at unknown angles from the simple line of Time, upon journeys that no one can predict" (*AtD* 533). Not only do they become the "Jews of mathematics," which might be seen as a form of harassment based on a constructed ethnicity; this racism is also extended by political/philosophical exclusion, as they assume the identity of Anarchists, who "always lose out" and now have to fear more severe modes of repression. However, it is especially noteworthy that the Quaternionists as Anarchists here distance themselves not from American capitalism, a dialectics that takes in a large part of the novel, but from the "Gibbs-Heaviside *Bolsheviks*." In this, the novel not only disintegrates the radical distinction between the upcoming ideologies of German fascism and Soviet communism as well as American capitalism; what is more, it also problematizes what for Badiou is the most important political truth procedure (*LoW* 72). *Against the Day* therefore problematizes the Bolsheviks' belief "that they are the inevitable future." In their suppression of other social groupings, they do not stress the absolutely universal appeal of the communist event, but, in the terms of the novel, create a "party of a single Established Coordinate System, present everywhere in the Universe, governing absolutely." This conflation of political and scientific systems, borrowing the Newtonian notion of absolute space and Cartesian "xyz" geometry, implies, once more, the inherent nexus between two realms that cannot be neatly separated. By appropriating scientific concepts, political communism is depicted as another metanarrative that assumes an absolute and inevitable place in the world. *Against the Day* thereby invests its poietical powers to delineate not only a world in which other truth procedures such as Bolshevism are undermined in their political sustainability—unmistakably rejecting Badiou's political affiliations; even more so, the novel shifts the focus from more common political procedures, such as the Bolshevist fidelity (*LoW* 72) and juxtaposes another subjective condition that has been overshadowed by political fundamentalism.

What is more, this hybridization of discourses is even extended in the third part of this constellation of otherness. The Quaternionists are thus banned from social life because of their nomadic disposition, as "drifters who set up their working tents for as long as the problem might demand, then [strike] camp again and move[] on, always ad hoc and local." The third paradigm of othering again combines two apparently distinct spheres. While for Badiou "political thinking demands a *displacement*, a journey which is always, dare I say, abnormal" (*IT* 63), *Against the Day* suggests that such a political condition might also be embodied by scientific procedures. A sociological mode of habitation, therefore, interweaves with the Quaternionist scientific modes of problem-solving. Since they do not adhere to a given and static methodological heuristics, they embody the nomad's roaming in deterritorialized spaces also in a mathematical sense. By projecting their scientific approaches to a sociological mode of life, *Against the Day* stresses the inseparability of such realms and exhibits the existential ramifications of a subject of the event that translates its scientific fidelity into a political mode of being, which is even more pronounced in the case of Yashmeen, as will be discussed in the final part of this chapter.

Quaternionists assume the status of a constellation of minorities, groups that are progressively and systematically excluded from the religious, economic, and social order of the turn of the century, and well into the twentieth century. This is specifically because *Against the Day* depicts Quaternionism as a common denominator, which scientifically embodies the identity markers of those suppressed in their very research goals. In other words, not only are they affected by the existent identities of Anarchists, heretics, and nomads; they essentially produce these characteristics on a scientific level. The defiance of stable structures, be they governmental, economical, or religious, is thus paralleled in their mathematical investigations. The religious inclination of Vectorists' notion of "God's intention" is "perverted" by integrating the imaginary component that essentially affects the entire notion of a "three-dimensional, and real" system. While the Hamiltonians' insistence on the "reality" of Time certainly has mathematical implications, the existence of time also relates to extra-scientific concerns. To this extent, the novel stresses the close affinity between Quaternionism and temporality in the sense of the historical reality of their exclusion.

One agent that executes such mechanisms of exclusion is the Vectorists who have a crucially different take on the Quaternionist event. In fact, Vectorism as depicted in this passage assumes the subjective status of reactivity and obscurity at the same time. In its reactive dimension, Vectorists deny the Quaternionist event as "simply inadmissible," they "den[y] the creative power of the event in favour of a deleted present" (*LoW* 58). As an obscure subject, they, however, even go "to war" and invoke "a full and pure transcendent Body, an ahistorical or anti-evental body" (*LoW* 59). Vectorism's epistemic limits, marked by the "Nothing they knew of Time," leads them to reject a different world model based on imaginary axes and "*impossible* numbers." While Quaternionists take that leap of faith and integrate this impossibility into the current mathematical situation, Vectorists perpetuate numbers only in their possible or real modality. As in the case of *The Road*, in order to preserve the world as it is, "earthly space they had fought over uncounted generations to penetrate, to occupy, to defend," they combine the reactionary stimulus of upholding "a present 'a little less worse' than the past" (*LoW* 55) and the obscurantism that directs terror at everyone (*E* 77), which also guided Brian Remy's fidelity to the simulacra event in *The Zero*.

This existential precariousness crucially affects the Quaternionist's ontological status itself. As subjects of events, they become the very premise that their scientific event introduces into the world. However, this does not "mean [they] only imagine now that [they] exist." Instead of a phenomenology of existence, where ontological entities are dependent on cognitive functions, they transform into an ontologically complex subject themselves. For while the "imaginary" part of them is empowered in senses that are to be investigated in the following, their confinement to the "real" also implies specific modes of exploitation, alienation, and exclusion. In a sense, this doubleness, floating between an immanent sphere of political, economic, or religious harassment and an evental movement beyond this "real" sphere is neatly contained in their spectral existence. They are "Ghosts. Ghosts." On the one hand, they are shut out from the "world" and are literally turned into dead remnants of themselves. However, on the other, they assume, as a subject of the event, a new form of empowerment, returning from those assumed gone with new abilities of resistance. Like the linguistic repetition, they bilocate and return endowed with a new subjective identity. In the following part, I will depict how Kit Traverse becomes one part of this scientific-political subject and transcends the determining forces that limit him. However, Kit will return to Vectorism, betray the Quaternionist event, and, ultimately, forsake his subjective fidelity.

Traversing the Webb

The character Kit Traverse manifests an intricate example for illustrating the creation of the scientific-political subject of the event. Starting out as a Vectorist, Kit transforms into a subject of the event when he accepts Quaternionism and embraces its new ontological imperatives. However, just as in the case of other subjects of events discussed in this study, his transformation is not a clear and linear development. Similarly to Sam's, Hailey's, and Sowell's creeping fidelity that initially tries to reject the event, Kit also at first denounces the event of Quaternionism. To this extent, one can particularly read the novel's often-bemoaned length as giving a fuller view of the necessarily ongoing fidelity that a subject of the event has to maintain. By following Kit over a span of some 30 years and a variety of geographic locations, Pynchon's expansive outlook gives a literary investigation of the theory of the subject of the event that necessarily requires repetitious affirmation and endurance. Only be reiterating the propositions of the event in various contexts and at various times, faced with different obstacles and the apparent waning of its claims, does a subject keep its status. If the other novels are restricted to relatively short narrated times and narrating times, *Against the Day* stretches both in order to shed light on the essential factor of persistence. In doubling the panoramic view on Kit's life, the reader is also confronted with the fact that a fidelity is a necessarily long and often tiresome process.

In the frame of Pynchon's poetics that incessantly undermines the stability of identities, Kit's subjective status is not a fixed unalterable continuum. Rather, the novel shows the need for a perpetual reaffirmation of the event if a subject wants to maintain its status and guarantee its reagency. While the other novels equally exemplify this continuous need for perpetuating evental points, *Against the Day* emphasizes with the character Kit the uncertainty of subjective processes of faithfulness. Nevertheless, Kit's fidelity to the Quaternionist event will bestow him with reagency, in that he abandons his Vectorist persuasion, his familial obligation, and the financial indebtedness to Scarsdale Vibe, which are not so much independent themes, but have reciprocal effects upon each other.[32] Heinz Ickstadt certainly has a point when he writes that "although he [Kit] is the most intellectual of them [the Traverse family], he is also the least aware of what is going on, a postmodern Parzival who misses asking the right question (or making the right commitment) at the right moment" (2010: 41). Nevertheless, I claim that he does make some right decisions that ascertain his status as a subject of the event, at least for a while.

A large part of *Against the Day* is devoted to the American Western setting that follows the Traverse family, consisting of Webb and Mayva and their children Frank, Reef, Lake, and Kit.[33] Webb's subscription to Anarchism, which was already briefly commented on, makes him a thorn in the side of the state and economic order. Corporate magnate Scarsdale Vibe, who metonymically personifies the incorporation of American, and also transnational, territories, eventually orders Webb's assassination by the two desperados Deuce Kindred and Sloat Frenso. The tragedy of Webb's murder is not only heightened by Lake ending up as Deuce's wife; in addition, Kit's scientific talent steers him into the grasp of Vibe's financial tutelage. Gaining his first experiences in physics, Kit starts out as an apprentice at Dr. Nikola Tesla's "high-voltage experiment" (*AtD* 97) in Colorado. Tesla's research in electrical engineering proves fertile for Kit's scientific orientation, for he now "thought of himself as a Vectorist, having arrived at that mathematical persuasion not by any abstract route but, as most had up till then, by way of Electricity, and its practical introduction, during his own early years, at an increasingly hectic clip, into lives previously innocent of it" (*AtD* 97). Already here, the novel introduces the scientific antagonism between Vectorism and Quaternionism, thereby neatly foreshadowing Kit's oscillation between the two camps. Although the novel has not mentioned the practice of Quaternionism by this point, the depiction of Kit becoming a Vectorist clearly addresses the other science. In describing the manner of Kit's pledge to Vectorism, the novel applies a negative definition, for Vectorism does not involve "abstract route[s]" but is a pragmatic, "practical" science. By conjuring a diametrically opposed notion of usefulness as opposed to mere theoretical abstraction, Vectorism is depicted as meeting the needs of an economically oriented world of market relations that Max Weber has so famously pointed out. This discursive opposition that concentrates on the sciences' ability to perpetuate capitalism's mechanisms is an ongoing topic within the novel and is probably best represented when Vibe asks Kit about his intentions to proceed with his mathematical studies: "*Useful* advanced mathematics? Or—" (*AtD* 330). For Vibe, scientific branches that do not contribute to economic progress are not even a cogent alternative, which is conveyed by his inability to even verbally express their alterity. According to Vibe, Kit is well advised to devote his mathematical talent to "become the next Edison" (*AtD* 331) and thus to subscribe to the workings of Capitalism in a "useful" manner.

This dialectics between the practicality of Vectorism and the uselessness of Quaternionism proves to be a major discursive characteristic in the clash between the two disciplines and will be contemplated in more detail at a later point. Yet, it also seems noteworthy that Kit is being introduced into this scientific discourse "by way of Electricity." For Scarsdale Vibe seeks to exploit Tesla's research of what he calls a "'World-System,' for producing huge amounts of electrical power that anyone can tap in to for free" (*AtD* 33). Already here, Kit's use of vectors, which will help

Tesla solve a mathematical problem, subliminally promotes the advent of a capitalist global order.[34] Moreover, the combination of Kit's initiation into Vectorist science with semantic clusters of "Electricity," "his own early years," the "increasingly hectic clip," and a loss of "innocence" evokes another scientific discourse that strongly affects the subjective formation in *Gravity's Rainbow*. Tyrone Slothrop's Pavlovian conditioning, which results in his psychic erections anticipating V-2 strikes, is there employed to show the subject's inevitable determination by pre-conscious mechanisms. Kit seems entrapped by similar modes of conditioning in which Vectorism is physically and psychologically "introduced" into him, like an intravenous fluid. Nevertheless, this subjective determination by Vectorism is simply a "mathematical *persuasion*" that is liable to be discarded by a more fundamental notion of fidelity.

For Kit, Vectorism "could have been a religion, for all he knew" with a "god of Current, bearing light, promising death to the falsely observant" (*AtD* 98). His mathematical books were like "Scripture and commandments and liturgy, all in this priestly Vectorial language" (*AtD* 89). Yet once more, science is likened to religion. Like the pre-secular grand narrative, Vectorism incorporates sacred structures and prescriptive rules, which make Kit insomniac with the paranoid obsession of hermeneutical decoding. The epistemologically insecure place of the subject is thus amplified by Kit's limited knowledge that hints at a realm beyond his subjective cognitive powers. Furthermore, his puritanical practices of deciphering are marked by a "hit-or-miss" (*AtD* 98) arbitrariness whose transformation from "mystery . . . into an understanding" (*AtD* 98) are less than given. His desire to "see" a transcendent form of reality, "directly, without equations" (*AtD* 98) remains initially futile, since he is equally at the mercy of salvation's uncertainty. The manner in which Vectorism dissimulates a similar evental disposition can be grasped when Kit seems to have a scientific enlightenment. Once,

> one night out west of Rico someplace a window opened for him into the Invisible, and a voice, or something like a voice, whispered unto him, saying, "Water falls, electricity flows—one flow becomes another, and thence into light. So is altitude transformed, continuously, to light." Words to that effect, well, maybe not words exactly. . . . And he found himself staring into the ordinarily blinding glow of a lamp filament, which he found instead unaccountably lambent, like light through the crack of a door left open, inviting him into a friendly house. With the stream in question roaring in sovereign descent just a few feet away. It had not been a dream, nor the sort of illumination he would someday learn that Hamilton had experienced at Brougham Bridge in Ireland in 1845—but it represented a jump from one place to another with who knew what perilous æther opening between and beneath. He saw it. The vectorial expressions in the books, surface integrals and potential functions and such, would henceforth figure as clumsier repetitions of the truth he now possessed in his personal interior, certain and unshakable. (*AtD* 98–99)

At first glance, this epiphany bears close similarities to an event. The eruptive nature that opens a window into an "Invisible," non-ontological realm and the literally illuminating manifestation of an aphoristic, quite esoteric insight of spirituality suggest an event-like happening.[35] However, on closer examination, this epiphanic moment does not entirely meet the criteria of a genuine event, in Badiou's sense. On the one hand, the mysterious words uttered to Kit are marked by continuity. By equating water with electricity and accentuating their fluidity and reciprocal transformation, the content of Kit's revelation insists on incessant "continuity," on evolutionary becoming rather than singular revolution. This holistic worldview, which denies the incisive character of events, is underlined by its effect on Kit. Kit looks into a merely "*ordinarily* blinding glow" that, although "unaccountably lambent," still does not amount to more than the "light through the crack of a door left open" ushering him into the comfortable warmth of a familiar hearth.

Once more, the novel combines the imagery of light with a specific ocular reception. Earlier, Vanderjuice described the scientific community as "squinting" (*AtD* 58). Here, Kit "stares" into the light as if mesmerized. Although he appears to be under a spell, Kit's "staring" implies more a position of voyeuristic desire than overwhelming disbelief toward the singularity of an event. Whereas both passages are related to an imminent danger of blinding, the lasting effect upon both I and eyes does in this instance only amount to a customary "glow" that may occasion a crack in a door but not its entire destruction and a consequent ushering through a gateway of new insights. Kit is, indeed, aware of this. He explicitly acknowledges that it was not like the event of Quaternionism that Hamilton experienced. Note the difference between what Kit describes as a "glow" but what in Hamilton's case was a "sort of illumination." What is more, the sentence "it had not been a dream, nor the sort of illumination he would someday learn that Hamilton had experienced at Brougham Bridge in Ireland in 1845" seems to imply a straightforward description of how Kit has learned of Hamilton's confrontation with the Quaternion event. Yet, the passage also seems to invite a reading according to which Kit will someday learn a similar form of illumination ("the sort of illumination he would someday learn"), where "that" does not figure as the object of a preposition, but as a conjunction. The peculiar temporal structure of the sentence also indicates the latter interpretation. For the sentence's evocation of incisive illuminations, unconscious processes and past events interweaves different forms of ontological levels in merging "subjective," "post-subjective," and "objective" temporalities. Whereas Kit's epiphany is a subjective experience, the passage's addressing of unconscious mechanisms and historical happenings conflates various ontological orders in order to show his determination by the scientific event. Added to this, Kit, who "would someday learn" of Quaternionism, is thus framed in future tense and past fact. As a form of hysteron proteron that implies a certain determination, this expresses the inevitability in respect of Kit's subjection to the Quaternionist event.

To this effect, Kit being able to "see it" should be conceived as a momentary epiphany rather than a subjective process in the light of an event. Although he experiences a development, attested by the spatial "jump from one place to another," it is still an individual movement. The "truth" that is now his is merely "in his personal interior," simply a cognitive process/progress and not a truth directed at a universal collective subject that the Quaternionist event maintains. In other words, Vectorism's revelation fosters his egoistic solipsism, without addressing a political dimension of collectivity—a dimension that is even more pronounced in Danielewski's *Only Revolutions*.

While "Kit's semi-religious attachment to Vectorism" (*AtD* 159) is certainly a persevering "persuasion" (*AtD* 97) that determines his subjective abilities, it is not the sole structure that has such effects upon his agency. The distinction between persuasion and fidelity is even extended by two other structures that play their part in Kit's subjective constitution and thereby usher in the political extent of his scientific fidelity. Both his familial obligations to Webb and his financial indebtedness to Scarsdale Vibe thus form two strains of responsibility that restrict Kit's freedom.

At first, Kit seems to abandon his family obligations by deciding to accept the proposition made by Vibe's stand-in Alex Foley (*AtD* 103). Kit endorses a scientific course of life not only because of his craving for mathematical research and to redeem his sense of belonging; his decision to accept Vibe's patronage also inexorably involves economic patterns of debt. The economic rhetoric of the passage repetitively evokes a semantic of biopolitical exploitation. For Kit's intention to become a scientist *"por vida,"* (*AtD* 103) as well as his readiness to sign a deal with the devil "for his life" is not only conceived in terms of a contractual, temporal "life." "For life" simultaneously implies an economic paradigm of exchange, in which Kit literally cedes his *"bios"* to Vibe.[36] By indebting himself to the industrial magnate, Kit enters an economic contract that lasts well beyond his ability to pay it off and makes his own life a commodity of exchange.[37] To this extent, Kit is literally "depending on the job," (*AtD* 103) a dependence on modes of production that promise a future point at which his life may be redeemed as soon as he has paid his dues.

His indebtedness to Vibe marks a key moment in Kit's loss of agency. The hysteron-proteron structure of this passage that first depicts his decision to "sign up with Foley's plan for his life" (*AtD* 103) and only then injects a flashback of their conversation again attests to this determination by the inversion of cause and effect. The way Kit's decision is being presented on a level of discourse, furthermore, attests to Kit's impulsiveness. In first presenting his decision and only later inserting the scene where Foley's proposal is elaborated, the passage's alinear *discourse* functions as a narrative means that paints Kit as a short-sighted character merely guided by his "yearning" and "desire" (*AtD* 103). Kit's inability to make decisions is also underlined by another temporal conflation, in which this "clarity of desire" that he assumes to be the basis for his decision is only ascribed retroactively ("that's how he'd think of it later") (*AtD* 103). Kit's passivity is generally accentuated in that "he [finds] himself, unaccountably." Next to a further economic dimension that lies in his literal lack of positive accounts (for he is indebted), he is also unaccountable in a legal sense. The abandonment of his "life" to Vibe that makes the magnate "untroubled and free" renders Kit merely an "element" that is outside the law.

Yet, Kit also abandons another aspect of his "life." His decision to accept the financial aid provided by Vibe clearly runs against everything that Webb embodies. When still alive, Webb thus expresses his utter disagreement: "They own you," (*AtD* 105) he warns Kit. Webb is aware of the economic "deal" (*AtD* 105) and its biopolitical implications. He expresses the property relations between Vibe and Kit in the present tense, thereby indicating the comprehensive grasp of Capital that abandons any form of past or future temporality: ownership in capitalism, Webb amplifies, is a permanent structure that cannot be thought outside of. Although Vibe individually personifies capitalism, he is here equated with a corporation, as well as with a "They," a recurring topos of paranoia and heteronomy in Pynchon's novels.

Although this marks the point of both Webb's alienation of his child and Kit's progressive incorporation into the Vibe family, the either-or structure of Kit's decision cannot be separated as neatly as Webb wishes to. The familial obligation to their father constitutes a dominant theme for all of Webb's children and serves as a persistent directive for their ethical demeanor that cannot be dissociated in cogent oppositions. This obligation is specifically evoked by Webb's assassination. For it seems as if Webb's death generates similar structures that determine his children in their possible modes of action.[38] Repeatedly, Frank and Reef try to avenge their father, while Lake's falling in love with Deuce is perceived by her family as well as other characters as a clear violation of familial commitments. However, still at the funeral site, Lake demystifies this antiquated narrative when she chides her brothers' plans: "You're off into that old world o' family vengeance, it has its claim on you now, you're both out lost in country you don't know how to get back in from" (*AtD* 217). What Lake calls the "old world o' family vengeance" reveals her brothers' family obligations to be conservative and outmoded myths. She, indeed, addresses this in topological terms and semantic borders. Frank's and Reef's position "out lost in a country" without the knowledge of how to return creates a spatial map on which vengeance appears as a frontier into a mythical notion of America. Fostering a religious eye-for-an-eye maxim, Frank and Reef are inescapably "claimed" by family obligations.

In this sense, the narrative strand that McHale identifies as the "dime-novel Western" (2011: 17) actually involves a reflexive rewriting of this particular genre, a "genre-poaching" (2011: 18).[39] The notion of the literary, narratological "event" that could in the framework of the Western be seen as the retribution and the return of order, which the novel seems to suggest can be arrived at by avenging Webb, is continuously deferred. "Messy and unsatisfactory," observes McHale, "each episode ends in an anticlimax of one kind or another" (2011: 23), while Celia Wallhead opines that "the travels of the characters give the impression of a 'plotless' novel" (2010: 293). Already in the beginning, *Against the Day* evokes the tropes of this particular genre and concomitantly stifles its formulaic themes and narrative "events." Professor Vanderjuice thus muses that "here's where the Trail comes to its end at last, along with the American Cowboy who used to live on it and by it" (*AtD* 53). Vanderjuice goes on to stockpile a variety of stereotypical cowboy traits: "No matter how virtuous he's kept his name, how many evildoers he's managed to get by undamaged, how he's done by his horses, what girls he has chastely kissed, serenaded by guitar, or gone out and raised hallelujah with, it's all back there in the traildust now and none of it matters" (*AtD* 53). Although Vanderjuice addresses the waning of the frontier—and the beginning of the novel at the Columbian World Exposition equally suggests Turner's presence—McHale argues that here, the novel emphasizes the "continuing vitality of the fictional West" as a discursive construct. Within the historical refraction of the 1890s through the embedding in the generic discourse of the dime novel,[40] *Against the Day,* nevertheless, rewrites the genre by adopting "a strategy of demystification and debunking, subjecting the western to a *revisionist* transformation" (McHale 2011: 23). While the literary and narratological structure of the Western thus commands specific readerly expectations that implicate an ethics of justice, the novel unmasks these narratives as part of a mythical construction of ideological nature.

Still, even though all of Webb's children at one time or another abandon their family obligations and thereby undermine the dominant mechanisms of the genre, his presence does not abate: "And Webb's ghost, meantime, Webb's busy ghost, went bustling to and fro doing what he could to keep things hopping" (*AtD* 218). Kit is continuously haunted by the spectral figure of his father, which reminds him in a Hamletian manner of his unfinished business.

Faced with the determining constraints of family obligation, financial debt, and scientific persuasion, Kit's lack of agency is probably best manifested when he finds himself on a ship to pursue his Vectorist studies at Göttingen. On board the S. S. Stupendica, Kit and his soon-to-be wife Dally Rideout, eventually notice the peculiar ontological status of the vessel: "It had begun to seem as if she and Kit were on separate vessels, distinct versions of the Stupendica, pulling away slowly on separate courses, each bound to a different destiny" (*AtD* 514). Instead of merely addressing notions of Dally's subjective sentimentality—"Daydreaming" (*AtD* 515) as Kit smirks—where the separation only takes place in her imagination, the ship soon transforms into two physically disparate vessels. The Stupendica's "secret identity, latent in her present conformation, though invisible to the average passenger" (*AtD* 515) is the Habsburgian battle ship S. M. S *Emperor Maximillian,* "a participant in the future European war at sea" but "so far as official history goes, never built" (*AtD* 515). As a product of bilocation, a mysterious phenomenon that is discussed recurrently throughout the novel though never comprehensively explained, the two ships are merged at their construction site into a single object. When the vessel now begins to disintegrate, Kit gets separated from Dally and cannot leave the warship. Once the "steel metamorphosis" (*AtD* 518) is completed, Kit, who finds himself in the lower levels, experiences the physical dimensions of the separation. The identities of the ship have disconnected and formed, like in a meiosis, two independent ships. While Dally and the "Elect" find themselves on the "Stupendica [which] continued its civilian journey" (*AtD* 523), Kit and the "Preterite" are trapped in the dreadnought that heads to Morocco, where it will engage in the Tangier Crisis. Symptomatic for Kit's lack of power is the "Chief Oberhauptheitzer" [*sic*!] (*AtD* 519) thwarting Kit's intentions to go back to the upper levels: "No, mister, no no—he does not understand—there are no staterooms, it is no longer the Stupendica up there. That admirable vessel has sailed on to its destiny" (*AtD* 519). Kit is, furthermore, denied the way up by a "bituminous hand, which propelled him rapidly through the fierce spasms of light and the ungodly steel clangor toward the bunkers at the side of the ship, out of which men were loading coal on to skids to be dragged to the boiler furnaces" (*AtD* 517). Through his Vectorist persuasion, he has unwillingly become a cog of the dreadnought's machinery, being coerced to power the ship that plays its part in the military gambits that will lead to the First World War.

Through Kit's adherence to the Quaternionist event, he will be able to abandon these structures of determination and becomes part of a faithful subject. While Kit at first attempts to recuperate from the loss of his father through a "plunge into advanced Vectorism. No looking over your shoulder" (*AtD* 325) and thus clings to Vectorism's escapist dimensions, he eventually accepts Prof. Vanderjuice's advice that interweaves physics and psychology and also science and politics: "When human tragedies happen, it always seems as if scientists and mathematicians can meet the situation more calmly than others. But it's as likely to be a form of escaping reality, and sooner or later comes the payback" (*AtD* 325). Vanderjuice undermines the rationalist stereotype of the scientific community and points to the unsustainability of their psychological coping strategies. Although he speaks of "scientists and mathematicians" in general, the impetus to escape reality seems particularly pertinent to the science of Vectorism with its construction of multiple dimensions beyond the given world. The multiple dimensions that Vectorism is able to conjure are not just a theoretical arithmetic but crucially relate to a very political and psychological practice. For while the impulse of constructing multiple parallel worlds certainly has an effect on the present world, if only by showing that other worlds are possible, Quaternionism's adherence to the "given world" (*AtD* 131) implies a more fundamental positioning *in medias res*. Instead of turning their back to the world at hand, Quaternionists essentially work within the perimeters of the given world without abandoning the radical potential to change this world, thereby engaging in the question of "How are we to be faithful to changing the world *within the world itself?*" (*TRoH* 67).

Moreover, Vanderjuice, whose "conscience was also showing signs of feeling, as if recovering from frostbite" (*AtD* 324), since he was similarly bought by Vibe, not only suggests one way out of Kit's indebtedness by convincing him " 'that [he] owe[s] them'—he would not say 'him'—'nothing' " (*AtD* 323) but also gets Kit into touch with Quaternionism. "Overflowing with an all-but-elated idea of how he might actually do someone some good," Vanderjuice confronts Kit with his first knowledge of Quaternionism:

> One day, chatting with young Traverse, he happened to pull an old copy of the British science journal *Nature* from a row of them on his bookshelf, and leaf through to one of the articles. "P. G. Tait on Quaternions. Regards their chief merit as being 'uniquely adapted to Euclidean space . . .' because—'lamp' this—'What have students of physics, as such, to do with more than three dimensions?' I invite your attention to 'as such'."
>
> "A physics student, as something else, *would* have need for more than three dimensions?" Kit puzzled.
>
> "Well, Mr. Traverse, if you ever considered becoming that 'something else,' Germany would seem the logical place for you. Grassmann's *Ausdehnungslehre* can be extended to any number of dimensions you like. Dr. Hilbert at Göttingen is developing his 'Spectral Theory,' which requires a vector space of *infinite* dimensions." (*AtD* 324)

Kit, who has curiously up until now solely been a Vectorist disciple without having crossed the Quaternion discourse is here initiated with a literal "row" on the Professor's bookshelf.[41] Tait, a fervent and rather polemical adherent of Quaternionism, figures as an outspoken part of the Quaternionist subject. His attempts to substantiate Quaternionism in the scientific *"Kampf ums Dasein"* made him engage in quite explicit disputes with Gibbs and Heaviside. By introducing Kit to the scientific dispute, Vanderjuice, on the one hand, quite basically points Kit to an alternative to the Vectorist system. Next to undermining the dominance of that particular scientific discourse, Vanderjuice more fundamentally ushers Kit into a different world of science that simultaneously accounts for his present situation. For the distinction between a science of extensional spaces, embodied in Grassman, Hilbert, or Minkowski, and a science that draws its potential from within the given, though complex, four axes, that is, Quaternionism, directly applies to the differentiation between escapism and realism.[42] Whereas Grassman just like Hilbert allows the projection of an infinity of dimensions, their "spectral theories" could be perceived as just such forms of "escaping reality" (*AtD* 325). This is then obviously also a metapoetical discussion that *Against the Day* reflects upon. Through the juxtaposition of two scientific paradigms, Pynchon addresses the relation between fiction and reality itself. While his fiction itself is often compared to the potential of other worlds, and which is only accentuated by his reflection on counter-factual subjunctives, Pynchon here conceives a theory of political fiction that is complex. As Pöhlmann has pointed out, this implies that it is part real and part imaginary, without giving in to any priority of any of these two modalities (2010: 25).

However, Vanderjuice does not directly influence Kit in telling him which scientific trajectory he is supposed to follow. All he does is incite Kit to ponder the possibility of becoming a "physics student as *something else.*" Within the plurality of possible scientific persuasions that Göttingen offers, Kit, indeed, becomes that something else, with the "need for more than three dimensions" adding the essential component of time to these axes. Realizing "that nothing known to the *alternate* universe of vector analysis could bring him comfort or help him see a way *out*" (*AtD* 322), Kit progressively, but at first unwillingly, loosens his Vectorist adherence and is propelled on a different path.

Although Kit initially never fully accepts the scientific event, since he continuously discards the "Quaternionist talk" (*AtD* 131)—"The gossiping never stops with you Quaternion folks, do you all have to swear some oath to always lead an irregular life?" (*AtD* 560)—he has entered a process of fidelity. Unlike the novel's depiction of Hamilton's encounter of the Quaternions, Kit's confrontation is not represented as a similarly material and physical encounter. As in the case of *The Road* and *The Zero*, the novel does not presume a physical confrontation with the event but, rather, invests efforts in delineating the process of fidelity that is just as constitutive of the subject of the event. Kit thus, rather, exemplifies a form of fidelity that is processual, in very much the same sense as Sam's and Hailey's abandonment of their solipsisms, or Sowell's slow realization of the political event of emancipation. For him, the event's singularity and eruptive manifestation is constituted over an expanse of time, which, nonetheless, brings about a fundamental change.

A key station within Kit's slow and reluctant adherence to the Quaternionist event is constituted by his arrival at the already mentioned Quaternionist convention at Ostend. After having finally disembarked the *Emperor Maximilian* and roamed Northern Africa, Kit arrives in Belgium. While reflecting on how to reach Göttingen, as he seems to be no longer supported by Vibe, Kit's "ruminations were broken in upon by a violent dispute over in the corner, among an unkempt, indeed seedy, band of varying ages and nationalities whose only common language Kit recognized presently as that of the Quaternions" (*AtD* 525). The narrator's description of the Quaternionists' poor appearance subscribes to their social exclusion. Kit's own transitory position, oscillating between Vectorist persuasion and Quaternionist fidelity, is marked by his superior stance toward the "embattled persuasion" (*AtD* 525). Part of his Vectorist past thereby tries to distance itself from the aberrational scientific minority. Nevertheless, Kit is able to recognize the "common language" (*AtD* 525) that they use, having seemingly been introduced to their scientific episteme. Despite the professed universality of mathematical language (Engelhardt 2013: 216), Kit crucially differentiates the Quaternionist episteme, hinting at its common, collective basis. His ability to understand them suggests that his mathematical knowledge has been expanded by the Quaternion discourse. The incisive nature of his recognition ("presently" [*AtD* 525]), furthermore, highlights his instantaneous incorporation of the Quaternionist event, instead of his simply having learned the language over a course of time. What, moreover, attests to his partaking in their collective subjectivity is the fact that they "*recognize him*" (*AtD* 525, my emphasis) both in his existentially unstable position and through his being engaged in a process of fidelity. Note also in this context that his inclusion into their collectivity does not necessitate a rite of interpersonal initiation, as if they were a Masonic sect. Kit's status as a subject of the event, rather, consists in his fidelity toward an event and not to the sectarian dogmas of a fraternal organization that relies on the exclusive mechanisms of semiotic rituals.

The crucial effect of the event shows results when he engages in a discussion with Yashmeen Halfcourt, the exotic object of desire of many of the novel's characters and a different instantiation of a scientific subject, as will be expanded on in the next part. Yashmeen, upon meeting Kit for the first time, takes him "for a mathematician" (*AtD* 590). Kit immediately distances himself from that ascription, responding "well . . . maybe not *your* kind," and describes himself as being "a sort of, hm . . . Vectorist" (*AtD* 590). Kit's reluctance in identifying with Yashmeen, who continuously mocks his Vectorist persuasion, again illustrates his denial of the event. However, Kit's equally hesitant self-description, according to which he is only a "sort of" Vectorist, amplifies his processual turn to the Quaternions. This can even be detected in his bodily behavior. By "*squar[ing]* his shoulders" and wiping "*imaginary* beer foam" (*AtD* 590, my emphasis) off his face, Kit has obviously internalized the Quaternion language not only as a linguistic jargon but also as body language.

When Kit wants to help Yashmeen with the mathematical "Riemann problem" (*AtD* 591), his Quaternion fidelity makes itself felt without his being aware of it. Despite both Yashmeen's allegation of Kit's Vectorist solution to the Zeta-problem and his construction of multiple dimensions, Kit is not simply working within a Vectorist epistemology. Crucially, his application of the Zeta-function to ordinary vectorial settings "as if it was mappable into the set of complex numbers" (*AtD* 591) implements a complex function on existing vectors systems. Instead of simply substituting the Vector system for a new paradigm, Kit effectively applies the event to the current situation and thereby fundamentally changes its ontological structure. The Quaternion disposition of transforming the "well-known" dimensions into complex axes is also hinted at in the "as if" (*AtD* 591) of his experimentation. Kit is not intending to solve the Riemann problem, but, more importantly, investigates the potential of altering the ontological stability of Vectorism by a subjunctive, even ethical operation.

Although Kit's confrontation of the Quatenionist event is not represented in the novel's narrative, *Against the Day* integrates a scene in which he bears witness to the founding event as it is exhibited at the "Museum der Monstrositäten, a sort of nocturnal equivalent of Professor Klein's huge collection of mathematical models" (*AtD* 632) at Göttingen. Upon being ushered "ZU DEN QUATERNIONEN" by Yashmeen, Kit

> descended dark stairways uncomfortably steep even for the moderately fit— as if modeled after some ancient gathering-place, such as the Colosseum in Rome, stained with Imperial intention, promises of struggle, punishment, blood sacrifice—and stood at last before a rubber curtain, waiting, until it was mysteriously drawn aside and he found himself injected into overamplified Nernst light at the verge of white explosion, and there he was, undeniably at the canalside in Dublin sixty years ago as Hamilton received the Quaternions from an extrapersonal source nearly embodied in this very light, the Brougham Bridge receding away in perfect perspective, the figure of Mrs. Hamilton gazing on in gentle consternation, Hamilton himself in the act of carving into the bridge his renowned formulae with a pocket-knife part real and part imaginary, a "complex" knife one might say. (*AtD* 634)

In contrast to the Vectorist epiphany that Kit experiences back in Colorado, this instance resembles more the singular reception of an event. As before, Hamilton is not depicted as a genius-discoverer, but one who rests passively, receiving the "extrapersonal source." The Quaternions' complex ontological status is, moreover, hinted at with their being "nearly embodied in this very light." Although their embodiment is only approximated, they, nevertheless, possess a body that only waits for the right form of illumination to become visible.

Despite the fact that Kit only views a reconstruction of Hamilton's "discovery," he, nevertheless, assumes the passive and receptive position at the mercy of an event. Once more, his lack of agency, finding "himself injected into overamplified Nernst light at the verge of white explosion" is underlined by photo-graphic imagery that, however, comes closer to the fundamental eruption of an event than the prior "glow" (*AtD* 98). Even though one could argue that Hamilton's presence in a museum obliterates the nonconformist nature of Quaternionism, the event having been normalized into an institutionalized setting, the fact that it is a museum of monstrosities, rather, suggests its abnormality.[43] To this extent, the display of the Quaternionist event does not solely figure as creating a place that regulates knowledge, since it assumes a different topographic location than other exhibited "events in the recent history of mathematics, such as Knipfel's *Discovery of the Weierstrass Functions* and the recently installed *Professor Frege at Jena upon Receiving Russell's Letter Concerning the Set of All Sets That Are Not Members of Themselves*" (*AtD* 633). Although the museum's display of items such as the "complex knife" or other "famous 'props' in the general mathematical drama, pieces of chalk, half-finished cups of coffee, even a thoroughly crumbled handkerchief" (*AtD* 634) obviously ridicules cults of authorship that foster a mythical form of the creator's aura, as well as the institution of the museum as a discursive site that orders knowledge, its presentation of the Quaternion event may also serve another function. Specifically through the location of the Quaternionist exhibition, it becomes clear to what extent it is not on the same footing as the other scientific "events." Placed at a subterranean level, Kit has to go at length to arrive at the Quaternionist site, which relates to the existential extortion that a fidelity requires. Thus, he has to descend "*uncomfortably steep*" steps that even pose problems for the physically adept; moreover, the comparison of the stairways with the ancient Roman place of slave battles insinuates, again, the existential precariousness of the Quaternionist subject of the event. Yet, correlating this site of struggle to an ancient place of summoning simultaneously renders it a locus of ritualistic reenactment. In the light of the institutional framework of lethal exploitation, the passageway to Hamilton's reconstruction also marks a site of resistance that gathers those faithful to the event and reminds them of their "promise of struggle" against the "Imperial intention" that may even demand "blood sacrifice." While Kit has confronted the Quaternionist event even before his visit to the exhibition, the material encounter with Hamilton's "discovery" adds to and perpetuates his fidelity.

One of the most explicit moments of Kit's reagency that he acquires through his fidelity manifests itself when he tries, together with his brother Reef, to assassinate Vibe in Venice. With the aid of Dally Rideout, who by now has become a resident of Venice, the two brothers pursue becoming the "agent[s] at last for Webb's vengeful ghost" (*AtD* 732) and bring down his murderer. However, the necessary closure of the revenge plot, in which Kit paradoxically strives to be an "*agent*" who is simultaneously guided by Webb's spectral unfinished business, remains inconclusive. While planning how best to assassinate Vibe, Reef thus suggests to Kit: "'A fella'd have to walk right up to old Scarsdale, face-to-face. Is where I guess you'd come in, Kit.' 'Maybe not,' Kit said" (*AtD* 737). Kit explains his reluctance to kill Vibe as too obvious an attempt that is bound to misfire. Yet, as soon as their plans do fail and another Anarchist who makes an attempt at the mogul's life is beaten to death in front of Vibe, Reef confronts Kit with his unwillingness to bring him down (*AtD* 746). What Reef takes to be a similar violation of family obligations as Lake's relationship with Deuce simultaneously attests to Kit's disengagement from his family creed as well as the debt of his life. By referring to an economic context once more, the "deal" (*AtD* 746) that Reef addresses is a different economic contract than the ones discussed before. For Reef, the revenge for his father follows a paradigm of exchange in which accounts can be settled by cancelling out lives. By taking Vibe's life, Reef expects a clean slate. Since Kit is unwilling to relapse to this economic and ethical narrative, he becomes for Reef a minor, a "kid," (*AtD* 746) and thus entirely without agency. However, Kit is not simply unwilling to get in on the deal. While Reef assumes that Kit is unable to enter a new arrangement through his contractual commitments that he still maintains to his "fairy godfather" (*AtD* 746), which resemble familial obligations, Kit's decision not to kill Vibe rests on different grounds. As a subject faithful to a scientific event, Kit realizes the political dimensions of this truth procedure. Through the active choice to reject the determining commitments to his conscience that tells him to redeem his father as well as the economic narrative that claims his life, his reagency manifests itself in moving beyond both structures.

On the one hand, he emancipates himself from the textual constraints that the Western genre imposes on him. Instead of seeking individual retribution, Kit opts for a more circumspect mode of retaliation in sparing Vibe's life, so as not to apply an analogous mode of action and thereby to fall prey to the same ethical "eye-for-an-eye" conundrum. Whereas Hume argues that *Against the Day* "seems more politically aggressive" (2011: 168) than Pynchon's prior novels, it seems as if Kit here actively rejects the use of violence as part of his fidelity. In keeping faith with the Quaternionist event, Kit thus breaks with Vibe's influence, as his Quaterionist work no longer proves to realize any profit. By following a scientific mode of thought that is not a form of "useful advanced mathematics," (*AtD* 330) Kit's subjective fidelity liberates him from the economic bonds that stick him to Vibe. In fact, although Kit has given his life to Vibe, the Quaternionist event endows him with a new subjective "bios" that compensates his loss and endows him with a new subjective identity that breaks the economic chains. Although Žižek observes: "We thus have two lives, the finite biological life and the infinite Life of participating in the Truth-Event" (1999: 170), the faithfulness to the Quaternionist event does not, in the case of Kit, result in an "infinite Life" since he abandons the "Truth-Event."

On the other hand, while being faithful, Kit disentangles himself from his family commitments in turning his back on the duties that his father's death seem to demand. In keeping faith to the event, Kit extends the individual narrative of revenge and lives up to his father's legacy in transferring his Anarchist conviction to scientific realms. In tune with the Anarchist tendencies latent in Quaternionism that have already been commented upon, Kit commemorates Webb's heritage in alignment with the Quaternionist event. He discards the lethal claims of revenge but simultaneously perpetuates the memory of his father by becoming a scientific Anarchist. Thereby, Kit applies the propositions that the event brings to light not exclusively in the domain of mathematics. By integrating the insights he gained from his subjective identity, he also transfers this knowledge on different situations. Instead of merely dwelling in the abstract spheres of theoretical mathematics, Kit lives up to the propositions of Quaternionism by projecting its materialist driving force on the "given world" (*AtD* 130). Unlike the escapist tendency of other forms of mathematics, he applies the eventual trace not exclusively to intra-scientific domains. Kit, like Sowell in Beatty's *Slumberland*, becomes a subject of the event by poaching Badiou's neatly separated truth conditions, showing how science and politics have common denominators and cross-fertilize.

To repeat, Kit's reagency that allows him to leave behind his scientific, familial, and economic debts only springs from the appearance of the event. Only by becoming a scientific-political subject of the Quaternionist event is he bequeathed the ability to abandon the structures that determine him. However, the fact that Kit becomes a part of the collective subject of Quaternionism that finds its first instantiation in Hamilton does not imply a passage toward a transcendent form of grace. As part of the Quaternionist subject, Kit equally has to face the mechanisms of exclusion that his fellow mathematicians have to go through. Reagency provides him with the capability to transcend these structures; still, this is not to be imagined as a miraculous gift that grants him supernatural powers. On the other hand, Kit likewise does not remain a subject of the event once having accepted the event. *Against the Day* thus shows that a faithful subject of the event is not an inexorable given once the process has been initiated. With Kit, the novel, rather, exemplifies to what extent an event necessitates persistent reaffirmation. Unlike Sam and Hailey in *Only Revolutions*, who continuously perpetuate the points of the event and thereby keep their love (and, by analogy, the event of their encounter) alive, Kit abandons his fidelity and relapses to Vectorism.

By the end of the novel, war-ridden Europe makes Kit return to the practicality of Vectorism: "Kit went to the address Viktor Mulciber had given him in Constantinople and was hired on the spot, and soon was turning his vectorist skills to matters of wing loading, lateral and longitudinal stability, so forth." (*AtD* 1068). Again, Kit's affiliation to Vectorism is described by the syntactical enumeration that mirrors the mathematical addition of dimensions. Like the Vectorist calculation with a plurality of extended axes, so does the sentence imply the return of Kit into this scientific camp by linguistic means. Moreover, Kit's relations with the arms-dealer Mulciber are indicative of his rejection of the Quaternionist fidelity.[44] While Quaternionists persistently attempted to prevent its technological exploitation for weapons,[45] Kit supports the Italian war effort with his mathematical skills. The materiality that is latent in his "turning [of] his vectorist skills to *matters*" suggests that Quaternionism does not provide a practical implementation. Unlike Quaternionism, whose impetus is to change the ontology of the world by providing its subject with a crucially different point of view instead of contributing to the national conflict with lethal technologies, Vectorism is depicted as a scientific discourse that plays its part in the Great War. For the recurrent narratorial enumeration that ends with the "so forth" suggests not only the multitudinous applicability of Vectorist calculations; what is more, the asyndeton also describes an ongoing chain of responsibility, in which the merely scientific problem of aerodynamics channels ineluctably into the death of people and fulfills Piet Woevre's diagnosis that "all mathematics leads, doesn't it, sooner or later to some kind of human suffering" (*AtD* 541). Kit thus takes in a position similar to the rocket scientists in *Gravity's Rainbow* that disintegrate the V-2's arch into bureaucratic segments of responsibility. As a consequence,

> Kit worked off and on at the interesting problem of how to pull a gigantic triplane out of a nosedive, and went up with Renzo for a couple-three more of those *picchiate*, most notably in August of 1917 during a Bolshevik-inspired strike of workers at the weapons factories in Torino. . . . Kit risked a look over at Renzo, demented even when at rest, and saw that here, approaching the speed of sound,

he was being metamorphosed into something else . . . a case of possession. Kit had a velocity-given illumination then. It was all political. (*AtD* 1071)

The individual dimension of Kit's scientific "interest" in the aeronautic problem only makes him realize the underlying structures of responsibility when he accompanies war-pilot Rezno on one of his trips. Despite his purely scientific intentions, Kit cannot overlook the political repercussions of his work. In fact, he finds himself once more part of an economic deal, since his scientific knowledge transforms not only Rezno into a glassy-eyed zombie. The ambivalence latent in the depersonalized "he" may also pertain to Kit. In that sense, Kit himself is "metamorphosed into something else" and the "case of possession" implies a structure of indebtedness to the technological needs of Rezno, and, by analogy, the war. Kit's "velocity-given illumination" makes him abandon the illusory belief that science and politics are separate spheres, which is epitomized when he is faced with Austria's intentions to invade Italy (*AtD* 1073). Kit is now forced "into abandoning his engineer's neutrality" and he begins to fly "missions, sometimes crewing for Renzo, sometimes alone. For a while he allowed himself to be seduced into the Futurist nosedive, with its æsthetics of blood and explosion" (*AtD* 1073). Unmistakably, Kit has abandoned his status as a faithful subject and betrays the event: unlike the universalist pretension of any event, he actively participates in the territorial gamble that cherishes "blood and explosion." In the vein of the Futurist celebration of *techne*, embracing what Filippo Marinetti celebrated in his 1909 "The Founding and Manifesto of Futurism," Kit is seduced by a modernist aesthetics of death. Kit returns to the scientific practice that determined his life prior to the event and thus perpetuates the social and political order that opposes, among other groups, the Quaternionist subject. Since "killing someone is always a matter of the (old) state of things" and can "never be a requisite of novelty" (*BE* 408), Kit's embrace of destruction makes him an unfaithful subject: "Unfaithfulness," Badiou explains in *Infinite Thought*, "is when a subject is constituted by faithfulness but that faithfulness disappears" (142). His faithfulness abates and he assumes the Vectorist reactive and obscure inclination that denied the Quaternionist event and simultaneously suppressed those faithful to it. Kit thus betrays the event in the words of Alberto Toscano: "The (ex-) subject of betrayal in fact *denies* having been seized by a truth, drowning his previous courage in deep scepticism and bowing to the imperative according to which we must avert the risks imposed by any truth procedure" (2006: 23). In dissociating himself from the event, he also resigns from the collectivity of the Quaternionist subject where his nosedive is a literal metaphor for his fall from grace: " 'Well full fuckin' circle,' is what he muttered to himself, 'ain't it' " (*AtD* 1068). *Against the Day* thereby shows to what extent the status of being a subject of the event should not be taken for granted. Only through an active and repeated reaffirmation of the event's points may a subject uphold his reagency and not succumb to an obscure reactive divergence when faced with a "moment of crisis":

What can go to crisis is the one or several "some-ones" who enter into the composition of the subject induced by this process. Everyone familiar with the moments of crisis faced by a lover, a researcher's discouragement, a militant's lassitude, an artist's sterility. Or again, with the lasting failure of someone to understand a mathematical proof. . . . And at this point, I am confronted with a pure choice between the "Keep going!" proposed by the ethic of this truth, and the logic of the "perseverance in being" of the mere mortal that I am. (*E* 78)

The last part of this chapter focuses on a different subject of the event that showcases a more sustained form of fidelity and inquires into what Badiou calls the "lasting failure of" not understanding "a mathematical proof." Yashmeen Halfcourt's mathematical subjectivity offers another process of faithfulness that is markedly different from Kit's haphazard status as a subject of the event as well as from those subjects discussed in the previous chapters. Yashmeen constitutes a scientific subject of the event that extends its mathematical fidelity on political realms and thereby establishes an entirely new subjective dimension.

The Zeta-Maniac

Like Kit Traverse, Yashmeen Halfcourt is at first confined by structures that are beyond her control. Only her fidelity to the mathematical Riemann event harbors the potential of endowing her with reagency. By integrating another mathematical event, *Against the Day* employs its fictional potential in showing the poietical creation of a multitude of events at the same time, without yielding to the same undifferentiated multitude of events that mark *Gravity's Rainbow*. In this, the novel stands out in the context of this study, since it is the only novel that implements more than just one event. Nevertheless, *Against the Day* clings to the emphatic nature of these events. In contrast to Badiou, who insists on the scarcity of events in order to preserve their singular character, Pynchon's juxtaposition of various events emancipates itself from the evental conditions of the "real" world and creates not only multiple alternate worlds, but also worlds that harbor alternate and multiple events. Moreover, by conjuring another mathematical event, the novel also dampens the rigid oppositionality that reigns between Vectorism and Quaternionism and offers a third position to this dialectics. While Yashmeen could also be seen as part of the Quaternionist subject, she adheres to a more specific event that, in remaining faithful to the history of science, cannot be subsumed under a generalized notion of Quaternionist mathematics.

In the beginning of the novel, Yashmeen is equally at the mercy of her stepfather, Auberon Halfcourt, who has left her under the protection of the mysterious neo-Pythagorean society "based upon the sacred Tetractys" (*AtD* 220). The T.W.I.T., one of Pynchon's ever-present secret societies that nods to the hilarity of acronyms, are supposed to protect her while Auberon has been sent on a colonizing mission to Inner Asia, more specifically, to Shambhala, which is of prime interest to the various nations in the novel. Nicholas Nookshaft, Grand Cohen of the "True Worshippers of the Ineffable *Tetractys*," (*AtD* 220) fills American private eye Lew Basnight in on Yashmeen's background story:

> Frankly as if she had not been standing a foot away, he began to acquaint Lew with the girl's history. She had been the ward of Lieutenant-Colonel G. Auberon Halfcourt, formerly a squadron commander in the Eighteenth Hussars, seconded some while ago to the Political Departement in Simla for the odd extra-regimental chore, and currently believed operating somewhere out in Inner Asia. Yashmeen, sent back here a few years previously for a British education, had been placed under the protection of the T.W.I.T. "Unhappily, to more than one element active in Britain, her degree of bodliy safety too readily suggests itself as a means of influencing the Colonel's behavior. Our custody hence extends rather beyond simple caution." (*AtD* 222)

This passage reverberates with colonial themes. Yashmeen, "who regarded Lew out of eyes from which a suggestion of the Oriental might not have been altogether absent" (*AtD* 221) continuously figures as an alluring object of desire.[46] Throughout the novel, Yashmeen, who already carries the botanically exotic in her name, has to serve as a projection site of various sexual cravings, "gathering appreciative looks from passersby male and female" (*AtD* 224). Moreover, her adoption by Auberon, a functionary in the British Imperial enterprise, renders her the object of colonial hegemony. As an intertextual reference to Shakespeare's *A Midsummer Night's Dream*, Auberon/Oberon thus embodies the partriarchal authority of the king of fairies. Shakespeare's Oberon not only "come[s] from the farthest step of India" (2005: 19) where he maintained a relationship with the "bouncing Amazon" (ibid.: 20) Hippolyta who gets kidnapped by Theseus; moreover, his colonial desire for Titania's "changeling boy" (ibid.: 21) converges the pedophilic and exotic cravings that seem equally latent in the relationship between Auberon and Yashmeen. Yashmeen could thus be identified with two objects of colonialist and patriarchal oppression, discursively othered and physically held captive.

What adds to her determination by Imperial discourse is manifested in her British education, being sent back "here" unmistakably constructing a spatial topography that distinguishes between civilized home and savage colony. Even more so, her passive position as a chess piece in the national gambit over territory renders her an object rather than the subject of discourse. Not only does the Grand Cohen relate her story as if she were absent and thereby offers various problems of subaltern representation and historiography but Yashmeen's being "sent back," and "having been placed" under T.W.I.T. protection also describes her powerless state in a grammatical sense. Even in the narratorial summary Yashmeen is constructed as passive and thereby being denied the ability of self-constitution or -representation. In accordance with this, Nookshaft extends the mere mode of protection to a "degree of bodily safety" that channels into disciplinary confinement.

Despite Yashmeen's insistence that she "can look after [her]self" (*AtD* 222), the organization assumes this mode of surveillance by concentrating its ocular attentions on her. In fact, the T.W.I.T.'s "protection" of Yashmeen oscillates between disciplinary and controlling measures. On the one hand, Nookshaft sends her "up to University, to Girton College, Cambridge, to study maths" (*AtD* 225) and thus confines her in a corrective institution (*AtD* 496). Yashmeen's confinement in the attic, "her tiny garret room" (*AtD* 496), once more points to the literary past and makes her a mad Bertha, a figure of alterity who is incarcerated in the colonial home without hope for escape. But this spatial confinement changes into a more ubiquitious mode of control when the T.W.I.T.'s monitoring is extended at the hand of a metonymical increase of national interest in her person. Because of the political significance of Auberon, Yashmeen is subjected to an international fight over territory, as well as to the local protective mechanisms of the supranational organization led by Nookshaft.

However, right after addressing her increasing confinement, the narrative goes on to depict Yashmeen's turn to mathematics, which involves the manifestation of the Riemann event. The discursive presentation of her determination, which is directly followed by the disruptive momentum of the event narratively first sets the scene of her immanent situation, literally secluded from interaction, and then offers a causal response that inhabits the potential of emancipation. In contrast to Kit's experience of the event, which is framed in various hysteron-proteron interweavings, Yashmeen's evental confrontation directly follows the exposition of her limitations. In a sense, the immediate juxtaposition of lack of agency and event conveys the contingent eruption of the event. This contingency thus also guides the description of the event:

> Against these, like a shoot in a garden, from some invisible bulb or seed far below, green, astonishing, emerged this all-but-erotic fascination with the thoughts of former Göttingen eminence G. F. B. Riemann. She secluded herself in the upper room with a number of mathematics texts and began, like so many of that era, a journey into the dodgy terrain of Riemann's Zeta function and his famous conjecture—almost casually thrown into an 1859 paper on the number of primes less than a given size—that all its nontrivial zeroes had a real part equal to one half. (*AtD* 496)

In writing "against" the colonialist discourse of oppression, the novel here employs a similar rhetoric that links postcolonial resistance with Yashmeen's mathematical faithfulness. The instantaneous eruption of her mathematical interest that is cushioned in a pastoral language of civilized nature is compared with the contingent and extraneous advent of a wild plant. This "shoot" that literally disrupts, even wounds, the Edenic harmony of the garden expresses the mathematical event that she accepts as a way out of her entrapment. Note that the source of her fascination is situated in an ontologically and epistemologically uncertain sphere. For the shoot stems from "some *invisible* bulb or seed *far below*" that is outside the topology of the garden but not absolutely transcendent. This uncertainty is extended by the connective that offers the alternatives of bulb "or" seed, two botanically different states of a plant that both harbor the semantic dimension of inception. Yet, this metaphorical innuendo of a revelatory moment is also conveyed in the "bulb," which points beyond its botanical meaning. In tune with the dominant theme of light that has, as was already observed in the previous part, a particular relation to manifestations of events, the bulb suggests an "astonishing" moment of illumination and the instantaneous revelation of an epistemological insight.

What adds to the evental structure of the passage is Yashmeen's "all-but-erotic" interest in Riemann's "thoughts" (and not Riemann himself). It suggests a position of disinterested fidelity—in a similar manner as the Quaternionists relate to Hamilton—that is markedly different from the otherwise omnipresent sexual eruptions of desire. Although the oxymoronic spatial conflation of her seclusion in her room and the simultaneous beginning of a mathematical rite of passage seems just a similar form of escapism that Prof. Vanderjuice addresses earlier in the novel, Yashmeen's mathematical investigations will eventually lead her out of both, the academic ivory tower and T.W.I.T.'s fortress, without losing sight of the "real."

While the Riemann event does not assume as expansive a role as the Quaternionist one, *Against the Day*, nevertheless, hints at a collective subject that launches on "a journey into the dodgy terrain." Thereby, Pynchon stresses that even microcosmic events may propel the possibility of subjective compositions. In a similar manner as the encounter in an amorous fidelity puts the political or scientific events that affect a vast mass of people into perspective, the novel inquires into a scientific practice that offers the potential of subjective empowerment for some individuals, if not for all of humanity.

Again, the topological description of this "dodgy" subjective process as a hazardous undertaking refers to the existential peril that a subject of the event has to face. Particularly in the field of positivist science, Riemann's "conjecture" remains methodologically problematic. Without sufficient proof for his hypothesis, Riemann was confronted with a moment of undecidability, "a wager" (*BE* 201). For Badiou, "this undecidability is an intrinsic attribute of the event" (*BE* 201) since the intricate place of the subject cannot discern the event from the perspective of the situation that it is part of. However, like the imminent contingency of Mallarmé's *A Cast of Dice* (*BE* 192), Riemann's leap of faith that is "almost casually *thrown*," proved to be on track and he resolved to produce his eponymous Zeta function. While the Riemann event is depicted not as elaborately as Hamilton's Quaternionist event, and without going into the details of the mathematical relevance of Riemann's differential geometry,[47] I want to trace Yashmeen's fidelity toward the mathematical problem, since it yields various interesting insights to her becoming a subject of the event.

Thus at Girton, Yashmeen's increasing lack of agency makes her leap into mathematics. Despite the escapist inclination of Yashmeen's coping strategies to flee the oppressive contraints that determine her, mathematics constitutes a privileged position. For while her sexual adventures (*AtD* 498) also serve a deviating effect, it is the mathematical problem that keeps occupying her mind. Like Riemann's own moment of undecidability, Yashmeen cannot ignore the persistence of Riemann's Zeta-function. Her epistemologically fragile position is thus underlined by the uncertainty latent in her "not quite [being] able" (*AtD* 498) to ignore the problem as well as in the ambivalent presence of Riemann himself: "*almost as if* he were *whispering* to her"

(*AtD* 489, my emphasis). What is more, the elliptical presentation of both Riemann's notes and her reflections highlights the probing manner of her intention to reach "the tantalizing possibility" (*AtD* 498). Still, unlike Riemann, who simply posited his conjecture through the event and ascertained his subjective fidelity by his wager, Yashmeen's investigation of the mathematical problem still adheres to hermeneutic/logical deduction. By analyzing Riemann's autobiographical "as-yet-uncatalogued memorandum" (*AtD* 489), she tries to infer answers from the textual documents in a logically prescribed manner. Like *Gravity's Rainbow*'s Pointsman, she adheres to "hermeneutics: a dizzying pursuit of clues, a peeling away of layers in search of a cause, a linear movement toward points of origin" (Melley 1994: 718). Still, her logical attempts of deduction are confounded as she is denied an ultimate "solution" to the problem.

Hence, although Yashmeen has accepted the Riemann event, where her engagement in solving the Zeta-function problem constitutes her fidelity toward the event, she assumes her faithfulness still in a teleological manner. This is to say that Yashmeen in the beginning presumes that the solution to the Riemann problem manifests a specific insight after which she can move on to other inquiries: initially, she thus takes the event to demand that she simply solve the scientific problem. However, as a genuine event, the Riemann problem, rather, constitutes an ongoing occupation in which the event has to be reaffirmed "point by point" without there being a final moment of conclusion.

After she has moved on to Göttingen to elaborate her mathematical studies under David Hilbert, one instantiation of Yashmeen's reagency manifests itself in her mathematical fidelity.

In Hilbert's class one day, she raised her hand. He twinkled at her to go ahead. "*Herr Geheimrat—*"

"'Herr Professor' is good enough."

"The nontrivial zeroes of the ζ-function . . ."

"Ah."

She was trembling. She had not had much sleep. Hilbert had seen this sort of thing before, and rather a good deal of it since the turn of the century—since his own much-noted talk at the Sorbonne, he supposed, in which he had listed the outstanding problems in mathematics which would be addressed in the coming century, among them that of the zeroes of the ζ-function.

"Might they be correlated with eigenvalues of some Hermitian operator yet to be determined?"

The twinkle, as some reported later, modulated to a steady pulsation. "An intriguing suggestion, Fräulein Halfcourt." Usually he addressed her as "my child." "Let us consider why this should be so." He peered, as if she were an apparition he was trying to see more clearly. "Apart from eigenvalues, by their nature, being zeroes of some equation," he prompted gently.

"There is also this . . . spine of reality." Afterward she would remember she actually said "*Rückgrat von Wirklichkeit.*" "Though the members of a Hermitian may be complex, the eigenvalues are real. The entries on the main diagonal are real. The ζ-function zeroes which lie along Real part = ½, are symmetrical about the real axis, and so . . ." She hesitated. She had seen it, for the moment, so clearly.

"Let us apply some thought," said Hilbert. "We will talk about this further." But she was to leave Göttingen shortly after this, and they would never have the chance to confer. As years passed, she would grow dim for Hilbert, her words those of an inner sprite too playful to frame a formal proposition, or to qualify as a fully habilitated Muse. And the idea itself would evolve into the celebrated Hilbert-Pólya Conjecture. (*AtD* 604)

Confronted with the unmistakable hierarchies that the institutional setting and especially Hilbert's patronizing chauvinism evoke, Yashmeen's ongoing occupation with the Zeta-problem makes her appear weakened. Yet, the marks of her bodily exhaustion simultaneously attest to her obstinate mathematical relentlessness. Despite the condescending gestures that Hilbert directs her, Yashmeen proposes a cogent mathematical hypothesis that deals with the Zeta-problem. Her "suggestion" is structured like Riemann's conjecture, since it is formulated as a question and thus substitutes her former mode of logical deduction for a more perilous hypothetical wager; what is more, the epistemic horizon of a "yet to be determined" operator equally conforms to Riemann's method of conjecture that implies a realist ontology in which phenomena exist beyond a subjective epistemic grasp. Her previous methodological approach toward the problem that rested on verifiable modes of deduction is substituted for a more epistemologically uncertain operation that approximates Riemann's own wager as well as the general leap of faith that an event implies.

Yet another dimension manifests Yashmeen's faithfulness, which also differentiates her fidelity from Kit's. In tackling the mathematical aporia, she tries to solve it by transferring the problem onto other domains of mathematical discourse. While Kit tries to solve the Zeta-problem by applying Quaternions to Vectorist calculations and thereby applies the propositions of the event on the mathematical situation, Yashmeen opts for a different interdisciplinary solution. She translates the Riemann problem into Hilbert's "linear algebra" (Berressem 2010: 350), and employs the concept of *Eigenvalues* to shed light on the Zeta-function. Unlike Kit's fidelity to Quaternionism that makes him integrate the ontological illegality of the event into other disciplines, Yashmeen's Riemann fidelity makes her apply other branches of mathematics to the evental proscriptions. Thereby she, nevertheless, succeeds in applying the new episteme to the mathematical situation in general in a different manner than Kit. Rather than incorporating the evental trace into other fields of mathematics and infecting them with its new form of knowledge, the fact that the Riemann event does not offer similar epistemic insights to work with as the Quaternions but, rather, posits an undecidable problem itself, thus affects other mathematical regions in a reverse move. In this sense, Yashmeen's status as a subject of the event can be grasped as a mediating figure, in which she spreads the contagious epistemological and ontological ramifications of the event to other fields by inquiring into their potential to work on the ζ-function. And indeed, Yashmeen's "suggestion" bears fruits, since it leads Hilbert to arrive at the "celebrated Hilbert-Pólya Conjecture," which proposes one solution to the Zeta-problem. Although Hilbert's ignorance of Yashmeen's role in his approach to the ζ-function could again be viewed in the light of his condescending disrespect of Yashmeen's mathematical abilities, which does not even qualifies her "as a fully habilitated Muse," she, indeed, fulfills her part in the collective Riemann subject. As a member of the subject of the Riemann event, her contribution to Hilbert and Pólya's advances is part of her evental faithfulness that makes her convert two eminent mathematicians who equally engage in the ζ-function problem and adapt a process of fidelity in coming up with their own conjecture. Her reagency allows her to make a crucial contribution to the field of mathematics and does, therefore, not rest on her individual persona. In the vein of her disinterested fidelity, she plays her part in the collective process of a scientific procedure.

A last point of observation that needs to be commented upon consists in the political dimension of Yashmeen's "suggestion." Whereas Kit increasingly attempts to rigidly separate science and politics, Yashmeen is extremely aware of the connection between the two spheres. The manner of her inter-mathematical approach to the Zeta-problem functions as a fundamental implication of the political. Her translation of the ζ-function into Hilbert's linear algebra that rests on the concept of *Eigenvalues* translates the Riemann problem not only into another scientific discourse but also fundamentally transposes a mathematical aporia into the realm of politics. For, as Berressem notes, the concept of *Eigenvalues* "could become more than a throwaway reference for Pynchon because it is possible to generalize from vectorial transformation|change to systemic transformation|change" (2010: 351). Since *Eigenvalues* are invariable constants within particular bodies or systems that remain unaltered even after the system has undergone change, this metaphor ideally relates to the notion of events and their systemic ramifications.[48] Nevertheless, the fundamental change that an event introduces to a specific system, be that mathematical or political, Yashmeen insists, is that the *Eigenvalue* of a system remains the same. By creating a connection between the mathematical concept of the *Eigenvalue* and interpreting it as the "spine of reality," the "*Rückgrat von Wirklichkeit*" Yashmeen stresses the similarity between the geometrical appearance of an Eigenvector and the most vulnerable part of an organism's skeletal structure in order to stress the fundamental political impetus of such reflections. Just as Quaternionism extended the conventional geometrical system by transforming the "real" three dimensions into a complex four-dimensional plane, Yashmeen emphasizes the materiality of such intramathematical problem-solving by highlighting the inexorably "real," "nontrivial" dimension despite all "complexity," repeatedly reiterating the word "real." Despite the imaginary component of the "Hermetian," Yashmeen discards the escapist stimulus in the same manner as the Quaternionists. Like their reluctance to think beyond the third dimension, the insistence on the "real axis" poaches the hermetic discourse of mathematics and allows the osmosis of political questions. In like manner as Quaternionism showed that its scientific insights cannot be thought without contemplating political problems of representation, the subject of the Riemann event methodologically intertwines both procedures and exhibits their inevitable dependence.

Whereas Yashmeen's eye for the political stems from her own precarious status that makes her the victim of matters of representation, at Göttingen she is also sought out by the "Otzovists," according to her, a

> new subset of heretics, this time against Lenin and his Bolshevists—said to be anti-Materialist, devout readers of Mach and Ouspensky, immoderately focused on something *they* call "the fourth dimension." Whether Dr. Minkowski, or in fact any algebraist in the street, would recognize it as such is another matter. But they have been able with little effort to drive the Materialists in Geneva quite mental with it. Lenin himself is said to be writing a gigantic book now, attempting to *refute* the "fourth dimension," his position being, from what I can gather, that the Tsar can only be overthrown in three. (*AtD* 616)

This confrontation between the scientific and the political bears remarkable connection points to Badiou's theory. Yashmeen's classification of the Otzovists as a "subset" draws on the set theoretical formulations that differentiate between individuals that are merely represented by the State and actually recognized citizens that are also presented. Without proper presentation, Otzovists are simply counted as a set by the Leninist state of the situation, in like manner as African Americans in Beatty's *Slumberland*. Their singular status is legitimated by their anti-materialism that makes them illegal under the regime of political Bolshevism, which tries to "refute" them. This is particularly striking since Badiou sees Lenin as part of the revolutionary subject faithful to the Communist event and, therefore, again reflects on other political truth-procedures.[49] However, here *Against the Day* disintegrates the collective political subject of the October Revolution into another "subset" by depicting its exclusion from that political order because of scientific divergences. The novel therefore complicates the hermetic existence of a political subject of the event by relating it to another truth condition, that of science. By indicating a fundamental absence of Badiou's theory—*what happens if subjects faithful to different events interact*—the novel addresses the complicated interrelation not only of various characters, nations and worlds, but also between mutually conflicting events in its encompassing look at the cultural milieu of the turn of the century.

Despite the common political persuasion, "these anti-Leninist Bolshies" (*AtD* 631) diverge from the political subject that Lenin represents by a scientific stance that diverges from Marxist materialism. In fact, what Yashmeen derogatorily shrugs off as their belief in "the fourth dimension," which features comparable escapist tendencies as in Vectorism, could be seen as a belief in the non-ontological existence of the event. For the event's anti-materiality, in the sense that it can neither be grasped physically, nor integrated into a historical teleology of production, indeed, "is another matter." However, the oscillation between a purely materialist philosophy that simply assumes change within the logic of History and an anti-materialist idealism is converged in Yashmeen in the sense of what Badiou terms the "materialist dialectic" (*LoW* 1).[50] She combines the materiality of political realities with the anti-material, "meta-physical" eruption of an event. Only through the combination of the two is it possible to "overthrow" the current political and scientific order.

Yashmeen's special position within this dialectic manifests itself through her extraordinary abilities. One such skill is the reason why the Otzovists seek her help. For their "single-minded concentration on Miss Halfcourt and her four-dimensional skills" (*AtD* 631) boils down to seeing in her an angelic figure of salvation. Through her mathematical, and, particularly, geometrical knowledge, they promise themselves redemption from the territorial expulsion from Russia. Yashmeen's mathematical skills are, however, "more than algebraists' whimsy" (*AtD* 602). Indeed, through her mathematical fidelity, she is bequeathed with the ability to leave the walls behind that previously confined her in both a literal and a metaphorical sense. "It started harmlessly enough," Yashmeen relates:

> when I was much younger, thinking about complex functions for the first time, really. Staring at the wallpaper. One night, at some god-awful hour, I understood that I couldn't get away with only one plane, I'd need two, one for the argument, one for the function, each with a real axis and an imaginary one, meaning *four axes*, all perpendicular to one another at the same point of origin, and the more I tried to *see* that, the crazier ordinary space became, until what you might call *i, j*, and *k*, the unit vectors of our given space, had each rotated an unknown number of degrees, about that unimaginable fourth axis, and I thought I had brain fever. I didn't sleep. I slept too much. (*AtD* 617)

Here it becomes clear that Yashmeen's "mathematical curse" (*AtD* 617) began already in childhood, and to what extent she differentiates herself from the Quaternionist subject. Although she also contemplates the quaternionist "*four axes*," she distances herself from "what" Kit, as a Quaternionist, "might call *i, j*, and *k*" but which she conceives in different ways. While this understanding of space, indeed, brings her to the limits of her mental capacities, it is only when she engages in the Riemann problem that she may fully grasp the consequences of this scientific branch. This, indeed, offers an intricate modulation of Badiou's notion of events, since Yashmeen seems to reject the Quaternionist event as not part of her scientific situation and, rather, engaging in a similar, though scientifically different event. Thereby, *Against the Day* undermines the universality of events within particular situations, since Yashmeen undermines the eventness of Hamilton's procedure and engages in a faithfulness that takes root in a related manifestation, which, nevertheless, evokes not only a different form of fidelity but also a different kind of event.

However, unlike Kit's introduction to Vectorism that determines him in various ways, Yashmeen's contact with mathematics endows her with peculiar gifts that are, however, "not always" (*AtD* 617) in her control. While she already subscribed to Quaternionist geometry when only a child, she will embrace with the Riemann event a specific form of complex geometry. Her mysterious ability to take a glimpse of "future, past, and present . . . all together" (*AtD* 617) is then extended by a more physical penetration of space. After conversing with Kit about the Zeta-problem, Yashmeen exhibits her special gift when she accidentally walks through a wall (*AtD* 592). The discrepancy between her active decision to exit Kit's room (which clearly differs from the passive position that follows when "she found herself" [*AtD* 592]) and the contingency inherent in her "mistake" (*AtD* 592) to do so is symptomatic for the concept of reagency. In contrast to a deliberative humanist potential, her reagency oscillates between chance and active choice. One aspect of her acquired abilities makes her see beyond the subjective appearances that represent the world according to human interpretation. Her ability to grasp a deeper level of reality lets her use the "function" of the door to "walk through a solid wall" (*AtD* 592). In tune with her advances in Riemannian geometry, she literally moves beyond a Euclidean understanding of space and enters a differential topology.[51] This branch of geometry that moves, like Quaternionism, beyond the absolute space of conventional coordinate systems and rests on differential algebra's calculation with "function[s]," presents Yashmeen with a means to crack the solid walls of physical reality as well as the metaphorical incarceration within structures of oppression.

But Yashmeen also transcends the walls that confine her in another sense. By once more emphasizing the political ramifications of science, she admonishes Kit: "Do none of you ever think beyond these walls? There is a crisis out there" (*AtD* 594). She realizes that "the political crisis in Europe maps into the crisis in mathematics" (*AtD* 594) and that any separation of science and politics is a mere fiction. On the one hand, this once more attests to her scientific-political subjectivity. Her topological understanding of space makes it translated through her geographical metaphor according to which politics "maps into" (*AtD* 594) mathematics. On the other hand, she again addresses her status as a subject of the event. By relating the event of "the infinite" (*AtD* 594) that manifested itself with the aid of Cantor's set theoretical formulations, she equally insists on the perilous environment that those faithful to an event have to face. However, what seems particularly remarkable is the analogy she draws between nations and mathematics. "Suicide" (*AtD* 594), which constitutes one of the most radical modes of resistance within the modern political order, is compared with the illegal status of a scientific concept that was renounced by mathematicians because of its metaphysical inclinations. Yashmeen's reflections on the Zeta-problem are fundamentally paralleled with a political mode of resistance. Her fidelity to the Riemann event makes her an inevitably political subject that tries to escape the grasp of national and state jurisdiction. Her thinking "beyond these walls" (*AtD* 594) is extended by her decision to leave the institutional confines of Göttingen, which functions as a specific mode of topological resistance.

By escaping the controlling *dispositif* that limits her agency, Yashmeen leaves Göttingen together with Kit and becomes a nomad that abandons the fixed coordinates of the Western world. To be sure, while this concept has become inflationary after Deleuze's and Guattari's deliberations in connection to their spatial dialectics,[52] I argue that she becomes a nomad only because of the manifestation of an event. Instead of a ubiquitous adaptation of this sociological concept within the fluctuations of smooth and striated spaces, *Against the Day* makes the case that her nomadic existence is fundamentally relying on her inquiry into the Riemann event. Thereby she stresses that it is not only "political thinking [that] demands a *displacement*, a journey which is always, dare I say, abnormal" (*IT* 63); particularly the disposition of a scientific fidelity equally propels her "displacement" and makes her engage on an "abnormal journey."

A crucial stop of her wandering through war-ridden Europe is a halt at Riemann's grave in Biganzolo, which illustrates her repeated affirmation of the event: instead of weeping and thereby bringing to light an individual form of worship, Yashmeen merely sweeps her hat in order to pay tribute to Riemann and not to indulge in any cult of personality (*AtD* 662). Even though she is mesmerized by the site that marks Riemann's death, her active response to the ritualistic surrounding undermines the sentimental code of conduct that the cemetery seems to "suggest" (*AtD* 662). As a consequence, her insistent negative declarations reject Riemann's death as an end to the Riemann event. By honoring Riemann, Yashmeen perpetuates her fidelity and thereby exemplifies to what extent an event does not end with the death of one of its first subjective instantiations, which *Slumberland* and *Only Revolutions* illustrate in even more pronounced ways. In a similar vein as Sowell or Hailey and Sam, she affirms the progression of the event well beyond the grave. In this, she once again actively resuscitates the event as well as her fidelity in asserting her uncompromising faithfulness.

Yet, while fidelity rests on the repeated confirmation of the event, Yashmeen also extends the radius of her subjective process, thereby not merely repeating it but adapting it to the new surroundings it faces. Indeed, while a point demands that the event "must be re-played in some way, as if it were returning in a changed, displaced form, but one forcing you 'to declare afresh'" (*IpoL* 50), Yashmeen, crucially, extends this re-enactment. Confronted with the ultimate form of sedentariness, she applies the Riemannian notion of space by assuming a nomadic identity. In this sense, the correlation between her commemoration of the Riemann event and her childhood reminiscence seems not coincidental. Especially her observation that she "should not remember it now" indicates the pressing and inevitable manifestation of a subjective insight that seems to take its origin in the narrative representation that constitutes a point of her fidelity.

It is at this moment when she remembers the "*stranniki*":

"In Russia, when I was a small child," Yashmeen continued after a while, "I should not remember it now, but I do, wanderers, wild-looking men, came to our doors seeking shelter as if they were entitled to it. They were the *stranniki*—once, they had led everyday lives like other men, had their families and work, houses filled with furniture, children's toys, pots and pans, clothes, all the tack of domestic life. Then one day they simply turned—walked out through the door and away from that, from all of it—whatever had held them there, history, love, betrayals forgiven or not, property, nothing mattered now, they were no longer responsible to the world, let alone the Tsar—only God could claim them, their only allegiance was to God. . . . The Government feared them more than it feared Social Democrats, more than bomb-throwers, 'Very dangerous,' Papa assured us—we knew he didn't mean dangerous to us—we also understood it was our duty to help them in their passage. Their holy mission. . . . We told each other stories about them, ambassadors from some mysterious country very far away, unable to return to that homeland because the way back was hidden. They had to keep wandering the world whose deceptions and melodramas, blood and desire, we had begun to sense, perhaps not seeking anything with a name, perhaps only wandering. People called them *podpol'niki*, underground men. Floors that had once been solid and simple became veils over another world. It was not the day we knew that provided the *stranniki* their light." (*AtD* 662–63)

The alternative existence that the *stranniki* embody thus seems a cogent mode of resisting the confines that Yashmeen faces. Clearly, one form of Pynchon's excluded middles (like Quaternionists, Anarchists, or Octovists) the nomads are depicted as another token "other." However, while they are compared to Anarchists in their use of explosives and disregard of property, their imminent danger to the state, rather, consists in their defiance of the regulated life that the state proscribes. As it is not possible to pin them to a specific and stable site of residence, the wanderers pose a threat to the spatial order upon which a nation rests. What seems, moreover, noteworthy in this context is the fact that they differ from traditional nomadic people, since the *stranniki* started out as sedentary people. To this extent, their decision to alter their sociological modes of habitation "one day," which implies a fundamental change of their situation, could be viewed as a response to processes of displacement; yet another possible interpretation, not necessarily independent from their political exclusion, implies a similar evental manifestation as Yashmeen experiences. Whereas the *stranniki* pledge allegiance to God, Yashmeen's fidelity to Riemannian geometry might manifest a scientific variation of an analogous theme. What for the nomad appears as a divine revelation is for Yashmeen a mathematical event that propels both on a "holy mission," which again relates to the close ties between science and religion in the novel. By the same token, the nomads' apparent destabilization of fixed spatial orders implies a fundamental ontological change that alters everything "that had once been solid and simple," penetrating into the very heart of the metonymical "home." And this is again hinted at with the metaphoric of light that plays once more on its ambivalent relation to fields of knowledge. Yashmeen's positing of a collective "we" that does not have epistemological access to "their light" marks the chasm between the *stranniki* as a subject of the event and Yashmeen and her family who do not inhabit the same situation. However, as a pointal reaffirmation of her subjective fidelity, she here acknowledges their common fate and adopts their mode of habitation under the name of the Riemann event.

Most importantly, by means of her extension of the propositions that the event prescribes, she comes to realize the ateleological driving force of their existence. The *stranniki* are not part of a diaspora. In spite of Elias's claim that a "longing for 'home' . . . permeates the novel's plot" (2011: 31), the *stranniki* personify a radical abandonment of home. To this extent, they question the very concept of both, a return home and a final point of arrival, which[1] affects Yashmeen's fidelity as well. Whereas before a sense of linearity guided her mathematical desire to solve the Zeta-problem, she now comes to the conclusion that the *stranniki* are "not seeking anything with a name"; the fact that they are "only wandering" offers her a way out of her isolation. However, her new identity comes at a price, as the passage goes on, for, as she explains, "leaving Göttingen. No. It was never [her] choice" (*AtD* 663). Once more, *Against the Day* illustrates the limitations that a subject of the event has to accept. Yashmeen's reagency that makes her leave the controlling grasp of the institutional *dispositifs* is not a free choice. Instead, under the unrelenting momentum of the event, her escape has to be viewed as a condition of an extra-subjective source. Moreover, while she affirms her status as a "*strannik*" (*AtD* 663) and thereby seems to augment the reach of the Riemann event for her subjective process, she concomitantly discards the purely mathematical dimensions of her fidelity. Just as Kit abandons his hope for an "alternate universe of vector analysis" (*AtD* 322), Yashmeen distances herself from her mathematical beliefs and their promise of "transcendence" (*AtD* 663). While Kit abandons his mathematical persuasion, Yashmeen's rejection of the "new geometry" (*AtD* 664) as childish reveries of naivety seems to amount to a similar rejection of the event. This is amplified by the fact that she repudiates her subjective status, since there was no evental manifestation, "no visitation, no prophecy, no plan," which consequently only made her able to walk "up on the wall" (*AtD* 664) but not outside of it. While Badiou would see this as a "moment of crisis," (*E* 78) I would insist that this does not constitute a similar mode of betrayal as in Kit's case of returning to Vectorism and forsaking his Quaternionist fidelity. Yashmeen, rather, embraces an extended form of her subjective status that is not exclusively mathematical. She lives up to her pretensions of applying the "nontrivial" implications of the Zeta-function onto political domains.[53] Whereas the "nontrivial zeroes of the ζ-function" (*AtD* 604) manifested an inherent mathematical problem, she translates the notion of triviality into politics and seems to reject mathematics as such, since to her it is only concerned with the triviality or nontriviality of a mathematical nature.

As a scientific and political subject of the event, Yashmeen practices what she preaches. In this sense, the fact that "her extraordinary eyes remained directed at the grave" (*AtD* 664) again plays with the ambivalence of ocular organ and subjective identity. Still under the sign of the event, the persistence of Yashmeen's fidelity, according to which she merely discards her monolithic mathematical identity only as a girl she "scarcely know[s] anymore" (*AtD* 664), does not entirely reject the "teachings" of the event. Although her reconceptualization as a scientific-political subject is still tinted in a tone of regret, marked by the semantic cluster that evokes with Yashmeen's "expulsion" a "terrible discontinuity" (*AtD* 664) of a diasporic existence, she is also endowed with specific moments of reagency. The permanent "state of departure" (*AtD* 664) thus manifests the nomadic potential to undermine the very foundation of the modern logic of sedentary life as a part of the national program of monitoring its citizens. Despite the fact that she thinks of herself as fallen from grace because of her Adamic expulsion from the garden she used to inhabit, this simultaneously implies an attack of the oppressive structures that held her captive before. In fact, the spatial outline that she draws, which implies the stability of fixed sites such as the "garden" of Western modernity, is undermined from within. Yashmeen's exclusion from the "center" implies her reagency, since she now has to live not outside of Europe but in a subterranean space that literally undermines its foundations.

Even though her escape from Göttingen might appear to be a naïve act of flight, she now endorses a spatial mode of resistance that antagonizes the political order from within. Adapting Riemann's "astounding re-imagination of space" (*AtD* 616) to a political form of resistance, Yashmeen's pointal fidelity marks another transformation of her subjective identity and thereby shows that the subject of the event is not defined by fixed and stable continuity but implies an ongoing process of redefinition. While Yashmeen's individual status as a scientific subject of the event lays the groundwork for the creeping process of emancipation, she now partakes in a collective scientific-political subjectivity. This is amplified by the passage's shift from an individual point of reference to a collective "We." While this echoes the transformation from a solipsistic "I" into a "US" in *Only Revolutions*, Yashmeen's newly affirmed collective stance establishes a more fundamental political vision. In contrast to Sam's and Hailey's "democracy of Two" that fashions a social bond out of two individuals, the evental subject that Yashmeen promotes proves to entail a collectivity of a larger scale. Through her affiliation with both the mathematical community and the politically excluded Otzovists, she becomes part of a more thorough enterprise that attempts to dismantle the existing order of control and, in a way similar to *Slumberland,* rejects a problematic, since it is an essentialist, group identity. Instead, the subject of the event integrates a collective process of fidelity without homogenizing this procedure within the framework of prescriptive laws of demeanor. Despite the fact that a deontological dimension exists in this ethics, which prescribes the fidelity to the event, the modes of how these fidelities may be realized is open to interpretation.

Within the framework of her newly formulated political praxis, she teams up with Kit's brother Reef and the sexually ambivalent Cyprian Latewood to roam the Balkans. This passage both spatially and textually marks a major shift in the novel's genre and concomitantly conforms to Yashmeen's nomadic subjectivity. Whereas the quest pattern is systematically undermined in all of Pynchon's novels to the degree that "failure to attain revelation is a hallmark of Pynchon's questing heroes," (1983: 22) as Molly Hite has shown, a key difference between a character like Oedipa Maas and Yashmeen Halfcourt consists in their varying expectations of revelation.[54] While *The Crying of Lot 49*'s quest heroine awaits in vain the epistemological solution of the Trystero mystery, Yashmeen abandons this teleological motivation in accordance to her nomadic existence. If Elias has a point when she argues that *Against the Day* might best be understood as a "postmodern pilgrimage" (2011: 29–30),[55] the fact that Pynchon increasingly undermines the stability of genre-conventions raises doubts about his trying to contain the novel within any particular genre at all.[56] By analogy, one could see the novel's overall appropriation and self-reflexive rewriting of particular genres as a journey without a goal. Rather than trying to arrive at a particular point at which some generic rules have been met, the novel walks the ways of various thematic and stylistic discourses, like the Western dime novel, only to assume another discourse, as that of the quest narrative, without ever redeeming a specific expectation. Although *Against the Day* massively employs historical genres,[57] one mode of undermining these classifications is the deferral of what these genres take to be their constitutive events ("revenge" in the dime-novel, "spiritual insight" in the quest narrative). Although attesting to modern literature's systematic critique of a narratological understanding of events, *Against the Day,* nevertheless, integrates a different register of event that is the driving force of subjects, not of plot. Thus, without going into the details of generic codes, it seems more illuminating to analyze how the novel's Quixotic (textual and spatial) passage of wandering complies with Yashmeen's altered status as a subject and how it endows her with reagency.

Next to having escaped the controlling reach of the T.W.I.T. and finally having left behind her teleological desire, Yashmeen also emancipates herself from the colonial and paternalistic bonds that her father maintained over her. In a last letter to Auberon, who simultaneously embodied Yashmeen's subject of control and object of desire, she severs her ties to him in conformity with her subjective status: "I had the obvious thought once that all this wandering about must have an object—a natural convergence to you [Auberon], and that you and I need only be reunited for all to come clear at last" (*AtD* 749). Having adopted the *stranniki*'s spatial movement that is not directed to a specific destination makes Yashmeen sequester her bonds to her colonial foster father. Indeed, she admits, "I find I cannot set aside your profession, the masters you serve, the interests which all this time out there in Inner Asia, however unconsciously, you have been furthering" (*AtD* 749). Auberon's perpetuation of the colonial enterprise, which also occasioned Yashmeen's confinement, can no longer be ignored by her. This realization again relates to her embrace of ateleology, for Auberon's search for Shambhala and its promise of religious redemption marks a spiritual and economic end point that she no longer agrees with.[58] It should come as no surprise that as soon as she surrenders the search for her father, she finds him; Auberon, who proves to be just as determined by colonialism, confesses to her: "For me, Shambhala, you see, turned out to be not a goal but an absence. Not the discovery of a place but the act of leaving the futureless place where I was" (*AtD* 975).

Despite their absolute defiance of any forms of linear directions, Yashmeen and her compatriot wanderers, who decide to "live among their kind, among wolves, Anarchists, and road agents" (*AtD* 888) do engage in political missions, as when they assume as their "main task" the detection of the "*Interdikt* line, and disabling it" (*AtD* 946). Nevertheless, they only approach this goal, without ever succeeding in bringing it to an end. The *Interdikt*, a gas line installed by the vicious characters Professors Renfrew and Werfner who share the "unhappy position among the Major Arcana" (*AtD* 226) of the Devil, and whose contrivance is supposed to emit poison gas on the Balkan residents, metaphorically represents the wake of modern industrial warfare, what Elias call the "military-industrial complex's true shrine of death" (33), that moves well beyond the territorial legitimacies of nations. The biological weapon of mass destruction that already foreshadows in its name the fundamental biopolitical ramifications of the twentieth century marks a definite aim for their active struggle. However, within the scope of a more fundamental mode of resistance, their mission gets deferred until it is substituted for matters of a more existential form. After some haphazard attempts to locate the lethal gas line, the narrator observes that "the topic of the *Interdikt* had not arisen again. Ljubica's birth had taken the question, for Yashmeen, to a far lower priority" (*AtD* 954). Confronted with the all-encompassing signs of death that are harbingers of the approaching European conflict, Yashmeen, rather, invests efforts in focusing on the child she has with Reef. While this insinuates a relapse to conservative familial structures that simply ascertains egoistic motivations of self-protection, I would argue that her shifting of priorities implies an active perpetuation of life, nomadic life to be exact. For when Cyprian confronts her: "You can't seriously mean to have a baby out there. It's primitive. It might as well be the jungle. You'll need to be near competent medical help." Yashmeen retorts: "You're still living in the last century, Cyprian. All the nomadic people of the world know how to have babies on the go. The world that is to be. We are out here, in it" (*AtD* 939). Keeping faith to the event, Yashmeen even integrates her child into the newly acquired subjecthood.[59] Particularly her emphasis on the future fashions a spatio-temporal order, a complex geometry of being simultaneously inside and outside, that grants her refuge as a nomadic subject of the event. Realizing that "the *national idea* depends on war" (*AtD* 938), Yashmeen creates a subjective community that antagonizes these structures of control by augmenting the perpetuation of life in the face of omnipresent "blood and explosion" (*AtD* 1073). In stark contrast to Kit's relapse to Vectorism and his role within the atrocities of World War I, Yashmeen all the more so upholds her fidelity by reaffirming the scientific part of her subjectivity.

Through the application of the ateleological pattern on her mathematical fidelity, she comes to the conclusion that "Mathematics once seemed the way" (*AtD* 749) but has now lost its pertinence for its linear inclinations. Once mathematics is no longer conceived as a "way," a means that propels her to a specific end, she retorts to the scientific part of her subjecthood:

> One day Yashmeen, out in the bora, just for a still-bracing Δt, had a relapse into her old Zetamania. She remembered that Littlewood, after struggling with a reluctant lemma one winter at Davos, through weeks of föhn . . . had reported that when that wind dropped for a day, the solution, as if by magic, was there. And no doubt because the bora, known in these parts as the "wind of the dead," descending out of the Karst, blowing uninterrupted for long enough, will also—with required changes of sign—have its effect upon the mathematical mind, as the brain lobes for this sort of thing began to relax, and strange and even counterintuitive thoughts to arrive from somewhere else co-conscious with the everyday, something similar happened now to Yashmeen. Just for the instant, the matter was illuminated, unequivocally, something as obvious as Ramanujan's Formula—no, something of which Ramanujan's Formula was a special case—revealed why Riemann should have hypothesized one-half as the real part of every $\zeta(0)$, why he had needed to, at just that point in his thinking . . . she was released into her past, haunting her old self, almost close enough to touch—and then of course it was gone again and she was more immediately concerned with the loss of her hat, flying away to join hundreds of others in migration to some more southerly climate, some tropical resort of hats where they could find weeks of hat *dolce far niente* to grow new feathers, allow their color to return or find new shades, lie and dream about heads that Fate had meant them to adorn. (*AtD* 816)

Just as Yashmeen starts to forget her mathematical past, she is haunted by the "wind of the dead" and finally solves the Riemann problem. In fact, only the ecological effect of the bora incites in her a physiologic condition of passivity. As soon as the mathematically active parts of her brain start to relax and she assumes a receptive posture that is not fixed on mathematical problem-solving, she is visited by the solution to Riemann's Zeta-function. Although the phrasing of the passage might suggest a topos of Romantic ingenuity, where she is a medium from the "co-conscious" forces that stem from a transcendental disclosure via nature, her passivity that grants her a specific epistemological understanding seems, rather, part of her status as a subject of the event. Within this framework, her transitory glimpse of the insight into the Zeta-problem depends on her abandonment of any belief in teleology. Only under the condition of relinquishing "all the work [they] have put in, the theorems, the proofs, the questioning, the breath-taken trembling before the beauty of an intractable problem" (*AtD* 664) that is directed at a determinable end is she allowed the "revelation" where her obsession with the ζ-problem shifts into (0), a function without origin and end. As Elias puts it, "the object of the question dissolves into the process of the quest, which becomes its own perverse revelation" (30).

This is amplified by the evanescence of the moment. The transitoriness indicates with the infinitesimal timespan of "a still-bracing Δt" how fleeting her understanding is. The time differential is particularly noteworthy, for it assumes an important place within Pynchon's oeuvre. In *The Crying of Lot 49*, dt is described as

> a vanishingly small instant in which change had to be confronted at last for what it was, where it could no longer disguise itself as something innocuous like an average rate; where the velocity dwelled in the projectile though the projectile be frozen in midflight, where death dwelled in the cell though the cell be looked in on at its most quick. (Pynchon 2006b: 89)

In a similar vein as Oedipa Maas, Yashmeen's fidelity forces her to confront change at last. However, while Oedipa's quest for the Trystero is permanently defined by epistemological uncertainty even though its presence makes itself felt in a manner that transcends a continuous notion of becoming, the event that breaks with the "average rate" of change endows Yashmeen with specific insights into her fidelity. Yashmeen thus obtains illumination of "something as obvious as Ramanujan's formula." Only through her mathematical faithfulness can she declare the obviousness of a highly intricate mathematical formula. In fact, she assesses the "obviousness," since she foresees Ramanujan's solution to the Zeta-problem, which will only occur in 1914.[60] What is more, her instantaneous correction that assumes Ramanujan's formula within the framework of the Zeta-problem makes her integrate other discursive offshoots within a larger narrative of the Riemann event, as she did in the case of Hilbert. Ramanujan's formula as a paradigmatic perpetuation thus becomes part of a collective procedure that works on the Riemann problem.

The second aspect of *The Crying of Lot 49*'s description of dt points to further intertextual dimensions by foreshadowing *Gravity's Rainbow*'s discussion of Δt.[61]

Ozier, among others, has convincingly analyzed the mathematical allusions in Pynchon's novel, particularly those stemming from the field of "mathematical analysis" (Ozier 1975: 194), and argues that Δt is closely tied to moments when some of the novel's characters undergo a fundamental transformation. According to Ozier, Δt marks for Leni Pökler a "radical loss of self" while Tyrone Slothrop experiences a more fundamental "expansion into pure Being" (ibid.: 203) when confronted with Δt. More generally, however, Δt implies the "infinitely small but nevertheless non-zero quantity" (ibid.: 195) that transcends structures of domination.[62] Whereas the "possibility of transcendence" (ibid.: 206) imminent in Δt does reverberate in Yashmeen's case, this plays out in a crucially different manner. Despite the fact that Yashmeen also senses "the moment, and its possibilities" (Pynchon 2006b: 161) that is implied in the Δt and she also proves to undergo a transformation, her change into a subject of the event is already long in progress when she faces Δt. Moreover, while for Leni or Slothrop, transformation implies a radical form of disintegration that even leads to Slothrop's material vanishing from the novel, Yashmeen's transformation to a subject of the event is no religious transcendence. As was already observed, Yashmeen profoundly rejects transcendence and opts for immanence within the political structures that she dismantles from within and with the help of her new subjective status. Equally so does she refrain from simply disappearing, "scatter[ing]" like Slothrop, faced with his thinning "'Temporal bandwidth' . . . the width of [his] present, [his] *now*" (Pynchon 2006a: 517). In the case of Slothrop, his being loosened by anti-paranoia and his losing track through anti-causality, the "Δt image, associated with the dissolution of his persona and with his disappearance from the novel, is a harbinger of the moment of transcendence in a pure personal present" (Ozier 1975: 199). Notwithstanding the liberating ramifications that his transcendence of determining structures implies, Slothrop's literal, since it is textual, escapism crucially differs from Yashmeen's handling of Δt. If Slothrop thins, Yashmeen thickens, in the sense that she reaffirms her presence in the real world and keeps faith to the political, that is material, dimensions of her subjective status. While the Δt marks the moment where she "solves" the Riemann problem and thereby relates back to the original source of the mathematical event, this intra-conditional form of reagency only lasts for just "an instant." Despite the literally instant gratification she (and the reader) takes in seeing her solve the problem she has been working on for a large part of her life, the political part of her evental subjectivity reminds her of the material concerns she has to take care of. If the time differential was a sign of change, harboring within its infinitesimally small range—"Δt approaching zero, eternally approaching, the slices of time growing thinner and thinner" (Pynchon 2006a: 161)—a singular point of agency, *Against the Day* undertakes "required changes of sign." For Yashmeen, Δt is only a "relapse into her old Zetamania," part of her subjective constitution—however, only a part. Without totally abandoning her previous purely scientific fidelity, she extends her subjective status by a political and social facet. As soon as the Δt passes and her mathematical insight fades, she is "more immediately concerned with the loss of her hat, flying away to join hundreds of others in migration to some more southerly climate." In the vein of Pynchon's overall concern of dismantling stable forms of identity, metaphorically hinted at with the change of hats/heads, *Against the Day* equally insists on the floating character of a subject of the event. However, Yashmeen's loss of hat/head merely indicates a loss of identity and not an entire loss of her status as a subject of the event. For the mathematical head/hat that flies to assemble with a community of nomadic fellows is part of a collective scientific-political subject that, on the one hand, oscillates between its scientific and political condition, and, on the other, requires permanent reaffirmation of these pointal markers. Whereas agency in *Gravity's Rainbow* could thus be said to rest within the infinitesimally small Δt, *Against the Day* shows with Yashmeen that reagency is an ongoing process that does not require the subject's disappearance.

To conclude, *Against the Day's* scientific-political subjects of the event add to *Only Revolutions's* and *Slumberland's* faithful subjects of events by emblematizing two different ways of a trans-conditional fidelity. Moreover, by depicting reactive and obscure tendencies that were already analyzed in *The Road* and *The Zero*, the novel integrates the full range of possible subjective creations. To some extent, *Against the Day* could thus be said to be a paradigmatic example of the concept of the "subject of the event," since it accounts for a variety of its registers. Its juxtaposition of a multitude of events that also affects realms beyond the conditions that Badiou theorizes makes it additionally expand the theoretical constraints that are latent in Badiou's approach. *Against the Day* thereby shows to what extent fictional narratives may produce a range of events, as well as reflect on the status of events in a historically metafictionist manner. Nevertheless, while such subjective creations as the subject of love in *Only Revolutions* or the aesthetic-political one in *Slumberland* uphold a continuous form of fidelity, Pynchon's long temporal vista allows the illustration of the necessarily prolonged struggle with subjective fidelities. By following Kit Traverse over some 30 years of his life, we as readers can observe how a faithful procedure may turn on itself, if taken for granted. Yashmeen's faithful extension of her subjective status that translates scientific matters into political realms shows how a subject of the event attains reagency in even transcending the condition where an event materialized and how a faithful spread into different spheres enhances a process of fidelity. The immortality that Badiou sees in a subject of the event is specifically expressed when Yashmeen exclaims: "We can do whatever we can imagine. Are we not the world to come? Rules of proper conduct are for the dying, not for us" (*AtD* 879). Placing a crucial emphasis on the imagination, Yashmeen shows that in keeping faith in a "world to come" she partakes in a procedure that leaves the mortal ground behind without suggesting an entire form of subjective transcendence. Pynchon thereby also shows that a minute analysis of works of fiction that might be discarded as merely "postmodernist" may offer the eruption of something that lies beyond the critical state of affairs of such fiction: "There lay as-yet-undiscovered notes of redemption, time-reversal, unexpected agency" (*AtD* 816).

Conclusion

The End as Enjambment

The predication of an "end" is an enjambment
that prohibits resolution when one is unaware
of how to proceed on to the next step.

Alain Badiou, "On a Finally Objectless Subject."

This study elucidated to what extent the discourse of the "end of the subject" in literature and theory is not the final word in the matter and how specific American novels published in the twenty-first century offer "unexpected" forms of "agency" (*AtD* 816). Unlike Badiou's diagnosis that the "predication of an 'end'" constitutes an enjambment that indicates the unawareness of "how to proceed," I see the poetic device as an appropriate term to conceive of the concept of the subject of the event as a response to the "death of the subject." By having shown how far selected American novels after 2000 imagine a different conception of the subject and of the event, these works, indeed, make a case for the subject in literature and thereby emphasize the potential of the novel to literally conceive of something "new." Through a crucial dialogue with Alain Badiou's thought, *The Road*, *The Zero*, *Only Revolutions*, *Slumberland*, and *Against the Day* created a form of events and subjects that were unthinkable in specific traditions of thought (theoretical and literary) that can be termed postmodern.

If the literary-theory of the subject of the event that is endowed with reagency could, indeed, be seen as an "enjambment" to this discourse of finality, this is by necessity not a return to a notion of the subject and the event prior to this critique. While being aware of the various traditions in American culture, the American novel of the new century does not content itself with merely stopping in its conception of subjects and events, as if having reached a final unbridgeable point. Simply abandoning the subject and declaring it dead, which would metaphorically imply the end of the poem, is not a cohesive alternative for these novels, either. Like an enjambment, it undermines the teleology of this discourse and offers a "next step." As a theoretical, literary, and cultural enjambment, the subject of the event does not merely continue as before but offers a uniquely new conception of these terms. While this is certainly a break with traditional notions of subject and event, it is, to repeat it once more, only an "*immanent break*" (*E* 42) and not a complete transcendence, since, to return to the image of the poem once more, the line does run on, albeit only on a different typographic level.

However, I want to conclude this study by also stressing that this final chapter could also be seen as an enjambment by going beyond the five novels that were analyzed in the main part of this study. This last part is then a run-on-line in that it attempts to briefly present a glimpse of two other American novels published in the new millennium that equally reflect on the creations of subjects of the event. Without implying that this is a wider cultural phenomenon—thereby preserving the exceptional "rarity" (*BE* 392) of events and subjects who act in faith to it that is distinct from a universal condition of subjectivity—I try to show that the reflection on events and subjects is a concern that is shared by specific works of fiction after 2000.

Although Jess Walter's *The Zero* undermined the status of "9/11" as an event and examined to what extent this occasions the creation of a reactive subject, this is not the only way in which literature might engage with such real life happenings. Equally so, fiction might invest its poietical powers in rewriting such happenings as events. In its projection of "as-if" worlds, the American novel might employ historiographic metafictional techniques, and instead of merely reflecting on the discursive reality of history put its energies in rewriting a mere happening as an event. As was already intimated in Chapter 2, Matt Ruff's *The Mirage* (2012) literally lives up to its title and creates an intricate effect of doubling the happenings of September 11, 2001. By inversing the world as we know it, the novel tells the story of the United Arab States that fight the "Christian fundamentalists" who on November 9, 2001

> hijacked four commercial passenger jetliners. They crashed two of them into the Tigris and Euphrates World Trade Towers in downtown Bagdad, Iraq, and a third into the Arab Defense Ministry headquarters. . . . The fourth plane, which is believed to have been bound for either the Presidential Palace in Riyadh or, possibly, Mecca . . . , crashed in Arabia's Empty Quarter after its passengers attempted to retake control from the hijackers. (Ruff 2012: 17)

The novel's satirical take on the incident not only mediates the happening in a radically different tone than the exclusively serious so-called 9/11 novels, but it is also a crucial instance of a literary work of art that fundamentally breaks with the factual imperatives that in the beginning guided the mediation of the attack.[1] Yet, the novel also inquires into the ontological stability of this mirrored world by letting "the *other* America" (ibid.: 312) percolate into the fictional world of the novel. When the novel's protagonists realize that this "geopolitical anomaly" (ibid.: 317) is merely "some sort of atonement" (Ruff 316), indeed, "not *a* judgment, it's *the* Judgment" (ibid.: 323), the novel's protagonist Mustafa seeks for a way out of this theological limbo. When at the end of the novel the jinn who occasioned the inversion of worlds is being shot by Osama bin Laden, another mirage takes place:

> All around the globe—in Berlin and the occupied territories; in London and Tehran, Kabul and Denver, Chicago and Jakarta, Islamabad and Corpus Christi, Los Angeles and Mumbai; in Alexandria and Alexandria—the storm scoured the landscape, roaring though the homes and hiding places of the powerful and the meek like some mighty voice: Refresh. Refresh. This is the day the world changes. (ibid.: 405)

The novel's epilogue "The City of the Future" then concludes the novel at this ambivalent moment of indecision. Does the death of the jinn destroy the phantasmagoric illusion that the novel created? Is it the "world he woke up in yesterday"? (ibid.: 410) Mustafa contemplates. He concludes that "if it is a new world, it is as apt to contain good surprises as bad ones" (ibid.: 410). Confronted with this narrative event, he decides to step up to its propositions and risk a radical wager: "the struggle of the future he must still face, and the struggle of the past he must learn to let go" (ibid.: 413). Unlike the novels discussed in the main part of this study, *The Mirage* ends at the moment where a subject of the event is created. While the novel therefore merely hints at a subject's reagency but stops short of considering it at large, it contemplates the poietical power of literature in respect of events. By creating a mirrored alternate world, the novel mediates on the capabilities of literature to produce events that take their root in the "real" world but inherently undermine this separation. Literature in this vein may compensate the scarcity of events in real life, while the novel not merely satisfies an escapist craving but in its satirical mirroring also comments on the political undercurrents that surrounded "9/11."

The novel's mediation on time is particularly evident in the last part, which gives expression to the manifestation of an event, and its creation of a "present" (*LoW* 51) by being depicted in the present tense is shared by another book that deals with a subject of the event: Richard Powers's *The Time of Our Singing* (2003). While the novel could be seen as inquiring into a similar direction as Beatty's *Slumberland*— the connection of aesthetics and politics in terms of African American citizens as related to the issue of time—Powers's novel shows a heightened awareness of temporal modalities, which becomes apparent not only in the novel's title but also in the various discussions of time on a diegetic and formal level. In a chronological telling of the story of the mixed-race children Jonah, Joseph, and Ruth Strom, the novel spans some 200 years in giving a shattering account of African Americans and "the condition of belonging" (Powers 2003: 488) up to the present but with a particular focus on the Civil Rights era. Ultimately, the three siblings are confronted with the same questions of aesthetic and political emancipation that are at the core of *Slumberland*. Yet, in addition *The Time Of Our Singing* also mediates on temporality as represented by their father, a white Jewish scientist who is comprehensively immersed in the problem of the existence of time. When at some point he concludes that "there is no time" (ibid.: 90), it becomes obvious to what extent this scientific standpoint ignores the political realities of the United States. Yet, by pointing to the necessarily interlinked spheres of science, politics, and art, the novel subscribes to *Slumberland*'s and *Against the Day*'s hybridization of these conditions and shows that the universal postulation of the inexistence of time may be undermined by other discourses. In similarly reflecting on the connection between art and politics as in *Slumberland*, Powers's book discusses the problem of minstrelsy in Jonah's performance of German classical music and thereby reflects on the relation between individual and aesthetic and political tradition. The conclusive event of the novel, which opens up an emphatically impossible phenomenon of temporal conflations that affects the novel in its entirety, engages in the book's complex temporal structure. At the narrative end of the novel, the story miraculously conflates the diegetic moment when the children's parents David Strom and Delia Daley first meet at Marian Anderson's performance at Lincoln Memorial in 1939 with their grandson Kwame's getting lost at the same site some half century later. This narrative event not only unshackles the stable realistic diegesis of the novel by implying a surreal phenomenon but also makes sense of the entire novel as a consequence of an amorous event. Although placed at the end of the novel, the temporal conflation suggests that this narrative event already took place at the first meeting of David and Delia. In a completely different manner than Danielewski's *Only Revolutions,* the novel, nevertheless, shows how the seeming impossibility of love is here played out in the context of the political milieu of the Jim Crow era. Delia's and David's racial identity therefore gives the condition of love a literally different color and shows that despite all differences, "Bird and fish can fall in love" (ibid.: 610). As a subject of an amorous encounter, the novel offers a unique example that shows scientific, aesthetic, and political realms as connected to the truth procedure of love and that become part of the reaffirmations of points that the subject of the event needs to maintain. Delia and David become a subject of the event that clings to their amorous encounter and maintains their love even when faced with the most pressing political modes of harassment. Equally so, David's reflection on the existence of time is not merely a scientific occupation but tries to make sense of the consequences of their encounter that proved to unshackle the stability of time as a unidirectional vector. His scientific engagement with the reality of time therefore does not deny the existence of history and racism but shows that if thought according to their amorous event, they have created a "present" (*LoW* 51) that lies outside of time. Moreover, the family's penchant for classical music also interlinks their children as a point of their fidelity. Even though their children do have to face similar modes of racial exclusion, David's and Delia's fidelity to their event shows that the impossibility of founding a Jewish black family in the United States of the mid-century can be overcome by a rigorous fidelity in the truth of their event. Again, as a subject of the event, their reagency, which makes them found a family that is aesthetically successful does not imply a wholesale transcendence of structures of oppression. David notes in this respect that "we were—what? 'Turning our backs on. Your mother and I said no; we were that struggle. This: making you children free, free to define. Free of everything'" (ibid.: 466). While especially the children do not become "free from everything," particularly from the event that only brought them into being, David and Delia comply with their grandson's urge to be faithful: "He [Kwame]'s fighting to bring himself into being, willing them the way on" (Powers 630). To the repetitive question whether the bird and fish may also "build a nest" (ibid.: 630), which implies the continuation of the amorous event in its reagent points, Kwame thus tells them: "The bird and the fish can make a bish. The fish and the bird can make a fird" (ibid.: 631). Kwame therefore also acts in fidelity to an event that lies, just as for *Slumberland*'s Sowell, out of his reach by resurrecting the amorous event of his dead grandparents and appropriating it to art. By "singing himself into existence" (ibid.: 631), he addresses not only the hybrid identity of his family but also the hybridity of truth conditions that are latent in his becoming of a subject of the event.

The Time of our Singing is, therefore, a paragonic instance of novels that create a subject of the event. By evoking a contingent, disruptive, and singular event, the novel addresses a subjective procedure that touches all four generic conditions and shows how its subjects become empowered by reagency. In this sense, the novel might be seen not only as a summary . . . but as an extension of the amorous, aesthetic, political, and scientific procedures in the last three chapters of this study. Moreover, like *Only Revolutions, Slumberland*, and *Against the Day*, Powers's novel juxtaposes a variety of historical happenings with the eruption of an authentic event and shows how its characters navigate the plurality of happenings by having to decide upon a singularity that ushers in a subjective procedure. In this vein, the novel returns to the epistemological crisis that was addressed in the beginning of this book of having to wage on the possibility of a "different world" for which there is no "clear name in any accepted language" (*TRoH* 1) yet.

This study showed that the American novel after 2000 engages in an essential debate by offering an enjambment to the question of the event and the question of the subject. In conceiving of subjects of events, my book wages on a new "name" not for an entire literary period but a concept that helps to make sense of a variety of texts in the millennium that fail to enter any "accepted language." To this extent, *The Road, The Zero, Only Revolutions, Slumberland, Against the Day, The Mirage*, and *The Time of Our Singing* respond to the question of "What is happening to us in the early years of the century"? (*TRoH* 1) by responding: what is happening to us might be a cultural milieu that requires an elaborate investigation of emphatic events both "real" and "fictional" and, if we are lucky (or foolish enough), this wager to profess one's fidelity might even make us subjects.

Notes

Introduction

1 See Jacques Derrida's *Apokalypse*, which includes the essays "Von einem neuerdings erhobenen apokalyptischen Ton in der Philosophie" and "No Apocalypse, not now." The latter, particularly, inquires into the rejuvenation of apocalypticism in America at the end of the twentieth century (1985: 91).

2 Badiou, indeed, sees America itself as an event, as Gernot Kamecke and Henning Teschke observe in their introduction to *Ereignis und Institution* (2008: 12), which was one of the first reflections on Badiou's thought in German academia.

3 The various attempts at detecting a concrete starting point of postmodernism thus runs against the very concept of postmodernism that radically undermines such beginnings and opts for differential movements. Jeremy Green contemplates a range of possible relations between postmodernism and its historical antecedent: "Should it [postmodernism] be seen as a subtle series of variations on established themes [of modernism], a devolution, an emancipation, or even a violent Nietzschean act of forgetting?" (21).

4 In *The Century*, Badiou notes that "the man of humanism has not survived the twentieth century" (166) and credits, despite the difference of their approaches, Nietzsche, Sartre, Foucault, Lacan, and Althusser for this attack. See particularly the final chapter "The joint disappearance of Man and God" in *The Century*.

5 Nancy notes that "the critique or the deconstruction of subjectivity is to be considered one of the great motifs of contemporary philosophical work in France, taking off from, here again and perhaps especially, the teachings of Marx, Nietzsche, Freud, Husserl, Heidegger, Bataille, Wittgenstein, from the teachings of linguistics, the social sciences, and so forth" (1991: 5).

6 There seem to be conflicting readings of this happening in Pynchon criticism. While one line of argument sees Slothrop's disappearance as a kind of transcendence that escapes all forms of determination, others are more skeptical about such an idealist reading. For a comprehensive summary of how critics have read Slothrop's disappearance, see Luc Herman and Steven Weisenburger (2013: 200).

7 See Melley's article "Bodies Incorporated: Scenes of Agency Panic in *Gravity's Rainbow*" as well as his monograph *Empire of Conspiracy: The Culture of Paranoia in Postwar America*.

8 The transgression of a topological order rests for Lotman on the clear postulation of binary values: there lies a "binary semantic opposition [that] lies at the foundation of the internal organization of textual elements: the world is divided up into rich and poor, natives and strangers, orthodox and heretical, enlightened and unenlightened, people of Nature and people of Society, enemies and friends" (1977: 237).

9 In Jerome Bruner's influential essay "The Narrative Construction of Reality," Bruner's constructivist approach positions events as an essential, subversive constituent

of narrative canonicity. Bruner, accordingly, argues that "not every sequence of events recounted constitutes a narrative" (1991: 11), thus acknowledging that, on the one hand, a narrative is a unique form of presenting events; implicit in Bruner's understanding of events is, yet, an unelaborated distinction between the canonical recounting of events and the status of their narrativity, the breach of canonicity. If events may be part of a recounting that is not a narrative (because of its lack of violation), events as such do not carry the disruptive, singular potential. Rather, it seems to be the *form* of the narrative presentation that determines the "singularity" of an event. Although the discursive mediation of events should not be omitted from the nature of events (and will be discussed in the following in more detail), Bruner seems to conflate a very distinct categorical classification of "singular" narrative events, and "generic" sequences of events that lack what William Labov has called the "tellability" of narrative. "Thus, tellability," writes Peter Hühn, "(and, ultimately, narrativity) can be said to depend on eventfulness" (2010: 2–3). See also Marie-Laure Ryan's entry on "tellability" in the *Routeledge Encyclopedia of Narrative Theory*, as well as David Herman's explanation: "Events, conceived as time- and place-specific transitions from some source state S (pond unfrozen) to a target state S' (pond frozen), are thus a prerequisite for narrative" (2005: 151).

10 See particularly Wolfe's and Franzen's notorious *Harper's* essays "Stalking the Billion-Footed Beat: A Literary Manifesto for the New Social Novel" and "Perchance to Dream," the latter of which was published as "Why Bother" in his essay collection *How to be alone*. Günter Leypoldt's "Recent Realist Fiction and the Idea of Writing 'After Postmodernism'" inquires into a more complex relationship between postmodernism and recent realist fiction. For a convincing critique of Franzen's call for a new realism, see Madhu Dubey's "Post-Postmodern Realism?"

11 Žižek notes in this respect: "The fundamental lesson of postmodernist politics is that *there is no Event*, that 'nothing really happens', that the Truth-Event is a passing, illusory short circuit, a false identification to be dispelled sooner or later by the reassertion of difference or, at best, the fleeting promise of the Redemption-to-come, towards which we have to maintain a proper distance in order to avoid catastrophic 'totalitarian' consequences; against this structural skepticism, Badiou is fully justified in insisting that—to use the term with its full theological weight—*miracles do happen . . .*" (1999: 155).

12 Derrida also notes the impossibility for an event to be repeated in *Eine gewisse unmögliche Möglichkeit vom Ereignis zu sprechen*: "Da das Sprechen an die Struktur der Sprache gebunden ist, ist es andererseits einer gewissen Allgemeinheit, einer gewissen Iterierbarkeit, einer gewissen Wiederholbarkeit unterworfen und muss schon deswegen die Singularität des Ereignisses verfehlen" (2003: 21). Since language is always caught up in a self-referring system, *speaking* about events always takes away their singularity. Although Derrida emphasized the importance of a concept of the event already in his seminal "Structure, Sign and Play in the Discourse of the Human Sciences," his epistemological orientation does not allow him to grasp an event as a totally pre-discursive phenomenon. Derrida alludes to the absence of events in structuralism when, right in the beginning of his 1966 essay, he wonders: "Perhaps something has occurred in the history of the concept of structure that could be called an 'event,' if this loaded word did not entail a meaning which it is precisely the function of structural-or structuralist-thought to reduce or to

suspect. But let me use the term 'event' anyway, employing it with caution and as if in quotation marks. In this sense, this event will have the exterior form of a *rupture* and a *redoubling*" (1978: 278).

13 As Steven Best and Douglas Kellner observe in *Postmodern Theory: Critical Interrogations, Communications and Culture*, "all postmodern theory lacks an adequate theory of agency, of an active creative self, mediated by social institutions, discourses, and other people" (1991: 283).

14 See, for instance, Murray Bookchin's *Re-enchanting Humanity. A Defense of the Human Spirit Against Antihumanism, Misanthropy, Mysticism, and Primitivism*, Jan D. Kucharzewski's, Stefanie Schäfer's, and Lutz Schowalter's essay collection *"Hello, I say, It's Me"*: *Contemporary Reconstructions of Self and Subjectivity*, or Todd F. Davis's and Kenneth Womack's *Mapping the Ethical Turn*. The ethical turn generally implies the increase in ethical questions starting in the 1990s (Böhm, Kley, Schönleben 13). Hubert Zapf even speaks of an "ethical agenda" that took hold with the development of "holocaust and trauma studies" (2012: 83). In arguing that the theoretical approaches such as deconstruction are unethical (Böhm et al. 2003: 13), I think such arguments do not do justice to this theoretical complex. Writing about literary production in general, Green discerns that the arguments for the end of postmodernism "entail[] a return to earlier modes and concerns. In this case, the way forward—beyond postmodernism—turns out to look very much like the way back—back to the less contentious issues and paradigms that postmodernism supposedly destroyed" (2005: 24–25). Badiou also comments on this trend when writing in *The Century*: "Let us note that a certain twenty-first century, under the sign of human rights as the rights of the natural living being, of finitude, of resignation to what there is, tries to return to man as a given" (169).

15 See, for instance, Böhm's, Kley's, and Schönleben's *Ethik—Anerkennung— Gerechtigkeit*, which follows not only the return of ethics but also the recent theorizing about notions of recognition, particularly in the work of Nancy Fraser, Axel Honneth, Charles Taylor, or Paul Ricoeur (2003: 19ff.). Badiou, indeed, provocatively argues in respect to the Levinasian trend of recognizing or respecting the Other: "all ethical predication based on recognition of the other should be purely and simply abandoned" (*E* xv). Since multiplicity and difference is all there is, Badiou, rather, stresses the orientation of ethics on the Same (*E* 25ff.).

16 See particularly Derrida's later writings or how this ethics of difference has been adopted by various politico-philosophical projects such as Michael Hardt and Antonio Negri's triloy *Empire*, *Multitude* and *Commonwealth*, or Appiah's *Cosmopolitanism*, for instance. For a critique of the ethics of otherness, see especially Badiou's chapter "Does the Other Exist?" in *Ethics*. In a nutshell, Badiou argues that Levinas's principle of the " 'Altogether-Other' " is the "ethical name for God" (*E* 22).

17 For a genealogy of the term, see, for instance, Stephen J. Burn's introduction to his *Jonathan Franzen at the End of Postmodernism*, or Mary K. Holland's *Succeeding Postmodernism*. The creativity to come up with a label for the new period is, indeed, remarkable. Post-postmodernism seems to strike the largest consensus (see, for instance, Trimmer, McLaughlin, or Kucharzewski and Schowalter), while there are also other neologisms circulating, which are depicted by Vermeulen and van den Aken: Lipovetsky or Virilio's hypermodernism, Kirby's pseudomodernism (what he later refashions as digimodernism), or altermodernism as conceived by Bourriaud.

Vermeulen and van den Aken have their own concept of metamodernism, which Holland,independently conceives. See also Raoul Eshelman's *Performatism, or, the End of Postmodernism*, which conceives of a theory of subjectivity after postmodernism that, however, stresses transcendence and theism, which is rejected within the scope of this study.

18 See Hoberek's introduction to the special issue of *Twentieth-Century Literature*, which is tellingly called "After Postmodernism," McLaughlin's "Post-postmodern Discontent," or his more recent "After the Revolution: US Postmodernism in the Twenty-First Century."

19 Green summarizes this critical assumption when writing that "some commentators even tried to lay the blame for the events of September 11, 2001 at postmodernism's door, as if to suggest that the trauma of the terrorist attacks on the U.S. will finally wake liberal intellectuals from their relativistic slumbers" (2005: 19).

20 For a more elaborate discussion of McCarthy's place in literary history, see Andrew Estes's introduction in his *Cormac McCarthy and the Writing of American Spaces*. For recent arguments of Pynchon's detachment from postmodernism, see, for instance, McHale (2007), Pöhlmann (2010), or Ickstadt (2008).

21 See, for instance, Burn's *Jonathan Franzen at the End of Postmodernism*, Daniel Grassian's *Hybrid Fictions: American Literature and Generation X*, or Nicoline Timmer's *Do You Feel It Too?*

22 See, for instance, Kristiaan Versluys's essay collection *Neo-Realism in Contemporary American Fiction*. However, the "'return of the real'" was also launched against postmodernism from an ecocritical perspective at a time "when it [ecocriticism] resolutely styled itself against postmodernism, eventually building a reputation for blaming our environmental problems on postmodern thought," (2012: 35) as Serpil Oppermann observes. For a more elaborate analysis of the link between ecocriticism and postmodernism, see her article "Rethinking Ecocriticism in an Ecological Postmodern Framework: Mangled Matter, Meaning, and Agency."

23 Burn argues that in such ostensibly realistic literature as Richard Powers, the "selective deployment of metafictional techniques [is] another way to reengage with the world beyond the book" (2005: 21). This is obviously ignoring that metafictional devices break the "willing suspension of disbelief" and therefore shatter the illusion of an escapist diegetical world, which leaves the equation that more realistic forms are more political (Burn 2005: 21) seriously wanting.

24 Chetwynd's paper was accessible as an audiofile but has been reworked into the article "Inherent Obligation: The Distinctive Difficulties in and of Recent Pynchon."

25 Kurachzweski, Schäfer, and Schowalter ask: "Can the subject be put on its feet again by approaches that aptly acknowledge postmodern insights about the powers and the discourses that shape us, without to revert to dogmas about human nature? How can we develop post-postmodernist positions without falling prey to stereotypical or even nonsensical stances that dismiss all postmodern theorizing as 'naively relativistic' and as ignorant of the paradoxes that come with many of its arguments" (2009: 3).

26 While the "culture wars" were primarily a political discussion, they also mapped on the institution of the university. Green argues that "neoconservative positions in the 'culture wars' of the 1980s and 1990s . . . deplored the turn within English departments to theory, multiculturalism, and an expanded canon, all—it was

claimed—at the expense of the study of great literature" (2005: 6). Green, indeed, observes an overlap between the ostensible end of postmodernism and the skepticism toward French theory when he writes tongue-in-cheek: "News of postmodernism's expiration can therefore be taken in good spirits, since urgent political and intellectual problems might now be addressed without a detour through the latest neo-Nietzschean mills flown from France. Everything that such a theoretical ruled out of court—history, capital, the subject—can now be brought back to the table, and not before time" (2005: 19).

27 In his essay "On a finally objectless Subject," Badiou claims that "what is demanded of us is an additional step in the modern, and not a veering towards the limit, whether it be termed 'post modern' or whatever" (1991: 24). Toth and Brooks argue that there are a variety of theorists who "echo the recent ethico-political 'turn'" (2007: 5) as in the work of the later Derrida. "Along with Derrida," Toth and Brooks write, they could have well included "the likes of Jean-Luc Nancy, Jean-Luc Marion, John D. Caputo and Slavoj Žižek" (ibid.: 5). It is noteworthy that Badiou is not on this list.

28 Particularly since the English publication of Badiou's major book *Being and Event*, critical reception has started to gain momentum. In his 2003 monograph *Badiou: A Subject to Truth*, Peter Hallward still points to the fact that Badiou is not included "in either of the two most substantial recent English surveys of French philosophy in the twentieth century" (2003: 349). Hallward and Slavoj Žižek (*The Ticklish* Subject) were among the first to critically engage with Badiou's work. In France, Badiou's key role could, however, already be seen in Deleuze and Guattari's discussion of *L'être et L'èvenement* in their *What is Philosophy?* A first critical engagement with Badiou's thoughts can be found in Hallward's edited *Think Again: Alain Badiou and the Future of Philosophy*, which includes essays by such seminal thinkers as Balibar, Rancière, Laclau, Nancy, and others. More recently, there were published not only Christopher Norris's Companion to *Being and Event*, but also John Mullarkey and Beth Lord's *Continuum Companion to Continental Philosophy*, in which Badiou takes up a major role. Among the first essays, particularly in literary and cultural studies, that dealt with Badiou's work are, for instance, Alexander Dunst's "Thinking the Subject Beyond its Death," Simone Pinet's "On the Subject of Fiction: Islands and the Emergence of the Novel," Julian Murphet's "Character and Event," and Gran Farred's "The Event of the Black Body at Rest: Mêlée in Motown." For a more elaborate consideration of Badiou's place in academia, see my article "Event{u}al Disruptions: Postmodern Theory and Alain Badiou."

29 In respect to the apparently problematic term of truths, Kamecke and Teschke ask whether the humanities and cultural studies can swallow a concept of truths (2008: 7). Particularly Badiou's notions of "fidelity," or "resurrection," reverberate with religious semantics. James Williams, for instance, insists that "where some distance was maintained between theological language in *Being and Event* in terms of time and history, with *Logics of Worlds* the language is much closer to a theological account of human time touched and salvaged by resurrection" (2012: 127). One reason for Badiou's apparent theology might be the fact that his *Saint Paul: The Foundation of Universalism* was one of the first of his books to be published in English. For a co-option of the theological undercurrents of Badiou, see Frederieck Depoortere's *Badiou and Theology*, which seeks to "introduce the thought of the

French philosopher Alain Badiou to a theologically interested audience" (2009: 1). Badiou's radical anti-theological persuasion can be seen in the prologue to *Saint Paul* where he insists that he reads Paul not as a religious subject but as a "poet-thinker of the event" (2007: 2), his persistence on the secular notions of infinity that finally can be thought with the help of Cantor in *The Century* (154), or his essay *Gott ist tot*.

30 Badiou himself comments on his political history in *Deleuze: The Clamor of Being*: "Then came the red years, 1968, the University of Vincennes. For the Maoist that I was, Deleuze, as the philosophical inspiration for what we called 'anarcho-desirers,' was an enemy all the more formidable for being internal to the 'movement' which made Deleuze and Jean-Francois Lyotard attack Badiou for his alleged 'Bolshevization' of the department" (2000: 2). While Badiou has persistently corrected his position, particularly allegations of his Stalinist sympathies, the figure of Mao remains an ambivalent figure in his thinking that one has to be aware of. Feltham argues that Badiou's Maoist period is only evident in his publications up to *Theory of the Subject* (2010: 16). For a comprehensive critique of Badiou's philosophy, see especially Mehdi Belhaj Kacem's *Après Badiou* as well as François Laruelle's *Anti-Badiou*.

31 In their introduction to a seminal essay volume that celebrated the English translation of *Being and Event,* Paul Ashton, A. J. Bartlett, and Justin Clemens inquire into the relation between master and disciple. If, indeed, Badiou's thinking is an event itself, those affirming its imperatives do not simply "apply" his theories but critically engage with his thought, negotiating it within the working premises of various fields: in my case, literary studies.

32 Badiou addresses this allegation and retorts that the discourse of "Anti-Americanism is meaningless. The American people have brought humanity admirable inventions in all orders of experience. But today there cannot be the least political liberty or independence of mind, without a constant and unrelenting struggle against the *imperium* of the USA" (*IT* 118).

33 In *Inästhetik und Mimesis,* Kacem shows that Badiou's theory embraces a form of mimesis of aesthetic and scientific paradigms. By relying on his definition of the event not only on set theoretical mathematics but also on Mallarmé's *A Cast of Dice,* Badiou succeeds in combining these spheres for a unique understanding of events that is closely linked to the study of literature: "Mallarmés Theorie des Ereignisses ist . . . negativ. Das heißt, dass das Mallarmé-Gedicht von dem Zweifel ausgeht, ob wirklich etwas geschehen ist; es spricht nicht von der positive aktuellen, vor unseren Augen liegenden Präsenz des Ereignisses; es spricht nicht einmal in tragischer oder melancholischer Weise von seinem Verschwinden oder von seinem Rückzug; sondern in eisiger, klinischer Weise, ich möchte fast sagen im Register des Kriminalromans, des Gerichtsmediziners: das Mallarmé-Gedicht geht von der neutralen, fast nicht auszumachenden Spur dieses entschwundenen Ereignisses aus. Wie oft im Kriminalroman gesagt wird: das Verbrechen war fast perfekt, man hat seine Spuren völlig beseitigt, und nur ein ausgezeichneter Untersuchungsbeamter, ein guter Spürhund wie Columbo, kann die winzige Spur finden, die beweist, dass es doch einen Raubmord gegeben hat. Und weiterhin wie in einem Krimi rekonstruiert die lange und peinlich genaue Untersuchung, wie man so sagt, den Faden der Ereignisse, das heißt das Ereignis selbst, insofern es tatsächlich stattgefunden hat. Und Badiou hat sein ganzes Leben der Entfaltung der Philosophie dieser

Gegen-Untersuchung in Bezug auf das Verschwinden des Ereignisses gewidmet, indem er nachwies, dass es ein Ereignis gibt, dass in immer aleatorischer, seltener und prekärer Weise irgend etwas stattfindet, in der Politik, wie anderswo, und sich mit seinen unauslöschlichen Folgen auf die ganze Menschheit auswirkt" (2010: 28). (Mallarmé's theory of the event is negative. That means that Mallarmé's poem doubts whether something has really happened; it does not speak of the positive, actual presence of the event; it does not even speak in a tragic or melancholic way of its disappearance or the withdrawal; but in a neutral, clinical way, I almost want to say in the register of a crime novel, like a forensic pathologist: Mallarmé's poem assumes the neutral trace of the withdrawn event that cannot be detected. How often we can read a crime novel where it says: the crime was almost perfect, the traces have been removed completely, and only an excellent detective, someone as good as Columbo, can find the evanescent trace, which proves who committed the felony. And like in a crime novel, the long and miniscule analysis retraces the traces of the event, if it happened at all. And Badiou has devoted his life to conceptualizing a philosophy of this counter-analysis in relation to the disappearance of the event, by showing that there is an event, that something happens, even though in an increasingly aleatory, rare and precarious manner, be that in politics, or somewhere else, and which has inexorable consequences on the entire humanity. [My translation]) Kacem's interconnection of Badiou's thought with ideas of criminology is interesting in terms of the hermeneutic inclination of literary studies.

34   Despite the resonances with a religious praxis, Badiou emphasizes that "the word 'fidelity' refers directly to the amorous relationship, but I would rather say that it is the amorous relationship which refers . . . to the dialectic of being and event, the dialectic whose temporal ordination is proposed by fidelity" (*BE* 232).

35   Badiou's examples of artistic subjective creations center on music, painting, and poetry. See particularly his *Handbook of Inaesthetics*, which is the most elaborate discussion of the truth condition of art and which tellingly leaves out the novel. In *Being and Event,* Badiou emphasizes the discussion of contingency in Mallarmé's poetry. "Poetry," he writes, "is the stellar assumption of that pure undecidable against a background of nothingness, that is an action of which one can only *know* whether it has taken place inasmuch as one *bets* upon its truth" (*BE* 192). As one of the four conditions, artistic fidelity centers on poetry, which becomes clear when Badiou writes that "art (more precisely, the poem)" (*IT* 124) is constitutive of subjects. Whereas Badiou avoids contemporary works of literature, almost always stressing modernist art (even when he talks about prose, he only talks about Samuel Beckett), which Hallward summarizes as "his uncompromisingly modernist conception of art" (2004: 1), the saliency of this topic is, in my view, a genuine concern of the American novel of the twenty-first century, because of the aforementioned background of the postmodernist critique of these concepts.

36   Badiou, at times, seems to consider the interconnection between generic procedures, as when he writes that "it is impossible to conceal the patent kinship [of scientific events] with the play of traces in art" (*LoW* 75). However, he immediately goes on to stress the difference between the two conditions: "This is usually clouded by the fact that in art what is at stake is the sensible and the variance of its forms, while in science it is the intelligibility of the world and the invariance of its equations. Science

thereby proves to be the reverse of art, which explains the spectacular isomorphism between their evental traces" (*LoW* 75).

37 See particularly, Book I of *Logics of Worlds*, 45–78. See also Alberto Toscano's "The Bourgeois and the Islamist, or, The Other Subjects of Politics." Toscano remarks that "Badiou already recognizes, in the *Théorie du sujet*, the need to think different subjective configurations, not all of which can be regarded as the ethical bearers of novelty and universality" (2006: 23).

38 In *Being and Event*, Badiou only conceives of a faithful subject of the event. It is only in *Ethics*, *Infinite Thought*, and *Logics of Worlds* that he expands on these subjective formalisms.

Chapter 1

1 The *OED* dates the term's first occurrence to the sixteenth century, deriving from the Latin "*eventus*, from *evenire* 'result, happen', from *e-* (variant of *ex-*) 'out of' + *venire* 'come'" (1993: 865).

2 See Marc Rölli's observation that specifically French philosophy has crucially engaged with the concept of the event (2004: 7). Moreover, he also sees postmodernism as extolling the concept, be it in mediatheoretical ways as simulacra, ontologically as difference or discourse-analytically as "Aussagen-Ereignisse" (2004: 7). For the importance of events in narratology, see, for instance, Wolf Schmid's *Elemente der Narratologie*, Jerome Bruner's "The Narrative Construction of Reality," David Herman's "Events," Ansgar Nünning's "Making Events—Making Stories—Making Worlds," or Peter Hühn's "Event and Eventfulness."

3 See Rölli's essay collection *Ereignis auf Französisch*, which gives a plethora of different thinkers of the event—from Bergson, Merleau-Ponty, and Lacan over Derrida, Levinas, and Foucault to Deleuze—and restricts itself merely to the French and German context.

4 Rölli argues that all later attempts that tried to define the event in a philosophical way have to be placed in the tradition of Heidegger—if they want to or not—and it is in this light that they have to prove their critical potential and their further power (2004: 9). By now, it seems to be a critical commonplace in Badiou studies to emphasize the differences from Gilles Deleuze's notion of events.

5 Rölli observes that the event and history are diametrically opposed. So writing a history of the event is bound to fail (2004: 14).

6 In this manner, I also address the mathematical foundations of Badiou's ontology only where necessary.

7 Next to the chapter entitled "Simple Becoming and True Change" in *Logics of Worlds* (363–80), Badiou also differentiates his notion of events from the ordinary call for change in the cultural and political milieu of recent times and in modernity in general: "They all say that the world is changing at a dizzying pace and that, if we are not to risk ruin or death . . . , we must adapt to this change or, in the world as it is, be but a mere shadow of ourselves. That we should energetically engage in incessant 'modernization', accepting the inevitable costs without a murmur. . . . To that end everyone must pedal: modernize, reform, change! What politician on the campaign trail can dispense with proposing reform, change, novelty?" (*TRoH* 2). "Let us say,"

Badiou writes in *Infinite Thought*, "that not everything that changes is an event, and that surprise, speed, and disorder can be mere simulacra of the event," (97) which is investigated in more detail in Chapter 3.

8 Badiou could thus be seen as adopting the middle perspective between Heidegger's single event and Deleuze's infinite events, which could also be said to be an assemblage of just one event. See, for instance, Hallward's observation of how Deleuze "presents the world itself as 'a pure emission of singularities,' as a continuous stream of events, each of which is an affirmation or expression of the one Event of life" (2003: 176). By endorsing the emphatic momentum of the former, he combines this revolutionary impetus with the plurality of events of the latter, being nevertheless rare to render them distinct from everyday occurrences.

9 Badiou's explicit and repeated rejection of the linguistic turn can be discerned when he critically observes that "contemporary philosophy institutes the passage from a truth-orientated to a meaning-orientated philosophy" (*IT* 34), which he seeks to undo. Indeed, one could argue that while Heidegger works against the forgetting of being, Badiou does so against the forgetting of truth. However, "for Badiou," as Hewson notes, "ontology is not a question of the 'meaning' of being: the 'content' of ontology is rather located wholly within the work of mathematics, and philosophical work is hence directed towards the event-character of truths belonging to science, love, art and [politics]" (Hewson 147). In *The Rebirth of History*, Badiou elucidates that for him, existence is intensional, while being is extensional (67). Christopher Norris equally remarks that for Badiou, the linguistic turn typifies not "a means of liberation from outworn ideas or misconceived pseudo-dilemmas but rather a means of distracting attention from problems that would otherwise occupy the forefront of any philosophical project" (2009: 3). While Badiou parenthesizes the eminence of language and insists that philosophy has to contemplate being in and for itself, this is not to say that language is not also involved in his analysis, or that he omits the fact that language is "the colour of philosophy, its tonality, and its inflexion" (*IT* 38). While it has often been argued that Badiou conceives set theory as another logical meta-language, he is eager to point out that set theory as ontology is itself only *a* situation (*IT* 131). See also Meditation Three of *Being and Event*, or when he writes that "philosophy privileges no language, not even the one it is written in. Philosophy is not enclosed within the pure formal ideal of scientific language. Its natural element is language, but, within that natural element, it institutes a universal address" (*IT* 38).

10 See Meditation One of *Being and Event*. Feltham notes that Badiou has in mind "a return to authenticity via a Heideggerian claim: modern philosophy under the banner of anti-Platonism has not only misrecognized the contemporary actuality and radicality of Plato, but also—*pace* Heidegger and the Platonic forgetting of being—it forgot the Cantorian event that revealed infinite multiplicity in the form of set theory. This claim is both Heideggerian in its form—the field of philosophy is structured by a forgetting—yet anti-Heideggerian in its content—we must have done with the philosophy of finitude" (2010: 20). Laruelle is particularly critical of this subtractive philosophy and connects it to Badiou's unabating Maoism. See particularly his *Anti-Badiou*, which bears the telling subtitle: *On the Introduction of Maoism into Philosophy*.

11 Jean-Jacques Lecercle notes in respect to Badiou's distinction between natural language and the language of ontology: "Is this merely a restatement of Carnap's

familiar positivist position? It is not: Badiou does not use the contrast between natural and artificial languages, and, more importantly for us, quite unlike Carnap, he raises the question of the poem: perhaps there is a way, after all, of saving language for philosophy, through a celebration of poetic practice" (208).

12 One of the basic assumptions of equating set theory with ontology is that both talk about multiples, the one as sets, the other as beings. For an introduction to Badiou's set theoretical ontology see, for instance, Feltham's introduction to *Infinite Thought* or Peter Hallward's chapter in *Badiou: A Subject to Truth*. Badiou observes in *Being and Event* that "the reason behind the choice of set theory is that it shows how all mathematical entities, including relations and operations, can be thought of as pure multiples" (*BE* 91). In the vein of Heidegger's anti-substantialist critique of metaphysics, Badiou employs set theory's thinking of the multiple to, on the one hand, think being without a process of unifying it—what he calls the "One" (*BE* 23)— while, on the other, to establish an infinite universe of multiplicities by the only operation of "belonging" that he develops in Meditation Eight. What is more, set theory simultaneously avoids a theologocentric act of creation that brings these beings into "existence" since it grounds its entire infinite but immanent universe of sets in the literal nothing: the void. By stipulating that the void is the "proper name of being" (*BE* 52), with the help of the axiom of the void and the axiom of the powerset, set theory can, indeed, evolve something out of nothing, as is explained in Meditation Five. Hallward observes that "only as founded on nothing or nothing but itself, can the concept of multiplicity be made properly absolute. Were the multiple to be founded on something (else) . . . its multiplicity would to some degree be constrained by this thing beyond its immanent logic" (2003: 82). Moreover, it has to be mentioned that ontology for Badiou is not a meta-discipline, a master narrative that can assume a regulating position, but, rather, it is itself a situation "being itself a consistent multiplicity, on pain of falling apart" (Feltham 2008a: 88).

13 While Russell's antinomy points out that the well-constructed formula "the set of all sets which does not contain itself" is logically a paradox, since this set has either to count itself or not, the axiom of foundation states: " 'If α is a nonempty set, then there is an element b of α such that there are no sets that belong both to α and b.' This axiom explicitly outlaws the paradoxical situation of sets belonging to themselves. It ensures that, given a certain set, it is impossible to count down indefinitely from the set to a member of that set and then to a member of that member. Eventually, we reach something that belongs to the set but that itself has no member: an 'urelement,' or the empty set, which is thus 'foundational' of all the other sets" (Hallward 2003: 339).

14 Žižek insists in *The Parallax View*: "Idealism posits an ideal Event which cannot be accounted for in terms of its material (pre)conditions, while the materialist wager is that we *can* get 'behind' the event and explore how Event explodes out of the gap in/ of the order of Being" (166).

15 While Badiou merges the event, evental site, and intervention in *Logics of Worlds* (see Book V), Feltham notes that they were "already fused in *Being and Event*" (2008a: 107).

16 Through this, set theory succeeds in constructing an anti-theologocentric discourse of being. "In line with Derrida and Lacoue-Labarthe's versions of Heidegger's critique of metaphysics," writes Feltham in this context, "set-theory ontology does not *posit* being as . . . either a form or object; rather it unfolds being as an implicit consequence of its axioms" (2008a: 91).

17   While Deleuze, for instance, purports an ontology of intensities, in Badiou's
     extensional approach, "the operative sense of a term is fixed entirely by the range of
     those objects, whether physical or abstract, to which it applies or extends and not
     by anything specific *about* those objects" (90). Deleuze and Guattari reject Badiou's
     notion of just one form of multiplicity in *What is Philosophy?* "It seems to us that
     the theory of multiplicities does not support the hypothesis of any multiplicity
     whatever.... There must be at least two multiplicities, two types, from the outset.
     This is not because dualism is better than unity but because the multiplicity is
     precisely what happens between the two. Hence, the two types will certainly not be
     one above the other but rather one beside the other, against the other, face to face,
     or back to back. Functions and concepts, actual states of affairs and virtual events,
     are two types of multiplicities not distributed on an errant line but related to two
     vectors that intersect, one according to which states of affairs actualize events and
     the other according to which events absorb (or rather, adsorb) states of affairs"
     (152–53). Although they argue for a duality of multiplicities, one might associate
     this duality as two concepts within a dialectical, yet monist, ontology. Peter Hallward
     observes that Deleuze's "worldly, qualitative multiplicity excludes Badiou's deductive,
     mathematical multiplicity; his fold is precisely a qualitative or 'antiextensional'
     concept of the Multiple . . . , at the opposite extreme from a resolutely set-theoretic
     understanding'" (2003: 175–76).
18   "Badiou's use of the term 'state' incorporates a classically Marxist understanding of
     the political state as much as it overlaps with a simple intuitive understanding of the
     'status quo'" (2001: ix), Hallward explains.
19   This bears close parallels to Jacques Rancière's notion of consensus: "Consensus is
     the reduction of these various 'peoples' into a single people identical with the count
     of a population and its parts, of the interests of a global community and its parts"
     (2010: 189). Note Rancière's adoption of the set theoretical terms counting and parts.
20   To be sure, the excessive relation between presentation and representation, or
     situation and state of the situation is easy to calculate with finite sets. However, since
     most of set theory's multiples are infinite sets, it becomes the question of how to
     account for such quantitative discrepancies. Feltham notes that in such cases "the
     quantity of the powerset is literally undecidable" (2008a: 95). In an interview with
     Badiou, Feltham observes that "set theory does not say that all sets are infinite"
     (*IT* 136). Badiou responds that this axiomatic postulation is grounded in a larger
     rejection of what he calls the "philosophies of finitude": "It is more interesting and
     more attuned to the necessity of the times than declaring that we are finite and all
     is finite, we are mortal beings for death and so on. We are being-for the-infinite"
     (*IT* 137). It is equally worth noting that Badiou's embrace of infinity tries to think
     this phenomenon outside of the theological spheres that it has been ascribed to
     traditionally: "We must liberate this category from the theological conception, and
     mathematics is the unique means to do so" (*IT* 137).
21   There are also natural situations, which are defined by a mixture of singular, normal
     and excrescent multiples (normal sets being both presented and represented,
     excrescent multiples being only represented without being presented).
22   Feltham traces this rejection of dialectical materialism: "There is no History, there
     are only separate histories" back to Badiou's earlier work: "Within Badiou's oeuvre
     this statement stands as the *epitaph* to the Marxist dialectic of history. Already
     committed in *Théorie du sujet* to the multiplication of dialectical sequences, to the

absence of any final unity of these sequences and to the permanence of division, here [in *Being and Event*] Badiou embraces a radical separation and possible contemporaneity of diverse historical sequences" (2008a: 98). See also *The Rebirth of History* where Badiou remarks that "*History does not contain within itself a solution to the problems it places on the agenda*" (42), thereby clearly distancing himself from Marx's Hegelian teleology of History.

23   Badiou differentiates himself from Heidegger in this respect when he observes that his conception of various "historical sequences" has "nothing to do with the Heideggerian conviction of a monumental history of being from the Greeks until the present day with its sequences of the forgetting of being, metaphysics, nihilism and so on. I think it is necessary to speak of historicity and not History" (*IT* 136).

24   Foucault hints at a particular blind spot of structuralist theory that Derrida also addresses in his seminal essay "Structure, Sign and Play": "Perhaps something has occurred in the history of the concept of structure that could be called an 'event', if this loaded word did not entail a meaning which it is precisely the function of structural—or structuralist—thought to reduce or to suspect. But let me use the term 'event' anyway, employing it with caution and as if in quotation marks. In this sense, this event will have the exterior form of a *rupture* and a *redoubling*" (1978: 278). Although Derrida ponders the concept of the event, particularly in his *Eine gewisse unmögliche Möglichkeit vom Ereignis zu sprechen*, his epistemological orientation, I would argue, does not let him grasp this phenomenon other than as an always deferred trace.

25   Feltham translates Mallarmé's poem as *A Cast of Dice*, while the conventional English translation is *A Throw of Dice*. See Pierre Macherey's "The Mallarmé of Alain Badiou."

26   See Norris, who observes: "What is so difficult to grasp about all this, as anti-realists are fond of pointing out, is the sense in which truth can possibly (non-contradictorily) be conceived as somehow latent within a given situation or state of knowledge and yet as surpassing the utmost powers of any available proof-procedure or investigative method" (2009: 231).

27   I thank Sebastian Thede for this insight.

28   Feltham notes that "nothing prescribes the occurrence of an event; the existence of an evental site is a necessary but non-sufficient condition. Here Badiou places the error of deterministic theories of change; they confuse the existence of an evental site with the existence of change" (2008a: 100).

29   Another such problematic concept constitutes his notion of the "Idea" (21), which he links to political struggles in *The Rebirth of History*. In *Infinite Thought*, Badiou explains that he has "the same conception of truth as Spinoza. Truth is an *index sui*. Truth is the proof of itself. There is no external guarantee" (130). James Williams' "A Critique of Alain Badiou's Denial of Time in his Philosophy of Events" insists that Badiou's conceptions of eternal truths are mere "fiction[s]" (130).

30   For a more elaborate investigation of the relation between Badiou and postmodern theory, see my article "Event{u}al Disruptions: Postmodern Theory and Alain Badiou." Žižek, for instance, also notes that "what Badiou is aiming at, against this postmodern *doxa* [of anti-metaphysical thinking] is precisely the resuscitation of the *politics of (universal) Truth* in today's conditions of global contingency. Thus Badiou rehabilitates, in the modern conditions of multiplicity and contingency, not only

philosophy but the properly *meta-physical* dimension: the infinite Truth is 'eternal' and *meta-* with regard to the temporal process of Being; it is a flash of another dimension transcending the positivity of Being" (1999: 151).

31 Upon being asked by Justin Clemens whether "in a situation everyone has access to knowledge," Badiou responds that his "thesis is that in a situation there is always an encyclopedia of knowledge which is the same for everybody. But the access to this knowledge is very different. We can speak in Marxist terms, we can say that in a situation there is an ideological *dispositif* [apparatus] which is dominant" (*IT* 129). It is obvious how the distinction between such *dispositifs* and truths runs against the grain of Foucault's forms of discursive knowledge.

32 In respect of political truths, Badiou notes that "when I speak of political truth, this does not involve a judgement but a process: a political truth is not 'I say I am right and the other person is wrong', or 'I am right to like that ruler and detest that opponent'. A truth is *something that exists in its active process*, which manifests itself, as truth, in different circumstances marked by this process. Truths are not prior to political processes; there is no question of confirming or applying them. Truths are reality itself, as a process of production of political novelties, political sequences, political revolutions, and so forth" (*TRoH* 87).

33 In *Theory of the Subject*, Badiou still believed that an evental manifestation is contingent upon destruction, a stance that he alters in *Being and Event*: "I don't say in *L'Etre et l'évenement* that destruction is always a bad thing. It can be necessary to destroy something for the newness of the event. But I don't think it is a necessary part of the newness. Because I think the newness is a supplementation and not a destruction" (*IT* 132).

34 While Badiou calls himself a "modern Platonist" (*TW* 54), and he has also devoted the very first chapter of *Being and Event* to Plato, Simon Duffy comprehensively shows how Badiou rejects an "orthodox Platonic realism, i.e. the independent existence of a realm of mathematical objects" but, rather, proceeds to characterize "the Plato that responds to the demands of a post-Cantorian set theory" (59).

35 Clemens has raised the problem of what he calls the " 'über-subject' or 'ultra-subject'," namely a subject that, for example, in the case of Christianity, "is still faithful to the event of Christ. . . A subject which has lasted over 2000 years and which *is* that subject in its very slow vanishing." (*IT* 131). Badiou replied that "there is no super subject. A subject is a subject of a definite situation" (*IT* 131). This implies that the subject of the Spartacus event is not the same subject of the resurrection of this event in the political milieu of the 1990s Germany.

36 While Badiou gives a straightforward definition of intervention as "any procedure by which a multiple is recognized as an event" (*BE* 202), the mathematical intricacies of this concept are more complex. See Meditation Twenty of *Being and Event* or Norris's commentary.

37 Žižek is eager to point out that Badiou's notion of undecidability "is radically different from the standard deconstructionist notion of undecidability. For Badiou, undecidability means that there are no neutral 'objective' criteria for an Event: an Event appears as such only to those who recognize themselves in its call" (2006: 167).

38 See particularly his *Saint Paul*, where he writes that he considers Paul a "poet-thinker of the event" (2) and not part of a religious truth procedure.

39   In a subchapter on the question of whether fidelity to an event is like a form of
     asceticism, Badiou remarks "that the ethic of truths compels so considerable a
     distance from opinions that it must be called literally *asocial*. This a-sociality has
     always been recognized for what it is—in the image of Thales falling into a well
     because he seeks to penetrate the secret of celestial movement; in the proverb 'Lovers
     have eyes only for each other'; in the isolated destiny of the great revolutionary
     militants; in the theme of 'solitary genius', and so on" (*E* 54).
40   He declares that "the subject, as local situated configuration, is neither the intervention
     nor the operator of fidelity, but the advent of the Two, that is, the incorporation of the
     event into the situation in the mode of a generic procedure" (*BE* 393).
41   Badiou is eager to point out that one must "carefully distinguish love from the
     'couple'. The couple is what, of love, is visible to a third" (*C* 187). This third position
     does not exist for Badiou, since "the phenomenal appearance of the couple, which is
     submitted to an external law of count, does not say anything about love. The couple
     names not love but the state (or the State) of love. It names not the presentation but
     the representation of love" (*C* 187).
42   For a more elaborate distinction between possible and impossible worlds, see my article
     "Words without Worlds—Worlds without Words. Impossible Ontologies in Nelson
     Goodman and Alain Badiou". Moreover, in contrast to Badiou, who, as Hallward
     notes, "reserves the legitimate meaning of the term 'poetic' for the nomination of the
     event" (2003: 124), I argue that it is literature in general, which, in investing its poietical
     potential may give the unfounded event a name. "Poetry is language directed to the
     expression of the void, language used without object or reference" (2003: 124).
43   Dan Ross enquires if it is "impossible to understand a situation ontologically without
     prior experience of the ontological essence of the situation," whereupon Badiou
     insists that "everybody who is engaged in faithfulness in the relation to an event has
     an understanding of the situation. So it is not a prerequisite to have prior knowledge.
     Prior knowledge is always necessary to understand the being, the ontological schema
     of the situation, the mathematical categories and so on, because we have to work for
     that sort of understanding: terrible work! But from the point of view of singular truth
     we have an access from the event itself and not from preconstituted knowledge. The
     truth creates the understanding of the process of truth and the subject *is* this sort of
     understanding. So, the truth needs nothing other than itself. It's very important. The
     truth is not a question of knowledge; it is the *defection* of knowledge" (*IT* 134–35).
44   In *Infinite Thought*, Feltham confronts Badiou with exactly this problem of differing
     fidelities, for which there is, according to Badiou, "no abstract answer. . . . It is a
     matter of the concrete situation. If I am faithful to a political event, after May '68
     on the one hand, and on the other hand I am in love with a woman, well, that's my
     situation. There is no abstract possibility for grasping this sort of situation" (130–31).
45   In *The Parallax View*, Žižek explains that Badiou's notion of "points" "refers to
     Lacan's *point de caption*, of course" (2006: 37).
46   In a brief aside concerning the relationship between aesthetic events, Badiou
     acknowledges: "It can also happen that an incalculable event comes to reveal in
     retrospect a configuration to be obsolete with respect to the constraints introduced
     by a new configuration" (2005: 13). This obviously raises questions about the eternal
     appeal of events and it should be interesting to analyze how this works, particularly,
     in a literary historical sense.

47 Melley makes some important observations concerning the etymological history of the concept: "In the *Oxford English Dictionary*, 'agency' usually means either 'active working' and 'action' or 'instrumentality' and 'intermediation.' In 1830, Coleridge wrote of 'personal free agency,' a coupling which appears to govern the recent sense of 'agency' as autonomy and freedom. For a concise history of the legal concept of agency, see James Beniger (132–42). In mid-nineteenth-century America, Beniger explains, the 'general laws of agency' (135) were established precisely because agents had become too autonomous and needed to be held legally responsible for actions which departed from the explicit demands of their (often distant) principles. In other words, the general laws of 'agency' made agents anything but autonomous" (1992: 712).

48 This also differentiates itself from Raoul Eshelman's notion of performatism, what he discerns in contemporary Anglophone art that is no longer postmodern, since Eshelman insists that this "ethics of perpetration" (2011: n.p.) lets "encapsulated subjects now influence others via active, whole, performative interventions and—if all goes well—experience transcendence as presence, plenitude, and finality rather than as absence, deferral, and regress. The mode of "all goes well" is by definition authorial or theist. It requires that some higher (authorial) agency "cooperate" in causing the performance to bring lovers together (*Amelie*), have characters experience plenitude (Ricky and Lester in *American Beauty*), achieve finality (Christopher in *The Curious Incident*), or revenge themselves totally on their tormentors (Grace in Dogville and Shoshanna in *Inglourious Basterds*)" (2011: n.p.). Not only does the subject of the event question such an "authorial or theist" agency and relate to an atheological event but, as the chapter on *Against the Day* shows, it is also radically opposed to transcendence and, rather, engages in Badiou's notion of an "immanent break" (*E* 42).

49 "Democratic materialism," writes Badiou in *Logics of Worlds*, "only knows individuals and communities, that is to say passive bodies, but it knows no subjects" (50).

50 Nina Power analyzes the relation between Badiou and Althusser in respect to the status of the subject and humanism in more detail in "Toward a New Political Subject?" She insists that "Badiou's unwillingness to give up on a term—humanity—that Althusser would have regarded as ideological in the extreme is ultimately part and parcel of Badiou's insistence that a theory of the subject is possible, indeed necessary" (170). See also the last chapter in *The Century* where Badiou calls his own approach a "*formalized in-humanism*" (178).

51 Similar lines of argument can be found in Althusser's subjective interpellation and Lacan's symbolic embededness of the subject.

52 Moreover, he admits in *Ethics* that he now acknowledges "that the event opens a subjective space in which not only the progressive and truthful subjective figure of fidelity but also other figures every bit as innovative, albeit negative—such as the reactive figure, or the figure I call the 'obscure subject'—take their place" (lvii). These "other figures" are analyzed particularly in Chapters 2 and 3.

53 He thus writes in *Ethics* that "the subject of revolutionary politics is not the individual militant—any more, by the way, than it is the chimera of a class-subject" (*E* 43). "To be sure," he goes on to explain, "the militant enters into the composition of this subject, but once again it exceeds him" (*E* 43).

54 See, for instance, John Mullarkey's article "Animal Spirits: Philosomorphism and the Background Revolts of Cinema," which regards Badiou's as an "anthropocentric ontology" (17).

55 See, for instance, Norris's summary that for most critics, Badiou is "an anti-ethical thinker" (2012: 39).

56 See *Mapping the Ethical Turn* or *Literature and Ethics*, where the editors note that "the past two decades have witnessed a veritable renaissance in ethical theory, the consequences of which can be seen now beyond the bounds of philosophy in literary and cultural studies. Hence, the so-called 'ethical turn' in criticism, indebted to a renewed interest in the legacy of Levinas, to the more proximate engagement in Jacques Derrida's late work with religious, ethical, and political themes, and to a number of crucial interventions in literary studies, beginning with J. Hillis Miller's *The Ethics of Reading*" (Jernigan et al. 2009: 7–8).

57 Badiou comments on the omnipresence of the term when writing that "ethics designates today a principle that governs how we relate to 'what is going on', a vague way of regulating our commentary on historical situations (the ethics of human rights), 'social' situations (the ethics of being-together), media situations (the ethics of communication), and so on. This norm of commentaries and opinions is backed up by official institutions, and carries its own authority: we now have 'national ethical commissions', nominated by the State. Every profession questions itself about its 'ethics'. We even deploy military expeditions in the name of 'the ethics of human rights'" (*E* 2).

58 Hallward also notes that "Kant's very procedure—the evacuation of all heteronomous interests and motives, the suspension of all references to 'psychology' and 'utility', all allusion to any 'special property of human nature' . . . , all calculation requires to obtain 'happiness' or 'welfare' . . .—bears some resemblance to Badiou's."

59 For Badiou's outstanding critique of "the ethics of the other," see his chapter "Does the Other Exist?" in *Ethics*, which launches a cogent attack on a variety of theories that focalize on the "'recognition of the other' (against racism, which would deny this other), or to 'the ethics of differences' (against substantialist nationalism, which would exclude immigrants, or sexism, which would deny feminine-being), or to 'multiculturalism' (against the imposition of a unified model of behavior and intellectual approach). Or quite simply, to good old-fashioned 'tolerance', which consists of not being offended by the fact that others think and act differently from you" (20).

60 Žižek observes the legacy of Althusser in Badiou's notion of conditions when writing that "Althusser entertained for a short time the idea of the four modalities of subjectivity: the ideological subject, the subject in art, the subject of the Unconscious, the subject of science. Is there not a clear parallel between Badiou's four generics of truth (love, art, science, politics) and these four modalities of subjectivity (where love corresponds to the subject of the Unconscious, the topic of psychoanalysis, and politics, of course, to the subject of ideology)?" (1999: 167). In *The Parallax View*, Žižek further wonders: "Do not the first three truth-procedures (science, art, and politics) follow the classical logic of the triad True-Beautiful-Good—the science of Truth, the art of beauty, the politics of the good?" (406).

61 Without going into the details of this argument, it is worth noting that the relation between philosophy and these conditions is, emphatically, not one of hierarchical superiority: "Poem, matheme, politics and love at once condition and insult

philosophy" (*IT* 101). "If philosophy had only to *interpret* its conditions, if its destiny was hermeneutic, it would be pleased to turn back towards these conditions, and to interminably say: such is the sense of what happens in the poetic work, the mathematical theorem, the amorous encounter, the political revolution. Philosophy would be the tranquil aggregate of an aesthetics, an epistemology, an erotology and a political sociology. This is a very old temptation, which, when one cedes to it, classifies philosophy in a section of what Lacan calls the discourse of the University" (*IT* 101). For a critique of this subtractive notion of philosophy, see particularly François Laruelle's *Anti-Badiou*.

62 This has been noted by a variety of critics. In their introduction to Badiou's *On Beckett*, Alberto Toscano and Nina Power observe in this context that "questions about the number and nature of the 'conditions' remain open" (xxvi). In "The Fifth Condition," Alenka Zupancic argues that philosophy itself has to be viewed as the fifth condition (201).

63 Žižek also reflects: "Is not love, then, Badiou's 'Asiatic model of production'—the category into which he throws all truth-procedures which do not fit the other three models?" (2006: 406).

64 Although Žižek goes to some lengths in showing that Badiou's *Saint Paul*—for Žižek, "Badiou's ultimate example of the Event"— inquires into a *religious* condition, which "does *not* fit any of the four *génériques* of the event he enumerates (love, art, science, politics)" (1999: 163), Badiou explicitly states that Saint Paul is for him an artistic subject (2003: 2).

65 Next to an ecological condition, Žižek also points to a further, to him, necessary condition: to circumnavigate what Žižek perceives as the "deadlock of Badiou's politics" is to restore to "*the 'economic' domain the dignity of Truth*, the potential for Events" (2006: 328).

66 Badiou, indeed, reflects on this problem when he comments in the interview: "It is a problem which is very interesting and complex. For instance, there are some similarities between politics and love . . .; a singular connection between artistic creation and political thought also, and also a connection between love and science because love and science are the two procedures which don't know that they are procedures, in fact. It is not the same with artistic creation. We know perfectly well that it is a procedure of truth in rivalry with science. It is not the same, naturally, for the other conditions. . . . there is some connection between politics and love, it's an old story because, for example, all the French tragedies, Racine, Corneille, speak about the link between love and politics, a perfect example. In Lacan, for example, we find some connection, very interesting, between love and science. The link between politics and artistic creation is very elaborate, for example, in the work of Deleuze. It's a very interesting field" (*IT* 192).

67 Norris notes in this context how far a fidelity "may often be manifest in very different ways within a single life-history, as with the two highly gifted French mathematicians Jean Cavaillès and Albert Lautman who were both Resistance members shot by the occupying German Forces. While their courage and sheer moral heroism are beyond doubt, they should both most aptly be seen, in Badiou's estimate, as thinkers whose deployment of rigorous, axiomatic-deductive procedures in their mathematical work was likewise displayed to striking effect in their perfectly consistent carrying-through of ethico-political precept into practice" (2012: 42).

68 In the same volume, Badiou argues that "science and politics are completely different thinkings. Why? Because in the science of physics the experiment is an artificial construction *which must be repeatable*. Mathematical writing corresponds to experiments solely when the repetition of an experiment gives the *same* result. This identity is inscribed in a mathematical equation. In politics, however, the relationship between writing and experience is completely different. A political situation is always singular; it is never repeated" (*IT* 61).

69 For the relation between philosophy and art, which is inherently connected to art's capability to evoke truths, see the introduction to *Handbook of Inaesthetics*.

70 Since I see ethics, with Badiou, as a situated, exceptional undertaking that is not evident in "the act of reading as such" (1) but only in such works where events are being negotiated, I distance myself from J. Hillis Miller's coining of that term in *The Ethics of Reading*.

71 This common stance toward the relation between ethics and aesthetics posits that literature's alienating power may conjure alternative worlds for ethical testing. See, for instance, Öhlschläger's introduction to *Narration und Ethik* (11).

72 In *Ethics*, Badiou explains that " 'some-one' is an animal of the human species, this kind of particular multiple that established knowledges designate as belonging to the species. It is this body, and everything that it is capable of, which enters into the composition of a 'point of truth'—always assuming that an event has occurred, along with an immanent break taking the sustained form of a faithful process" (44–45).

Chapter 2

1 See, for instance, Badiou's *Infinite Thought* where he insists that only "people are capable of truth" (53).

2 While the reason for his ignorance of an ecological truth condition certainly lies in the fact that Badiou pursues a larger scope while such environmental concerns are relatively young, this does not lessen the necessary interconnection between historico-culturally specific reflections, which, in the case of this study, are reflected by novels "after 2000" and his more abstract approach. Indeed, Badiou mocks in *The Century* the "petty-bourgeois . . . age of ecology," with its concern for the "environment" and its "opposition to hunting—whether it is the hunting of foxes, whales or man" (176).

3 This irreversible direction toward all-encompassing death is observed, among others, by Ben de Bruyn, who argues that if compared to Mary Shelley's *Last Man* or Alan Weisman's *The World Without Us*, "*The Road* is much more pessimistic about the earth's regenerative capacities. The weather may still leave its mark on human houses and artefacts, but there is no return of life, neither weeds nor animals" (2010: 779–80). George Monbiot's review of the novel equally observes that the novel "considers what would happen if the world lost its biosphere" (2007: n.p.).

4 See, for instance, John Vanderheide's article "Varieties of Renunciation in the Works of Cormac McCarthy," where he argues that McCarthy's entire oeuvre displays a "kind of vital pessimism" (2006: 66). "In the first of his two interviews with Richard Woodward," as Euan Gallivan remarks, "McCarthy stated that 'the notion that the species can be improved in some way, that everyone could live in harmony, is a really

dangerous idea' . . . , and this new novel does little to suggest that he has altered his stance" (2008: 105). There seem to exist two opposed camps in McCarthy criticism, the one advocating his "nihilism," the other viewing "McCarthy in more humanistic terms," (2008: 133–34) as Randall S. Wilhelm observes.

5 I dwell more elaborately on Badiou's conception of "Evil" in the subsequent part of this chapter and the following chapter on *The Zero*.

6 To this extent, my reading of the novel critically distances itself from part of the criticism of the novel, which tends to focus on its anthropocentric aspects, often even reading the book as a tale of a return to liberal-humanist agency (see Heather Duerre Humann's article), or religious ethics (see Wielenberg). Among notable exceptions, such as Vanderheide (2008) or Gallivan, Wilhelm's article on the novel's still lives equally showcases a shift from the centrality of the human. Although Wilhelm focuses on the book's representation of objects, he nevertheless tries to read such scenes as a reflection of human concerns, making him conclude: "Although the father's end can be seen as tragic and suffering, an ugliness that seems all too at home in this apocalyptic landscape, it is the father's deeds that remain beautiful, that engender in the reader a sense of moral goodness and trenchant humanity that make *The Road* McCarthy's most spiritually-concerned text" (2008: 141).

7 While ecocentrism certainly implies the thinking of the whole biosphere as an inherently interconnected system and often implies a "misanthropic" (Garrard 2013: 25) tendency, I suggest that the novel's ecological event does not create a distinction between human and non-human life in a romanticizing prioritization of the latter or the simplified scapegoating of the former. Rather, by propelling a distinction between animate and inanimate beings, the event introduces an ontological difference that seems less attuned to a problematic concept of non-human "nature."

8 See, for instance, Thomas Schaub, who observes how "the world has been destroyed—whether by nuclear blast and subsequent nuclear winter or by the impact of a large meteorite—is less important than that the world has caught fire and turned everything but a few survivors to ash" (2009: 154). Estes equally remarks that "*The Road* does not depict the apocalypse itself and one measure of its austerity (which contributes to its aesthetic impact) is its silence on the event(s) that brought about the ruined present state of the world" (2013: 198).

9 This distinction between the world before and the world after the event is important, for the novel could also pose a fictional world that is a wasteland within the fictional logic of this world.

10 Estes argues that "McCarthy's language draws upon the King James Bible and that *The Road* is heavily indebted to Revelations" (2013: 193). See also, among others, the articles by Wielenberg, Schaub, Vanderheide, or Susan J. Tyburski.

11 In the vein of Badiou's radically secular philosophy, it would be misleading to call such transcendental acts *events*. See, for instance, his *Saint Paul*, or *Gott ist tot*.

12 Generally, the complexity of the novel's narrative situation, which for Estes "presents a hybridization of many forms" (2013: 206), seems to lie in deciding whether the narrative voice is simply an extra-heterodiegetic agency, or, which I see as more probable, narrated by an autodiegetic one. While most of the criticism has argued for the former, the continuous smooth transitions between external and internal focalization, as well as the father's relation to narration in general, seem to indicate otherwise. This argumentation, however, opens another narratological question that boils down to the distinction between the experiencing and narrating I, which

is problematized through the questionable spatiotemporal position that a narrating I would have to assume.

13   Unlike the Puritanical imagination of apocalypse, as in Increase Mather's *The Day of Trouble is near* or Michael Wigglesworth's "The Day of Doom," the event initiates not a singular "day" of destruction but is marked by processuality.

14   See also the chapter on *Against the Day* for its use of metaphors of light to convey dispositions of the event.

15   Peter Freese argues that the "truly apocalyptic is never interested in the end only but always searches for a new beginning" (1997: 17) and goes on to show that particularly the Puritanical founding fathers saw an inherent interconnection between the New World and the apocalyptic clean slate (ibid.: 24). In fact, one might also already see apocalyptic implications in the Columbian "discovery" of America. Lois Parkinson Zamora observes that Columbus "immediately initiated what was to become a perennial imaginative association of America with the promise of apocalyptic historical renewal" (1990: 7). Freese also notes that "in his letter to Doña Juana de la Torre, Columbus quotes from Isaiah and Revelation, and in his compendium of scriptural and other excerpts he sees his explorations as ushering in a more perfect age" (1997: 23). Particularly through its Puritanical belief in the New World as more than merely a geographical clean slate, Freese argues that "from its very beginning, American culture was deeply concerned with 'the end'" (ibid.: 24).

16   For Freese, religious apocalypse and scientific entropy (as the ultimate end of the universe in thermodynamical discourse) constitute "two competing paradigms of the end" (ibid.: 17). However, since the heat death of the universe, rather, amounts to a slowly encroaching process, a negative perpetual becoming so to speak, *The Road's* clear position of a singular event undermines this interpretation.

17   Buell attests that "the image of nuclear holocaust helped reactivate apocalyptic thinking precisely by providing a more convincing secular frame of reference for the apocalyptic paradigm than had been available since the so-called Enlightenment started to undermine the credibility of sacred history" (1995: 298–99). However, this is not to say that other eras were not as much influenced by apocalypticism. Buell notes that "the vision of the world or microcosm thereof coming to a cataclysmic end governs Cooper's *Crater*, Poe's *Eureka*, Melville's *Moby-Dick*, Twain's *Connecticut Yankee*, and Donnelly's *Caesar's Column*, to name but a few examples. Borderline cases like Stowe's *Uncle Tom's Cabin* swell the list immensely. In early modern America the roster continues with London's *Iron Heel*, Faulkner's *Absalom, Absalom*, and West's *Day of the Locust*" (1995: 296). See also Zamora's *Writing the Apocalypse*.

18   Estes observes that "by many accounts, the first post-apocalyptic novel is Mary Shelley's *The Last Man*," (2013: 194) spawning the genre in the nineteenth century. Freese, however, argues that "it seems that by now 'post-apocalyptic' has come to denote a new, and genuinely 'postmodern,' genre" (1997: 43).

19   For a comprehensive history of the concept, see, for instance, Demian Thompson's *The End of Time*, Freese's *From apocalypse to entropy and beyond*, or Greg Garrard's chapter on "Apocalypse" in his *Ecocriticism*. A rather playful reflection on apocalypse can be found in Derrida's *Apokalypse*. For a particular focus on the sociocultural context of apocalypticism, see Buell's chapter on "Environmental Apocalypticism" in his *The Environmental Imagination* (1995: 296ff.) as well as in

Emory Elliott's essay "'Saints' and 'Strangers'—America's Chiliastic Dualism." The semantic shift that included destructive connotations in the term is palpable not just since popular Hollywood movies for whom the "meaning of 'apocalyptic' as a mere synonym for 'catastrophic,' 'cataclysmic' or 'disastrous'" (1997: 27), which seems too superficial for Freese. While apocalypse in Michael Wigglesworth's long poem "The Day of Doom" is, for instance, already described in the negative sense when it says: "Till God began to pour/ Destruction the world upon/ In a tempestuous shower" (1947: l.21–24), it still retains the "essential tension between old and new, destruction and renewal, threat and promise" (Freese 1997: 27).

20 Freese argues more generally that "the visionary anticipation of the *eschaton* is one of Western man's essential means of coming to terms with the terrors and wonders of existence" (ibid.: 42).

21 In a sense, one could argue that the novel's critique of apocalypse reconceptualizes post-apocalypse not simply as a temporal indicator that merely states that something is set *after* the apocalypse. More intricately, the novel, rather, criticizes apocalypse through the prefix "post" as poststructuralism, for instance, criticized structuralism.

22 The ambiguity of this biblical marker also invites other intertexts. While, later in this chapter, I will show a further possible connection to Ex. 1:17, Carl James Grindley also sees parallels to Rev. 1:17 (2008: 12).

23 Read in the apocalyptic tradition, this passage recalls Wigglesworth's "The Day of Doom," which also ties the apocalypse to a piercing form of lightning in its fifth stanza: "For at midnight brake forth a Light, which turn'd the night to day."

24 Badiou explains: "I will term evental site an entirely abnormal multiple; that is, a multiple such that none of its elements are presented in the situation. The site, itself, is presented, but 'beneath' it nothing from which it is composed is presented. As such, the site is not a part of the situation" (*BE* 175). Evental sites are, by definition, necessary constituents of events. See Meditation 17 of *Being and Event*. In *Logics of Worlds*, he renames this concept as "Trace (of an event) or evental trace" (596).

25 I choose to speak of ecological discourse instead of ecological or even environmental literature or texts, as Buell, for example, still has it in his *The Environmental Imagination* (1995: 6ff.), since this seems to imply that there is literature without "ecology" or "environment." Buell, in fact, prefers the term "'environmental criticism' or 'literary-environmental studies'" rather than "ecocriticism," since the latter is for him "less indicative" than the former two (2005: 11). This conceptual distinction is taken up by Buell when he argues for first- and second-wave ecocriticism, for example, in his "Ecocriticism: Some Emerging Trends." For a genealogy of the field, see Cheryll Glotfelty and Harold Fromm's introduction to *The Ecocriticism Reader*. For a problematization of various ecological and critical concepts, see, for instance, Timothy Morton's *The Ecological Thought*.

26 Both Garrard and Buell observe the problems with such anti-anthropocentric perspectives for ecocriticism as a positive political praxis. Trying to imagine a world without the human, let alone the animate, is not only a phenomenological problem of mediation but, for Garrard, also futile in the context of ecocriticism: "Only if we imagine that the planet has a future, after all, are we likely to take responsibility for it" (2013: 105).

27 Badiou defines the present as such: "We will call present, and write π, the set of consequences of the evental trace, as realized by the successive treatment of points"

(*LoW* 52). A present is, therefore, fundamentally dependent on a subject that continuously reiterates his/her fidelity to an event and perpetuates the present.

28   Badiou thereby vigorously rejects relativist ethics that undermine the possibility of "Good" and "Evil." Rather than employing the terms in a universalist manner, however, Badiou only sees these ethical processes as ineluctably related to an event and, consequently, to subjective procedures. See his *Ethics* as well as the subsequent chapter on Jess Walter's *The Zero*, which gives a more tangible example of this notion of "evil."

29   Tim Edwards, for instance, writes that "McCarthy's most recent novel offers a landscape blasted not by natural violence [as in Blood Meridian] but by human violence" (2008: 55). Edwards even goes so far as to see the cause of the bleak landscape as a nuclear attack: "In fact, in *The Road* the machine in McCarthy's garden is in fact 'The Bomb' itself, whose apocalyptic arrival as '[a] long shear of light and then a series of low concussions'" (ibid.: 45) leaves behind a cauterized world, frozen in nuclear winter—and, significantly, a landscape (deathscape, really) bleak and decidedly unromantic, a landscape, in a sense, without meaning" (ibid.: 56). Grindley, among others, also sees indicators of nuclear apocalypse (2008: 12).

30   Garrard shows that "several of the most influential books in the environmentalist canon make extensive use of the trope [of apocalypse], from Carson's *Silent Spring* through Paul Ehrlich's *The Population Bomb* (1972) to Al Gore's *Earth in the Balance*. Apocalyptic rhetoric is deployed in the activist literature of Earth First!, the philosophical reflections of Bill McKibben and the poetry of Robinson Jeffers. Even the commonplace notion of 'environmental crisis' is inflected by it" (101–02). Nevertheless, Garrard cautions that "the long-term dangers this approach [the apocalyptic one] poses for environmentalist causes may outweigh its rhetorical usefulness" (2013: 108), since "just like Christian millenialism, environmental apocalypticism has had to face the embarrassment of failed prophecy even as it has been unable to relinquish the trope altogether" (ibid.: 109). Buell equally insists that "in the era of *Cat's Cradle*, *Doctor Strangelove* and *Star Wars* it is hard for apocalypticism to keep a straight face" (1995: 300).

31   In respect of Rachel Carson's *Silent Spring*, Garrard notes: "So the founding text of modern environmentalism . . . relies on the literary genres of pastoral and apocalypse, pre-existing ways of imagining the place of humans in nature that may be traced back to such sources as *Genesis* and *Revelation*, the first and last books of the Bible" (2013: 2).

32   See Garrard (2013: 93ff.) or Thompson (1996: 3ff.).

33   Buell remarks upon this circular structure when writing that "we create images of doom to avert doom: that is the strategy of the jeremiad," while he is not certain "whether the same logic applies to the rhetoric of environmental apocalypse" (1995: 295). In *Writing for an Endangered World*, Buell also notes the oxymoronic disposition of ecoapocalypse as exhibited by Mahasweta Devi's Bengali novella "Pterodactyl": "As with all ecocatastrophe writing, the story's apocalypticism presumably aims to disconfirm itself" (2001: 232).

34   See, for instance, Estes, who argues that "the nightmare vision of a possible future in *The Road* shows readers all that stands to be lost in a catastrophe—natural, technological, or otherwise" (2013: 209). De Bruyn equally reads a cautionary function in the novel: "If we continue to carelessly fill our shopping carts and to

ignore the environmental problems which force some of us today to wear mouth masks, McCarthy suggests, our children may have to wear masks everywhere and carry their entire world in a grocery cart, like fundamentally homeless vagrants" (2010: 780).

35 While the proleptic dimension of ecoapocalypse certainly also lies on the level of reception, conjuring a horrific future in relation to the extra-textual present, this rhetorical and political strategy nevertheless insists that the present evils of human pollution initiate this apocalyptic holocaust.

36 The next chapter on *The Zero* outlines just such a mistaken perception of an event since, in the case of the novel's depiction of "9/11," one can apply an analysis of continuities that reject its nomination as an event.

37 Estes equally observes that the novel's event undermines nature-culture dichotomies: "Because the text never divulges the cause of the disaster we are never sure of whether the apocalyptic world of the text is the result of a natural phenomenon (a comet, for example), a religious event (the Rapture) or a manmade catastrophe (nuclear war)" (2013: 205).

38 Buell gives a summary of the concept of deep ecology: "a term introduced by Norwegian philosopher Arne Naess to distinguish Naess's biotically egalitarian vision of 'organisms as knots in the biospherical net or field of intrinsic relations' from 'shallow' environmentalist campaigns against 'pollution and resource depletion' chiefly for the 'health and affluence of people in the developed countries'" (2005: 137). Ecocentrism implies for Buell a "view in environmental ethics that the interest of the ecosphere must override that of the interest of individual species. Used like the semi-synonymous biocentrism in antithesis to anthropocentrism, but whereas biocentrism refers specifically to the world of organisms, ecocentrism points to the interlinkage of the organismal and the inanimate" (2005: 137). Timothy Morton's notion of the "ecological thought" expresses a similar philosophy: "The ecological view . . . is a vast, sprawling mesh of interconnection without a definite center or edge. It is radical intimacy, coexistence with other beings, sentient and otherwise—and how can we so clearly tell the difference? The ecological thought fans out into questions concerning cyborgs, artificial intelligence, and the irreducible uncertainty over what counts as a person. Being a person means never being sure that you're one. In an age of ecology without Nature, we would treat many more beings as people while deconstructing our ideas about what counts as people. Think *Blade Runner* or *Frankenstein*: the ethics of the ecological thought is to regard beings as people, without a concept of Nature" (2010: 8).

39 To be sure, Badiou also does not exclusively stress that subjects have to be human. Repeatedly, he thus speaks of works of arts being a subjective procedure, for instance, within an artistic generic procedure (*LoW* 68). Nevertheless, he seems to have humans in mind for subjective processes, which becomes particularly manifest when he speaks of the "'some-one' [that] is an animal of the human species" (*E* 44) or of his more recent figure of the subject as a "body" (see *Logics of Worlds*).

40 While a deconstructive reading would certainly point to the necessary interrelation between animate and inanimate entities, which seem just an extension of the binary between human and non-human or culture and nature that my reading seeks to avoid, I insist that the *The Road*'s ecological event introduces and insists upon this distinction, which might not have been discernible from the pre-eventual point of

view. Indeed, I read the novel and its event as reflecting on the possibility to think an inanimate world without an animate being to perceive it. This comes close to the recently elaborated thoughts of Graham Harman's object-oriented philosophy. See particularly his *The Quadruple Object*. For a circumspect introduction into this "speculative realism," see Julius Greve's "Object-Oriented Utopianism." See also Diedrich Diedrichsen's account of a new sense of the inanimate in contemporary culture in "Beseelung, Entdinglichung und die neue Attraktivität des Unbelebten."

41 Wilhelm intriguingly reads this scene as a still life (2008: 131).

42 Although set only in the former United States, there are also indications that the event is a global one.

43 Ellis writes on this passage: "Unraveled, and impossible to restore to their former relation in a complex system, they can be mourned for their loss even as anyone with children to worry about must hope that other arrangements might yet arise, and that one's own apocalypse might not spell the end for a generation to follow. This ambivalent nightmare expresses most forcefully these deepest fears, and yet its ending enacts a small promise of hope against that dimming away of the world" (2008: 36).

44 In fact, *Logics of Worlds* conceptualizes four subjective directions. Yet, the form of resurrection, which is analyzed in Chapter 5, could be seen as a subcategory of the faithful subject.

45 See particularly Badiou's chapter "On the Problem of Evil" in his *Ethics*. There, he argues that the Nietzschean notion of being beyond good and evil—or rather "beneath Good and Evil" (*E* 59)—accounts for normal situations. If, however, an event happens, there opens a window in which subjective fidelities occasion the distinction between faithful and reactive or obscure processes (*E* 59ff.). One also has to note that these positions are not absolute. To remain a faithful subject, it needs to repeatedly affirm the points of an event. While such a continuous subjective process will be depicted in the case of the amorous subject in Danielewski's *Only Revolution*, Pynchon's *Against the Day* shows that the failure of a subject to uphold its fidelity may just as well forsake its positive status and render it a reactive form.

46 See for instance, Kunsa, who observes that "the boy's mother committed suicide in fear of falling prey to such atrocities [of being eaten]. The father ponders a similar fate not a few times, but he does not acquiesce to suicide's lure; rather, he honors his responsibility" (2009: 59). This negative verdict is attested by Thomas A. Carlson, when he writes that "the mother's hopelessness, the failure of her heart, or the turn of her heart toward that darkness and death in which sorrowing itself is swallowed up, relate fundamentally if negatively to the question of world and time and their founding conditions in the openness of a possibility, which means founding a futurity and its past, that simply no longer appears to her. In the absolute closure of such possibility, in the total absence of death, she suggests, there is not only no life to live or love but also—what amounts to the same—nothing more to say, no story still to tell" (2007: 56). See also Wielenberg (2010: 9) or Wilhelm, who writes that "although the wife's reasons for committing suicide and merciful murder may seem logical, even rational, given the potential threats of rape, torture and cannibalism, McCarthy seems to drive the point home here that such a philosophy is untenable, even im- moral in the face of human suffering, whether there is a God or not" (2008: 135).

47 This dimension thus also attests to Badiou's antihumanism that he admits in his *Ethics* (5), which thereby distinguishes his theory from a simple return to humanistic notions of the subject.

48 See, for instance, Luce Irigaray's ecofeminist approach, as in her essay "There Can Be No Democracy without a Culture of Difference," as well as Christopher Cohoon's accompanying commentary "The Ecological Irigaray."

49 See particularly Sandra M. Gilbert's and Susan Gubar's seminal study *The Madwoman in the Attic*.

50 Estes is a notable exception.

51 Just one of a multitude of such instances can be grasped when the father, who continuously wants to uphold his rational superiority over his environment, is represented as such: "He'd little idea where the cart was and he thought that he was getting stupid and that his head wasn't working right" (*TR* 103). See also Estes (2013: 206).

52 See, for instance, Kunsa, Humann, or Ellis.

53 Faced with a "loss of memory, world and language" (2010: 783), De Bruyn, in referring to Robert Pogue Harrison, sees the father enacting processes of "lexification": father and son are "carrying the ancestral fire, the fire of lexification and human world-making, across the waste" (ibid.: 783).

54 Wilhelm notes that "objects become, then, intimately connected with the protagonists' very existence, some even to the point where they become psychologically embodied, and when they are lost or left behind, engender in the mind anxiety and something akin to the human sense of loss" (2008: 131–32).

55 Wilhelm equally argues that the father "performs the centuries-old ritual of preparing the meal as a sign of civilized humanity. . . . Since 'culture' has been destroyed in this narrative and belongs to the void in a sense, the father's replication of the civilizing function of still life seems a strategic attempt to maintain a sense of dignity and a meaningful connection to human history as a means of surviving in this raw new world, where barbarity and the threat of cannibalism continuously loom" (ibid.: 132).

56 This functionalizing relation to objects is equally observed by Wilhelm: "The father also seems to imbue other artifacts with agency, linking these objects to ancient still life elements as ritual helpers along the route of this nightmarish journey towards an afterlife" (ibid.: 132).

57 While Estes is certainly right that "the canned good is no longer in the realm of the simulacra, the free-floating play of signifiers irrevocably severed from any signified, but a unique item (or it will soon be unique as production has utterly ceased)" (2013: 203), the attitude that the father exhibits to these goods is marked by the wish to reinstate these modes of production.

58 The most obvious of such scenes is when they discover a bunker, which harbors "the richness of a vanished world" (*TR* 147). The paradisiac utopia that this nuclear bunker symbolizes may be grasped in the description of its contents as well as in the father's reaction to it: "Crate upon crate of canned goods. Tomatoes, peaches, beans, apricots. Canned hams. Corned beef. Hundred of gallons of water in ten gallon plastic jerry jugs. Paper towels, toiletpaper, paper plates. Plastic trashbags stuffed with blankets. . . . Oh my God, he said. . . . I found everything. Everything" (*TR* 146–47).

59 Following Benesch's definition of "technology" as "both a value system and a system of variegated technical applications, or, put differently, as an ideological symbolic pattern and a network of production" (2008: 8), narrative could certainly be viewed in such terms and simultaneously viewed as a structural symbolic order as well as a concrete facet of man-made appliances.

60 See particularly Daniel Luttrull's essay "Prometheus Hits *The Road*: Revising the Myth," which gives a historical account of the myth from Hesiod to Nietzsche. See also Estes, Kunsa, or Wielenberg, among others.

61 Estes goes on to show how the novel constructs a binary between more advanced forms of technology that father and son use, while the "bad guys" are often represented as employing inferior appliances.

62 Jane Bennett's influential and provocative *Vibrant Matter: a political ecology of things* is an interesting reference in this context. In chapter four, "A Life of Metal," she extends the Deleuzian vitalism she established in the foregoing chapters by considering whether the idea of "the conative drive or motility of simple or protobodies" can "be pulled away from its mooring in the physiological and organic" (2010: 53). She attempts to animate things that from an anthropocentric perspective are usually seen as inanimate. In referring to Deleuze's and Guattari's reflections on metal in *A Thousand Plateaus*, she suggests that metal like the shackles that hold Prometheus in Aeschylus's *Prometheus Bound* are not simply dead but, indeed, vibrant matter. "The aim here," she writes, "is to rattle the adamantine chain that has bound materiality to inert substance and that has placed the organic across a chasm from the inorganic" (ibid.: 57). While one could, indeed, use Bennett's analysis of the metal that holds Prometheus as a foil that undermines the binaries of animate and inanimate in *The Road*, I would like to uphold this binary for a particular reason. Instead of animating the inanimate, I read *The Road* as fictionalizing the event of the inanimate. This means that I reject endowing matter with organic properties, since this "*esprit de corps*" (ibid.: 60) is for me again inherently anthropocentric.

63 Luttrull's undimmed humanism can also be grasped when he writes that the novel argues "that humanity (or, more specifically, humaneness) does not rely upon the biosphere but rather stems from something innately human that transcends environment, finding its origin somewhere within the human consciousness or soul" (2010: 20).

64 This is not to say that there are no thematic echoes in *The Road* that have not already cropped up in his former novels. As I mentioned earlier, the general skepticism toward the "human" is an ongoing concern in McCarthy's fiction.

65 See, for instance, Estes's chapter on the novel.

66 Wilhelm has a different, more positive reading of this scene, arguing that "the father conceptualizes the son as an icon of religious significance and suggests the potential sacredness of the human mind" (2008: 136).

67 In both instances, the boy's defiance of the monological language acquisition by his father, with the latter wondering about a phrase he used, "where did you get that?" (*TR* 155), could be seen as an indicator of the son's emancipation from his father's didactic input. However, one might also interpret it as the son becoming a self-sustaining system that has now acquired the ability to produce language itself rather than merely reflecting what it has learned, thereby playing into the hands of the father's scheme of perpetuating human existence and, with it, language.

68 See, for example, Glotfelty and Fromm's introduction.

Chapter 3

1 By referring to the happenings of September 11, 2001 as "9/11," this chapter tries to point to the exceptionalist absorption of the incident in its nomination and thereby undermines its status as an event. This rejects Derrida's argument that "by pronouncing 9/11 we do not use language in its obvious referring function but rather press it to name something that it cannot name because it happens beyond language: terror and trauma" (Borradori 2003: 148).

2 See, particularly, the special issue of *American Studies*, guest-edited by Andrew Gross and Maryann Snyder-Körber.

3 See, especially, Sabine Sielke's article "Why '9/11 is [not] unique' or: Troping Trauma."

4 It is obviously difficult to arrive at a clear and ultimate interpretation of how works of fiction relate to "9/11." Martin Randall's *9/11 and the Literature of Terror* does, however, make a convincing case in showing how fictional narratives dealing with September 11 that have become canonical, particularly seemingly realist novels such as Don DeLillo's *Falling Man*, Claire Messud's *The Emperor's Children*, Martin Amis's collection *The Second Plane*, Ian McEwan's *Saturday*, or even the more experimental *Windows on the World* by Frédéric Beigbeder, simply memorialize and sacralize rather than critically reflect on the happenings (Randall 7). Critics have also attempted to paint a linear movement of responses to 9/11, some arguing for a "transition of narratives of rupture to narratives of continuity" (Keniston et al. 2008: 3), others for the exact opposite development (Randall 2011: 1).

5 See Baudrillard's *The Spirit of Terrorism* or *Philosophy 9/11* edited by Timothy Shanahan.

6 After Francis Fukuyama's much debated eponymous diagnosis of the end of history, Baudrillard regards "9/11" as a stimulus for terminating the reign of neoliberalism and globalization (Hetzel 273). See Thorsten Schüller's essay "Kulturtheorien nach 9/11" for a summary of how postcolonial studies engaged in a new sense of conflict.

7 Birgit Däwes observes how "'change' has turned into the most prominent association with the date" (2011: 72). Däwes mentions Marianne Hirsch, Dori Laub and René Girard as proponents of evoking radical aesthetic, historical and cultural changes (ibid.: 72–73). Even though Alfred Hornung's essay "Flying Planes Can Be Dangerous" draws a longer line of what he perceives to be "ground zero fiction," detecting first generic aspects in novels that were written before 2001, he nevertheless argues that 9/11 "reinstated a sense of concrete reality" (2004: 390), since "with the collapse of the buildings and the real deaths of people, postmodern assumptions and cherished ideas also collapsed and were grounded" (403). Whether fiction in the twenty-first century, particularly in relation to "9/11," actually follows this "groundedness" will be discussed in the following. Mita Banerjee also argues that "September 11 . . . could well be considered not only the ground zero of American literature and the American nation, but also the ground zero of the very paradigm of postcolonial studies" (2007: 309). See also Roger Rosenblatt's article in the *Time Magazine* "The Age Of Irony Comes To An End."

8 Habermas even suggests seeing "9/11" as "the first historic world event in the strictest sense: the impact, the explosion, the slow collapse—everything that was not Hollywood anymore but, rather, a gruesome reality, literally took place in front of the 'universal eyewitness' of a global public" (Borradori 2003: 28).

9   It seems not only questionable to insist that "9/11" had a large-scale impact on literary production but the attempt to conceive of a whole literary genre, what Hornung and Däwes term, although on slightly different grounds, "Ground Zero fiction," or Randall the "literature of terror," also falls prey to definitional unclarity and becomes consequently so encompassing that it renders itself oblique. This can be seen, for example, in Däwes's very inclusive understanding of "9/11" novels, also taking into consideration, for instance, Dave Egger's *Zeitoun*, which, simply because of its temporal setting and discussion of coercion and arbitrary imprisonment, is supposedly part of this genre. Däwes's attempt to furnish a working set of "9/11" novels, however malleable her conception of the genre, ultimately cannot evade the risk of homogenization. Arguing that there is a "process of 'rewriting'" (2011: 70) eminent in all "9/11" novels is just not true. The tip of the iceberg is probably Richard Gray, who argues that "it is surely right to see [Cormac McCarthy's] *The Road* as a post-9/11 novel" (2011: 39).

10 Däwes equally attests that "after September 11, the nexus between historical circumstances and their narrative representation has come into particular focus through the terminology of the 'event'" (2011: 70).

11 Hollywood's symbolic premediation of September 11 has been commented on by a variety of critics. See, for instance, Slavoj Žižek, who writes that "America got what it fantasized about" (2002: 16) in such movies as *Independence Day*, or *Escape from New York*. See also Däwes (2011: 99–105), Gray (2011: 9–11), Michael Rothberg's "Seeing Terror, Feeling Art. Public and Private in Post-9/11 Literature," E. Ann Kaplan's *Trauma Culture* (2005: 13), or Judith Greenberg's introduction to *Trauma at Home: After 9/11* (2003: xx).

12 In *Infinite Thought*, Badiou claims that "the 'war against Islamic terrorism' takes over from the Cold (and Hot: Korea, Vietnam, Cuba . . .) War against communism" (107) and therefore attests to the continuity of this political incident. While denying the happening the status of an event, Badiou nevertheless mourns the "death of many thousands of common people and ordinary workers deep in the heart of a great metropolis" (106).

13 See, for example, Jacques Derrida's essay "Deconstructing Terrorism" in Borradori's *Philosophy in a Time of Terror*, Noam Chomsky's *9–11*, Michael Hardt's and Antonio Negri's *Multitude*, or David Holloway's *9/11 and the War on Terror*.

14 Hoth argues that realistic depictions of September 11 are dominating (2011: 114).

15 *Only Revolutions* integrates the happening in its chronomosaic, a historical column that lists various, often haphazard, historical "events." The novel's collocation of the by now iconic signifiers "North Tower" and "South Tower" with "Beckham's kick" or the death of "Nathan Chapman" (S277) thus simultaneously questions the equivalence of "9/11" to an "absolute event" (Baudrillard 2002: 4). By juxtaposing various "historical" happenings in a dispersed conglomerate of data, which will be discussed in more detail at a later point of this study, *Only Revolutions* is representative of part of the discourse surrounding, constructing, and undermining "9/11" and its nomination as an event.

16 In portraying a literally inversed world in which the United States is a rogue state while the United Arab States declares a War on Terror, *The Mirage* readily assumes its fictional potential in order to create a world in which "9/11" has the status of an event. The novel thereby extends a mere historiographic metafictional technique in

order to create a world in which "9/11" is radically different and implies the potential for faithful subject formation.

17　McLaughlin, among others, argues in respect to *Against the Day* that "the novel in its structure and its themes works against the desire of power to reduce 9/11 to a single narrative" (2013: 291). *Bleeding Edge*, Pynchon's most recent novel, is set in New York City during the time of the attack. While it mediates the radical impact it had on the city's inhabitants, it simultaneously rejects the discourse of the death of irony as well as the happening's absolute contingency when its character Conkell "foresmells" the attack, thereby obviously alluding to Slothrop's erections before the V-2 rockets strike.

18　Badiou defines the obscure subject in two different ways. His *Ethics* proposes the definition that is taken by this chapter. In contrast to *Ethics*, *Logics of Worlds* does not comment any longer on the possibility of an obscure subject also coming into existence by mistaking a happening for an event. However, while in *Logics of Worlds* it is "Islamism" that for Badiou manifests "the present-day incarnation of the obscure subject" (Toscano 2006: 29), I want to suggest that such obscure subjective processes can also be seen on the part of the American people itself.

19　Badiou depicts how the religious as well as philosophical conception of Evil is conducted in negative terms: "Ethics is conceived here [according to Kant's categorical imperative] both as an *a priori* ability to discern Evil (for according to the modern usage of ethics, Evil—or the negative—is primary: we presume a consensus regarding what is barbarian), and as the ultimate principle of judgment, in particular political judgment: good is what intervenes visibly against an Evil that is identifiable *a priori*" (*E* 8).

20　In *Infinite Thought,* Badiou equally argues that "'terrorism' is a non-existent substance, an empty name" (110).

21　For similar arguments that connect September 11 with sublimity, see Miles Orvell's "After 9/11: Photography, the Destructive Sublime, and the Postmodern Archive," or Terry Castle's *New Yorker* 9/11 encyclopedia entry on Karlheinz Stockhausen, subtitled "The unsettling question of the sublime."

22　Hallward notes that in Badiou's system, "only those who remain actively faithful to the implications of an event can grasp them at all. To 'perceive' an event as an event is in no sense to appreciate it at a safe distance (as Kant admired the French Revolution, say). The truth is true only for its subjects, not for its spectators" (2003: 128).

23　See, for instance, Baudrillard's claim that the attack finally caused the breakdown of the reign of simulacra.

24　By experiencing the victims' suffering by way of mediation, the spectator does not need to distance himself/herself from the experience of death in order to cope with it. A form of distancing is already implied by the medium (my translation).

25　See Don DeLillo's "In the Ruins of the Future," where he approaches the created moment of unrepresentability from a spatial perspective: "There is something empty in the sky. The writer tries to give memory, tenderness and meaning to all that howling space." Even Derrida tunes in into that rhetoric: "We do not know what we are talking about. . . . 'Something' took place. . . . But this very thing, the place and meaning of this 'event,' remains ineffable, like an intuition without concept . . . out of range for a language that admits its powerlessness and so is reduced to pronouncing mechanically a date, repeating it endlessly . . . a rhetorical refrainment that admits to not knowing what it's talking about" (Borradori 2003: 86). Particularly, trauma studies have focused on the matter of how the traumatic event has led to moments of inexpressibility. For a critique of this approach, see Sielke's "Why '9/11 is [not] unique' or: Troping Trauma."

26 Randall writes: "Not only has a certain kind of realist fiction generally failed to identify and describe the 'wounds' left after the attacks but that furthermore other more hybrid forms have helped to reveal the profound difficulties of representing such a visually resonant, globally accessible and historically significant event" (2011: 3).

27 Another such comic instance is when Brian's son Edgar mourns his father's death, knowing full well that Brian is alive and kicking.

28 See Giorgio Agamben's *Homo Sacer: Sovereign Power and Bare Life.*

29 Agamben thereby shows that Carl Schmitt's notion of sovereignty, according to which he is sovereign "who decides on the state of exception" (Schmitt in Agamben 1998: 11), has to be viewed in the light of processes that only create the liminal figure of the *homo sacer.* In this context, the *homo sacer* is not simply an exclusion necessary for the constitution of political orders but, rather, constitutes, like the sovereign, the very foundations of every form of politics as biopolitics.

30 In *The Rebirth of History,* Badiou reflects on such national processes of stereotyping, which he calls "*separating names*" (77).

31 Badiou, however, also claims that the attack was a crime that "formally, is fascist" (*IT* 107).

32 Agamben gives an overview of anthropological, psychological, and sociological discussions of the ambivalent nature of the sacred in the second chapter of *Homo Sacer.*

33 Through the place's analogy to such sites as Guantanamo Bay and Abu Ghraib, there is a particular parallel to Agamben's diagnosis of Nazi concentration camps, which for him are the epitome of biopolitics (1998: 166ff.). Agamben goes on to say that "if the essence of the camp consists in the materialization of the state and in the subsequent creation of a space in which bare life and the juridical rule enter into a threshold of indistinction, then we must admit that we find ourselves virtually in the presence of a camp every time such a structure is created, independent of the kinds of crime that are committed there and whatever its denomination and specific topography" (ibid.: 174). Moreover, Agamben insists that "as the absolute space of exception the camp is topologically different from a simple space of confinement," (ibid.: 20) such as disciplinary institutions.

34 For a superb introduction and overview of postmodernist crime fiction, see Susan Elizabeth Sweeney's "Crime in postmodernist fiction."

Chapter 4

1 See, for example, Sascha Pöhlmann (2009: 65), Hanjo Berressem (2012: 217), Katherine N. Hayles (167), or Brian McHale (2011: 141).

2 See Pöhlmann, who points to this critical commonplace (2012: 5).

3   While the relation to the other is certainly palpable even in their very first words that contain the other character ("Samara" [H1] and "Haloes" [S1]), I insist, with Badiou, that only an event makes it possible to construct a whole world that depends on this difference. In *In Praise of Love*, Badiou writes that "it is essential to grasp that the construction of the world on the basis of difference is quite distinct from the experience of difference. Levinas's vision starts from the irreducible experience of the face of the other, an epiphany that is grounded in God as 'the Almighty Other'. The experience of otherness is central, because it is the foundation stone of ethics. In a great religious tradition, love also becomes an ethical sentiment *par excellence*. In my view, there is nothing particularly 'ethical' about love as such" (24).

4   McHale makes a similar argument about the novel being the most typical poem in world literature in his eponymous essay. He particularly sees segmentivity and structurality as decisive aspects of the book's lyric character.

5   Influences on this type of textual representation can be traced back to modernist poets such as E. E. Cummings, but it arguably only flourished in its technological realization with postmodernist writers such as Raymond Federman, B. S. Johnson, John Barth, and Kurt Vonnegut. See *The Routledge Companion to Experimental Literature* edited by Joe Bray, Alison Gibbons, and Brian McHale. In his essay "Print interface to time: *Only Revolutions* at the crossroads of narrative and history," Hansen argues that Danielewski's novel "is, in its own right, a revolution in literary form, composition and typography," which he connects to the book's inherent immersion in the "digital textual condition" (2011: 178–79). Joe Bray and Alison Gibbons observe that the novel's structural idea harkens back to Milorad Pavić's *The Inner Side of the Wind, or The Novel of Hero and Leander* (2011: 5).

6   "Chronomosaic" is a term introduced by Danielewski himself. It refers to the list placed at the center of each double page. Critics have attempted to show the interconnection between the chronomosaic and the two narratives: see, for instance, Pöhlmann, who calls it the "history gutter," or Hansen's essay.

7   Sean O'Hagan puts *Only Revolutions* in a row with Pynchon's *Gravity's Rainbow*, Burroughs' *Naked Lunch*, and Joyce's *Finnegans Wake*. Danielewski's mentioning of Jacques Derrida in an interview leads Leonard to perceive "an affinity between his [Derrida's] understanding of representation and subjectivity and Danielewski's" (51). McHale, moreover, in referring to his theory of the postmodernist ontological dominant, writes that unlike modernist narratives, *Only Revolutions* disallows the integration of Sam's and Hailey's stories into a comprehensive unity (2011: 141).

8   Evans explains that the big Other is not only manifested in language but also finds its first "subjective" expression in the mother (1996: 133). One might further speculate whether the chronomosaic could be seen as the symbolic order that determines their subject formation. However, as I will show in the following pages, there is a crucial difference between chronomosaic and Hailey's and Sam's narrative that escapes the subjective determinism that is latent in the symbolic order.

9   See Vladimir Propp's *Morphology of the Folktale*.

10 See Hayles's essay on the novel's relation to data and information.

11 This is also not to say that there are no connections between the narratives and the chronomosaic. Instead, "the characters' colloquial language is appropriate to the period" (Hayles 2011: 167). In Sam's narrative, for example, there appear "BEATNIKS" (S270) when the history gutter dates 1956. On January 26, 2003, Sam

and Hailey "ricochet away by Iraqi forces, UN forces" (H280). Hayles, like Hansen, is convinced that the novel achieves "a hybridisation of narrative with data, temporality with spatiality, and personal myth with collective national identity" (159). However, she also concedes that any concrete "correlation with the narratives are elusive at best" (2011: 165–66).

12 A very basic problem to the insistence on the narrative dependence on the history gutter is the fact that if Sam's narrative would start with the coinciding beginning of the chronomosaic on November 22, 1863, he would never meet Hailey, since her narrative life would only commence on November 22, 1963. Additionally, Hailey's accompanying chronomosaic ends in 2006, while she continues to live.

13 Despite its global aspiration, one cannot deny the fact that the novel in both Hailey's and Sam's narrative as well as in the chronomosaic "is set firmly in the U.S.A." (Pöhlmann 2009: 66). Pöhlmann, moreover, notes that the history gutter creates the "illusion of objectivity" (ibid.: 72) in concealing the historiographer's voice, which he takes to be that of the Creep.

14 Although McHale sees a similar structural paradigm latent in Sam's and Hailey's narratives, I will show in the following how the relation to the event still presents a critical difference. Moreover, this does not mean that Hailey's and Sam's narratives do not also imply forms of enumeration and list making. Particularly their cataloging of animals, plants, and cars have to be considered as underlying the enumerative principle, what Hayles differentiates as a form of data collection rather than the chronomosaic's data "assemblage" (2011: 163). A plain difference subsists in the fact that the chronomosaic lists what would generally be defined as events, while Sam and Hailey list animate and inanimate objects. Sharing the structural mode of making lists does not imply that its relation to events is the same as well.

15 The systemic movements of différance that inhabit every list would somewhat undermine Umberto Eco's historical argument of the beginning of the excessive list with Rabelais (2009: 250). Eco, however, for me seems to have a point in arguing that the excessive list as well as the chaotic enumeration show an increase in modern and postmodern literature (ibid.: 254). Eco distinguishes between the excessive list and, in referring to Leo Spitzer, the chaotic enumeration (ibid.). While excessive lists may, nevertheless, be coherent and conjunctive (ibid.: 279, 321), chaotic enumerations cannot be subsumed under a grander principle (323). Eco's general distinction between lists that concentrate on a signified and others focusing on its constituent signifiers (ibid.: 324) seems problematic as an approach.

16 Particularly because Danielewski constructed the chronomosaic by asking for input from his fan community, Hansen raises the question as to what extent the various historical incidents can be seen as "an allegory of his [Danielewski's] generation's collectively experienced and collectively selected history" (2011: 187).

17 Van Hulle's connection to *Finnegans Wake*, the novel's own citing of *Tristan and Isolde* and *Romeo and Juliet*, or parallels to Whitman (Pöhlmann 2012: 5) are just a few examples indicating such an intertextual awareness. See also Berressem's article for a more elaborate account of the novel's literary forerunners.

18 Paul Crumbley's *Inflections of the Pen* makes a prominent point in orthographically discriminating up to sixteen dash types for what generally was printed as a simple em-dash. As a consequence, one has to be aware that the dashes cannot be reduced to a single function because of "the varying significance of Emily Dickinson's marks" (Lindberg-Seyersted 1976: 30).

19 Pöhlmann's essay points to the similarities between Whitman and Danielewski in terms of aesthetics and politics (2012: 5ff.). Hayles equally attests that their narratives are conveyed in "free verse" (2011: 164).

20 DuPlessis conceives of this, according to McHale, as "the kind of writing that is articulated by sequenced, gapped lines and whose meanings are created by occurring in bounded units . . . operating in relation to . . . pause or silence" (2011: 144).

21 Eleanor Wilner, for instance, holds that "the dash, that verbal sign which both divides and connects, which rushes forward and yet, simultaneously, arrests" (1971: 126) thus interconnects, rather than sequesters.

22 Although Derrida's crossing out implies two lines that chiasmatically meet in the middle, an appropriation from Heidegger, Hayles sees a similar reference in the novel's anti-concordance located by the end pages (2011: 168). A key difference that marks the *sous rature* of the event is, however, that the em-dash effaces nothing, while there is still language visible in the anti-concordance. One might also speculate to what extent the novel, which visually is grounded on spheroid motives, count-as-ones, here introduces a mark that approximates ontology's proper form of being, the void Ø as Badiou delineates in Meditation One of *Being and Event*.

23 Next to these canonical couples, Pöhlmann, moreover, observes the novel's referencing of Bonnie and Clyde, Eva and Adolf and Baader and Meinhof (2009: 67), the latter two certainly problematizing the very idea of couples.

24 Evans argues that the often-quoted sentence "il n'y a pas de rapport sexuel," traditionally translated as "there is no such thing as a sexual relationship" should "better be rendered 'there is no relation between the sexes'" (1996: 181). For me, both translations grasp the relational impossibility that is important for Badiou's argument.

25 Sex is, according to Badiou, not the only constituent element of the generic procedure of love. Founding a family, or "the birth of a child [are] part of love" (*IpoL* 33). However, one should not conclude that these aspects are "the fulfillment of love" (*IpoL* 33), but they are, rather, symbolic repetitions that perpetuate the encounter.

26 I would distinguish this reading from, what for Pöhlmann is a continuous ontological paradigm: "They themselves are constantly becoming" (2009: 69). Only after the emergence of the event is this process of becoming a subject initiated. Moreover, this process is not one of identitarian flux. They cannot simply choose to assume their prior identity after they have accepted the event.

27 Strictly speaking, "couple" is a problematic term. Badiou is eager to point out that one must "carefully distinguish love from the 'couple.' The couple is what, of love, is visible to a third" (*C* 187). This third position does not exist for Badiou, since "the phenomenal appearance of the couple, which is submitted to an external law of count, does not say anything about love. The couple names not love but the state (or the State) of love. It names not the presentation but the representation of love" (*C* 187).

28 See particularly Pöhlmann's "The Democracy of Two."

29 Pöhlmann, like Hayles, writes that Hailey and Sam are "mythical characters" (2009: 67). I would specify this argument in insisting that they only become mythical figures at the end of the novel, when confronted with the death of the other. While they do convey a "mythical quality, [being] at once particular and universal" (ibid.: 67), one could ascribe their own characterization as mythical creatures to their exuberant self-aggrandizement. Their becoming constituents of a mythical

narrative only at the end would make sense in the light of their having to address a larger audience, which is fundamental for the creation of every myth.

Chapter 5

1 This obviously recalls Jacques Rancière's important book *The Politics of Aesthetics*. In contrast, Badiou sees politics and aesthetics as "two distinct truth procedures" (*C* 152). For a more elaborate account of the relationship between art and politics, see his chapter "The infinite" in *The Century*.

2 Such an essentialist category is certainly wanting, which already intimates itself in the question of whether Frederick Douglass was an "African American" or if one can compare Wright's naturalism with Whitehead's postmodernism, a consideration that is pertinent to Warren's argument. In the course of this chapter I will propose an alternative of how one might gather such literary works into one "set."

3 In his essay "Post-Black, Old Black" Paul C. Taylor's observes that the essentialist understanding of "black artists" "limits artists to black influences and black topics, and saddles them with the burden of inhabiting the art world most saliently as Black Artists. So if they do not draw principally on, say, black vernacular cultures, or express perspectives on racialized themes like lynching, slavery, or Civil rights, then they aren't black enough to gain entry to the art world on the only terms available to them" (2007: 632). By adding Richard Powers's *The Time of Our Singing* to this list, questions of authorial essentialisms might be questioned to an even more complex extent. Powers's novel interrogates similar issues as *Slumberland*, by even touching upon all four generic conditions. I will elaborate on the novel's creation of a subject of the event in the conclusion of this book.

4 For a seminal, essentialist take on black identity, see particularly Langston Hughes's "The Negro Artist and the Racial Mountain." For a nationalist point of view, see especially "The Negro-Art Hokum" by George S. Schuyler. See also Taylor's essay for an overview of the post-black discourse. Taylor observes that "the idea of post-blackness . . . derives from the work of [Thelma] Golden" (2007: 626). Particularly her curatory work at the Studio Museum in Harlem is said to have initiated the discourse on Post-Blackness. The concept of "Post-soul" had been circulating before that, probably first in Nelson George's 1992 *Baps, B-Boys Buppies, Bohos: Notes on Post-Soul Black Culture*.

5 There he writes that "every faithful subject can also reincorporate into the eventual present the fragment of truth whose bygone present had sunk under the bar of occultation. It is this reincorporation that we call resurrection" (*LoW* 66). While Badiou has also written about the notion of resurrection in *Saint Paul*, it relates more to the process of Jesus's resurrection as an event itself and not the actual process of resurrecting a bygone event. Also, while Toscano conceives of resurrection as a sovereign subjective procedure next to faithfulness, reactivity, and obscurantism, I see it as simply a subspecies of a faithful process.

6 In the following, I will refer to this political event as the event of emancipation. Since the resurrection of the Spartacus event always implies a new event and does not rest on the detection of an "original" founding event, my interpretation of the event of African American emancipation does not specifically rely on deciding

upon a first event but is more interested in the guiding structure of fighting the excess of representation over belonging. In *Infinite Thought* Badiou defines equality as meaning that "a political actor is represented under the sole sign of his or her specifically human capacity" (53). He goes on to note the importance of understanding that " 'equality' does not refer to anything objective. It is not a question of an equality of status, of income, of function, and even less of the supposedly egalitarian dynamics of contracts or reforms. Equality is subjective. . . . Such equality is in no way a social program. Moreover, it has nothing to do with the social. It is a political maxim, a prescription. Political equality is not what we want or plan, it is what we declare under fire of the event, here and now, as what is, and not what should be" (*IT* 54).

7   In *Infinite Thought* Badiou explains that his emphasis on the destructive qualities of events that he still maintained in his *Theory of the Subject* are grounded in the fact that back then, "political truth was paradigmatic" (133) for him. Although he has certainly widened his scope since then and also contemplates the productive energies of events, these forms of "creativity" (*IT* 132) are more to be situated in the fields of art, science, and love.

8   It is telling that Badiou's examples for political events are revolutions. See, for instance, his *Logics of Worlds*, which lists the political sequences "73-71 BC for Spartacus, 1905-1917 for Bolshevism, 1792-94 for the Jacobins, 1965-68 for the Cultural Revolution in China" (72). While Badiou's early work, particularly *Theory of the Subject*, still upholds a notion of "creative destruction," he modifies this into "subtractive destruction" in his later work. See Colin Wright's article "The violence of the new: Badiou's subtractive destruction and Gandhi's satyagraha." However, even though Badiou alters his understanding of political violence, his political procedures all too often imply a notion of material revolution. See also his *The Rebirth of History*, where he writes that "collective mass action can only take the form of a riot, at best directed towards its historical form, which is also called a 'mass movement' " (40).

9   I have written more elaborately on this matter in the theoretical part of this book. For Badiou's simultaneous debt and development of Marx's dialectical materialism, see his preface to *Logics of Worlds*, where he conceives of a "materialist dialectic" (1–5).

10 See Badiou's notion of the community as expressed in Chapter 10 of *Conditions*. Badiou's notion of the community shares some similarities with Rancière's notion of the ethical community: "The political community thus tends to be transformed into an ethical community, into a community that gathers together a single people in which everyone is supposed to be counted. Only this procedure of counting comes up against that problematic remainder that it terms 'the excluded'. However, it is crucial to note that this term itself is not univocal. The excluded can mean two very different things. In the political community, the excluded is a conflictual actor, an actor who includes himself as a supplementary political subject, carrying a right not yet recognized or witnessing an injustice in the existing state of right. But in the ethical community, this supplement is no longer supposed to arise, since everyone is included. As a result, there is no status for the excluded in the structuration of the community" (2010: 189). Chapter 2 of *The Road* also illustrates that the absolute contingency of an event may also call for the abandonment of human life itself, which clearly runs against the grain of a Marxist teleology, which is essentially focused on working humans.

11 Warren is particularly critical of this gesture: "I think it important to see that a political and social analysis centered on demonstrating that current inequalities are simply more subtle attempts to reestablish the terms of racial hierarchy that existed for much of the twentieth century misunderstands both the nature of the previous regime and the defining elements of the current one" (2011: 5). See also Glenda Carpio who approves of Warren in claiming that it is an "empty goal of pointing to the obvious as if it were a revelation—mainly, that racism persists and that we should look to the history of racial trauma to discover why" (2013: 386).

12 One certainly has to differentiate between race and racism, a distinction that is not always being upheld in the criticism. My argument insists that even though in a post-race time, that is, a time where race as a stable essentialist concept is maintained, there are still racist practices dominating in (American) society.

13 Sowell ponders: "I suppose being East German was a lot like being black—the constant sloganeering, the protest songs, no electricity or long-distance telephone service" (*SL* 118). For an analysis of East Germany and its inhabitants in the novel, see Elisa Schweinfurth's article " 'They looked German, albeit with even tighter pants and uglier shoes, but there was something different about them': The Function of East and West Germany and the Fall of the Berlin Wall in Paul Beatty's *Slumberland*."

14 George Blaustein has equally observed that "*Slumberland* is about two supposedly grand historical 'ends': the formal end of Jim Crow with the crossing of the color line, and the oft-cited 'end of history' that followed the fall of the Berlin Wall" (2010: 730).

15 To repeat Badiou's purism, he writes in *Saint Paul* that "the crucible in which what will become a work of art and thought burns is brimful with nameless impurities; it comprises obsessions, beliefs, infantile puzzles, various perversions, undivulgeable memories, haphazard reading, and quite a few idiocies and chimeras. Analyzing this alchemy is of little use" (2003: 2).

16 Warren generally insists that with the end of the Jim Crow era, the collective project of African American literature lost its basis (2011: 2).

17 In "Author as Producer," Benjamin inquires into the relation between a political tendency and literary quality. He contends that political progressiveness is tantamount to literary quality. However, this implies for him that a work of art is only progressive, that is, it supports the proletarian class struggle, if it concomitantly revolutionizes the formal constraints of the medium it is engaging in.

18 One can glimpse this literary awareness, for example, in the opening scene's allusion to Ellison's *Invisible Man* (Blaustein 2010: 727) or the title of Part 3 "The Souls of Black Volk" (*SL* 107). Madhu Dubey argues in respect to Beatty's previous novel *White Boy Shuffle* that his "frenziedly eclectic style, characterized by pastiche and heteroglossia, is as thoroughly postmodern as [Ishmael] Reed's, even as it evacuates this style of any kind of liberatory political possibility" (2011: 168). While the same techniques are employed in *Slumberland*, I argue that this is part and parcel of a "liberatory political possibility" that takes root in an event.

19 Taylor cites Soraya Murray and Derek Conrad Murray's definition of "post-black": "Terms like 'post-black,' and 'post-soul aesthetic' . . . are being coined to try and capture what appears to be a distinctive shift in a generation that has grown up after the civil rights era" (qtd. in Taylor 2007: 640).

20 See Michelle Alexander's *The New Jim Crow: Mass Incarceration in the Age of Colorblindness* for a more thorough investigation of how disciplinary measures and

practices of incarceration still prevail in contemporary America. Marlon Ross also notes that "as Michelle Alexander and others have pointed out, Jim Crow effectively still exists because one set of racial barriers and exclusions has been replaced with another set designed to lock out the majority of African Americans after the legal disestablishment of segregation" (2013: 398). Taylor equally observes that "race may have declined in significance in the sense that the causes of racial stratification have less than ever before to do with overt exclusion and racism. But it remains profoundly significant in light of the distinctly racialized patterns of disadvantage that result from, for example, the ostensibly race-neutral policies that govern policing and wealth transference" (2007: 636).

21 One has to say that *Slumberland* offers a rather naïve take on Germans who readily incorporate the cultural narratives they consume, some never reflecting these narratives in the slightest.

22 As a matter of fact, in reflecting on the sociological mechanisms of simplification, the novel, uses a similar form of stereotyping, thereby pointing simultaneously to the problematic structure of this psychological work as well as its inevitability.

23 By assuming a poststructuralist/psychoanalytic stance, as Lott does, one could certainly point to ways in which minstrelsy embodies "less the incarnation of an age-old racism than an emergent social semantic figure highly responsive to the emotional demands and troubled fantasies of its audiences" (2012: 6).

24 The set theoretical relations of belonging ($\in$) and inclusion ($\subset$) are the most fundamental and, indeed, sole operators in Badiou's mathematical ontology. Yet, they are not merely mathematical symbols but, through the polyvalence of their names, also directly apply to political spheres. For a thorough investigation of the political dimensions of Badiou's set theory, see Norris, who writes that Badiou sketches out "a conception of political justice grounded in the clear-cut distinction between two set-theoretical concepts, namely those of *belonging* and *inclusion*" (2009: 91).

25 It also rejects a notion of difference, by which Warren observes that "merely including the Negro within American society as it exists would be tantamount to the Negro's giving up something significant—something lofty—for something tawdry, to accepting a mess of pottage for one's birthright" (2011: 27), which was ultimately a "scam perpetuated by a black elite for securing its dominance" (ibid.: 28).

26 Those committed to a meaningful African American literature, after all, did not want merely "to assimilate African Americans into the dominant order as it was," since mere inclusion "would be tantamount to the Negro's giving up something significant—something lofty—for something tawdry, to accepting a mess of pottage for one's birthright" (ibid.: 27).

27 As has been shown in the theory chapter of this study, the fact that evental truths are eternal and infinite also means that political fidelity toward an event is an endless struggle without an end in sight.

28 See, for instance, Ali's *Mixed-Race, Post-Race: Gender, New Ethnicities and Cultural Practices*. In fact, the very concept of "post-racism" faces similar problems of immanence as "postmodernism," "poststructuralism," "postcolonialism," etc. To be sure, post-race discussions certainly do not argue for the absence of racism in society but rather undermine the concept of race from a systemic point of view.

29 For the proponents of an ethics of recognition, see Böhm's, Kley's, and Schönleben's introduction to *Ethik—Anerkennung—Gerechtigkeit*, which singles out Charles Taylor, Paul Ricoeur, or Emmanuel Levinas.

30 This would then be a possible way of gathering works of art that embody political faithfulness into a set. Instead of speaking of "black" or African American literature, one could see a family resemblance in such works in their participation in politico-aesthetic fidelities.

31 See also his chapter "Philosophy and the 'Death of Communism,'" where he asks: "How could the 'death of communism' be the name of an event once we remark that every historical [political] event is communist, inasmuch as 'communist' designates the trans-temporal subjectivity of emancipation?" (*IT* 98). In fact, Badiou goes on to argue, "The ruin of the Party-State is a process immanent to *the history of States*" (*IT* 104) and not immanent to communism itself.

32 In fact, although Taylor rightly observes that "'post'[Black]-talk implies an end of history argument" (2007: 626), I seek to reverse the argument within my interpretation of the novel, maintaining that the novel's post-History talk is situated in its investigation of the end of the blackness argument.

33 Norris, to repeat it again, observes that Badiou "maintains that certain episodes commonly thought of as major, even epochal events—such as the collapse of soviet-type communism in 1989–1991 or the 2001 attack on the Twin Towers in New York—should instead be viewed as the dramatic, yet in many ways perfectly intelligible (if not predictable), outcome of developments already in train." (2009: 160–61).

34 Although Blaustein has already remarked that *Slumberland* "anticipates Warren's critique but is also symptomatic of it" (2010: 726), my reading of the novel suggests a different, more critical relation between the novel and Warren's arguments.

35 In fact, Warren's argument to radically historicize African American literature is antithetical to postmodernist attempts to undo historical categories, particularly of literary historical nature.

36 To glimpse part of the lively dispute, see the special issues of both the *MLA* and the *PMLA*, which feature various responses to Warren's controversial claims. In the same issue of *PMLA*, Warren himself responds to his critics (2013).

37 Warren distances himself from a larger view of African American literature that seeks to establish its influences in African culture (2011: 2), such as Henry Louis Gates Jr. in *Signifying Monkey*, and equally refrains from seeing post–Jim Crow black literature as part of this constellation (ibid.: 6).

38 Black literature in the Jim Crow era would, according to Warren, be "evaluated instrumentally, in terms of whether or not it could be added to the arsenal of arguments, achievements, and propositions needed to attack the justification for, and counteract the effects of, Jim Crow" (ibid.: 10).

39 Taylor observes that the beginning of the "post-black" or "post-soul" era is to be situated after the end of the Civil Rights Movement, which marked the "decline of soul culture, reflected in popular music and film, again in part, by the rise of an urban-inflected, hyper-materialistic nihilism and the fall of a rural-inflected, gospel-tinged optimism" (2007: 625).

40 See, for instance, Nelson's juxtaposition of the 1960s "we-shall-overcome tradition of noble struggle, soul and gospel music, positive images, and the conventional wisdom that civil rights would translate into racial salvation" and the 1980s–1990s "going-for-mine-materialism, secular beat consciousness, and a more diverse, fragmented, even postmodern black community" (2001: 1).

41 See, for instance, Daniel Grassian's rather unreflected study on the so-called Hip Hop generation.

42 Sowell lists his acoustic references in a comical merge of high and low culture, combining properly musical as well as mundane sounds: "Brando's creaking leather jacket in *The Wild One*, a shopping cart tumbling down the concrete banks of the L-A-River, Mothers of Invention, a stone skimming across Diamond Lake, the flutter of Paul Newman's eyelashes amplified ten thousand times, some smelly kid named Beck who was playing guitar in front of the Church of Scientology, early, early, early Ray Charles, Etta James, Sonic Youth, the Millenium Falcon going hyperdrive, Foghorn Leghorn, Foghat, Melvin Tormé, aka 'The Velvet Fog,' Issa Bagayoho, the sizzle of an Al's Sandwich shop cheesesteak at the exact moment Ms. Tseng adds the onions." (*SL* 34–35).

43 See, for instance, Dykes D. Oswald's article on the code, which observes that "the law of reparation in the Code is complicated with some difficult questions about the social classes into which the population was divided" (1904: 84).

44 In the sphere of art, Badiou often picks individuals to designate an event, such as the "Schoenberg-event" (*LoW* 80), but also refers to the Cantor-event in mathematics (*LoW* 38). However, this does not rely on a Romantic notion of authorial creation but, rather, sees the subject Schoenberg as a medium that brings an artistic event into being.

45 "When the tune ended, it was evident from his downcast gaze that he'd been deeply moved, but he was too embarrassed to praise it and too dumbfounded to trash it." (*SL* 176) Thorsten thus asks Sowell: "Did you know that before World War II, the percentage of Jews in Germany was zero point eight-seven-two? To blame such a small percentage of people for the world's problems, it's embarrassing. To be threatened by primitive races like yours that can't think, or heathen races that can only deceive and nothing else, this shows our own inherent inferiority, and I hate the Jews for this, I hate you for this. I've never even met a Jew, and who knows, I might even be Jewish, but I hate them anyway" (*SL* 177).

46 While Badiou often refers to the Schoenberg-event or the Cantor-event, he has in mind more than the simple equivalence of human individual and event. By saying that Charles Stone bears the trace of the event of emancipation, I do not want to suggest that he *embodies* this event but, rather that he bears the trace of it, which makes him more than a mere faithful subject.

47 See *Ethics*, where he states that reactive fidelities are "an Evil from which there is no return" (80).

48 See Du Bois's eponymous biography as well as Hughes's poem "October 16." In Ellison's *Invisible Man*, "John Brown's Body" is being performed at a Marxist assembly and is being used for their propaganda (1995: 339).

49 See also David S. Reynold's *John Brown, Abolitionst*, where he emphasizes the revolutionary impetus of Brown, having "*killed* slavery" (2005: ix).

50 See, in this context, Gary Alan Fine's article "John Brown's Body: Elites, Heroic Embodiment, and the Legitimation of Political Violence," in which he argues that "Americans define themselves as a people repelled by the idea of violent political action" (1999: 225).

51 See especially Eagleton's chapter "The Writer and Commitment" in *Marxism and Literary Criticism*.

52 See also Eagleton's chapter on the question of "Form and Content."

53 Again, in danger of generalization, one could see the South's response as tantamount to an obscure fidelity, denying the truth of black emancipation and stressing the particularity of white sovereignty, while the North's reaction tries to normalize the event according to state interests.

54 " 'John Brown's Body' put Brown's death to work in service of the state," as Nudelman observes (2001: 641).

55 Du Bois is eager to point out that "his family was not rigidly Puritan," being "born into a religious atmosphere; not that of stern, intellectual Puristanism, but of a milder and a more sensitive type" (2001: 9). For Badiou's essentially post-Marxist understanding of a collective subject irrespective of class belonging, see Toscano who observes that "one of the lessons of the Chinese Cultural Revolution, according to Badiou, is that the bourgeoisie too engages in politics, and not simply by means of exploitation or coercion" (2006: 17).

56 Badiou himself points to Jesus's resurrection in *Saint Paul* (2003: 4) and views Paul not as a religious but as a "poet thinker" (ibid.: 2).

57 Badiou somewhat counterintuitively also sees the fidelity to the Christ event, that is, his resurrection, as a truth procedure that forms the Christian subject (ibid.: 13). However, "it is not Christ who is the hero of subjectivity for Badiou, but Paul" (Ashton et al. 2006: 8).

58 Nudelman also observes that "from the moment John Brown was sentenced to death, his body became a source of controversy and political struggle" as the South tried to "remove the body from public view," while the North "hoped the public display of Brown's body would secure the status of the martyred hero" (2004: 4).

59 See Nudelman, who writes that "Brown's body could not be long forgotten; each time the song was sung his rotting corpse was brought back into view. When soldiers sang 'John Brown's Body', they did not simply celebrate Brown's death or its redemptive aftermath but rather the very process of transformation through which corpses, in all their gruesome and seemingly intractable materiality, are reinterpreted as group spirit" (2001: 640).

60 See Foucault's seminal essay "Of other Spaces," in which he comments on the exclusion of burial sites with the advent of the society of discipline (1986: 25).

61 This recalls Benjamin's notion of revolutionizing form in "The Author as Producer." However, in contrast to Badiou's somewhat myopic view of aesthetic events, which are for him, like for Benjamin, engaging in the change of form, Benjamin accounts for the political relations these revolutionary art forms assume. If Badiou could thus be said to follow the formalist line of Marxist literary criticism, he distances himself from this stance by not letting political matters seep into the aesthetic condition. See also the introduction to *Handbook of Inaesthetics*, where he argues that aesthetic events are simply concerned with formal configurations (2005: 13).

62 See also Badiou's "The Subject of Art," in which he notes that "it's the emergence of a new possibility of formalization, or if you want, it's an acceptance like form of something which was inform" (2009: n.p.). While Badiou subscribes to the view that "significant developments in literary form, then, result from significant changes in ideology" (Eagleton 2002: 23), he grounds this transformation of form in the eruption of an aesthetic event.

63 This notion of the sensible and form, causing a "transformation in the rules of visibility themselves" (*TRoH* 69), recalls Rancière's notion of the "distribution

of the sensible" (2004: 12). While Rancière importantly points to the necessary interconnection of aesthetic and political regimes (ethical, representational, and aesthetic) that Badiou neglects in his account of politics and aesthetics, Badiou's notion of the event allows for thinking of changes within these regimes, which, as I would argue, Rancière does not account for.

64 Blaustein equally observes that "Stone and Sowell represent two exaggerated models of artistic genius, one creative and one synthetic" (2010: 728), which could be related to this duality of idealist genius and materialist, "synthetic genius" (ibid.: 729).

65 Whereas Gerald Early argues in his essay "What is African-American literature" that black literature "no longer has to be obsessed with the burden or expectation of political protest or special pleading for the humanity of the race or the worth of its history and cultures as it had done in the past" (qtd. in Warren 2011: 113), *Slumberland*, rather, assumes its political role through aesthetic means, as Benjamin would have it.

66 Indeed, if viewed from a Marxist perspective, the relation between aesthetic and political events, or form and content, are necessarily reciprocal. It seems striking that Badiou does not account for this political dimension of art when he sees the latter as being concerned with changes in form that classical Marxism would see as responding to changed social circumstances.

67 See his chapter entitled "The Future of the Past" (2011: 81ff.).

Chapter 6

1 See Sascha Pöhlmann's notion of "cosmographic metafiction" in "Cosmographic Metafiction in Sesshu Foster's *Atomik Aztek*."

2 Particularly Lew Basnight and Cyprian Latewood are often read as attaining a sovereign subjective status. See, for instance, Michal Harris's "The Tao of Thomas Pynchon," or Michael Jarvis's "Very Nice Indeed: Cyprian Latewood's Masochistic Sublime, and the Religious Plurlism of *Against the Day*."

3 Badiou observes that the faithful scientific subject sustains, "after the upsurge of ε [the event], the consequences of a mathematico-experimental modification, takes the name of results (principles, laws, theorems . . .), whose consistent entanglement exposes within appearing everything that gathers around ε. The complete present which is engendered, point by point (difficulty by difficulty), by the faithful subject whose fomalism is borne by the consistency of the initial results, is commonly named a (new) theory" (*LoW* 75).

4 Badiou's opinion about the relation between science and policits is ambivalent. In *Infinite Thought*, he insists that these discourses are different "because in the science of physics the experiment is an artificial construction *which must be repeatable*. Mathematical writing corresponds to experiments solely when the repetition of an experiment gives the *same* result. This identity is inscribed in a mathematical equation. In politics, however, the relationship between writing and experience is completely different. A political situation is always singular; it is never repeated" (*IT* 61). Yet at times, he seems to be aware of the interrelation between these two truth conditions. Norris observes in this respect: "Fidelity . . . may often be manifest in very different ways within a single life-history, as with the two highly gifted French

mathematicians Jean Cavaillès and Albert Latuman who were both Resistance members shot by the occupying German forces. While their courage and sheer moral heroism are beyond doubt, they should both most aptly be seen, in Badiou's estimate, as thinkers whose deployment of rigorous, axiomatic-deductive procedures in their mathematical work was likewise displayed to striking effect in their perfectly consistent carrying-through of ethico-political precept into practice" (2012: 42).

5 See particularly Timothy Melley's article "Bodies Incorporated: Scenes of Agency Panic in 'Gravity's Rainbow' " as well as his monograph *Empire of Conspiracy*. Melley's notion of "agency panic," which implies "the crisis of apparently imperiled individual autonomy" (1994: 709) already manifests itself in the novel's very beginning. He thus writes that "the first line of the novel contains an agency dilemma characteristic of those to follow" (ibid.: 709). For him, "the bizarre but unmistakable geographical relation between Slothrop's penis and the subsequent landing of the rockets—is the novel's most significant, and most commented upon, agency problem" (ibid.: 709).

6 Lance Ozier sees this differently when he argues that "we are confronted with Pynchon's mathematical images of death-transfigured woven into a sustained affirmation of possibility" (1975: 207).

7 One can thus read Dr. Edward W. A. Pointsman's subscription to Pavlovian physiology as a counternarrative toward the notion of *a priori*, self-determined subjects, while LaPlace's attempts to calculate probabilities ultimately denies human action in the face of contingency. Roger's girlfriend Jessica thus tellingly asks him: "Why is your equation only for angels, Roger? Why can't we do something, down here? Couldn't there be an equation for us too, something to help us find a safer place?" (2006a: 55). While the Poisson distribution, indeed, calls for the rejection of any kind of anticipation, one could, however, interject that the absolute rejection of cause and effect also poses various problems for agency.

8 Pöhlmann observes that "just as *Gravity's Rainbow* drew on chemistry and physics and Mason & Dixon on (para)geography and astronomy, Against the Day looks to mathematics and uses it as a leitmotif that offers a vast variety of ideas, images and structures for the literary text, and it is also used metaphorically itself" (2010: 25).

9 I particularly thank Nina Engelhardt for her comments on the mathematical parts of this chapter.

10 However, the hermeneutic function of mathematics does echo *Gravity's Rainbow*, if one accepts Ozier's argument that "one thread into the labyrinthine revelations of Gravity's Rainbow runs by way of Pynchon's scientific and mathematical references" (1975: 194). Toon Staes observes that "Pynchon's 2006 novel does not emphasize the harrowing effects of the scientific worldview as much as Gravity's Rainbow does. Rather, *Against the Day* narrativizes how the modern scientific method became geared towards the justification of the prevailing society" (2010: 101). While Staes's reading seems to focus on the negative impetus of the sciences, I want to show that the sciences also harbor the potential for creating a subject of the event.

11 Despite being based on different footings, this verdict has also been proposed by, among others, Brian McHale (2007: n.p.), Pöhlmann (2010: 9), and Kathryn Hume, who observes that "*Against the Day* seems to represent a new departure for Pynchon" (2011: 168).

12 See, for instance, Hume, who posits that there are three "paths of life" that inhabit the potential of resistance: "the via media, the Convent, and Dynamite" (178). The

scientific-political subject of the event does not seem to be part of any of these 'paths of life.' See also Graham Benton's "Daydreams and Dynamite: Anarchist Strategies of Resistance and Paths of Transformation in *Against the Day*."

13 In their introduction to Badiou's *On Beckett*, Alberto Toscano and Nina Power observe in this context that "questions about the number and nature of the 'conditions' remain open" (xxvi).

14 This interconnection is consistent with earlier Pynchon novels, particularly *Gravity's Rainbow*. Steven Weisenburger thus notes "the points of connection between (on the one hand) procedures of science and technology and (on the other) the rituals of religion and occultism" (1988: 2). Such convergences may be detected in the entirety of Pynchon's oeuvre.

15 Nina Engelhardt equally observes that "changes in the perception of mathematics and its relation to the world tie in with the wider epistemological shift around the turn of the century, beginning with Friedrich Nietzsche's perspectivism and the implied loss of objective truth and finding a close correspondence in Ferdinand de Saussure's notion that linguistic signs do not refer to actual objects in the world but relate to each other only" (2013: 215). She goes on to note the close connection between the novel's temporal setting and the crisis of mathematics: "The foundational crisis in mathematics was prepared for since the nineteenth century, reached its apex after the First World War and abated in the mid-1920s, thus covering a period corresponding to the time span treated in *Against the Day*" (ibid.: 216).

16 See Terry Reilley's "Narrating Tesla in *Against the Day*."

17 Simon de Bourcier's monograph *Pynchon and Relativity* gives a detailed historical account of the Æther and analyzes its narrative function in *Against the Day*.

18 Many critics have noted the critical role of light in the novel. See Ickstadt (2010: 42), or Leyla Haferkamp's "'Particle or Wave?': The 'Function' of the Prairie in *Against the Day*." In her reading of the novel, Hume argues that light "signal[s] spiritual material" that is tied to *Against the Day*'s "Catholic or at least Christian" (2011: 172) vocabulary. I disagree that the novel is as outspokenly Christian as Hume sees it, as the various alternative religions seem to indicate. See, especially Harris's and Coffman's articles.

19 For an explanation of the current uses of quaternions, see R. Mukundan's "Quaterions: From Classical Mechanics to Computer Graphics and Beyond."

20 For a comprehensive account of this struggle, see Michael J. Crowe's *A History of Vector Analysis*, especially Chapter 6, "A Struggle for Existence in the 1890's."

21 For an elaborate account of Quaternionism, see Engelhardt's "Mathematics, Reality and Fiction in Pynchon's *Against the Day*."

22 Crowe thus notes: "Although Hero of Alexandria and Diophantus in ancient times had encountered the question of the meaning of the square root of a negative number, and although Cardan had in his 1545 Ars Magna used complex numbers in computation, nevertheless complex numbers [*sic!*] were not accepted by most mathematicians as legitimate mathematical entities until well into the nineteenth century. This is hardly surprising since numbers such as $\sqrt{-1}$ seem to be neither less than, greater than, nor equal to zero" (6).

23 To a similar extent, Quaternionism's principle of non-commutativity runs against the grain of conventional mathematical laws. In ordinary algebra, there is no problem in exchanging variables such as $ab = df$ into $ba = fd$. Quaternionist mathematics,

however, forbids such substitutions. As Engelhardt explains: "In everyday calculations, multiplication is commutative, meaning that it makes no difference if three is multiplied by four or four by three: 3 x 4 = 4 x 3. In contrast, with Quaternions, the time of calculating with an element in relation to the next element is crucial: $i \times j = -j \times i$" (2013: 219).

24 Crowe insists that "Hamilton's discovery of quaternions was in the tradition of the work done on complex numbers" (1967: 23). In fact, "at least five men, working independently of each other, had by 1831 discovered and published the geometrical representation of complex numbers" (ibid.: 11).

25 "A Quaternion, put simply, thus consists itself of a real and an imaginary axis, what Hamilton terms a scalar and a vectorist part" (ibid.: 32).

26 See Freud's *Der Witz und seine Beziehung zum Unbewussten*.

27 Norris notes that "there are three main features that distinguish Badiou's account of such episodes [of revolutionary change] from the widely influential treatment to be found in Thomas Kuhn's book *The Structure of Scientific Revolutions*. One is of course that Badiou seeks to theorize the conditions of possibility for the occurrence of such transformative events through a set-theoretical investigation of the points at which some existing (whether social or scientific) ontology comes under paradigm-breaking strain from unexpected developments within or outside its home territory. The second is the far greater stress he lays on those exemplary figures (or 'militants') whose life histories, commitments, discoveries, conversion experiences, holdings-out against political pressure or orthodox scientific belief, and so forth, he sees as providing a necessary focus or rallying point for the various dedicated groups—of whatever kind—that form in their historical wake. The third, somewhat in contrast to these, is Badiou's clear-eyed recognition of the forces that have always been ranged against any such threatening mobilization of the socially excluded or politically oppressed" (2009: 154).

28 Although Quaternions are not as relevant to contemporary mathematics and physics as Hamilton wished them to be, Quaternionism's import for modern science should not be underestimated. Thomas Hill, for instance, writing in 1857 argued: "It is confidently predicted, by those best qualified to judge, that in the coming centuries Hamilton's Quaternions will stand out as the greatest discovery of the nineteenth century" (Hill in Crowe 1967: 37). Moreover, Erwin Schrödinger also underlined Hamilton's fundamental role, when he note: "While these discoveries (Quaternions, etc.) would suffice to secure Hamilton in the annals of both mathematics and physics a highly honourable place, such pious memorials can in his case easily be dispensed with. For Hamilton is virtually not dead, he himself is alive, so to speak, not his memory. I daresay not a day passes—and seldom an hour—without somebody, somewhere on this globe, pronouncing or reading or writing or printing Hamilton's name. That is due to his fundamental discoveries in general dynamics. The Hamiltonian principle has become the cornerstone of modern physics, the thing with which a physicist expects every physical phenomenon to be in conformity . . ." (Schrödinger in Crowe 1967: 17). I again refer to Crowe's *A History of Vector Analysis*, although its methodological approach in positing a historical hermeneutics somewhat complicates Quaternionism's status as an event. See also R. Mukundan who notes that "Quaternions, now used in computer graphics, games programming, and virtual reality systems, and thus in the creation of other worlds and spaces, were first employed in 'aerospace applications and flight simulators'" (2011: 97).

29 Nikola Tesla articulates a similarly post-subjective form of scientific revelation:
    " 'Back in the San Juans we always blamed it on the altitude.' In the Velebit, rivers
    disappear, flow underground for miles, re-surface unexpectedly, descend to the
    sea. Underground, therefore, lies an entire unmapped region, a carrying into the
    Invisible of geography, and—one must ask—why not of other sciences as well? I was
    out in those mountains one day, the sky began to darken, the clouds to lower, I found
    a limestone cave, went in, waited. Darker and darker, like the end of the world—but
    no rain. I couldn't understand it. I sat and tried not to smoke too quickly the last
    of my cigarettes. Not until a great burst of lightning came from out of nowhere did
    heaven open, and the rain begin. I understood that something enormous had been
    poised to happen, requiring an electrical discharge of a certain size to trigger it. In
    that moment, all this"—he gestured upward into the present storm clouds, which
    all but obscured the giant toroidal terminal nearly two hundred feet above, whose
    open trusswork formed a steel cap of fungoid aspect—"was inevitable. As if time had
    been removed from all equations, the Magnifying Transmitter already existed in that
    moment, complete, perfected. . . . Everything since, all you have seen in the press,
    has been theatrical impersonation—the Inventor at Work. To the newspapers I can
    never speak of that time of simply waiting. I'm expected to be *consciously scientific*,
    to exhibit only virtues likely to appeal to rich sponsors—activity, speed, Edisonian
    sweat, defend one's claim, seize one's chance—If I told them how far from conscious
    the procedure really is, they would all drop me flat" (*AtD* 326–27).
30 Benesch notes that "contrary to ordinary . . . scientific texts generally posit
    themselves as non-texts or representations of unequivocal, factual truths. By the
    same token, scientific authors do not 'possess' the ideas conveyed by a book or a
    journal article in the same way literary authors have copyright to the ideas conveyed
    by a novel" (2009: 5).
31 See Badiou's *Saint Paul*.
32 Ali Chetwynd has interrogated the notion of obligation in late Pynchon. Yet, while
    he also underlines the "competing obligations he [Kit] bears to his father's legacy and
    to the benefactor who had his father killed," (2015: n.p.) he does not account for Kit's
    scientific persuasion.
33 Chetwynd, in fact, argues that "of all the threads of plot in *Against the Day*, Thomas
    Pynchon's longest and most densely populated novel, that which follows Kit Traverse
    can lay best claim to centrality" (2015: n.p.).
34 Kit indeed becomes "a roving electrical apprentice—'Could call me a circuit rider,
    I guess'—journeying one mountain valley to the next, looking to keep from ever
    going down into another mine, taking any job that happened to be open, long as
    it was something, anything, to do with electricity. Electricity was all the go then in
    southwest Colorado, nearly every stream intersecting sooner or later with some
    small private electrical plant for running mine or factory machinery or lighting
    up towns" (*AtD* 98). Toward the end of the novel, the fantastical aeronauts "The
    Chums of Chance" float over the increasingly illuminated earth and the narrator
    notes: "While crossing the continent the boys had expressed wonder at how much
    more infected with light the nighttime terrains passing below had become—more
    than anyone could ever remember, as isolated lanterns and skeins of gas-light had
    given way to electric street-lighting, as if advanced parties of the working-day were
    progressively invading and settling the unarmed hinterlands of night" (*AtD* 1032).
    In the novel's ambivalent representation of the theme of light, it is here negatively

connoted. Tesla's initial experiments with electricity have advanced to a progressive, capitalist invasion of America's "hinterlands of night."

35   For general overviews of *Against the Day*'s Eastern spiritual innuendos, see Harris's "The Tao of Thomas Pynchon," or Christopher K. Coffman's "Bogolism, Orphism, Shamanism: The Spiritual and Spatial Grounds of Pynchon's Ecological Ethic."

36   While this resembles Agamben's process of transforming "*bios*" into "*zoē*" and thereby guarantees the sovereignty at the cost of a *homo sacer*, the process here is not framed in a state of exception with Kit, deprived of all qualities, becoming bare life.

37   See David Graeber's *Debt*, for a historical/ethnographic genealogy of the concept of debt and its relation to life.

38   Indeed, neither of the children reacts to Webb's death as if it were an event, but rather in respect of the preceding family structures that were already in operation before he died.

39   McHale's article does a remarkable job in identifying not only the various genres that make up *Against the Day*'s story world; he, moreover, argues that the novel's use of mass media genres relates to their historical inception and thereby "historicizes *doubly*, on the one hand, by refracting the era's historical realities through the genres of its own self-representations; on the other, by indicating where we stand with respect to this distant era and its characteristic genres" (2011: 26).

40   "By the 1890s," notes McHale, "when the chronology of *Against the Day*'s storyworld begins, typical dime-novel westerns often featured sympathetic outlaw heroes who engaged in forms of 'social banditry,' seeking redress and retribution for wrongs done to them by powerful landowners and corrupt politicians. . . . This, of course, is exactly the situation of the Traverse boys in Pynchon's Wild West narrative. The Traverses, like the James Boys of the dime novels, are good-guy outlaws bent on justifiable revenge; the middle brother, Frank, even shares a first name with one of the James brothers" (ibid.: 20).

41   Historically, Kit would have heard of the Quaternionism-Vectorism battle by 1903, the date of this passage. See Crowe's *A History of Vector Analysis*.

42   Amy J. Elias argues that in *Against the Day*, "characters who lose themselves in escapism or egoism lose the capacity for action and moral connection with others" (2011: 36). In his *Style of Connectedness*, Thomas Moore insists that Pynchon "condemns the paranoid cop-out, which is passivity, mere mindless pleasures, and that includes merely escapist indulgence in mysticism" (1987: 231).

43   Badiou considers the relation between institution and the transmission of knowledge in a short article "What is a philosophical institution?," in *Conditions*.

44   The *Pynchonwiki* observes that "Mulciber is an alternative name of the Roman god Vulcan, the god of fire and volcanoes, and the manufacturer of art, arms, iron, and armor for gods and heroes. Mulciber is also the name of a character in John Milton's Paradise Lost, the architect of the demon city of Pandemonium."

45   While there exists a "Quaternion-ray weapon" (*AtD* 445) that has the anachronistic range of an Atomic bomb, this weapon cannot be operated at ease, since it seems to fire back on those using it.

46   The homogenizing simplification latent in Orientalist discourse might thus also be grasped in the fact that Yashmeen is actually Russian. Within an Orientalist reading of Yashmeen's submission to colonial discourse, I do not suggest that there are processes of resistance that undermine the Imperial order. However, unlike a

deconstructionist approach, à la Homhi Bhabha, I argue that her ability of successful resistance only springs from the reagency she acquires as a subject of the event.

47 Walter Penrose observes that "perhaps the most important unsolved mathematical problem today is the Riemann hypothesis, which is concerned with the zeros of this analytically extended Zeta function, that is, with the solutions of $\zeta(z) = 0$" (2004: 133). Riemann's topology has also been taken up by Deleuze and Guattari for whom his geometry, indeed, marked "a decisive event" (1987: 532). However, unlike Deleuze's and Guattari's notion of smooth and striated space, I argue that Yashmeen's becoming a nomad that roams through smooth spaces and thereby dismantles the hegemony of striated spaces from within only comes to her as part of her reagency. In this sense, I see the subversive potential that is latent in smooth space not as a systemic mode of reistance but as a form of resistance that is dependent on the manifestation of an event.

48 Berressem explains that *Eigenvalues* or -vectors were introduced in the context of the "modeling of mathematical transformations by way of the identification of those vectors within the transformation that remain invariant and the measurement of the scalar changes of these vectors, such as those brought about by operations of stretching or compression" (2010: 350).

49 See, for instance, Badiou's "Philosophy and the 'death of communism'" in *Infinite Thought*.

50 Badiou writes in the preface to *Logics of Worlds* that his own materialist dialectic can be summarized by the sentence: "*There are only bodies and languages, except that there are truths*" (4).

51 Haferkamp summarizes Deleuze's and Guattari's adaptation of Riemannian geometry when writing that "Riemann space as smooth space is the accumulation of 'patches of space,' it consists of a heterogeneous multiplicity of 'shred[s]' of Euclidean space' and is best defined as 'an amorphous collection of pieces that are juxtaposed but not attached to each other' . . . thus allowing for ambiguity in the spaces between" (2010: 314).

52 See Deleuze's and Guattari's concept of the nomad and its habitation in smooth spaces in Plateau "1227: Treatise on Nomadology—The War Machine" in *A Thousand Plateaus*.

53 "The Riemann zeta function," explains the *Pynchonwiki*, "has two classes of zeros, the trivial zeroes being at negative even integers (-2, -4. . .), the non-trivial complex numbers, believed (but not proven) to have Re(z)=1/2."

54 Wallhead, in fact, interlinks Pynchon's undermining of the quest genre by relating *Against the Day*'s lack of literary "events" to Kipling's *Kim*. She thereby interlinks both novels' narratological critique of "events" regardless of literary historical differences and relates it to the status of the subject when writing that "the lives and trajectories seem plotless because the characters are caught in quests which they do not control" (2010: 296).

55 Elias's notion of the pilgrimage accounts for Yashmeen's defiance of teleology, since "unlike quest, pilgrimage asserts that whether or not one receives the boon, one's prayers have been answered" (35).

56 See McHale's "Genre as History." Despite the fact that Elias acknowledges that genres "should be understood as flexible sets of narrative classes" (2011: 29) and notes that "its [the novel's] generic characteristics and contradictions thus seem to

place *Against the Day* closer to picaresque than quest, yet neither genre adequately contains the novel" (ibid.: 32), she, nevertheless, proposes the "postmodern pilgrimage" as a genre that "uniquely accounts for the novel's dominant motifs and symbols" (ibid.: 30). Elias's observation that "in *Against the Day*, the battle against genre is intense indeed. Pynchon's text frustrates readers' generic expectations" (2011: 43) does not stop her from positing her own generic reading. Benton rightly observes that "Pynchon's formal techniques—which favor heterogeneity, over uniformity, spontaneity over conformity, and fragmentation over consolidation—align with an anarchist aesthetic that reflects a sustained skepticism toward all typologies and classification of genre" (2011: 191).

57　McHale writes that "Pynchon appropriates the conventions and materials of genres that flourished at the historical moments during which the events of his story occur" (2011: 19).

58　Next to the major European powers that, as Gaspereaux informs Captain Sands, "are bringing in their forces" so that "chances increase day by day for some sort of sustained conflict over possession of the city, in regimental strength if not larger" (*AtD* 448), non-governmental corporations, like ". . . the Standard Oil, or the Nobel brothers" (*AtD* 444) also have a lively interest in the city. Just before they reach Shambhala, the aeronautic crew Chums of Chance meet Lyle and Leonard, "a couple of oil prospectors headed for their next likely field of endeavor" (*AtD* 440). The Chums soon learn that "this whole Shambhala story of theirs is just a pretext" (*AtD* 441) for the economic aspirations of industrial corporations.

59　It is justified to ask whether Ljubica is part of this particular subject of the event, since she is literally born into the situation without having confronted the event in the first place. This obviously recalls *The Road*'s son and his reactive status.

60　See the *Pynchonwiki*'s entry on Srinivasa Ramanujan.

61　See particularly Ozier's "The Calculus of Transformation: More Mathematical Imagery in Gravity's Rainbow" for a thorough analysis of Δt and other mathematical metaphors in the novel.

62　Ozier thus observes that "for Leni Pökler the mathematical characteristics of the Δt as an infinitely small but nevertheless non-zero quantity represent the moment of personal commitment as an equally infinitesimal but thereby pure personal present which contrasts with the scientifically rational world her husband [Franz Pökler] inhabits" (1975: 195). *Against the Day* (2006)

Conclusion

1　Even if Walter's novel bent the mimetic *dispositif* of "9/11," it still refrained from alienating the happening to such an extent as Ruff's novel does.

Bibliography

Agamben, Giorgio ([1995] 1998), *Homo Sacer: Sovereign Power and Bare Life*, translated by Daniel Heller-Roazen, Stanford: Stanford University Press.

Alexander, Michelle (2012), *The New Jim Crow: Mass Incarceration in the Age of Colorblindness*, New York: New.

Ali, Suki (2003), *Mixed-Race, Post-Race: Gender, New Ethnicities and Cultural Practices*, Oxford: Berg.

Ashton, Paul, A. J. Bartlett and Justin Clemens (2006), "Masters & Disciples: Institution, Philosophy, Praxis," in Paul Ashton, A. J. Bartlett and Justin Clemens (eds), *The Praxis of Alain Badiou*, 3–12. Melbourne: re.press, 2006.

Ashton, Paul, A. J. Bartlett and Justin Clemens, eds (2006), *The Praxis of Alain Badiou*, Melbourne: re.press, 2006.

Babel, Reinhard, Nadine Feßler, Sandra Fluhrer, Sebastian Huber and Sebastian Thede, eds (2014), *Alles Mögliche: Sprechen, Denken und Schreiben des (Un)Möglichen*, Würzburg: Königshausen & Neumann.

Back to the Future (2009), Directed by Robert Zemeckis. 1985. CA: Universal Studios Home Entertainment. DVD.

Badiou, Alain ([1988] 2007), *Being and Event*, translated by Oliver Feltham, London: Continuum.

Badiou, Alain ([2005] 2007), *The Century*, translated by Alberto Toscano, Cambridge: Polity.

Badiou, Alain ([1992] 2008), *Conditions*, translated by Steven Corcoran, London: Continuum.

Badiou, Alain ([1997] 2000), *Deleuze: The Clamor of Being*, translated by Lousie Burchill, Minneapolis, MN: University of Minnesota Press.

Badiou, Alain ([1993] 2001), *Ethics: An Essay on the Understanding of Evil*, translated by Peter Hallward, London: Verso.

Badiou, Alain (1994), "Gilles Deleuze, *The Fold: Leibniz and the Baroque*," translated by T. Sowley, in Constantin V.Boundas and Dorothea Olkoswski (eds), *Gilles Deleuze and the Theatre of Philosophy*, 1–69, London: Routledge.

Badiou, Alain ([1998] 2002), *Gott ist tot: Kurze Abhandlung über eine Ontologie des Übergangs*, translated by Jürgen Brankel, Wien: Turia + Kant.

Badiou, Alain ([1998] 2005), *Handbook of Inaesthetics*, translated by Alberto Toscano, Stanford: Stanford University Press.

Badiou, Alain (2005), *Infinite Thought*, translated by Oliver Feltham and Justin Clemens, London: Continuum.

Badiou, Alain ([2006] 2009), *Logics of Worlds: Being and Event II*, translated by Alberto Toscano, London: Continuum.

Badiou, Alain ([1989] 1999), *Manifesto for Philosophy*, translated by Norman Madarasz, Albany, NY: SUNY Press.

Badiou, Alain (1991), "On a Finally Objectless Subject," translated by Bruce Fink, in Eduardo Cadava, Peter Connor and Jean-Luc Nancy (eds), *Who Comes after the Subject?*, 24–31, New York: Routledge.

Badiou, Alain ([2011] 2012), *The Rebirth of History*, translated by Gregory Elliott, London: Verso.

Badiou, Alain ([1997] 2003), *Saint Paul: The Foundation of Universalism*, translated by Ray Brassier, Stanford: Stanford University Press.

Badiou, Alain (2009), "The Subject of Art," *The Symptom*, 6: np. Accessed September 4, 2015, http://www.egs.edu/faculty/alain-badiou/articles/the-subject-of-art/.

Badiou, Alain and Nicolas Truong ([2009] 2012), *In Praise of Love*, translated by Peter Bush, London: Serpent's Tail.

Badiou, Alain and Slavoj Žižek ([2005]2009), *Philosophy in the Present*. Translated by Peter Thomas and Alberto Toscano. Cambridge: Polity.

Banerjee, Mita (2007), "Postethnicity and Postcommunism in Hanif Kureishi's *Gabriel's Gift* and Salman Rushdie's *Fury*," in Joel Kuortti and Jopi Nyman (eds), *Reconstructing Hybridity: Post-colonial Studies in Transition*, 309–23, Amsterdam: Rodopi.

Barth, John ([1956, 1958] 1988), *The Floating Opera and The End of the Road*, New York: Anchor Books.

Bartlett, A. J. and Justin Clemens, eds (2010), *Alain Badiou: Key Concepts*, Durham: Acumen.

Baudrillard, Jean (2002), *The Spirit of Terrorism and Other Essays*, translated by Chris Turner, London: Verso.

Beatty, Paul (2008), *Slumberland*, New York: Bloomsbury.

Becker, Karl (2010), "The New World of the Post-Apocalyptic Imagination." Master's Thesis, California State University.

Bedient, Calvin (1990), "Kristeva and Poetry as Shattered Signification," *Critical Inquiry*, 16 (4): 807–29.

Bell, Bernard W. (1990), "The African American Literary Tradition," in Martin Coyle, Peter Garside, Malcolm Kelsall, John Peck (eds), *Encyclopedia of Literature and Criticism*, 1136–47, Oxford: Taylor and Francis.

Benesch, Klaus (2009), "Diverging Cultures, Competing Truths? Science, Technology, and the Humanities: An Introduction," in Klaus Benesch, Meike Zwingenberger (eds), *Scientific Cultures – Technological Challenges: A Transatlantic Perspective*, 1–13, Heidelberg: Winter.

Bender, Gretchen and Timothy Druckrey, eds (1994), *Cultures on the Brink: Ideologies of Technology*, Seattle: Bay Press.

Benjamin, Walter (1970), "The Author as Producer," translated by John Heckman, *New Left Review*, 1 (62): 83–96. Accessed September 4, 2015. http://newleftreview.org/static/assets/archive/pdf/NLR06108.pdf.

Bennett, Jane (2010), *Vibrant Matter: A Political Ecology of Things*, Durham: Duke University Press.

Benton, Graham (2011), "Daydreams and Dynamite: Anarchist Strategies of Resistance and Paths of Transformation in *Against the Day*," in Christopher Leise and Jeffrey Severs (eds), *Pynchon's Against the Day: A Corrupted Pilgrim's Guide*, 191–213, Newark: University of Delaware Press, 2011.

Berressem, Hanjo (2010), "'Vectors and [Eigen]Values': The Mathematics of Movement in *Against the Day*," in Sascha Pöhlmann (ed.), *Against the Grain: Reading Pynchon's Counternarratives*, 349–68, Amsterdam: Rodopi.

Berressem, Hanjo (2012), "The Surface of Sense, The Surface of Sensation and The Surface of Reference: Geometry and Topology in the works of Mark Z. Danielewski," in Sascha

Pöhlmann (ed.), *Revolutionary Leaves: The Fiction of Mark Z. Danielewski*, 199–221, Newcastle upon Tyne: Cambridge Scholars Publishing.

Berressem, Hanjo (2010), "'Vectors and [Eigen]Values': The Mathematics of Movement in *Against the Day*," in Sascha Pöhlmann (ed.), *Against the Grain: Reading Pynchon's Counternarratives*, 349–68. Amsterdam: Rodopi.

Berressem, Hanjo and Leyla Haferkamp, eds (2009), *Deleuzian Events: Writing|History*, Berlin: Lit.

Besena, Bruno (2004), "Ein einziges oder mehrere Ereignisse? Die Verknüpfung zwischen Ereignis und Subjekt in den Arbeiten von Alain Badiou und Gilles Deleuze," translated by Ralf Krause, in Marc Rölli (ed.), *Ereignis auf Französisch*, 313–34, München: Wilhelm Fink.

Best, Steven and Douglas Kellner (1991), *Postmodern Theory: Critical Interrogations, Communications and Culture*, Houndsmille, Basingstoke, Hampshire: Macmillan.

Bickley, William and Michael Warren (1989), *Family Matters*, ABC/CBS. Television.

Blaustein, George (2010), "Flight to Germany: Paul Beatty, the Color Line, and the Berlin Wall," *Amerikastudien*, 55 (4): 725–38.

Böhm, Alexandra, Antje Kley and Mark Schönleben (2011), "Einleitung: Ethik – Annerkennung – Gerechtigkeit," in Alexandra Böhm, Antje Kley, Mark Schönleben (eds), *Ethik – Annerkennung – Gerechtigkeit*: philosophische, literarische und gesellschaftliche Perspektiven, 11–34, München: Fink.

Böhm, Alexandra, Antje Kley and Mark Schönleben, eds (2011), *Ethik – Annerkennung – Gerechtigkeit*: philosophische, literarische und gesellschaftliche Perspektiven, München: Fink.

Bookchin, Murray (1995), *Re-enchanting Humanity. A Defense of the Human Spirit Against Antihumanism, Misanthropy, Mysticism, and Primitivism*, London: Cassell.

Borradorio, Giovanna (2003), *Philosophy in a Time of Terror: Dialogues with Jürgen Habermas and Jacques Derrida*, Chicago: University of Chicago Press.

Boundas, Constantin V. and Dorothea Olkoswski, eds (1994), *Gilles Deleuze and the Theatre of Philosophy*, London: Routledge.

Bowden, Sean and Simon Duffy, eds (2012), *Badiou and Philosophy*, Edinburg: Edinburgh University Press.

Bray, Joe and Alison Gibbons (2011), "Introduction," in Joe Bray and Alison Gibbons (eds), *Mark Z. Danielewski*, 1–16, Manchester: Manchester University Press.

Bray, Joe and Alison Gibbons, eds (2011), *Mark Z. Danielewski*, Manchester: Manchester University Press.

Bray, Joe, Alison Gibbons and Brian McHale, eds (2012), *The Routledge Companion to Experimental Literature*, Oxon: Routledge.

Brontë, Charlotte ([1847] 2006), *Jane Eyre*, London: Penguin Classics.

Bruner, Jerome (1991), "The Narrative Construction of Reality," *Critical Inquiry*, 18: 1–21.

Buell, Lawrence (2011), "Ecocriticism: Some Emerging Trends," *Qui Parle: Critical Humanities and Social Sciences*, 19 (2): 87–115.

Buell, Lawrence (1995), *The Environmental Imagination: Thoreau, Nature Writing, and the Formation of American Culture*, Cambridge, MA: Harvard University Press.

Buell, Lawrence (2005), *The Future of Environmental Criticism: Environmental Crisis and Literary Imagination*, Malden, MA: Blackwell.

Buell, Lawrence (2001), *Writing for an Endangered World: Literature, Culture, and Environment in the U.S. and Beyond*, Cambridge, MA: Harvard University Press.

Burn, Stephen J. (2008), *Jonathan Franzen at the End of Postmodernism*, London: Continuum.

Cadava, Eduardo, Peter Connor and Jean-Luc Nancy, eds (1991), *Who Comes after the Subject?*, New York: Routledge.

Cantor, Georg (1883), "Über unendliche, lineare Punktmannigfaltigkeiten V," *Mathematische Annalen*, 21: 545–91. *SpringerLink*. Web. October 4, 2013.

Carlson, Thomas A. (2007), "With the World at Hear: Reading Cormac McCarthy's The Road with Augustine and Heidegger," *Religion & Literature*, 39 (3): 47–71.

Carpio, Glenda (2013), "What Does Fiction Have to Do with It?," *PMLA*, 128 (2): 386–87.

Carroll, Robert and Stephen Prickett, eds (2007), *The Bible: Authorized King James Version with Apocrypha*, Oxford: Oxford University Press.

Castle, Terry (August 2011), "Stockhausen, Karlheinz. The unsettling question of the Sublime," *NYMag.com*, 27. Accessed August 8, 2015. http://nymag.com/news/9-11/10th-anniversary/karlheinz-stockhausen/.

Chetwynd, Alistair (April 7, 2011), "Inherent Obligation: Ethical Relations and The Demands of Patronage in Recent Pynchon," Paper presented at the *International Pynchon Week: Of Pynchon And Vice: America's Inherent Others*, June 9, 2010.

Chetwynd, Alistair (2014), "Inherent Obligation: The Distinctive Difficulties in and of Recent Pynchon." *English Studies*, 95 (8): 923–48.

Chomsky, Noam (2011), *9-11: Was there an Alternative?*, New York: Seven Stories.

Coffman, Christopher K. (2011), "Bogolism, Orphism, Shamanism: The Spiritual and Spatial Grounds of Pynchon's Ecological Ethic," in Christopher Leise and Jeffrey Severs (eds), *Pynchon's* Against the Day: *A Corrupted Pilgrim's Guide*, 91–114, Newark: University of Delaware Press.

Cohoon, Christopher (2011), "The Ecological Irigaray?," in Axel Goodbody and Kate Rigby (eds), *Ecocritical Theory: New European Approaches*, 206–14, Charlottesville, VA: University of Virginia Press.

Connor, Steven (2010), "I Believe That the World," in Vera Nünning, Ansgar Nünning and Birgit Neumann (eds), *Cultural Ways of Worldmaking: Media and Narrative*, 29–46, Berlin: Walter de Gruyter.

Coyle, Martin, Peter Garside, Malcolm Kelsall and John Peck, eds (1990), *Encyclopedia of Literature and Criticism*, Oxford: Taylor and Francis.

Craig, Jennifer and Warren Steele, eds (2009), *R|EVOLUTIONS: Mapping Culture, Community, and Change from Ben Jonson to Angela Carter*, Newcastle upon Tyne: Cambridge Scholars Publishing.

Crockett, Clayton (2013), *Deleuze beyond Badiou: Ontology, Multiplicity, and Event*, New York: Columbia University Press.

Crowe, Michael J. (1967), *A History of Vector Analysis*, Notre Dame: University of Notre Dame Press.

Crumbley, Paul (1997), *Inflections of the Pen: Dash and Voice in Emily Dickinson*, Lexington: Kentucky University Press.

Danielewski, Mark Z. (2006), *Only Revolutions*, New York: Pantheon Books.

Danielewski, Mark Z. (March 17, 2012), "Only Revolutions." Reading at Haus der Berliner Festspiele, Berlin.

Davis, Todd F. and Kenneth Womack, eds (2001), *Mapping the Ethical Turn: A Reader in Ethics, Culture, and Literary Theory*, Charlottesville: University of Virginia Press.

Däwes, Birgit (2011), *Ground Zero Fiction: History, Memory, and Representation in the American 9/11 Novel*, Heidelberg: Winter.

de Beistegui, Miguel (2005), "The Ontological Dispute: Badiou, Heidegger, and Deleuze," translated by Ray Brassier, in Gabriel Riera (ed.), *Alain Badiou: Philosophy and its Conditions*, 5–58, Albany, NY: SUNY Press.

de Bourcier, Simon (2012), *Pynchon and Relativity: Narrative Time in Thomas Pynchon's Later Novels*, London: Continuum.

de Bruyn, Ben (2010), "Borrowed Time, Borrowed World and Borrowed Eyes: Care, Ruin and Vision in McCarthy's *The Road* and Harrison's Ecocriticism," *English Studies*, 91 (7): 776–89.

Deleuze, Gilles and Félix Guattari ([1980] 1987), *A Thousand Plateaus: Capitalism & Shizophrenia*, translated by Brian Massumi, Minneapolis: University of Minnesota Press.

Deleuze, Gilles and Félix Guattari ([1991] 1994), *What is Philosophy?*, translated by Hugh Tomlinson and Graham Burchell, New York: Columbia University Press.

DeLillo, Don (1986), *White Noise*, New York: Penguin.

DeLillo, Don (2009), "In the Ruins of the Future," *The Guardian*. December 22, 2001. Accessed September 4, 2015. http://www.theguardian.com/books/2001/dec/22/fiction.dondelillo.

Depoortere, Frederieck (2009), *Badiou and Theology*, London: T & T Clark.

Derrida, Jacques ([1983] 1985), *Apokalypse*, edited by Peter Engelmann, translated by Michael Wetzel, Wien: Passagen.

Derrida, Jacques (1998), *Archive Fever: A Freudian Impression*, translated by Eric Prenowitz, Chicago: University of Chicago Press.

Derrida, Jacques (2003), *Eine gewisse unmögliche Möglichkeit vom Ereignis zu sprechen*. 2001, translated by Susanne Lüdemann, Berlin: Merve.

Derrida, Jacques ([1967] 1997), *Of Grammatology*, translated by Gayatri Chakrovorty Spivak, Baltimore: Johns Hopkins University Press.

Derrida, Jacques ([1966] 1978), "Structure, Sign and Play in the Human Sciences," translated by Alan Bass, in *Writing and Difference*, 351–70, London: Routledge

Diedrichsen, Diedrich (2012), "Beseelung, Entdinglichung und die neue Attraktivität des Unbelebten," in Irene Albers and Anselm Franke (ed.), *Animismus – Revisionen der Moderne*, 289–300, Zürich: diaphanes.

Douglass, Frederick ([1845] 2009), *A Narrative of the Life of Frederick Douglass, An American Slave*, Cambridge, MA: Harvard University Press.

Dreyfus, Hubert L. and Harrison Hall, eds (1992), *Heidegger: A Critical Reader*, Oxford: Blackwell.

Dubey, Madhu (2011), "Post-Postmodern Realism?," *Twentieth–Century Literature*, 57 (3, 4 and 57): 364–71.

Du Bois, W. E. B. ([1926] 2000), "Criteria of Negro Art," in Winston Napier (ed.), *African American Literary Theory: A Reader*, 17–23, New York: New York University Press.

Du Bois, W. E. B. ([1909] 2001), *John Brown*, New York: Random House.

Du Bois, W. E. B. ([1903] 2007), *The Souls of Black Folk*, Oxford: Oxford University Press.

Duffy, Simon (2012), "Badiou's Platonism: The Mathematical Ideas of Post-Cantorian Set Theory," in Sean Bowden and Simon Duffy (eds), *Badiou and Philosophy*, 59–78, Edinburg: Edinburgh University Press.

Dunst, Alexander (2009), "Thinking the Subject Beyond its Death," in Jan Kurcharzewski, Stefanie Schäfer and Lutz Schowalter (eds), *"Hello, I Say, It's Me." Contemporary Reconstructions of Self and Subjectivity*, 73–88, Trier: WVT.

Eagleton, Terry ([1976] 2002), *Marxism and Literary Criticism*, London: Routledge.

Eco, Umberto (2009), *Die Unendliche Liste*, translated by Barbara Kleiner, München: Carl Hanser.

Edwards, Jonathan ([1723] 1977), *Apocalyptic Writings*, edited by Stephen J. Stein, New Haven: Yale University Press.

Edwards, Tim (2008), "The End of the Road: Pastoralism and the Post-Apocalyptic Waste Land of Cormac McCarthy's *The Road*," *The Cormac McCarthy Journal*, 6: 55–61.

Elias, Amy J. (2011), "Plots, Pilgrimage, and the Politics of Genre in *Against the Day*," in Christopher Leise and Jeffrey Severs (eds), *Pynchon's* Against the Day: *A Corrupted Pilgrim's Guide*, 29–46, Newark: University of Delaware Press.

Eliot, Thomas S. ([1920] 2005), "The Lovesong of J. Alfred Prufrock," edited by Randy Malamud, New York: Barnes & Nobles.

Eliot, Thomas S. ([1922] 2005), *The Wasteland*, edited by Randy Malamud, New York: Barnes & Nobles.

Elliott, Emory (2010), *National Dreams and Rude Awakenings: Essays on American Literature, from the Puritans to the Postmodern*, edited by Matthew Elliott and Winfried Fluck, Heidelberg: Winter.

Ellis, Jay (2008), "Another Sense of Ending: The Keynote Address to the Knoxville Conference," *The Cormac McCarthy Journal*, 6: 22–38.

Ellison, Ralph (1995), *Invisible Man*. 1952, New York: Vintage.

Engelhardt, Nina (2013), "Mathematics, Reality and Fiction in Pynchon's *Against the Day*," in Zofia Kolbuszewska (ed.), *Thomas Pynchon and the (De)vices of Global (Post) modernity*, 212–31, Lublin: Wydawnictwo KUL [John Paul II Catholic University Press].

Eshelman, Raoul (2008), *Performatism, or, the End of Postmodernism*, Aurora, CO: Davies Group.

Eshelman, Raoul (2011), "Performatism, Dexter, and the Ethics of Perpetration," *Anthropoetics*, 17 (1). Accessed June 13, 2014. http://www.anthropoetics.ucla.edu/ap1701/.

Estes, Andrew Keller (2013), *Cormac McCarthy and the Writing of American Spaces*, Amsterdam: Rodopi.

Evans, Dylan (1996), *An Introductory Dictionary of Lacanian Psychoanalysis*, London: Routledge.

Everett, Percival (2001), *Erasure*, London: Faber and Faber.

Farred, Gran (2007), "The Event of the Black Body at Rest: Mêlée in Motown," *Cultural Critique*, 66: 58–77.

Feltham, Oliver (2005), "An Introduction to Alain Badiou's Philosophy," in *Infinite Thought*, 1–28, London: Continuum

Feltham, Oliver (2008), *Alain Badiou: Live Theory*, London: Continuum.

Feltham, Oliver (2008), "Badiou und Deleuze: ein oder zwei Begriffe des Ereignisses?," in Gernot Kamecke and Henning Teschke (eds), *Ereignis und Institution: Anknüpfungen an Alain Badiou*, 29–42, Tübingen: Narr.

Feltham, Oliver (2010), "Philosophy," in A. J. Bartlett and Justin Clemens (eds), *Alain Badiou: Key Concepts*, 13–24, Durham: Acumen.

Fine, Gary Alan (1999), "John Brown's Body: Elites, Heroic Embodiment, and the Legitimation of Political Violence," *Social Problems*, 46 (2): 225–49.

Foerster, Norman, ed. (1947), *American Poetry and Prose*, 3rd ed., Boston: Houghton Mifflin.

Foucault, Michel ([1969] 1972), *The Archeology of Knowledge and the Discourse on Language*, by A. M. Sheridan Smith, New York: Pantheon.

Foucault, Michel (1986), "Of Other Spaces," translated by Jay Miskowiec, *Diacritics*, 16 (1): 22–27.

Foucault, Michel (1982), "Subject and Power," *Critical Inquiry*, 8 (4): 777–95.

Franzen, Jonathan (2002), *How to be Alone*, New York: Picador.

Freese, Peter (1997), *From Apocalypse to Entropy and Beyond: The Second Law of Thermodynamics in Post-War American Fiction*, Essen: Blaue Eule.

Freese, Peter and Charles B. Harris, eds (2004), *Science, Technology, and the Humanities in Recent American Fiction*, Essen: Die Blaue Eule.

Freud, Sigmund (1905), *Der Witz und seine Beziehung zum Unbewussten*, Leipzig: Deuticke.

Gaitanidis, Anastasios (2007), "Narcissism and the Autonomy of the Ego," in Anastasios Gaitanidis and Polona Curk (eds), *Narcissism – A Critical Reader*, 13–30, London: Karna.

Gaitanidis, Anastasios and Polona Curk, eds (2007), *Narcissism – A Critical Reader*, London: Karna.

Gallivan, Euan (2008), "Compassionate McCarthy?: *The Road* and Schopenhauerian Ethics," *The Cormac McCarthy Journal*, 6: 98–106.

Garrard, Greg (2012), *Ecocriticism*, London: Routledge.

George, Nelson (1992), *Baps, B-Boys Buppies, Bohos: Notes on Post-Soul Black Culture*, New York: Harper Collins.

Gilbert, Sandra M. and Susan Gubar (1979), *The Madwoman in the Attic: The Woman Writer and the Nineteenth-Century*, New Haven: Yale University Press.

Glotfelty, Cherryl and Harold Fromm, eds (1996), *The Ecocriticism Reader: Landmarks in Literary Ecology*, Athens, GA: University of Georgia Press.

Glotfelty, Cherryl and Harold Fromm (1996), "Introduction," in Cheryll Glotfelty and Harold Fromm (eds), *The Ecocriticism Reader: Landmarks in Literary Ecology*, xv–xxxvii, Athens, GA: University of Georgia Press.

Goethe, Johann Wolfgang von (1986), *Goethe, Johann Wolfgang: Sämtliche Werke nach Epochen seines Schaffens*, München: Hanser.

Goodbody, Axel and Kate Rigby, eds (2011), *Ecocritical Theory: New European Approaches*, Charlottevilles, VA: University of Virginia Press.

Graeber, David (2011), *Debt: The first 5,000 Years*, New York: Melville House.

Grassian, Daniel (2003), *Hybrid Fictions: American Literature and Generation X*, Jefferson, NC: McFarland.

Grassian, Daniel (2009), *Writing the Future of Black American Literature of the Hip Hop Generation*, Columbia, SC: University of South Carolina Press.

Gray, Richard (2011), *After the Fall: American Literature since 9/11*, Malden: Wiley-Blackwell.

Green, Jeremy (2005), *Late Postmodernism. American Fiction at the Millennium*, New York: Palgrave MacMillian.

Greenberg, Judith, ed. (2003), *Trauma at Home After 9/11*, Lincoln: University of Nebraska Press.

Greenberg, Judith (2003), "Introduction," in Judith Greenberg (ed.), *Trauma at Home After 9/11*, xvii–xxiv, Lincoln: University of Nebraska Press.

Greve, Julius (2014), "Object-Oriented Utopianism. A Jamesonian Perspective on the Possible Worlds of Graham Harman," in Reinhard Babel, Nadine Feßler, Sandra

Fluhrer, Sebastian Huber and Sebastian Thede (eds), *Alles Mögliche: Sprechen, Denken und Schreiben des (Un)Möglichen*, 69–88, Würzburg: Königshausen & Neumann.

Grindley, Carl James (2008), "The Setting of The Road," *Explicator*, 67 (1): 11–13.

Gross, S. Andrew and Maryann Snyder-Körber, eds (2010), *Trauma's Continuum: September 11th Reconsidered. Special Issue of Amerikastudien/American Studies*, 55 (3).

Gutierrez, Cathy (2005), "The Millennium and Narrative Closure," in Stephen D. O'Leary and Glen S. McGhee (eds), *War in Heaven/Heaven on Earth: Theories of the Apocalyptic*, 47–60, London: equinox.

Haferkamp, Leyla (2010), " 'Particle or Wave?': The 'Function' of the Prairie in *Against the Day*," in Sascha Pöhlmann (ed.), *Against the Grain: Reading Pynchon's Counternarratives*, 307–22, Amsterdam: Rodopi.

Hall, David D., ed. (2004), *Puritans in the New World: A Critical Anthology*, Princeton: Princeton University Press.

Hallward, Peter (2003), *Badiou: A Subject to Truth*, Minneapolis, MN: University of Minnesota Press.

Hallward, Peter (2004), "Introduction: Consequences of Abstraction," in Peter Hallward (ed.), *Think Again: Alain Badiou and the Future of Philosophy*, 1–20, London: Continuum.

Hallward, Peter, ed. (2004), *Think Again: Alain Badiou and the Future of Philosophy*, London: Continuum.

Hallward, Peter (2001), "Translator's Introduction," in Alain Badiou (ed.), *Ethics*, vii–xvlvii, London: Verso.

Hansen, Mark B. (2011), "Print Interface to Time: Only Revolutions at the Crossroads of Narrative and History," in Joe Bray and Alison Gibbons (eds), *Mark Z. Danielewski*, 178–99, Manchester: Manchester University Press.

Hardt, Michael and Antonio Negri (2004), *Multitude. War and Democracy in the Age of Empire*, New York: Penguin.

Harman, Graham (2011), *The Quadruple Object*, Winchester: Zero Books.

Harris, Michael (2010), "The Tao of Thomas Pynchon," in Sascha Pöhlmann (ed.), *Against the Grain: Reading Pynchon's Counternarratives*, 213–30, Amsterdam: Rodopi.

Hauschild, Christiane (2009), "Kommentar zu Jurij Lotmans 'Zum künstlerischen Raum und zum Problem des Sujets'," in Wolf Schmid (ed.), *Russische Protonarratologie*, 283–90, Berlin: Walter de Gruyter.

Hayles, Katherine N. (2011), "Mapping Time, Charting Data: The Spatial Aesthetic of Mark Z. Danielewski's Only Revolutions," in Joe Bray and Alison Gibbons (eds), *Mark Z. Danielewski*, 159–77, Manchester: Manchester University Press.

Heidegger, Martin (1989), *Beiträge zur Philosophie (Vom Ereignis). Gesamtausgabe*, vol. 65. Frankfurt am Main: Vittorio Klostermann.

Heidegger, Martin ([1989] 1999), *Contributions to Philosophy (from Enowning)*, translated by Parvis Emad and Kenneth Maly, Bloomington, IN: Indiana University Press.

Heidegger, Martin ([1989] 2012), *Contributions to Philosophy (of the Event)*, translated by Richard Rojcewicz and Daniela Vallega-Neu, Bloomington, IN: Indiana University Press.

Herman, David ([2005] 2008), "Events," in David Herman, Manfred Jahn and Marie-Laure Ryan (eds), *Routledge Encyclopedia of Narrative Theory*, 151–52, London: Routledge.

Herman, David, Manfred Jahn and Marie-Laure Ryan, eds ([2005] 2008), *Routledge Encyclopedia of Narrative Theory*, London: Routledge.

Herman, Luc and Steven Weisenburger (2013), *Gravity's Rainbow, Domination, and Freedom*, Athens, GA: University of Georgia Press.

Hewson, Mark (2010), "Heidegger," in A. J. Bartlett and Justin Clemens (eds), *Alain Badiou: Key Concepts*, 146–54, Durham: Acumen.

Hite, Molly (1983), *Ideas of Order in the Novels of Thomas Pynchon*, Columbus: Ohio State University Press.

Hoberek, Andrew (2007), "Introduction: After Postmodernism," *Twentieth Century Literature*, 53 (3): 233–47.

Holland, Mary K. (2013), *Succeeding Postmodernism: Language & Humanism in Contemporary American Literature*, New York: Bloomsbury.

Holloway, David (2008), *9/11 and the War on Terror*, Edinburgh: Edinburgh University Press.

Holloway, David (2002), *The Late Modernism of Cormac McCarthy*, Westport: Greenwood Press.

Hornung, Alfred (2004), "Flying Planes Can Be Dangerous: Ground Zero Literature," in Peter Freese and Charles B. Harris (eds), *Science, Technology, and the Humanities in Recent American Fiction*, 67–73, Essen: Die Blaue Eule.

Hoth, Stefanie (2011), *Medium und Ereignis: '9/11' im amerikanischen Film, Fernsehen und Roman*, Heidelberg: Winter.

Huber, Sebastian (2012), "Event{u}al Disruptions: Postmodern Theory and Alain Badiou," *COPAS*, 13: 1–18. Accessed May 2, 2014. http://copas.uni-regensburg.de/article/view/54/172.

Huber, Sebastian (2014), "Words without Worlds—Worlds without Words. Impossible Ontologies in Nelson Goodman and Alain Badiou," in Reinhard Babel, Nadine Feßler, Sandra Fluhrer, Sebastian Huber and Sebastian Thede (eds), *Alles Mögliche: Sprechen, Denken und Schreiben des (Un)Möglichen*, 253–68. Würzburg: Königshausen & Neumann.

Hughes, Langston (1959), "October 16," in *Selected Poems*, 6, New York: Knopf.

Hughes, Langston ([1926] 2000), "The Negro Artist and the Racial Mountain," in Winston Napier (ed.), *African American Literary Theory: A Reader*, 27–30, New York: New York University Press.

Hühn, Peter (2009), "Event and Eventfulness," in Peter Hühn, John Pier, Wolf Schmid and Jörg Schönert (eds), *Handbook of Narratology*, 80–97, Berlin: Walter de Gruyter.

Hühn, Peter, ed. (2010), *Eventfulness in British Fiction*, Berlin: Walter de Gruyter.

Hühn, Peter (2010), "Introduction," in Peter Hühn (ed.), *Eventfulness in British Fiction*, 1–13, Berlin: Walter de Gruyter.

Hühn, Peter, John Pier, Wolf Schmid and Jörg Schönert, eds (2009), *Handbook of Narratology*, Berlin: Walter de Gruyter.

Humann, Heather Duerre (2010), "Close(d) to God, Negotiating a Moral Terrain: Questions of Agency and Selfhood in *The Road* and *Sophie's Choice*," *Interdisciplinary Literary Studies*, 12 (1): 65–79.

Hume, Kathryn (2011), "The Religious and Political Vision of *Against the Day*," in Christopher Leise and Jeffrey Severs (eds), *Pynchon's Against the Day: A Corrupted Pilgrim's Guide*, 167–89, Newark: University of Delaware Press.

Hutcheon, Linda (1988), *A Poetics of Postmodernism: History, Theory, Fiction*, New York: Routledge.

Ickstadt, Heinz (2008), "History, Utopia and Transcendence in the Space-Time of *Against the Day*," *Pynchon Notes*, 54–55: 216–44.

Ickstadt, Heinz (2010), "Setting Sail *Against the Day*: The Narrative World of Thomas Pynchon," in Sascha Pöhlmann (ed.), *Against the Grain: Reading Pynchon's Counternarratives*, 35–48, Amsterdam: Rodopi.

Irigaray, Luce (2011), "There Can Be No Democracy without a Culture of Difference," in Axel Goodbody and Kate Rigby (eds), *Ecocritical Theory: New European Approaches*, 194–205, Charlottesville, VA: University of Virginia Press.

Irsigler, Ingo and Christoph Jürgensen, eds (2008), *Nine Eleven: Ästhetische Verarbeitungen des 11. September 2001*, Heidelberg: Winter.

Jameson, Frederic (1991), *Postmodernism, or, the Cultural Logic of Late Capitalism*, Durham: Duke University Press.

Jarvis, Michael (2012), "Very Nice Indeed: Cyprian Latewood's Masochistic Sublime, and the Religious Pluralism of *Against the Day*," *Orbit*, 1 (2): Np. Accessed February 4, 2014. https://pynchon.net/articles/10.7766/orbit.v1.2.45/.

Jensen, Alexander S. (2008), "The Influence of Schleiermacher's Second Speech *On Religion* On Heidegger's Concept of *Ereignis*," *Review of Metaphysics*, 61 (4): 815–26.

Jernigan, Daniel, Neil Murphy, Brendan Quigley and Tamara S. Wagner (2009), "Introduction: Questions of Responsibility," in Daniel Jernigan, Neil Murphy, Brendan Quigley and Tamara S. Wagner (eds), *Literature and Ethics: Questions of Responsibility in Literary Studies*, 1–14, Amherst: Cambria Press.

Jernigan, Daniel, Neil Murphy, Brendan Quigley and Tamara S. Wagner, eds (2009), *Literature and Ethics: Questions of Responsibility in Literary Studies*, Amherst: Cambria Press.

Kacem, Medhi Belhaj (2011), *Après Badiou*, Paris: Grasset & Fasquelle.

Kacem, Medhi Belhaj (2011), *Inästhetik und Mimesis*. 2010, translated by Ronald Voullié, Berlin: Merve.

Kamecke, Gernot and Henning Teschke (2008), "Einleitung," in Gernot Kamecke and Henning Teschke (eds), *Ereignis und Institution: Anknüpfungen an Alain Badiou*, 7–14, Tübingen: Gunter Narr.

Kamecke, Gernot and Henning Teschke, eds (2008), *Ereignis und Institution: Anknüpfungen an Alain Badiou*, Tübingen: Gunter Narr.

Kant, Immanuel ([1790] 1987), *Critique of Judgment*, translated by Werner S. Pluhar, Indianapolis: Hackett.

Kaplan, Ann E. (2005), *Trauma Culture: The Politics of Terror and Loss in Media and Literature*, New Brunswick: Rutgers University Press.

Keniston, Ann and Jeanne Follansbee Quinn (2008), "Introduction," in Ann Keniston, and Jeanne Follansbee Quinn (eds), *Literature after 9/11*, 1–15, New York: Routledge, 2008.

Kolbuszewska, Zofia, ed. (2013), *Thomas Pynchon and the (De)vices of Global (Post) modernity*, Lublin: Wydawnictwo KUL [John Paul II Catholic University Press].

Kunsa, Ashley (2009), "'Maps of the World in Its Becoming:' Post-Apocalyptic Naming in Cormac McCarthy's *The Road*," *Journal of Modern Literature*, 33 (1): 57–74.

Kuortti, Joel and Jopi Nyman, eds (2007), *Reconstructing Hybridity: Post-colonial Studies in Transition*, Amsterdam: Rodopi.

Kurcharzewski, Jan, Stefanie Schäfer and Lutz Schowalter (2009), "Introduction," in Jan Kurcharzewski, Stefanie Schäfer and Lutz Schowalter (eds), *"Hello, I Say, It's Me.": Contemporary Reconstructions of Self and Subjectivity*, 1–12, Trier: WVT.

Kurcharzewski, Jan, Stefanie Schäfer and Lutz Schowalter, eds (2009), *"Hello, I Say, It's Me.": Contemporary Reconstructions of Self and Subjectivity*, Trier: WVT.

Lacan, Jacques ([1966] 2007), *Écrits. A Selection*, translated by Alan Sheridan, London: Routledge.

Lacan, Jacques (1988), *The Seminar. Book I. Freud's Papers on Technique, 1953–54*, translated by John Forrester, Cambridge: Cambridge University Press.

Laruelle, François ([2011] 2013), *Anti-Badiou: On the Introduction of Maoism into Philosophy*, translated by Robin Mackay, London: Bloomsbury.

Latour, Bruno (1993), *We Have Never Been Modern*, Cambridge, MA: Harvard University Press.

Lecercle, Jean-Jacques (2004), "Badiou's Poetics," in Peter Hallward (ed.), *Think Again: Alain Badiou and the Future of Philosophy*, 208–17, London: Continuum, 2004.

Leonard, Philip (2010), "'Without Return. Without Place': Rewriting the Book and the Nation in Only Revolutions," *Writing Technologies*, 3: 42–63.

Leypoldt, Günter (2004), "Recent Realist Fiction and the Idea of Writing 'After Postmodernism'," *Amerikastudien*, 49 (1): 19–34.

Lindberg-Seyersted, Brita (1976), *Emily Dickinson's Punctuation*, Oslo: Universitetsforlagets Trykningssentral.

Lotman, Jurij ([1971] 1977), *The Structure of the Artistic Text*, translated by Ronald Vroon, Ann Arbor, MI: Michigan Slavic Contributions.

Lott, Eric (1992), "Love and Theft: The Racial Unconscious of Blackface Minstrelsy," *Representations*, 39: 23–50.

Lott, Eric (1993), *Love & Theft. Blackface Minstrelsy and the American Working Class*, New York: Oxford University Press.

Luttrull, Daniel (2010), "Prometheus Hits The Road: Revising the Myth," *The Cormac McCarthy Journal*, 8 (1): 17–28.

Macherey, Pierre (2005), "The Mallarmé of Alain Badiou," in Gabriel Riera (ed.), *Alain Badiou: Philosophy and its Conditions*, 109–15, Albany, NY: SUNY Press.

Macquarrie, John (1994), *Heidegger and Christianity: Hensley Henson Lectures, 1993-1994*, New York: Continuum.

Mainberger, Susanne (2003), *Die Kunst des Aufzählens*, Berlin: Walter de Gruyter.

Marinetti, Filippo ([1909] 1973), "The Founding and Manifesto of Futurism," in Umbro Appolonio (ed.), *Futurist Manifestos*, 19–24, New York: Viking.

Mather, Increase ([1674] 2004), "The Day of Trouble is Near," in David D. Hall (ed.), *Puritans in the New World: A Critical Anthology*, 343–48. Princeton: Princeton University Press.

McCarthy, Cormac (2006), *The Road*, London: Picador.

McHale, Brian (December 20, 2007), "What was Postmodernism?," in Joseph Tabbi (ed.), *The Electronic Book Review*, Np. Accessed September 4, 2015. http://www.electronicbookreview.com/thread/fictionspresent/tense.

McHale, Brian (2011), "Genre as History: Pynchon's Genre-Poaching," in Christopher Leise and Jeffrey Severs (eds), *Pynchon's Against the Day: A Corrupted Pilgrim's Guide*, 15–28, Newark: University of Delaware Press.

McHale, Brian (2011), "Only Revolutions, or, The Most Typical Poem in World Literature," in Joe Bray and Alison Gibbons (eds), *Mark Z. Danielewski*, 141–58, Manchester: Manchester University Press.

McLaughlin, Robert (2004), "Post-Postmodern Discontent: Contemporary Fiction and the Social World," *Symploke*, 12 (1/2): 53–68.

Bibliography

McLaughlin, Robert (2013), "After the Revolution: US Postmodernism in the Twenty-First Century," *Narrative*, 21 (3): 284–95.

McParland, Robert (2010), "The Faithful Lightning: John Brown's Body and New Historicism," *Pennsylvania Literary Journal*, 2 (1): 114–32.

Meillasoux, Quentin (2011), "History and Event in Alain Badiou," *Parrhesia*, 12: 1–11.

Melley, Timothy (1994), "Bodies Incorporated: Scenes of Agency Panic in 'Gravity's Rainbow,'" *Contemporary Literature*, 35 (4): 709–38.

Melley, Timothy (2000), *Empire of Conspiracy: The Culture of Paranoia in Postwar America*, Ithaca, NY: Cornell University Press.

Miller, Adam (2008), *Badiou, Marion and St Paul: Immanent Grace*, London: Continuum.

Miller, J. Hillis (1987), *The Ethics of Reading*, New York: Columbia University Press.

Mitchell, Domhnall (1999), "Inflections of the Pen: Dash and Voice in Emily Dickinson by Paul Crumbley," in Paul Crumbley (ed.), Rev. Of *Inflections of the Pen*, *American Literature*, 71 (1): 180–81.

Monbiot, George (October 30, 2007), "Civilisation Ends with a Shutdown of Human Concern. Are we there Already?," in Cormac McCarthy (ed.), Rev. of *The Road*, *The Guardian*, np. Accessed September 4, 2015. http://www.theguardian.com/commentisfree/2007/oct/30/comment.books.

Moore, Thomas (1987), *The Style of Connectedness: Gravity's Rainbow and Thomas Pynchon*, Columbia, Missouri: University of Missouri Press, 1987.

Morrison, Toni ([1970] 1999), *The Bluest Eye*, New York: Vintage.

Morton, Timothy (2010), *The Ecological Thought*, Cambridge, MA: Harvard University Press.

Mukundan, R. (2002), "Quaternions: From Classical Mechanics to Computer Graphics and Beyond," in *Proceedings of the 7th Asian Technology Conference in Mathematics 2002. CiteSeerX – Scientific Literature Digital Library and Search Engine*, 97–106. Accessed September 4, 2015. http://citeseerx.ist.psu.edu/viewdoc/summary?doi=10.1.1.106.7361.

Mullarkey, John (2013), "Animal Spirits: Philosophomorphism and the Background Revolts of Cinema," *Angelaki*, 18 (1): 11–29.

Müller, Timo and Michael Sauter (2012), "Introduction: Ecocritical Extensions," in Timo Müller and Michael Sauter (eds), *Literature, Ecology, Ethics: Recent Trends in Ecocriticism*, 7–11, Heidelberg: Winter.

Müller, Timo and Michael Sauter, eds (2012), *Literature, Ecology, Ethics: Recent Trends in Ecocriticism*, Heidelberg: Winter.

Nancy, Jean-Luc (1991), "Introduction," in Eduardo Cadava, Peter Connor and Jean-Luc Nancy (eds), *Who Comes After the Subject?*, 1–9, New York: Routledge.

Nancy, Jean-Luc ([1993] 1997), *The Sense of the World*, translated by Jeffrey S. Librett, Minneapolis, MN: University of Minnesota Press.

Napier, Winston, ed. (2000), *African American Literary Theory: A Reader*, New York: New York University Press.

Nickerson, Catherine Ross, ed. (2010), *The Cambridge Companion to American Crime Fiction*, Cambridge: Cambridge University Press.

Norris, Christopher (2009), *Badiou's Being and Event*, London: Continuum.

Norris, Christopher (2012), *Derrida, Badiou and the Formal Imperative*, London: Continuum.

Nudelman, Franny (2001), "'The Blood of Millions': John Brown's Body, Public Violence, and Political Community,"*American Literary History*, 13 (4): 639–61.

Nudelman, Franny (2004), *John Brown's Body: Slavery, Violence, and the Culture of War*, Chapel Hill: University of North Carolina Press.

Nünning, Ansgar (2010), "Making Events – Making Stories – Making Worlds: Ways of Worldmaking from a Narratological Point of View," in Vera Nünning and Ansgar Nünning and Birgit Neumann (eds), *Cultural Ways of Worldmaking: Media and Narrative*, 191–214, Berlin: Walter de Gruyter.

Nünning, Vera, Ansgar Nünning and Birgit Neumann, eds (2010), *Cultural Ways of Worldmaking: Media and Narrative*, Berlin: Walter de Gruyter.

O'Hagan, Sean (September 24, 2006), "I wouldn't say this is unreadable . . . ," in Mark Z. Danielewski (ed.), Review of *Only Revolutions*, *The Observer*, Accessed January 14, 2014. http://www.theguardian.com/books/2006/sep/24/sciencefictionfantasyandhorror.features.

Öhlschläger, Claudia (2009), "Narration und Ethik. Vorbemerkung," in Claudia Öhlschläger (ed.), *Narration und Ethik*, 9–21, München: Wilhelm Fink.

Öhlschläger, Claudia, ed. (2009), *Narration und Ethik*, München: Wilhelm Fink.

O'Leary, Stephen D. and Glen S. McGhee, eds (2005), *War in Heaven/Heaven on Earth: Theories of the Apocalyptic*, London: equinox.

Oppermann, Serpil (2012), "Rethinking Ecocriticism in an Ecological Postmodern Framework: Mangled Matter, Meaning, and Agency," in Timo Müller and Michael Sauter (eds), *Literature, Ecology, Ethics: Recent Trends in Ecocriticism*, 35–50, Heidelberg: Winter.

Orvell, Miles (2006), "After 9/11: Photography, the Destructive Sublime, and the Postmodern Archive," *Michigan Quarterly Review*, 45 (2): np.

Oswald, Dykes D. (1904), "Code of Hammurabi," *The Juridical Review*, 16 (1): 72–85.

Oxford English Dictionary, s. v. "event" (1993), *OED*. Vol. 1. A-M, Oxford: Oxford University Press.

Oxford English Dictionary, s. v. "Haleskarth" (1961), Vol. 5. H-K, Oxford: Oxford University Press.

Oxford English Dictionary, s. v. "Propaganda" (1993), Vol. 2. N-Z, Oxford: Oxford University Press.

Oxford English Dictionary, s. v. "propagate" (1993), Vol. 2. N-Z, Oxford: Oxford University Press.

Ozier, Lance W. (1975), "The Calculus of Transformation: More Mathematical Imagery in *Gravity's Rainbow*," *Twentieth Century Literature*, 21 (2): 193–210.

Penrose, Walter (2004), *The Road to Reality: A Complete Guide to the Law of the Universe*, London: Jonathan Cape.

Petersen, Christer (2008), "Tod als Spektakel: Skizze einer Mediengeschichte des 11. Septembers," in Ingo Irsigler and Christoph Jürgensen (eds), *Nine Eleven: Ästhetische Verarbeitungen des 11. September 2001*, 195–218. Heidelberg: Winter.

Pinet, Simone (2003), "On the Subject of Fiction: Islands and the Emergence of the Novel," *Diacritics*, 33 (3/4): 173–87.

Pluth, Ed (2012), *Badiou: A Philosophy of the New*, Cambridge: Polity.

Pöhlmann, Sascha, ed. (2010), *Against the Grain: Reading Pynchon's Counternarratives*, Amsterdam: Rodopi.

Pöhlmann, Sascha (2010), "Cosmographic Metafiction in Sesshu Foster's *Atomik Aztek*," *Amerikastudien*, 55 (2): 223–48.

Pöhlmann, Sascha (2012), "The Democracy of Two: Whitmanian Politics in *Only Revolutions*," in Sascha Pöhlmann (ed.), *Revolutionary Leaves: The Fiction of Mark Z. Danielewski*, 1–32. Newcastle upon Tyne: Cambridge Scholars Publishing.

Pöhlmann, Sascha (2010), "Introduction: The Complex Text," in Sascha Pöhlmann (ed.), *Against the Grain: Reading Pynchon's Counternarratives*, 9–34, Amsterdam: Rodopi.

Pöhlmann, Sascha, ed. (2012), *Revolutionary Leaves: The Fiction of Mark Z. Danielewski*, Newcastle upon Tyne: Cambridge Scholars Publishing.

Pöhlmann, Sascha (2009), "Shining on the Nothing New: Re-Making the World in Mark Z. Danielewski's Only Revolutions," in Jennifer Craig and Warren Steele (eds), R|EVOLUTIONS: *Mapping Culture, Community, and Change from Ben Jonson to Angela Carter*, 64–82. Newcastle upon Tyne: Cambridge Scholars Publishing, 2009.

Poppe, Sandra, Thorsten Schüller and Sascha Seiler, eds (2009), *9/11 als kulturelle Zäsur: Repräsentationen des 11. September 2001 in kulturellen Diskursen, Literatur und visuellen Medien*, Bielefeld: Transcript.

Power, Nina (2012), "Toward a New Political Subject? Badiou between Marx and Althusser," in Sean Bowden and Simon Duffy (eds), *Badiou and Philosophy*, 157–73, Edinburgh: Edinburgh University Press.

Power, Nina and Alberto Toscano, eds (2003), " 'Think, pig!' An Introduction to Badiou's Beckett," in *On Beckett*, xv–xxxiv, Manchester: Clinamen Press.

Powers, Richard ([2003] 2004), *The Time Of Our Singing*, London: Vintage.

Propp, Vladimir ([1928] 2003), *Morphology of the Folktale*, translated by Laurence Scott, Austin, TX: University of Texas Press.

Pynchon, Thomas ([2006] 2007), *Against the Day*, London: Random House.

Pynchon, Thomas (2013), *Bleeding Edge*, New York: Penguin.

Pynchon, Thomas ([1966] 2006), *The Crying of Lot 49*, London: Penguin.

Pynchon, Thomas ([1984] 2000), "Entropy," in *Slow Learner*, 81–98, London: Vintage.

Pynchon, Thomas ([1973] 2006), *Gravity's Rainbow*, London: Penguin.

Pynchon, Thomas (October 28, 1984), "Is it O.K. to be a Luddite?," *New York Times Book Review*, 40–41. Accessed September 18, 2013. https://www.nytimes.com/books/97/05/18/reviews/pynchon-luddite.html.

Pynchonwiki, s.v. "Mulciber, Victor" (2006), Edited by Tim Ware. November 21. Np. Accessed September 4, 2015. http://against-the-day.pynchonwiki.com/wiki/index.php?title=M.

Pynchonwiki, s.v. "nontrivial zeroes" (2006), Edited by Tim Ware. November 21. Np. April 20, 2013. http://against-the-day.pynchonwiki.com/wiki/index.php?title=ATD_588-614.

Pynchonwiki, s.v. "Quaternions" (2006), Edited by Tim Ware. November 21. Np. Accessed September 4, 2015. http://against-the-day.pynchonwiki.com/wiki/index.php?title=Q.

Pynchonwiki, s.v. "Ramanujan Srinivasa Ramanujan" (2006), Edited by Tim Ware. November 21. Np. April 24, 2013.

Pynchonwiki, s.v. "Riemann zeta function" (2006), Edited by Tim Ware. November 21. Np. April 1 2013. http://against-the-day.pynchonwiki.com/wiki/index.php?title=ATD_489-524#Page_496.

Rancière, Jacques ([2002] 2004), "Aesthetics, Inaesthetics, Anti-Aesthetics," translated by Ray Brassier, in Peter Hallward (ed.), *Think Again: Alain Badiou and the Future of Philosophy*, 218–31, London: Continuum.

Rancière, Jacques (2010), *Dissensus: On Politics and Aesthetics*, translated by Steven Corcoran, London: Continuum.

Rancière, Jacques ([2000] 2004), *The Politics of Aesthetics*, translated by Gabriel Rockhill, London: Continuum.

Randall, Martin (2011), *9/11 and the Literature of Terror*, Edinburgh: Edinburgh University Press.

Reilly, Terry (2011), "Narrating Tesla in *Against the Day*," in Christopher Leise and Jeffrey Severs (eds), *Pynchon's Against the Day: A Corrupted Pilgrim's Guide*, 139–63, Newark: University of Delaware Press.

Reynolds, David S. (2005), *John Brown, Abolitionist: The Man Who Killed Slavery, Sparked The Civil War, and Seeded Civil Rights*, New York: Knopf.

Rhys, Jean ([1966] 2000), *Wide Sargasso Sea*, edited by Angela Smith, London: Penguin.

Rickli, Christina (2009), "Trauer- oder Traumageschichten? Amerikanische Romane nach 9/11," in Sandra Poppe, Thorsten Schüller and Sascha Seiler (eds), *9/11 als kulturelle Zäsur: Repräsentationen des 11. September 2001 in kulturellen Diskursen, Literatur und visuellen Medien*, 103–20, Bielefeld: Transcript.

Rickli, Christina (2008), "Wegweiser aus dem Trauma? Amerikanische Romane nach dem 11. September," in Sebastian Domsch (ed.), *Amerikanisches Erzählen nach 2000*, 126–45, München: Text + Kritik.

Riera, Gabriel, ed. (2005), *Alain Badiou: Philosophy and its Conditions*, Albany, NY: SUNY Press.

Rimmon-Kenan, Shlomith (1996), *A Glance beyond Doubt: Narration, Representation, Subjectivity*, Columbus: Ohio State University Press.

Roffe, Jon (2012), *Badiou's Deleuze*, Montreal: McGill-Queen's University Press.

Rölli, Marc (2004), "Einleitung," in Marc Rölli (ed.), *Ereignis auf Französisch*, 7–40, München: Wilhelm Fink.

Rölli, Marc (2009), "virtuality and Actuality: A Note on Deleuze's Concept of the Event," in Hanjo Berressem and Leyla Haferkamp (eds), *Deleuzian Events: Writing|History*, 72–84, Berlin: Lit.

Rölli, Marc, ed. (2004), *Ereignis auf Französisch*, München: Wilhelm Fink.

Rose, Tricia (1994), "Give me a Break (Beat)! Sampling and Repetition in Rap Production," in Gretchen Bender and Timothy Druckrey (eds), *Cultures on the Brink: Ideologies of Technology*, 249–58, Seattle: Bay Press.

Rosenblatt, Roger (September 24, 2001), "The Age Of Irony Comes To An End," *Time Magazine*. Accessed 13 May, 2012. http://content.time.com/time/magazine/article/0,9171,1000893,00.html.

Ross, Marlon B. (2013), "This is *Not* an Apologia for African American Literature," *PMLA*, 128 (2): 395–98.

Rothberg, Michael (2008), "Seeing Terror, Feeling Art: Public and Private in Post-9/11 Literature," in Ann Keniston, and Jeanne Follansbee Quinn (eds), *Literature after 9/11*, 123–42, New York: Routledge.

Ruff, Matt (2012), *The Mirage*, New York: Harper Collins.

Schaub, Thomas H. (2009), "Secular Scripture and Cormac McCarthy's *The Road*," *Renascence*, 61 (3): 153–69.

Scheffer, Bernd (2004), "'. . . wie im Film.' Der 11. September und die USA als Teil Hollywoods," in Matthias Lorenz (eds), *Narrative des Entsetzens: Künstlerische, mediale und intellektuelle Deutungen des 11. September 2001*, 81–104, Lorenz. Würzburg: Königshausen & Neumann.

Schmid, Wolf (2005), *Elemente der Narratologie*, Berlin: Walter de Gruyter.

Schmid, Wolf, ed. (2009), *Russische Protonarratologie: Texte in kommentierter Übersetzung*, Berlin: Walter de Gruyter.

Schüller, Thorsten (2009), "Kulturtheorien nach 9/11," in Sandra Poppe, Thorsten Schüller and Sascha Seiler (eds), *9/11 als kulturelle Zäsur: Repräsentationen des 11. September 2001 in kulturellen Diskursen, Literatur und visuellen Medien*, 21–38, Bielefeld: Transcript.

Schuyler, George S. ([1926] 2000), "The Negro-Art Hokum," in Winston Napier (ed.), *African American Literary Theory: A Reader*, 24–26, New York: New York University Press.

Schweinfurth, Elisa (2011), " 'They Looked German, Albeit with Even Tighter Pants and Uglier Shoes, but There Was Something Different about Them': The Function of East and West Germany and the Fall of the Berlin Wall in Paul Beatty's *Slumberland*," *COPAS*, 11: Np. Accessed November 2, 2013. http://copas.uni-regensburg.de/article/view/123/147.

Severs, Jeffrey and Christopher Leise, eds (2011), *Pynchon's Against the Day: A Corrupted Pilgrim's Guide*, Newark: University of Delaware Press.

Shakespeare, William ([1595] 2005), *A Midsummer Night's Dream*, London: Penguin.

Shanahan, Timothy, ed. (2005), *Philosophy 9/11: Thinking about the War on Terrorism*, Chicago, IL: Carus.

Sielke, Sabine (2010), " 'Why '9/11 is [not] unique' or: Troping Trauma," *Amerikastudien*, 55 (3): 385–408.

Smith, John H. (2012), "On the *Novelle* and/as *Ereignis*," *Seminar*, 48 (2): 417–39.

Spinosa, Charles (1992), "Derrida and Heidegger: Iterability and *Ereignis*," in Hubert L. Dreyfus and Harrison Hall (eds), *Heidegger: A Critical Reader*, 270–97, Oxford: Blackwell.

St. Clair, Justin (2014), "Pynchon's Postmodern Legacy, or Why Irony Is Still Relevant," *LA Review of Books*, September 21, 2013: Np. Accessed June 12, 2014. https://lareviewofbooks.org/review/pynchons-postmodern-legacy-or-why-irony-is-still-relevant/.

Staes, Toon (2010), " 'When You Come to a Fork in the Road'—Marcuse, Intellectual Subversion and Negative Thought in *Gravity's Rainbow* and *Against the Day*," in Sascha Pöhlmann (ed.), *Against the Grain: Reading Pynchon's Counternarratives*, 97–111. Amsterdam: Rodopi.

Sweeney, Susan Elizabeth (2010), "Crime in Postmodernist Fiction," in Catherine Ross Nickerson (ed.), *The Cambridge Companion to American Crime Fiction*, 163–77, Cambridge: Cambridge University Press.

Taylor, Paul C. (2007), "Post-Black, Old Black," *African American Review*, 41 (4): 625–40.

Thompson, Damian (1996), *The End of Time: Faith and Fear in the Shadow of the Millennium*, Hanover, NH: University Press of New England.

Timmer, Nicoline (2010), *Do you feel it too? The Post-Postmodern Syndrome in American Fiction at the Turn of the Millenium*, Amsterdam: Rodopi.

Toscano, Alberto (2006), "The Bourgeois and the Islamist, or, The Other Subjects of Politics," *Cosmos and History*, 2 (1/2): 15–38.

Toth, Josh and Neil Brooks (2007), *The Mourning After: Attending the Wake of Postmodernism*, Amsterdam: Rodopi.

Tyburski, Susan J. (2008), " 'The Lingering Scent of Divinity' in The Sunset Limited and The Road," *The Cormac McCarthy Journal*, 6: 121–28.

Urban Dictionary, s.v. "switch up." Def. 1. Accessed June 2, 2013. http://de.urbandictionary.com/define.php?term=switch+up.

Urban Dictionary, s.v. "turnt out." Def. 1. Accessed June 3, 2013. http://de.urbandictionary.com/define.php?term=TURNT+OUT.

Vanderheide, John (2008), "Sighting Leviathan: Ritualism, Daemonism and the Book of Job in McCarthy's Latest Works," *The Cormac McCarthy Journal*, 6: 107–20.

Vanderheide, John (2006), "Varieties of Renunciation in the Works of Cormac McCarthy," *The Cormac McCarthy Journal*, 5: 62–73.

van Hulle, Dirk (2011), "Only Revolutions and the Drug of Rereading," in Joe Bray and Alison Gibbons (eds), *Mark Z. Danielewski*, 200–15, Manchester: Manchester University Press.

Vermeulen, Timotheus and Robin van den Akker (2010), "Notes on Metamodernism," *Journal of Aesthetics & Culture*, 2: np. Accessed February 18, 2013. http://www. aestheticsandculture.net/index.php/jac/article/view/5677/6306.

Versluys, Kristiaan, ed. (1992), *Neo-Realism in Contemporary American Fiction*, Amsterdam: Rodopi.

Wallace, David Foster ([1996] 2006), *Infinite Jest*, New York: Little, Brown.

Wallhead, Celia (2010), "Kit and *Kim*: Espionage in *Against the Day*," in Sascha Pöhlmann (ed.), *Against the Grain: Reading Pynchon's Counternarratives*, 291–306, Amsterdam: Rodopi.

Walter, Jess (2006), *The Zero*, New York: Harper Collins.

Wansing, Rudolf (2004), "Im Denken Erfahren: Ereignis und Geschichte bei Heidegger," in Marc Rölli (ed.), *Ereignis auf Französisch*, 81–102, München: Wilhelm Fink.

Warren, Kenneth (2013), "A Reply to my Critics," *PMLA*, 128 (2): 401–08.

Warren, Kenneth (2011), *What Was African American Literature?* Cambridge, MA: Harvard University Press.

Wayans, Keenen Ivory and Damon Wayans (1990), *In Living Color*, Los Angeles, CA: Fox Network. Television.

Weisenburger, Steven (1988), *A Gravity's Rainbow Companion: Sources and Contexts for Pynchon's Novel*, Athens, GA: University of Georgie Press.

Whitehead, Colson (2006), *Apex Hides the Hurt*, New York: Anchor Books.

Wielenberg, Erik J. (2010), "God, Morality, and Meaning in Cormac McCarthy's *The Road*," *The Cormac McCarthy Journal*, 8 (1): 1–16.

Wigglesworth, Michael ([1662] 1947), "The Day of Doom," in Norman Foerster (ed.), *American Poetry and Prose*, 3rd ed., 45–49, Boston: Houghton Mifflin.

Wilhelm, Randal S. (2008), " 'Golden Chalice, Good to House a God': Still Life in *The Road*," *The Cormac McCarthy Journal*, 6: 129–46.

Williams, James (2012), "A Critique of Alain Badiou's Denial of Time in his Philosophy of Events," in Sean Bowden and Simon Duffy (eds), *Badiou and Philosophy*, 113–31, Edinburg: Edinburgh University Press.

Wilner, Eleanor (1971), "The Poetics of Emily Dickinson," *ELH*, 38 (1): 126–54.

Wolfe, Tom (1989), "Stalking the Billion-Footed beat: A Literary Manifesto for the New Social Novel," *Harper's Magazine*, November: 45–56.

Wright, Colin (2011), "The Violence of the New: Badiou's Subtractive Destruction and Gandhi's Satyagraha," *Subjectivity*, 4 (1): 9–28.

Wright, Richard ([1940] 2005), *Native Son*, New York: Harper Collins.

Zamora, Lois Parkinson (1990), *Writing the Apocalypse: Historical Vision in Contemporary U.S. and Latin American Fiction*, Cambridge, MA: Cambridge University Press.

Zapf, Huber (2012), "Absence and Presence in American Literature," in Timo Müller and Michael Sauter (eds), *Literature, Ecology, Ethics: Recent Trends in Ecocriticism*, 83–94, Heidelberg: Winter.

Žižek, Slavoj (2006), *The Parallax View*, Cambridge, MA: MIT Press.

Žižek, Slavoj (1999), *The Ticklish Subject: The Absent Center of Political Ontology*, London: Verso.

Žižek, Slavoj (2002), *Welcome to the Desert of the Real*, London: Verso.

Zupancic, Alenka (2004), "The Fifth Condition," in Peter Hallward (ed.), *Think Again: Alain Badiou and the Future of Philosophy*, 191–201, London: Continuum.

Index